Leaving My Self Behind

HARVEY MUDD

Leaving My Self Behind

THE PORCUPINE PRESS

The Porcupine Press
115 Chemin du Clos de Segaras
30700 Montaren
France
porcupinepressfr@gmail.com

Published 2018 by The Porcupine Press
Printed in the United States of America
Second printing
20 19 18 17   1 2 3 4

ISBN: 978-0-990859-7-03
Library of Congress Control Number: 2015959198

What you have done is safe and fruitful. Work and learn in evil days, in insulted days, in days of debt and depression and calamity. Fight best in the shade of the cloud of arrows.

Ralph Waldo Emerson, *The Journals*

I at least have so much to do in unraveling certain human lots, and seeing how they were woven and interwoven, that all the light I can command must be concentrated on this particular web, and not dispersed over that tempting range of relevancies called the universe.

George Eliot, *Middlemarch*

Other books by this author

Soulscot
Stations
The Plain of Smokes
A European Education
Spinoza's Dog

For Jim Levy,
who has gone the distance with me and for my
children, Mariana, Sam, and Elena.

Contents

Part III: The Journey Resumes

Part IV: The Pursuit of Happiness

Part V: The World as It Is

Part VI: Living and Its Consequences

Part VII: The Lost Years

Part VIII: Where Things Stand So Far

Part IX: Leaving

Part I

A Journey Begins

If I'm not seen again
In the old places, on the village ground,
Say of me: lost to men.
Say I'm adventure-bound
For love's sake.
Lost (on purpose) to be found.

San Juan de la Cruz, *The Spiritual Canticle*

1

Leaving Home

The gangplank was just wide enough for the wheelchair so Jim and I, in our awkward struggle with gravity, were holding up a line of our fellow passengers. There were no verbal complaints—civilized people do not generally grouse about the handicapped and Jim, for the moment, qualified as handicapped—but I could hear the rustle of impatience. We were embarrassed but not ashamed. Jim pressed one hand against his belly, against the surgical incision, the other hand over his mouth to suppress laughter. Laughing hurt. I pushed, practically doubled over with laughter myself. At the top of the gangplank, a young officer in a white hat watched us with sublime indifference. His involvement with us would not begin until we reached the deck. The ship loomed over us, its walls smooth, hard, and black. Motionless in the water, indifferent to tides and currents, the SS United States was the largest and fastest ocean liner in the world. It would take us to Europe in record time. The year was 1960.

As I struggled up the gangplank, I looked down and felt the return of an old vertigo. For the previous eighteen months I had struggled against irrational fears, of falling from a tall building or, worse, succumbing to the impulse to jump from the Brooklyn Bridge. I had not allowed myself to walk across that famous bridge, which I knew well in the way I would know many things in my life, from literature, in this case from Hart Crane's poem *To Brooklyn Bridge*.

Out of some subway scuttle, cell or loft
A bedlamite speeds to thy parapets,
Tilting there momently, shrill shirt ballooning ...

I feared that I might be my own kind of bedlamite, a disconnected and despairing wanderer in the cold-hearted city, and that I too might jump, my shirt ballooning for a terrible moment before the water came up to claim me. To protect myself, I had hunkered, for nearly twelve months, in a virtual cell, a little studio apartment in the west Village, confined there by fear of what might happen to me if I were to venture out. I came to realize that it was living that I most feared; the sunlight, self knowledge, the task of finding a place for myself in the hustle and pulse of the city of New York. Oblivion, the dark embrace of the cold river, had appealed to me for a time, not a very long time, but long enough and strongly enough that I avoided the bridge, stayed in, and read Hart Crane.

But with help from a gifted psychiatrist, I had made it. I had "saved my soul alive," as one of the Old Testament prophets puts it. The water no longer offered any attraction. Below the gangplank were the ordinary waters of New York Harbor, half Hudson River, fresh, half Atlantic Ocean, salt, with its surface soiled by iridescent swirls of oil. The water sloshed against the steel hull of the ship. I felt no dread of any sort, surprisingly, given how sheltered my life had been, no anxiety about what lay ahead. Metaphorically, kidding with myself, I said, "There are no submarines and it is not iceberg season." It was a remarkable transformation. Indeed, I could hardly remember the frightened young man that I had been. Suicidal thoughts, months of extreme loneliness, social panic, the sense, quite literally, of being non-existent, of being a hollow person, without a self, had faded as completely as does the memory of a toothache or a nightmare.

Jim fought to contain himself, but in spite of the stabs of pain he laughed. I laughed because I felt exhilarated. We laughed together because we seemed, even to ourselves, to be comical figures. We were American twenty-year-olds embarking for parts unknown, unknown to us at least. We didn't have a plan, neither itinerary nor schedule. We had no clear sense of where we were going or what we would do when we got there. We would improvise.

The ship backed out into the Hudson, started seaward, and passed the Statue of Liberty. I thought of John Keats' poem about discovering Homer's *Odyssey*. He described the feeling as comparable to the explorer "standing silent upon a peak in Darien" and seeing the Pacific Ocean for the first time. Keats' emotion on reading Homer, the thrill of the sublime—that favorite emotion of the Romantics—was the very emotion that I felt as the ship passed through the Verrazano Straits and into the vastness of the open sea.

I had been a serious reader since I was nine years old. When I was supposed to be asleep, lights out, I would read under my sheets with a flashlight. I would wake myself at five in the morning to read. I had loved popular tales of the sea, but after I discovered Joseph Conrad at age fourteen, books took on a deeper dimension. In Conrad there were things unknowable, unmapped continents, rivers without sources and valleys in shadow. From that time forward, from Joseph Conrad, literature became my guide. Books helped me understand my experiences, placing them in the context of other searches. Fiction held truths. The emotions that my experiences produced had names and analogies thanks to stories and poetry. And those same books guided me into experiences that I would not have had and that have contributed so significantly to my understanding of myself and the world. Would I have been as open to experience as I've been without Odysseus' example? I came to accept that the unexpected was very often essential, the necessary destination.

So off Jim and I went, to foreign places, willing to get lost but never alone, always in the company of books. Literature was becoming my true homeland, a place where I always felt comfortable. Even the most desolate stories offered rewards.

The adventure that Jim and I embarked upon had been in the works for at least six years, ever since, as freshmen in high school, we had formed our friendship and had decided that we needed to reach beyond our comfortable circumstances and the predictable futures that our backgrounds almost certainly guaranteed. By the time we were sixteen, we had both decided that we were destined to become something other than what would have been expected of us. Through the hormonal fogs and minor rebellions of adolescence, the constant was that we both wanted to be writers.

For Jim, breaking the mold was a goal less radical than it was for me. His mother had had literary ambitions, desires frustrated by alcohol and an unhappy marriage, but her love of books was profound and she shared this with her son and with me. Dead now fifty some years, she wanders about in my psyche still, a rumpled wraith with a glass of Scotch in one hand, the ice melting, and with a cigarette, the ash growing longer, in the other. Jim's father was a Beverly Hills psychoanalyst, a secretive man with Mediterranean attitudes toward women and food. We suspected, without really knowing about such arrangements, that he kept a mistress.

My family, by contrast, was more than just conventional; we were of the rarefied social strata that had rigid parameters of behavior. The idea that my father might have a mistress was both unthinkable and unlikely; he was the epitome of propriety, well anchored to job and the family's reputation. My family was prominent enough in Los Angeles that the family name alone presented an obstacle for me. I was always the young man identified by the frequent question "any relation to...?". I was named for my grandfather; I loved and admired my grandfather, but I felt burdened by his name, and by what I felt, as I grew older, as an unearned preference. He had earned it; I hadn't. His wealth was considerable, yet he was genuinely humble and modest. He was generous and philanthropic but was never ostentatious about it: that a prominent college bears his name was not his idea; it was named for him, after his death, by my father and my grandmother. Alive, he would have declined the honor. He had a sort of courtly modesty, like a prince of the realm who would step aside if someone better qualified than he had appeared on the scene. No one, in my knowledge of him and his life, ever did. He died suddenly and relatively young, so age never crippled him. While he was alive pettiness never diminished him, and no scandal touched the family. I never heard him utter an envious or spiteful word about anyone. He was never rude to a waiter; there was no trace of arrogance. At his memorial service in 1955, the African American man who had polished his shoes in the lobby of his office building for thirty years was present, sitting in the pews for the general public. I recognized this man for I had, on more than one occasion, sat next to my grandfather on the elevated shoeshine platform, four wooden seats, with eight metal footrests, as his shoes were polished. I had watched them interact; they conversed about family, sports, and politics. And at his memorial, I watched this aging black man weep.

There was so much to admire in my grandfather. Nevertheless, I needed to distance myself from him and from the city where he was so prominent so that I might have a chance to become my own person. This trip, Jim's and my adventure, was part of that effort, probably the first real step. My father had experienced this kind of family pressure; it was inherent, innocently enough, in a family like ours. He had followed in his father's footsteps going into the family firm. He had done it well and honorably for many years. In his sixties, however, he veered off the path and staged a late life rebellion, a dramatic change of direction. Because of his experience with his father, he seemed to understand my dilemma and from high school on had encouraged me, often just by giving no direction, to find my own way. It was my grandfather's money that made the trip possible but with my father's tacit encouragement.

My mother, on the other hand, knew exactly what she wanted me to be. She did not think an unstructured trip, two young men footloose in Europe, without institutional sponsorship, "a year abroad," would fit into her plan for me. She opposed the trip. I knew, instinctively, that what she wanted of me and for me was inauthentic, so before I had any sense of who I was or might be, the battles I fought with her, from roughly age six on, were painfully unequal. The trip had purpose of redressing that imbalance. I would return as someone substantial. It turned out to have been a good start, but the life project of dealing with my mother and her effects on my psyche would go on to the end of her life. And, in fact, beyond.

Four days before we boarded the ship, Jim and I had been in Los Angeles, at my house, packing. My mother was having a formal dinner party that night. Film industry personalities were included among the guests, not stars, for that wasn't her style, too flashy; but executives and studio lawyers. I had asked the lace-collared maid who was serving hors d'oeuvres to ask my mother if she would come to the kitchen for a moment. I had a question and, being in blue jeans, I knew better than to appear in the living room filled with beautifully dressed women and men in dark suits. I'd done that before and had felt like a stray dog that had wandered into a garden party. Everyone had been polite but had been relieved when I'd been chased out. Sending a message to my mother was the better way. My question was an easy one. I wanted to borrow an old suitcase of hers that had gathered dust in the attic for a decade. My mother appeared. I asked the question.

"How dare you interrupt my dinner party for such a question?" was her reply. "No, you may not." Without acknowledging Jim's presence, she turned and walked out. Jim was not surprised. He knew my mother. I took the suitcase anyway, and returned it eighteen months later. It had not been missed. Into the suitcase went clothes for a year, the books I had promised myself that I would read.

I worried still about my long-term physical survival, for I had had a serious cancer. Mortality was not an abstract issue for me. One of the books in the suitcase that I carried with me had been the letters of John Keats. He had died young, at age twenty-six; I thought his letters might help me deal with my own fear of dying. I don't remember if they did or not, but I loved those letters, so very wise for a young man. The paperback that I carried with me in 1960 still sits on my bookshelf.

I watched the lights of Manhattan Island drop below the horizon. Halfway across the Atlantic, an early winter storm came up. There was no porthole in our cabin, no natural light or natural air, so I spent as much time as I could on deck leaning on the rail. To center myself, I hummed, deep down in my chest, the *Ode to Joy* passage from Beethoven's Ninth Symphony. It induced an almost trance-like state, a spiritual calm, not a cure for seasickness, but nevertheless helpful. This musical phrase, its repetitions in rising pitch, was something that I had adopted, almost as a mantra, in high school. I would sneak out of my dormitory after lights out and make my way through the sleeping campus to a favorite euca-lyptus tree, where I would sit and listen to the tiny dry bells of the seed pods as they knocked gently, one against another, and the gray blades of the leaves as they rustled in a breeze. When I was sure that I had not been observed, when no lights were turned on in a faculty residence, and no flashlight was bobbing along the trail I'd taken, I would remove a forbidden cigarette from my shirt pocket and, shielding the flare of the match behind the tree trunk, would have a quiet smoke. I would sometimes sit for as long as half an hour and hum the *Ode to Joy*, send-ing it, almost as a prayer, into the star-filled California night. And now again, the Beethoven, this time cast into the teeth of an Atlantic storm.

The stormy sea was like a zinc tray held by a swaying waiter. The waiter held the tray not balanced perfectly, but tilted slightly, and upon this surface the ship slid slowly toward Europe.

"To Brooklyn Bridge" came to mind again. The ship was a bridge and on it I was crossing a great water, and safely, with no dark thoughts, not a one. A day out of Le Havre, on the French side of the Channel, the sun came out. The sea sparkled.

And Thee, across the harbor, silver-paced
As though the sun took step of thee...

2

The Arc of the Narrative Begins

My family, on both sides, had come to the New World in the seventeenth century; my father's family in 1635, my mother's somewhat later, but still in plenty of time to participate in the forging of the nation. Both ancestral lines stayed near the place of their landing for a century or more, Maryland for my paternal ancestors, and Philadelphia for my mother's, but then the wave of Manifest Destiny caught them and they joined the flow of Americans into the empty lands of the West—empty except for Native Americans whose resistance inevitably faded before greater numbers and superior force. It was to Missouri for my father's family in the 1830s. After the Civil War, my mother's ancestors made the perilous journey in covered wagons to the West Coast. They had encounters with the Apache, the last spasm of Native American resistance. My father's people were part of the mineral exploration of the west. My grandfather was born in the silver boom town of Leadville, Colorado in 1888; then they too, finally, went to California, the promised land, where I was born, in 1940, almost two years before the attack on Pearl Harbor.

My childhood was both privileged and unhappy. Nothing truly terrible ever happened to me. I did not live through the German bombings of London as had my contemporaries, the children of family friends. I had no direct experience of the war. Childhood does not explain a life, but, as Jean Jacques Rousseau explores in the *Confessions*, those years create the person who will, at a certain point, attempt to become a creative, conscious, and compassionate human being, or will try but fail, or who won't bother to make the effort. All those outcomes are shaped by the experiences of childhood, shaped, not predicted. Sigmund Freud, two hundred years later, comes to the same conclusion. I am with both Rousseau and Freud in this understanding of the ages of man. Childhood matters, so I have given it some attention.

My childhood, in which I include most of my adolescence, ended with an emotional collapse, a breakdown, at age nineteen. But I managed to land in the care of a good psychoanalyst, and that made all the difference.

"When you arrived in my office," my doctor had said, "you seemed to be a young man without a self." The idea that I had a "self," that I was a unique being, had never before entered my mind.

"Is the self the same as the soul?" I had asked him.

"We start with nothing." he replied. "We build ourselves out of experience, out of what we do. We earn our souls by how well we do it. How hard we try counts too."

His understanding of my childhood, after a month of talk, was that there had been so little emotional nourishment that a full human being had never formed. It was a sort of handicap, but one entirely invisible. I looked like a normal young man, physically healthy, intelligent, tall, brown hair and eyes, and reasonably good-looking. Furthermore, I had had every advantage that money could provide. How could I not thrive? Nevertheless, I felt hollow, as if I were just a shell. I had been born into a kingdom stocked with the finest of things, overstocked even, but understocked with maternal love, support, and approval. I had formed an *idea* of the kind of person I wanted to become, someone creative, an artist of some kind, but it was just an idea, something that I had lifted out of books. This bohemian persona, an act really, had kept me going for a while. I had stayed just ahead of a host of chaotic emotions until, in 1959, I couldn't anymore. Things came apart: self-control failed; self-love failed; shame and embarrassment lost their potency; and I imploded.

It had taken nineteen years to reach that point. The relatively stable years of late adolescence, ages sixteen and seventeen, had been resting on ground that had turned to quicksand at the first trauma—it was a love that failed. But I was lucky. I found the right doctor.

In that fall of 1960, after eighteen months of intensive psychotherapy, five days a week in the first six of those months, I was ready to actually do something. The doctor had given me the sense that whatever my condition might be called, it was, to a great extent, who I was and would always be. It would be fatal only if I could let it be. The doctor, like a father taking his hands off the bicycle seat and letting his offspring go wobbling off on his own, had set me free, to make my way as best I could. He gave me the sense that it would be good enough. It was an extraordinary gift. "Good enough" was good enough for me. And that was my state of mind when Jim and I decided to cross the Atlantic to explore the Old World.

My destination was Spain. I had a romantic notion that I was more Spanish than American. This was a sort of unconscious foundling story that I used to explain my feelings of estrangement from my birth family. My parents, so reserved, proper, and remote from what I thought of as real life—how little I knew of real life then—could not, I was sure, be my real parents. Certainly not my spiritual parents. The Spanish were a passionate people, or so I had read, and by going to Spain, I would fill in the details of my imaginary ancestry. I even fantasized about becoming a Spaniard, never considering that one could not change nationalities just by checking a box on a form. I wasn't unhappy with America in those days, but America—by that I meant family—expected me to be someone I didn't want to be. I wanted to be a writer: and surely, one could do that better in a place where the women were exotic, the landscape harsh, and the past, its bones and castles, was visible on the horizon. That I spoke only the most rudimentary Spanish, high school Spanish II at best, did not seem to be an obstacle. All the necessary components of this fantasy would, I assumed, fall into place. Having surmounted the effects of an unhappy childhood, having pulled through a breakdown, and having passed without incident through the five-year watchful period thought necessary for most cancers, I considered that I was, indeed, a lucky young man.

I live now in the Old World, in France. I am an expatriate, not a French citizen, but a legal resident. What started as an adolescent fantasy about being part of another culture has become reality. The path through time, 1960 to 2016, that I took to this result was that of a man who was always experimenting, always testing himself, becoming more mature, better informed, and more sure of his values. But to have come to the last phase of my life—I am now seventy-six years old—as a voluntary exile was not something that I would have wished for. After my Spanish year, I knew, without question, that I was an American. Language, culture, outlook, and political values made me one. Moreover, and perhaps more important, I was viscerally, sensually, an American. I remember walking out of the airport in Los Angeles, returning home in 1961, and thinking to myself that I knew the smell of the air and the color of the sky. Only LA looks like this, tastes like this. Even the preposterous, ungainly, palm trees and the garish billboards were a welcome sight. It was, thus, as an American that I went into my twenties and into the tumultuous, indeed, tormented, world that unfolded in the 1960s.

3

The Old World

I had been to Europe once before, in my fifteenth year, 1955. We were three, my father, my grandfather's oldest friend, Hamish Robertson, and me. Hamish was our guide; he bought the rail tickets, negotiated with taxi drivers, and translated, as needed, the French, German, and Italian that we encountered on that trip. Based in London, he handled the European business of my grandfather's company.

After my grandfather, Hamish was the most important adult in my life and would remain so until his death in the early 1980s. He was knowledgeable about things cultural, knew the best places to eat in dozens of cities and was completely at ease with the necessary and practical. He knew when to bribe an Italian policeman, and that one shouldn't attempt to bribe a French policeman. Despite always insisting that he was a Scotsman, he was a citizen of the world, at home almost anywhere in Europe. He was, for me, the keeper of history. He had lived it and shared with me his sense of its importance.

Hamish and I had a special friendship. He always called me "young Harvey." My grandfather, the first Harvey, had died three months earlier. I filled a void for Hamish and he filled one for me. I addressed Hamish, at his insistence, by his given name even though, by convention, owing to his age, I would have expected to say "Mister Robertson." There is no part of my memory in which he was not a presence. During the war a number of English children, his grandchildren, had come to live with my grandparents in Los Angeles. These children, with their strange accents, homesick and quietly fearful for their parents, brought the fact of the war home to us sheltered American children. By way of explaining the presence of these children—they occupied all the spare rooms in my grandparents' house—I was shown pictures in *Life* or *The London Illustrated News* of the children of the London poor sheltering in the subway tunnels during bombing raids.

After the war, Hamish came to California every year until my grandfather's death in 1955—a long journey by ship and then across the continent by train. I always looked forward to his visits. He was different from us Californians. He had a kind of sophistication and cultural depth that we lacked or, in a sort of reverse snobbery, we pretended that we didn't need. Hamish had been responsible for selecting much of the furniture and decorative fixtures—the silver table service, for instance, Georgian and the best available—in my grandparents' Tudor-style mansion on Benedict Canyon Drive. (At 7000 square feet, it would not have qualified as a mansion by today's standards.) My grandparents' house, despite the Beverly Hills address, was, in Hamish's view, located in the wilderness. He had come down to breakfast one morning when I was also visiting and announced that he had seen a coyote crossing the well-manicured lawns. "Lots of deer too," my grandfather added, "and possums, raccoons, and various birds of prey." Hamish was most impressed. Nature still existed in America; in Europe, it had been domesticated away. "Not a wolf or a bear left. The only predators *we* have are men." Remarks like that, which I didn't always understand, reinforced the sense of menace that I had felt during the war years. This dark undertone occasionally cropped up in his conversation, but he was always funny and mischievous. Life was to be enjoyed, engaged with, not feared.

On that 1955 trip, after Germany, where my father and Hamish conducted business, and on our way to Italy, we passed through Paris. We dined at the four-star *Tour d'Argent*. It was a memorable meal, my first at a "grand restaurant." There was a view of Notre Dame from the dining room and a menu that had no prices beside the dishes; it was assumed that if you were at *le Tour*, you didn't care about prices. Besides, said Hamish, to associate the art of cuisine with money was crass, a habit of the *arrivistes*—with a teasing wink—the Americans who could be counted on to select the most expensive item on the menu. My previous experience of a fancy restaurant had been the Thursday dinner, cook's day off, at the country club, where the most exotic dish was herring marinated in sour cream and where the salad was Jello molded into a circle and elevated to gourmet status by suspending tiny marshmallows in its quivering orange body. My horizons were expanding.

Hamish ordered sweetbreads, which, he explained, were glands from the neck of a calf. He cut off a bit and put it on my plate. Sweetbreads, exotic and previously unknown, settled the food issue for me: thereafter I would eat anything at least once. Baby birds in their nests in the Levant and fried ants in Mexico were now possible.

After the meal, my father retired to our hotel, the George V, and Hamish, with my father's permission, took me out on the town.

"As a special treat, young Harvey, I am going to introduce you to the finest, the rarest, plum brandy in the world."

We took a cab to the Place Pigalle in Montmartre, which, in those years, was the center ring for the nightly show of Parisian street walkers, a place where one could see women of the night leaning on lampposts, the living clichés of the Parisian "darkside." There were many prostitutes displaying themselves that night, women loitering in doorways or strolling slowly along Boulevard Clichy, some older than fit my image of what a prostitute should look like. The women wore gaudy makeup and outrageous outfits, skirts slit to mid-thigh, gold lamé dresses, skin-tight turtlenecks that exaggerated their breasts, fake leopard skin and spiked heels. As Hamish and I exited the cab, a little group of women approached, thinking, perhaps, that this was the older man breaking in the boy, a logical conclusion, I suppose, for why else does one come to Pigalle at 10 p.m. The offer of the forbidden but, at this stage of my life, completely unknown excited me. Women excited me. If I had not been with Hamish, however, I would have been quite terrified. I felt as if I had stumbled into an arena inhabited by predatory animals, Daniel in the lion's den came to mind—the stories one learns in Sunday School have unexpected uses—but I had a guide. Hamish deflected the women, politely, indeed, more than politely, with charm and gallantry, expressing no disdain.

"I told them," he said, winking at me, "that we are on an even more important mission, the plum brandy."

We walked up a narrow street—which fifty years later, when I lived in the neighborhood, I tried to find but couldn't with certainty—then turned into a dimly-lit blind alley, a sort of mews, and came to a small and unpretentious building, the last building in the *impasse*. The encounter with the women of the street still pumping adrenaline into my adolescent brain, it occurred to me that perhaps the plum brandy was a screen for something else, something that Hamish would not have revealed to my father, or to me either, in case I might "chicken out." I was, therefore, in quite a state as we came to this strange little building. Hamish stooped, lit his cigarette lighter, and studied the names by the bell. He rang, said a few words in French, the door opened, and we found ourselves in a tiny courtyard filled with pots of geraniums and some larger potted plants, including a bedraggled palm tree. There were metal trashcans arranged neatly in a corner. Then a door opened, light streamed out, and Hamish approached.

"*Commandante* Robertson, *bienvenu*." It was a woman's voice, pleasant, her tone one of happy surprise. I still could not see the owner of the voice. Hamish removed his hat, bent his head down, kissed her on both cheeks, and they embraced. Then she, a diminutive woman with white hair, appeared from behind his wide body. She looked at me and smiled.

Hamish introduced me as his "young American friend." He spoke now in both languages, translating for each of us. I felt very proud to be called his friend. I have forgotten the woman's name but I have her face still in memory, wrinkled but beautiful. She stepped aside and invited us in.

It was a small, tidy room, but richly textured with color and fabrics: a worn Persian carpet of reds and purples on the floor, curtains with a

floral pattern, and a stuffed chair covered with red velvet. There was a
lamp beside the chair with a shade made of paper on which was painted,
with painstaking detail, a chateau; the windows of the chateau were cut
so that the light from the bulb showed through them, giving the impression that the chateau was inhabited. There was an open book on a little
table by the chair so I assumed that the woman had been reading. In the
middle of the room there was a round table covered with a lace table
cloth; straight chairs were placed around it; and there we sat, Hamish,
this strange little woman, and I. There was a candle on the table, which
she lit.

Hamish turned to me and explained that they had met in Picardie
during the last year of the Great War, when he was recovering from a
combat injury. Her family had been producers of excellent brandies,
both apple and plum, and she still had a cellar full of these ancient
bottles, now very vintage, which she had inherited from her father. She
now supported herself by selling the bottles to exclusive clients. For the
most favored clients, like Hamish, there was an opened bottle and an
always open invitation.

"And I still have a bottle set aside for my Major, who never comes
to visit me enough," she said in French. He covered her tiny hand with
his very large masculine hand. Then she withdrew her hand, very gently,
and stroked his. They paused in this attitude: a sparrow taming a hawk.
After a moment, she disappeared and returned shortly with a bottle covered with dust. She showed me the label. "Commandante Robertson"
was written on it. She uncorked it and poured three glasses. We sat and
sipped. No one spoke. Outside were the faint noises of the city.

Having nothing to compare it to, I could not properly appreciate
the quality of the brandy, but I felt keenly that there was something
special in the occasion. After a while, the two old friends talked briefly in
French without including me. Hamish, large and solid, all six foot three
inches of him, seemed tame and tender. I sensed that they were flirting
or recalling ancient flirtations. Then, slowly, he disengaged, indicating
me, as if to say that he should return me to our hotel. My bedtime. He
picked up his hat, and, with appropriate courtesies, we departed. As we

returned through the Place Pigalle, the street women again approached, but perhaps sensing the aura of emotional richness that surrounded me, retired. We caught a cab.

In the cab Hamish said to me, "There is much you could learn from that fine lady, young Harvey." The cab threaded its way out of Montmartre and soon reached the Place de la Concorde and the broad avenues. He put his hand on my knee and said, apropos of nothing we had been talking about, "Read Shakespeare. It's all there." Hamish was often cryptic. Was "It's all there" everything one needed to know or an explanation for the events of the evening? He sank into pensive silence. The river of headlights carried us down the Champs-Elysées. When we returned to the hotel it was after one in the morning.

"It's long past my bedtime," was the last thing he said as he opened the door to his room. I went to the room I shared with my father, who was sound asleep and did not wake. As I lay in bed, I realized that Hamish had gone to considerable trouble over this evening. It had been not just the brandy that he wanted to share with me; it had been the totality of the experience: the fine meal, the secret cache of plum brandy, the lady, who was, perhaps, a woman he had once loved, the night streets of Paris and its inhabitants, and a glimpse, just a hint, of his past, his history in the Great War.

Over the years Hamish had told me a great deal about the First World War, about the horrors of trench warfare, the mud, the smell of death and cordite that the wind could not remove, the mind destroying artillery bombardments, disease, and the stupidity of the high command. Hamish had been gassed by his own side—the wind had shifted, blowing chlorine gas back on the British lines—and had been hospitalized in Picardie, and while his lungs healed, the convalescing young officer, dashing and handsome (I'd seen pictures), had stumbled onto the farmer who made the brandy and who had a beautiful daughter. I pictured Hamish walking slowly along country roads, carrying the stick that he always did when I knew him, returning again and again to the farmhouse, not for the brandy, but for the girl. I have invented this part of the story. I never had the courage or social know-how to ask any further. Hamish and I were not, after all, peers. He was my Virgil. I could ask about life, but I knew, somehow, that I was not to ask too much about *his* life. The war, Hamish often said, was an experience outside of time, in another dimension, and some of it was best left to lie in that distant place.

4

Foundations

I had been encouraged to be curious, to look into things, to ask questions. This permission came from my paternal ancestors, my father and grandfather. For my mother, there was no practical use for curiosity, but my father actively fostered it. It was scientific curiosity first of all, but it included a wide range of interests. In childhood it meant the traditional investigations: a chemistry set or a collection of rocks, and fossils. I sensed that nothing—except sex, perhaps, for my father was very repressed in that area—was off limits. I was forever taking things apart to see the inner workings, objects like a radio or the toaster. I apparently had little aptitude for reassembling the victims of my curiosity, sometimes requiring help from my father. My favorite toy as a ten-year-old was an Erector Set; my father spent hours with me building cranes and towers. I was curious about everything that humans had made: cathedrals, dams, and bridges, and my father could almost always tell me something about how these structures had come about.

My father also introduced me to the natural world through camping trips and through more formal lessons about natural history. A geologist by training meant that a drive through road cuts came with lessons about the physical makeup of that particular slice of the earth. I learned to see glacial rubble, ancient sea beds, the signs of uplifts or of ancient volcanism.

He owned a rural property in the Santa Monica Mountains an hour and a half outside of Los Angeles. The family went most weekends to "the ranch." On the boundary between a still undeveloped world and the expanding sprawl of Los Angeles, it could not be called wilderness, but it was wild. There were coyotes and rattlesnakes. The hills were covered with mesquite and manzanita scrub, the dry forests of Southern California that now burns so regularly. Los Angeles was close enough that at night we could see the glow of the city. There were open fields, studded with ancient live oaks, on which my father grazed cattle. It was a tax-loss operation, but that was incidental. He loved the land, the dirt, the heat of summer and the rains of winter. Those same fields had seen the cavalry charges of the 1935 epic of the Raj, *Lives of a Bengal Lancer*. Gary Cooper had walked these same fields in the uniform of a British officer. I thought this was very special because I knew about Gary Cooper. My father had taken me to see *High Noon* when I was twelve; it was the only movie I ever saw with my father; the story of moral courage meant something to him and has ever since to me. I revisit the film every ten years or so. The downside to going to the ranch was carsickness that I often experienced as we wound our way into the mountains, past the movie set for *How Green Was My Valley*, John Ford's film about a Welsh mining town. A childhood awareness of the power of the made-up world of the movies contributed to my certainty that fiction could sometimes contain much that was true. The final landmark on the road through the mountains to the ranch, beyond which I could seldom go without having to ask my father to stop the car so I could stand on the roadside and vomit, was a run-down vacation spa called Seminole Hot Springs. It was an incongruous place, an example of the triviality of the Hollywood way of invention: I knew that the Seminoles were a Florida Indian tribe; there was a larger-than-life statue of an Indian wearing the headdress of a Plains Indian, a Sioux or a Mandan. When we reached the top of the ridge, the road straightened and my stomach settled down.

We children had lots of chores— unloading the car came first, then bringing in firewood and building a fire in the winter, and throughout the year, picking up after the family dogs, pulling weeds—but we also had a great deal of fun. I learned to shoot a .22 rifle at tin cans (shooting at animals was prohibited unless the animals were pests; we had none of any significance). I learned to ride a horse and to drive a manual transmission car.

My father and my brothers and I hiked in those rugged mountains. I watched buzzards circling in the hot air, encountered rattlesnakes, which, if we came across them far from the house, we allowed to go on their way. This rule was evidence of an ethical relationship with nature that my father passed on to me. When there was nothing to fear, we should not be afraid. The only creatures we killed on sight were the black widow spiders that we found in the firewood pile or in dark corners of the garage. Tarantulas as large as my father's hand were harmless, so they always got a free pass. When I was ten I had a thing about beetles. I would get down on my knees and follow a beetle as it bumbled around in the dirt. My father would fold up his long frame and crouch beside me with a field guide to beetles in hand and find the name of the particular little beast that we were watching. The ranch, because it was so large (360 acres) and because we had no neighbors, was a wonderful place for all sorts of experiments, a place where errors were likely to be less serious. I learned to drive there, something I achieved on a WWII-vintage Jeep that one had to double clutch in order to shift to a lower gear, a lost art, a lost inconvenience. I bumped more than once into fence posts and rocks, but was forgiven. When at age twelve I announced at dinner one evening, when we were still in the city, that I had made dynamite with my chemistry set in the basement, my mother was dismissive: "Don't be silly, dear," she said. When I told my father what the ingredients were, common chemicals that one could get from a hardware store, my father thought there might be something to my claim. He overrode my mother's objections and rewarded me with an attempt to see if it worked. Because he was in the mining industry, he had access to fuse and blasting cap, which we took with my homemade dynamite (packed in a cylindrical Quaker Oats container, with the smiling Quaker in his black hat) to the ranch and succeeded in blowing a four-foot wide crater in the dirt. My father was proud of me, while making me promise never to make dynamite again.

I learned about the life and death of animals. I saw a pig slaughtered. (I actually looked away and was haunted for days by the terrible squeals.) A horse had hooked its hoof on a strand of barbed wire fence and had cut an artery in the area immediately behind its fore hoof. There was a great deal of blood. In this case my mother showed remarkable calm and resourcefulness. She ran to her bathroom and returned with a box of Kotex sanitary napkins and then helped me free the horse. We packed the Kotex into the wound. I held them in place while my mother returned to the house to call the vet. We stayed with the horse, calming it until the vet arrived. I was much impressed by my mother in this incident.

There were moral lessons too, not didactic, but by example. One day, my maternal grandmother came to the ranch for a summer barbeque. She no longer drove herself, but came in her Bentley driven by her African American chauffeur, an older man with white frizzy hair whom I remember well; his name was Dan Fields. After my grandmother was settled with lemonade, my father offered to show Dan some of the workings of the ranch. (Dan must have shown curiosity, but I don't know how this event began.) It was hot, midday. My father, Dan, and I, then eleven or twelve, got into the Jeep and drove to the barn area at the other end of the property. At the barn, my father was in shirtsleeves but Dan still wore his uniform black jacket and cap. My father invited Dan to shed his jacket, which he did, laying it carefully on the seat of the Jeep. We then walked around the barn area looking at animals and machinery. Dan stopped at the tractor, a small John Deere tracked machine. He asked if he could sit in it. My father assented and Dan climbed onto the seat with its yellow vinyl cushion. My father then asked if Dan would like to drive it. Dan's delight with this idea was unmistakable. My father then climbed up behind Dan and with one hand on Dan's shoulder, reached over and explained the controls and the gear shift. Dan worked the gear shift (the motor not yet running) and seemed to have trouble finding the correct notches. My father reached over and put his hand on Dan's hand and guided him through the sequence, first thru fourth, with reverse down and to the right. A few more instructions and they started the engine. My father got down and in first gear, which would not do much more than three miles per hour, Dan drove the tractor around the barn compound. My father and I watched and I think we applauded. The sight of my father's large white-skinned hand resting on Dan's gnarled black hand made a great impression on me, telling me something about my father and his attitudes about human beings. His values about the humanity that we all share became mine. As I recall this incident I realize how very important example, even the smallest gesture is in the raising of a child.

There was also a great deal of talk. My father, informally and without any stuffy or didactic affectations, created a sort of "gymnasium" in the classical Greek sense of the word, a place where ideas were discussed and debated. It came into existence without intention and its meetings were by the swimming pool and only at night. At first I was the only pupil, but whenever I had a friend stay for what we called "sleep-overs," that boy was always welcome. My best friend, Danny, was a frequent participant; eventually my brothers were included. By the time my sisters were old enough for these philosophical evenings, I'd already gone off to college, but I believe the tradition continued. For me, however, aged eleven through fourteen, it was an enriching experience.

It was for my father as well. He clearly enjoyed discussing serious questions, things philosophical, theological, and theoretical. Questions about God and the infinite, the idea of the curvature of space-time, and the evolutionary history of the physical planet became part of my mental geography.

My father and I would lie on outdoor chaises, wrapped in blankets in the fall and spring. The method was Socratic. My father posed questions. He rarely presented an opinion or certainty, except when it concerned the sciences, things like tectonic plate theory, or evolution, or cosmology. He knew the difference between opinions and facts. He was an M.I.T. graduate, was scientifically very literate, and valued facts highly. Since there were more unknowns than certainties in the field of cosmology,

we talked a lot about black holes and Einstein's theories while lying on
our backs by the pool and looking up at the stars; it was as if we might
see some part of the answer. In those days the smog had not reached the
mountains and the night skies were dazzling. In the background there
was always the sound of crickets. Questions about God were matters
that interested him as much as they did me. Did one need religion to be
a good person, to know right from wrong? Did one need God to explain
the world? My father identified himself as an agnostic. He made no
objection, however, to my receiving a religious education.

    And I received one. Until my father built the house at the ranch
and the family spent the whole weekend in what, to my father, was
the more spiritual setting, Sunday mornings were dedicated to making
a Christian out of me. My mother took me to St. James Episcopal on
Wilshire Boulevard and while she attended the service, I sat in a classroom in the basement of the rectory with other boys and girls my own
age and listened to Bible stories, Jonah and the whale and others, similar and didactically palatable for eight and nine-year-olds. The story of
Abraham's sacrifice of his son, Isaac, and God's substitution of a goat for
the boy, was most interesting to me and very distressing: Abraham's willingness to kill his son because God told him to do it, did not, I thought,
even at that young age, speak well of either God or Abraham. There were
workbooks of some sort. I think we may have colored in such things as
Noah's Ark and David holding his sling at the ready while staring up at
the giant Goliath. After the service, the minister, still wearing his cas-
sock, would come to our classroom and give theological instruction. The
New Testament was his purview.

    God had a son, an idea I did not understand, but which was pre-
sented as generally agreed upon, so I don't remember balking at the
idea. I knew that His son was killed in a particularly horrible way—
there were crosses strategically placed in the church buildings, none
with the body hanging from them, but there were enough illustrations in books which, even much cleaned up and scrubbed of agony,
meant that I knew what crucifixion meant. I, at nine, was a literalist.
I understood: he died. But then, we were told, the son came back to

life. The business of a dead person coming back to life bothered me. The minister—an older man, in a position of authority, who wore such sumptuous clothes at Easter that I thought he must be a sort of king—had said that we must believe it was true and since he said so, it must be. Nevertheless, the idea troubled me. I already knew a lot about death from what I knew about the war—there was no way a child born in 1940 could have avoided knowing something about death. There'd been so many soldiers and civilians killed, and none, as far as I had heard, had come back to life. We would have heard about it. It would have been talked about at the dinner table. Perhaps I had come across information about the war that was inappropriate for my age, or perhaps there was something in my personality that made me especially susceptible to "knowing" about such things. Whatever the reason, I was a child with doubts. If what the minister was telling us, repeating the story each Sunday about the dead man who came back to life, was true and it was so important, why didn't my father come to church and sit with my mother and repeat those pledges that began with "I believe...," pledges I was being taught to repeat by rote. Perhaps my father didn't believe. I worried about such things, questions that would, five or so years later, become fodder for our nighttime conversations, the gymnasium by the swimming pool.

The idea of a God who was everywhere and in charge of everyone and everything, would also become part of our informal curriculum. Since I knew about the wars, I wondered why God, if He had really been in charge, would have wanted so many terrible things to happen. Concepts like "free will" were not in my arsenal of rationalizations. The idea of a God who loved me was even more difficult. Why me? The message that I had received from my mother, who was often critical and never affectionate, was that I wasn't especially lovable. She said that she loved me, but in the absence of kind words or the sensual experience of affection, simple cuddling, I didn't feel that she did. People, I began to understand, could talk about love without meaning it. How did the minister know that God loved me? I'd never experienced it. How did the minister know about God? Perhaps he didn't really know; perhaps some

other minister had told him when he was little and impressionable, just
as he was telling me.

Eternity was another of those big ideas that had cropped up in Sunday
school and that I had trouble with. A future that stretched beyond next
week or my next birthday was an abstraction. The distant past was as
well. For a child it is hard to imagine a world that existed before he or
she had existed. But I finally got my young mind around "the past." This
understanding came to me rather suddenly, through a simple lesson that
my paternal grandfather orchestrated at just the right time in my life. It
was my first experience of what I now think of as an epiphany, epiphany
in its secular sense.

 Twice a month, between the ages of eight and ten, I spent the
weekend with my paternal grandparents. I looked forward to these
visits. My father would take me to his parents' house, driving across
flatland Los Angeles, up Third Street, past miles of little shops, dry
cleaners and gas stations, then onto Santa Monica Boulevard. I always
watched for the little red trolleys of the Pacific Electric Railroad as they
rolled by on their noisy metal wheels from downtown to the beach.
I wanted to ride the trolleys but since my father, a native son, found
driving pleasurable, I never had the chance. There was little traffic in
those days so we could get to Beverly Hills in fifteen minutes. When
we reached Beverly Hills he turned off Santa Monica Boulevard and
entered a world of fine houses on streets lined with palm trees that
were so tall and spindly that it was hard to believe that they could stay
standing up. We drove into the hills, then through the stone columns
that marked the entrance to the quarter mile of private driveway that
led to the house. Carrying a little overnight bag, I would mount the
limestone steps, pausing sometimes to dip my fingers in the fountain
with its glistening mosaic of pussy willows and butterflies. My father
stayed in the car until the front door opened and I entered the house.
He wanted me to go up the steps on my own, to sense that I was
entering my grandparents' world not as a child, but as a young man
in the making. The downstairs maid always opened the door; she was

an elderly woman, always in a black dress with a white lace collar, who had been with my grandparents for thirty years. The two little dachshunds would bound up to me. Then my grandmother would appear. She was tall and a bit like Eleanor Roosevelt in that she was always active in good causes and was not considered especially pretty. She was very warm and I loved her. She was from a family called Esterbrook, people who made fountain pens, and she had once been the national president of the Girl Scouts of America. I was a Cub Scout, learning to tie knots and trying to accumulate merit badges, so this meant something to me. Then my grandfather would appear and ask me, always, if I'd tied my own shoes. It was a joke between us. I would solemnly tell him that I had.

The library, with its dark paneled walls, ceiling height bookshelves, and stained glass windows that made little puddles of colored light on the oriental carpet, was one of my favorite rooms in the house. I was allowed to take any book off the shelf. Some were very old and valuable. I remember one book in particular, a book with hundreds of ancient woodcuts about mining in the Middle Ages: gears, pulleys and cutaway views of tunnels, men with picks wearing odd clothing. I couldn't read a word of it. It was Latin. This book, *De Re Metallica*, by Georgius Agricola had been translated from the Latin by Herbert Hoover. Hoover had been a friend of my great grandfather's; they were both mining engineers. My grandfather's copy of *De Re Metallica* was an original, from 1556; it smelled different from the books I usually read. I ran my fingers lightly over the illustrations and could feel the lines where the image had been pressed into the paper.

One afternoon, my grandfather took me into the library and sat me on the sofa. This was done in a deliberately formal manner that told me that something special was going to happen. He sat beside me and opened a folio-sized book containing color reproductions of watercolors depicting a place called Nineveh. The images were Victorian notions of what that ancient city, the Assyrian capital, had looked like at the apex of its power, tiled palaces, markets covered with brightly colored awnings, hanging gardens, and pleasure boats under sail along a great river called the Tigris. We kept turning the pages. There were maps. I had had a children's book about Abraham Lincoln that had maps of Illinois and the Mississippi river with tiny drawings of sternwheelers on the river, of wheat fields, forests, and wild animals placed appropriately. Abraham Lincoln's childhood had been in a real place, one which could be understood in a different way through a map called "Illinois." I had learned that the world could be understood symbolically through maps. I loved maps, the way of seeing the world from a great height.

After the watercolor tour of Nineveh and Assyria from the map-maker's altitude, there were, in this same book, sepia photographs of fallen columns, of stone heads emerging from the desert, and of crumbled mud-brick walls. The broken statuary and eroded walls would have sobering implications for me today, but didn't then. My grandfather had not intended a *sic transit gloria* message. Hamish would have, but his influence on my intellectual development had not yet begun. In preparatory school, a mere five years later, that afternoon with my grandfather came back to me as a flash of recognition when I read Shelley's poem about the fate of empires.

> *And on the pedestal these words appear:*
> *'My name is Ozymandias, king of kings:*
> *Look on my works, ye Mighty, and despair!'*
> *Nothing beside remains. Round the decay*
> *Of that colossal wreck, boundless and bare*
> *The lone and level sands stretch far away.*

Shelley's poem thrilled me. It still does. It traced outlines of a world that I was just beginning to perceive, the underlying narratives of fragility and impermanence. Reading Shelley's poem was probably the first time I experienced the power— the magic—of poetry. Nineveh, both the facts and the legends, had combined with Shelley's "Ozymandias" and together, the one catalyzing the other, an intoxicating, almost hallucinatory, insight had resulted. My Shelley "moment" was crucial in creating the idea that I wanted to be a poet. The world was intriguing, both as itself *and* how we imagined it, and the language of poetry was the way to express this.

My grandfather closed the book. He then reached into his jacket pocket and took out a little square piece of baked clay about 2 ½ inches on a side, 3/8 inch thick. It had strange marks on it, marks like the pecks of a bird's beak. He put it into my hand.

"The little marks are a kind of writing, an alphabet that is called cuneiform," he said. "This is a bill of sale for wheat. It comes from Nineveh or one of the other great cities of Mesopotamia." He paused, to emphasize what he would say next. "It is almost four thousand years old."

My eyes opened wide. Four thousand years was indeed very old! My understanding of time and its linear passage, and how much of it had already passed began here, with a message pressed into a piece of wet clay by a scribe who lived in a city that no longer existed. This little object lay in my open palm. My grandfather then reached over and closed my fingers around it. After a pause he said, "The past belongs to the living; you must never lose it."

On that occasion, I took his meaning literally, that I should take good care of the thing itself. As I grew older, I came to understand that it was the knowledge of the past that one should not lose. One should not forget. I did take care of the tablet too, for twenty-five years, until, during the time of the hippies, someone I had welcomed into my house stole it.

I handled the little clay tablet carefully. It seemed full of talismanic power. I stroked it, thinking, I suspect, of Aladdin's lamp, and a "genie" did appear, a formless spirit, but a genie nonetheless: imagination. I imagined that the ancient world of the Mediterranean unfolded before me and I, floating above it, could see the ancient cities and empires, Rome, Assyria, and Egypt. I imagined places that no longer existed. I could see the land too, the mountains, the deserts, the rivers, and deltas. I was opening my mind to a narrative that included the ancient past. Eventually I replaced the fables with history. Mesopotamia was the central part of this story; it led to an adult interest in all aspects of the Middle East, its history and geography. In time I would read many of the English Arabists, including all of T.E. Lawrence (he "of Arabia"). Charles M. Doughty's *Travels in Arabia Deserta* remains for me one of the great adventures, the equal of Marco Polo's.

Thirty years later, the fantasy of floating above the world reappeared in my adult work, not as a conscious reprise, but rather as something that emerged from deep in my unconscious. I was remembering those sepia photographs of shattered Assyrian statuary emerging from the sand. In my third book, *The Plain of Smokes* I wrote

> *... miraculous*
> *how the unexpected landscapes*
> *appeared as prelude*
> *on the kitchen table...*
> *...Asia Minor by afternoon*
> *Troy's outline*
> *in the rake of low sun,*
> *trace of walls and agony*
> *beneath the sand*

* * *

Through a bit of grandfatherly magic, I had discovered that Time had depth. Layers of previous days lie beneath the present day. As they went by, the days did not dissolve like the wake of a ship on the sea; they accumulated and were preserved in some form or another, as newspapers in an archive or as memory. Some of the past was dark, some rich with treasure, some of great importance. The little clay tablet had launched me toward a lifelong involvement with history generally and histories specifically, the history of my family, of my country, and of other cultures, of wars, injustices, and crimes. It was, in part, the search for the past, to see evidence of it, that inspired Jim's and my trip to Europe.

5

Landfall

The gray weather returned. When we disembarked at Le Havre, a light rain was falling. It was early morning and the lights along the docks were still on, haloed in the mist. The quays were wet. There weren't many of us who disembarked; most were going on to Southampton. Two serious-looking policemen stood at the foot of the gangplank and watched as we came down the gangplank. The romantic notions of travel that had accompanied me on the crossing— Lord Byron, at twenty-two, off to Greece to swim the Hellespont, that sort of thing—dispersed into the mist. Foreignness, somewhat intimidating, began here.

Jim and I crossed the quay and entered a gray metal-sided building. An immigration officer sat behind a plain wooden table on which, arrayed neatly side by side, were two rubber stamps with varnished wood handles. Entry allowed or entry denied. He asked us what we were going to do in France. At least I think that is what he asked. Neither Jim nor I spoke a word of French. It was an awkward moment, but since the official had probably seen many young Americans like us, it was merely awkward, not tense. Most came either for adventure or for study. I would have said to him, if I'd been able, that I came not for casual adventure, but for experience in capital letters. As to study I might have said that I wanted to see for myself a place with a past. My own country doesn't have much. I didn't want to be taken for a college boy on a lark. "I would like to see buildings more important than a department store."

But I said nothing. The official talked and my blank look explained my position. He shrugged his shoulders and picked up his stamp, thumped it down on my passport. *Le douanier* glanced at our bags; since drugs weren't much of an issue in those days, they were not opened. He waved us through and we were in Europe.

Jim and I left the customs hall and found ourselves on the street. Where was the rail station and how would we find it? Our dictionary told us how: follow the signs to *Gare*. There were few people out at this hour, mostly men in dark coats and hats, all walking, it seemed, in ways different than the ways Californians walk, more serious perhaps, with different sorts of things on their minds than we Californians usually had on ours. As we would discover very soon, they did in fact have serious things on their minds. France was facing a political crisis, one we little understood at the time.

On that gray French morning, with not an English word in sight, it suddenly struck us that we were unreachable. If someone died in Los Angeles, we would not know of it for months. We had left American Express Madrid and Rome as possible contact points, possible, but without dates. And if one of us stepped off a curb the wrong way, took a wrong turning and was lost, it might be forever. I had read in Prescott's *Conquest of Mexico,* how Cortez had burned his boats on the beaches of Veracruz: there was to be no turning back. A little vicarious heroics didn't hurt; it boosted morale.

Jim and I were so determined to untether ourselves from the known and comfortable that we had recognized, on the boat, that if we stayed together, insulated in our bubble of English language, our cultural and personal familiarity, we would learn little, experience less, and risk nothing. We decided, therefore, that we would separate, Jim to Italy, and I, staying with the original plan, would go to Spain.

But we stayed together for the next four days. We took the train to Paris, and gradually the undistinguished landscape, flat fields with copses of trees, became the city, the zinc roofs and red clay chimney pots, the station under its nineteenth century roof of iron and glass, a place familiar from pictures and postcards. When we arrived at the Gare

St Lazare we found a city in a condition of taut self-control, fearful, not panicked, but seriously apprehensive. Soldiers with automatic weapons patrolled the station and the streets outside, and there were few people on the streets. We had not come into a postcard scene of imposing buildings and noble statuary, but into a dangerous moment in the history of the French republic. Not accustomed to the idea that politics had serious consequences, we felt, vaguely, with American naivety, that we had stumbled into a movie. But it was not a fiction; it was a real crisis, a threat of civil war at the worst, or, at the minimum, a military *coup d'etat*. Already having lost its colony in Indochina in 1954, France, in that September, was on the brink of conceding that it had lost the crown jewel of its colonies, Algeria. There were concerns about a widespread mutiny by Algerian-based elements of the French army. Black vans filled with police were parked everywhere in Paris. Tanks had been parked in the middle of the Champs-Élysées to prevent a landing by glider. Three gendarmes, with machine guns strapped across their chests, stopped us to check identity papers. We had left our passports in our hotel. Because the words for "passport" and "hotel" are identical in French and English, we managed to convince the policemen that one of us would go back to the hotel and the other would stay behind, effectively in custody, as a hostage. Jim, because he had been a star runner in prep school, would go for the passports while I would stay. As I watched Jim run off I had a moment's panic, the silly notion that he might just keep running and that I would end up in jail. But soon enough he reappeared, panting, with two passports in hand. The problem was resolved.

The situation that we had stumbled into upset a number of my conceptions of how things stood in the world. I had thought that the Pax Americana had brought the world back into balance. But, as we saw in Paris those three days, disorder was as present and insistent as it had always been. In my childhood, the late 1940s through the 1950s, the threat of nuclear annihilation had been constantly in the background. But since it hadn't happened and continued not to happen year after year, it faded into the background; I think people treated it as someone else's problem, much the way climate change is treated today. Thus, an extreme civic crisis, a political failure of democracy, as France faced that year, came as a great surprise.

What Jim and I witnessed on the streets of Paris showed me that disorder, like the Colossus in Goya's painting, still stalked the earth. The forces of malevolence, of hate and misrule, were at work; France, as a mature democracy, was facing an existential threat. Because it was a threat from within, it seemed almost more serious. An enemy outside the wall is easy to understand: one turns to face it. When the enemy is a part of what you have imagined as yourself, a sort of political autoimmune disease, it seems more dangerous.

I saw, or wanted to see, contrasts that reflected favorably on the United States. I believed America, the City on the Hill, to be above all such troubles. America had won the war. America led the world. America was a model. America had settled its internal issues. A part of me firmly believed all this. As if to emphasize my sense of American superiority, I remarked to Jim that I had never seen soldiers carrying rifles on American streets. How conveniently I had forgotten that just three years earlier I'd seen the pictures of American soldiers with rifles escorting African American teenagers, kids my own age, into high school in Little Rock, Arkansas. Could this be America? No, I had decided, it was another country or a sort of colony, one called The South. As to overseas colonies, America had none, or so I believed. In that same year, however, what I didn't know, and what few outside the Eisenhower administration knew, was that the United States was assuming the ambitions, along with the responsibilities and delusions, of France's colonial enterprise in Southeast Asia. France's Indochina nightmare would become America's, the Vietnam War. History, another name perhaps for the Fates of Greek mythology, was weaving a snare that America was not to escape.

In that moment in 1960, however, Jim and I were only inconvenienced. We continued as planned. We would stay in touch through the mail drop at American Express. Since we had no itinerary, letters might sit for weeks, even months. We discussed the issues of solitude and isolation, but nonchalantly, as if being almost completely out of touch did not matter. We kept it light.

"If you marry a gypsy girl, I'll make sure your mother comes to the wedding," he said. We imagined his letter to my mother. "Dear Mrs. Mudd, you will be pleased to learn… services to be held on a hillside somewhere near Granada. Bring your walking shoes." Jim and I batted this joke back and forth a bit, while standing on the rail platform waiting for the train to Rome. I swore that like Odysseus I would tie myself to the mast and resist the call of the sirens, and he, Jim, must swear to do the same. It was a vow of emotional chastity, which probably meant physical chastity as well, that we took seriously. Jim broke the vow mid-year when his girlfriend from the States came to visit. And I, at least in my heart, had broken the emotional part of the vow by the time I crossed the Spanish frontier. The fantasy of meeting a gypsy girl accompanied me for most of the year. I had a specific girl in mind. I'd seen her picture in a book about Spain that I'd found in a used bookstore in New York. I was easily smitten, genetically a romantic, with fantasies fueled by an almost complete lack of experience with real women.

6

I Find the Road

As I stood on the platform and watched Jim's train leave for Rome I knew that I had come to a significant landmark; "adulthood begins here" was the perception. The soot-coated glass ceiling and the black steel girders that created the canopy called up the old movies that I'd watched in Greenwich Village cinemas the year before. How many soldiers had left from these same platforms, how many spies, how many rejected lovers? One came to the Gare du Lyon, one left or was left behind, and was never the same again. I too was being transformed, as was the world I came from. California, the bright sun, the palm trees, all that was in process of becoming unreal. This, the *Foreign*, was the real, and now the foreign was compounded by *alone*, but there would be no going back. Was I up to it? I was not sure. Yet that same day I managed to purchase a four-year-old Citroën DS 19. How I figured out how to find and buy a used car, I do not remember. Then, somehow, I found my way out of Paris, and set off for Spain.

I had none of the usual guidebooks. For what to see I had only the suggestions that I had picked up from Hamish. I was in many things his follower. In 1954, for instance, I had sat in on a conversation between Hamish and my father about classical music in which Hamish had mentioned that he preferred the Baroque over the more emotional Brahms and Rachmaninov, the music that my father liked and that I had grown up hearing on the Victrola. When I returned to school I went to the

41

librarian who suggested that I try Vivaldi. There were two music booths with earphones; I listened and was hooked. Vivaldi became part of my emotional survival kit. I was carrying a 10-inch record of the *Gloria* with me on the trip, along with a portable record player that was about the size of a briefcase. Today's smart phone has better sound.

I learned to appreciate things that we usually associate with "culture" from Hamish. The historical styles of architecture, for instance, what arch went with what period; 14th century Italian painting—Giotto, as the first humanist, was his favorite; Roman and Greek antiquity—he quoted Horace in Latin. He mentioned books I might never have heard of like the *Essays* of Montaigne. My father had guided me into natural history, but when it came to things cultural or historical, I was Hamish's pupil. I was like a puppy; Hamish would throw the ball and I would go chasing after it.

He had insisted, for instance, that I see the cathedral of Notre Dame des Chartres. It was not on the direct route to Spain and I was not the least religious, but I took the detour anyway. It turned out to be an important experience, for through this visit I came to understand something about the core idea that kept Hamish so willingly engaged with the world despite having lived through two world wars. It was an aggregate of objects, ideas, and values that he called "civilization."

Civilization was what stood between mankind and his worse impulses. By that word he had meant the efforts, across centuries, to select the best *and most enduring* among all the possibilities that life offered. To make rubble or to kill was easy. To create and then to preserve was infinitely more difficult. It was neither religion nor government that guided man toward good choices: it was a yearning to be better, a feeling that came out of natural law. Civilization was a projection of our best values and it mirrored those values back to us and thus enhanced our sense of our own worth. This, he said, was the persuasive argument for a liberal education. It was a conversation that he had often with my grandfather; he feared that the modern world, with its emphasis on money and technology, was diminishing the human spirit, that specialization would result in the loss of connection to the larger whole. Rationality, a love of beauty, and the will to create, these were what stood between people of good will and the barbarian. He had a great fear of the barbarian.

In 1955, Hamish took my father and me to see the ruins of Christopher Wren's Church of St Mary-le-Bow; it had been hit by a German bomb in 1941. St Mary's, when I saw it, was little more than jumbled piles of marble, broken walls, and no roof. "But we will restore it," Hamish said. Wren's plans for St Mary-le-Bow still existed and there were hundreds of photographs, so now, instead of clearing away the rubble to make way for something new, the English would rebuild the church. To a child of Los Angeles, where no building could be called truly old or worth saving, and where redevelopment was the default way of thinking, to restore a building to its original condition was a novel idea.

"It was a fearful time, young Harvey," he said. "German bombers overhead every night for two months. Thousands of tons of bombs fell on this city." He paused, looked at the skeleton of what he had described as the most beautiful church in London. His expression was grim.

"In a truly civilized world," he said, "one would not be subjected to random violent death. A mother should be able to walk her pram in Regent's Park without fearing that a bomb will fall on her. Absence of violence is what makes all else possible."

This image of the pram in the park was typical of Hamish's style: ironic, dry, understated. "All else?" I supposed that he meant everything that mattered, St Mary-le-Bow mattered. Rebuilding, restoring, was integral to his belief, his credo. One did not let the barbarian get away with it by letting his depredations stand.

Hamish was nominally Church of England, but without, as he once said to me, "a credulous or superstitious bone" in his body. He believed, however, that religions generally, including Christianity in its original moral sense—as opposed to its historical institutional existence—enabled some of the best aspects of mankind. St Mary-le-Bow represented for him more than the building. It was the spiritual home for thousands of poor East Londoners in the seventeenth century, and even more important to him, it was a work of great beauty.

His mood lightened. The grim expression faded and he turned to me, looking down, for I had not yet reached my full height, and with a mischievous look, he said:

"Churches matter. Being an angel is hard work, young Harvey, going out day after day, trying to keep us miserable creatures on our best behavior. Think of a church as a kind of inn, or a pub even, where the angels go to get refreshed, exchange notes and tips, work up plans for sorting us. And we do need sorting, if for no other reason so that we don't have to keep rebuilding."

We walked on. We walked over an iron grate, a vent apparently for the underground. A train whooshed past beneath us. "The Central Line to Bank," he observed, offhand, almost as a notation. His city had layers, strata, and he was aware of them. It was like his sense of history. There was meaning beneath us. The past.

"Perhaps you'll come back to see St Mary when she's restored. This site will be a hive of activity for a decade, workmen, engineers. Some enterprising chap will set up a coffee bar for the workers. I'll come once a month to watch." He reflected a moment. "There's another church you should see someday, another place where the angels stop…"

Chartres did not disappoint. As one approaches the town from the northeast, the cathedral rises out of yellow wheat fields like a sailing ship appearing over the far edge of the ocean. I found the town square and parked. As I examined the famous array of saints and apostles on the façade, I recast it the way Hamish might have, had he been with me; instead of saints, I thought of all those who had had a hand in its creation, the architects and engineers, the stone cutters, day laborers, carpenters, glass workers, and tradesmen, the muleteers who brought the stone, the bakers and brewers who provisioned the workers, prostitutes who gave pleasure to even the poorest of them on a Saturday night. There had been, no doubt, priests or monks who had taken their turn on the winches or who got down on their knees in the gravel to give comfort to the worker who had fallen from the scaffold. The building towered above me, taller than the ship on which I'd crossed the Atlantic. It was eerily quiet that Monday, almost a holy silence, though it occurs to me now that it might just have been lunchtime.

This was indeed a beautiful building; I needed no Christian faith to see that. And it was very old, I memorized the date the cornerstone had been set, 1194. I keep in my mind a handful of landmark dates to help me navigate the labyrinth of history: the year both Shakespeare and Cervantes died, a day apart in April, 1616; the year Muslim Granada fell to the Christians, 1492, the same year Columbus set off to find the route to the Indies; the year Cortez landed on the coast of Mexico, the years of the American Civil War, a handful of other dates that for some reason have struck me as being meaningful. The year of the Declaration of Independence, 1776, was among them. For Hamish, America had a place among the great projects of civilization, an ambitious plan fueled by noble ideas. Democracy was the core idea, a belief in a common good guided by collective wisdom. Wisdom, Hamish emphasized, not passions or appetites, not ambition or greed.

On the long drive from Paris to Spain, I stayed in little hotels and, lying on narrow beds, I read Stendhal's *The Charterhouse of Parma*. The protagonist of the novel, Fabrice, a young Italian nobleman of dubious paternity and younger than I was as I read the book, stumbles into the final battle of the Napoleonic Wars. Waterloo, Fabrice is sure, will mark the zenith of French glory. So this precocious adolescent reinvented himself as a Frenchman, specifically as a French soldier. He stole a dead soldier's uniform and believed that by doing so, he became a soldier and would become a part of history. But his perspective was a lowly one; he was not on the hilltop with the generals. He saw mud and smoke, a few bodies, and a lot of dead horses. His French comrades stole his horse. At one point, Fabrice asked a sergeant whom he encountered if he was in the battle yet. He saw little and understood less, and in the end, was on the losing side.

Fabrice quit the field without flourish. He hitched a ride on a peasant's hay cart. In Stendhal's young hero, I saw something of myself as I was then and am still. Engaged with life but without illusions. Fabrice discovered that he lived in a world full of lies, misconceptions, and failed efforts, but he remained persistently true to himself. Accidents, contingency, (and lazy plotting on Stendhal's part) determined most of what happened to Fabrice. The insight I took away from the novel is that we have little control over where and how we end up. If Stendhal had made the plot tighter and neater, the novel would have emerged as a lightweight romance; what Stendhal gives us is realism, wry and unlikely, but still truthful.

Contingency, I think, is the rule rather than the exception. It is the pattern that starts with our births. It is trite, but no less true, that we do not choose our parents. Nor, to extrapolate from that, do we choose our country of birth, who our neighbors are going to be, what natural disasters or diseases will reshape our landscapes, where the barbarians will come from, or what will emerge as the spirit of the age we inherit. And luck, more often than not, determines how we come out of it. Hamish told me that it was as much luck as courage that had won the war: good weather and fewer bad decisions than the Germans had made. A lot of luck. He had his own example. He lived in London during the German bombings of 1940-41, the raids that destroyed St Mary-le-Bow. A five-hundred pound German bomb had fallen into his backyard, smashing into his greenhouse; it had not exploded.

"I had been sitting in my study. I'd not gone to the shelter because our part of the city was never bombed. That the German pilot was off course was just my bad luck. But then the bloody thing didn't explode; my good luck. It took the bomb squad a week to get it out of my yard."

7

Spain at Last

I entered Spain at Irun, the old smugglers' gateway, and headed west along the coast. My destination was Altamira. I'd known about the caves of Altamira and their Paleolithic wall paintings of bison and gazelles for several years—from a few slides projected on a screen in a high school art history class—and visiting the caves had become a commitment, a pilgrimage for me, like the tomb of Saint James had been for the devout of the Middle Ages. My interest had something to do with the age of the site, 15,000 B.C. It was more than historical interest. I felt that Altamira would provide a glimpse into the ancient soul of humanity, long before humans began to write about either the soul or the gods. My interest also had to do with animals. And it had something to do with caves.

I was afraid of heights and of falling, but even as a child I was unafraid of caves. Tom Sawyer and his gang had had a hideout in a limestone cave overlooking the Mississippi and it was there they planned to be highway robbers. Fictional caves are where the fantasies of boys are born. I had had mine. As soon as I learned to read, I hid beneath my sheets with a flashlight and read long after my bedtime. This was my first cave. And I had been to a real and most impressive cave, a working copper-lead-zinc mine that my father had taken me to when I was eleven. It was in the state of Chihuahua, in northern Mexico, an exotic strangeness (my first visit to a foreign country) which added much to the experience. It was much more than a cave; it was a vast network of caverns, manmade halls, galleries, and tunnels, deep in the earth, 3000 feet down, accessible by a cage elevator. The air got cooler as we descended and then got warmer as we entered levels that were warmed by the earth's molten core. The sense of the weight of the earth overhead, the density of the rocks, and total darkness—our guide showed us by switching off the lights for twenty seconds—never bothered me. Huge fans hummed in the background and moved the warm air out and brought fresh air in; pumps removed water that would have flooded the shafts. The walls of the tunnels were whitewashed and the whole area was spotlessly clean. I watched a group of Mexican miners, men with little lamps flickering on their hard hats, emerge from a tunnel. They were talking and laughing, their white teeth bright against coppery brown skin. Then a little train appeared pulling dozens of open cars filled with raw ore. The mine face, where there was heavy machinery and dust, was half a mile away, at the end of a tunnel. I wasn't allowed to go further, but I would have.

For a time, I felt sure that I would follow my father and become a mining engineer, but gradually a greater interest emerged, archaeology. Perhaps the connection was in the caves, of things buried or hidden, waiting to be found. At my father's ranch there was a deep overhang of rock where people, now known as the Chumash, had camped hundreds of years earlier. The tribe has vanished, wiped out by the white man's diseases or worse, by intention. The rock walls of the overhang were blackened by smoke but, standing out against the black on the walls and the ceiling, were faint red markings. There were wavy lines and, quite clearly, a lizard. Perhaps the markings were no more than graffiti, gestures that said, "We were here," but perhaps they were more, magic I thought. I would often go—always alert for rattlesnakes—and sit under the overhang. In winter, if it was raining, I watched the sheets of rain fall on the fields and the silent dark masses of the oak trees, and imagined the little fires that had warmed Indians who sheltered from the rain, In summer, I would shelter in the cave from the heat of the July sun. I would look out at my father's yellow fields. What I did while I sat there was "to think," whatever that meant at age nine or ten. I was a solitary child, and no one worried about it. I was content in my solitude; perhaps I was happier being away from the tensions of the assembled family, out from under my mother's close vigilance. I would think about these vanished people and I felt sadness. The usual ten-year-old sadness has to do with some personal disappointment or loss; but this was different. I would look up at the smoked ceiling of the overhang and wonder who had painted the little red lizard. A child? A shaman? I decided that the wavy lines were rattlesnakes.

At Altamira, there are enormous red bison, herds of gazelles, and the imprint, in negative, of human hands. The hands of the painters, of the hunters. Except for pockets of scattered bones found by paleontologists, little was known about these beings, the animals or the humans, but here they were again, almost alive, saved by art. I visited the caverns before the damage from human breath had been noted, before the caves had been closed and replaced by a replica. It was a rainy day in October. I was completely alone, but in the company of ghosts that were even older than my grandfather's Mesopotamia. An ancient time, a time before Hamish's civilization had properly begun, but I knew that I was in the presence of its beginnings. From cave to the gothic vaults at Chartres, from bison on the wall to the stained glass windows, it was all of a piece, a continuum.

After an hour or two, the damp of the cave penetrated my coat so I went back outside. There too it was damp and cold. But there, in the air, time moved. I watched the rain fall and the light fade.

The dark came early. Without a watch, I often lost track of the hour. The day after my visit to the caves, I wandered in a medieval cloister and hadn't heard the monk announce closing time. Perhaps he hadn't, had just assumed that no one would have been so daft as to be wandering about in those cold and grey precincts in the twilight. Pounding on the door produced nothing. I was locked in. I spent a cold, damp night hunkered down between two stone caskets. One had the date carved on its lid, 1267, and the remains of a bishop inside; his skull was illuminated through a small crack each time I lit a cigarette. The monk who opened the cloister at nine in the morning was most apologetic and made me a hearty breakfast of fried ham.

I continued on to Santiago de Compostela where, on my first evening in the city, unaccustomed to cars driving along city streets without head-lights, I stepped in the path of a tiny Seat automobile in which there were a father, a mother, and four small children. I was knocked down, but did not appear (to myself, after checking bones) to be seriously injured. The father, utterly distraught, urged me to go to the hospital; the word for hospital being identical in both languages, I understood that much. Then I went through a comical exercise of pretending that I understood what he was saying. People had gathered around to stare at the wounded Yankee, or whatever sort of foreigner they thought me to be.

"Hospital, Señor. ¿No ira? ¿No ira?"

Now what, I thought, does "ira" mean? He kept repeating the word. Then it came to me. "Ira" was like the English "ire," anger. He wanted to know if I was angry. Not at all, I tried to assure him, smiling, shrug-ging; all was well. I was not the least bit angry; I was mortified at having stepped off the curb and into the path of his car, frightening his chil-dren, ruining his family outing.

I looked at him directly and as calmly as possible—I was shaking within, having been hit by a car in a strange land—I said, "no ira, no ira," and walked away. He followed, jabbering urgently. A block or so later, away from the crowd of gawkers, I discovered the reason for his concern: the back of my pant leg was wet with blood. I found a doctor's office—everything in Spain stays open late—and had my first experi-ence with second-world medicine. There were bloody sheets on the examining table and gauzes from removed bandages, stained yellow and brown, tossed about on the floor. The doctor was a homosexual. He made an awkward pass—which I deflected, causing embarrassment—but he managed, somewhat less clumsily, to get six stitches into the gash on my leg. A tetanus shot, and I was released into the night. I retired to my simple hotel, which turned out to be situated practically underneath a magnificent set of church bells that went off at six in the morning. I disposed of my torn pants and quite sore and bruised, left the hotel, did the requisite tourist visit to the tomb of Saint James the Apostle, James the killer of Moors. I remember nothing of it, probably because my leg hurt.

About five in the evening I set off on the road toward Soria which I wanted to visit because of the poet Antonio Machado, whose work I loved. I had no plan about where to spend the night. The route went through the city of Leon. I passed through a drab, dimly lit city center. The movie theater, which, at just past nine in the evening, was empty-ing, its lights flickering off. There were few pedestrians, all of whom were bundled and wrapped against the bitter cold of the approaching Castilian winter. I made a wrong turn and found myself thoroughly lost in a working class barrio that seemed not even up to second-world standards. The houses were grey stone, two and three stories high, with no lights showing, for all were shuttered against the cold. There was no commerce of any kind. The streets were lit by naked light bulbs hung from posts that were so far apart that there were deep shadows between feeble puddles of light. It was clearly an older part of the city, with narrow streets going every which way. I was completely lost.

I saw a man walking toward me. In the headlights I could see from his posture and gait that he was older. He was dressed in an overcoat, with a black beret on his head, and a scarf wrapped around his neck so that it covered the lower half of his face. I pulled up beside him and asked, as best I could, for directions to the next city on the route. "A Burgos." He pulled the scarf from his face and began to give directions, but it quickly became clear that I did not understand, and so, without a moment's hesitation, he came around to the passenger side of the car, opened the door and got in. I had a moment of apprehension but it passed. The man, very lean, almost gaunt, was probably in his late six-ties. He smiled and pointed back the way I had come. I turned the car around and off we went. He directed me with his finger, left, right. After about fifteen minutes of negotiating unmarked streets, we came to what was clearly the edge of the city. He pointed and said "Burgos." But how was he to get home? I objected with my few words, "Su casa, Señor.

¿donde?" He smiled, wagged his finger in a typical Spanish gesture of negation, offered me his hand, which I took; then he opened the door and got out into the bitter cold. The dead city and a long walk lay before him. He pointed again, waved, and walked away.

To Burgos then. When I set out it was well past ten at night. Mile after mile and no inn appeared. I finally pulled over, wrapped myself in my two coats and went to sleep in my car. Sometime deep in the night, there was a knock on my window. I awoke. A man was looking at me, a man whose face was entirely wrapped in a thick woolen scarf except for his eyes, which were hidden by goggles. He wore a leather cap and a long leather coat. I was frightened and was tempted to start the car and drive away. When the man saw that I was awake, he stood up and saluted, and then pointed to a badge on his leather coat. He was the highway patrol. I rolled down the window and managed to assure him that I was all right. I demonstrated that the car functioned. All this was done with simple words and pantomime. He nodded, saluted again, and, like my Good Samaritan earlier that night, walked away. Behind my car, I heard his motorcycle engine roar to life. A motorcycle, I thought, on a night like this! He pulled beside me for a moment, saluted again, and sped off. I watched his tail light disappear. The cold highway was like a ribbon of black satin gleaming in the light of a full moon.

Both these encounters filled me with a sense of profound gratitude. The modest generosity of the older man who had set me back on my route and the sense of duty that motivated the policeman were gestures I was not accustomed to, acts of disinterested decency. The wealthy, it occurred to me, are sheltered from the worst aspects of humankind, but in their comfortable houses and chauffeured automobiles, cared for by people on salary, they seldom experience the best. The "kindnesses" that they receive are paid for, never given. Until these two encounters in Spain, on the same night, I had not realized that there was something valuable that my father and people similarly sheltered were missing. I've never forgotten those two encounters.

Not long afterwards I realized that "ira," the word that the man who had run into me with his car had used, was the future tense of the verb "to go." "Won't you go to the hospital" was what he was asking, pleading. He probably thought he'd done me serious harm. Poor man. I had left him shaken and feeling guilty. I too felt guilty. I resolved to work at languages.

I pushed on to Soria, the austere land that had inspired some of the most beautiful poetry in the Spanish language. I thought of finding a house to rent in Soria, but after a month on the harsh plateau of Castile, the gray skies and the cold, I decided I needed sunlight. I headed south to explore Andalusia.

8

Al Andalus

I drove south, heading for the only place in Andalusia that I knew anything about, Granada. I had read Washington Irving's 1828 *Tales of the Alhambra* when I was fourteen. I had mental images of tortoise-shell cats occupying abandoned palaces and of an old lady who built her cooking fires in a corner of the room where the king had held audiences. The smoke from her fires had blackened the wondrous carved ceilings, the stalactites of plaster no longer white as new snow, now old and sooty. The old lady fed the cats—there were dozens, Washington Irving wrote, perhaps hundreds, several generations of them—and together they shared the beautiful red palace with the ghosts of the Arab kings and this solitary old lady. In Washington Irving's time the fountains no longer ran. A romantic ruin, now restored; I knew I must see it with the same level of attention that I'd given to Chartres. I was serious about being a tourist, a posture that kept me from feeling lonely.

Of even greater interest for me in respect to Granada was the poet Federico Garcia Lorca. I loved Lorca's poetry. The *Gypsy Ballads* had been a revelation; the imagery of mountain passes, daggers and cold moons, women with satin-smooth thighs, colors that appeared out of nowhere, the themes of passion and revenge, a totality of emotion, cadence, and imagery that was like nothing I had encountered before, either in fantasy or in fiction. In my imaginary travels, when I was a preteen, I had visited the planet Mars—I read all of Robert Heinlein's novels—but Heinlein's

Mars seemed a bit like Southern California. Lorca's world was much stranger and I was drawn into it. I wanted to follow the way of the gypsy, rather in the sense that boys imagine running off and joining the circus, but now with a bit of Eros in the mix. Imagination provided a good half of my inner life in my early years. Poets were the closest I came to having prophets; poetry for me was Scripture; and Lorca was one of the Evangelists. I have moved away from him as my tastes have matured, but he was there in the beginning. My favorite among the poems began with these lines:

> *Green, how I love you green,*
> *green wind, green branches*
> *the ship on the sea*
> *the horse in the mountains...*

Lorca had been murdered by fascist thugs in Granada in 1936. He was poet and martyr. It seemed inevitable, necessary even, that I would go to Granada. But on the way I stopped in Cordoba, just for a look around.

I had never heard of Cordoba and I knew nothing about its history. I came to the city quite by accident. It was midday and I was hungry. Following my tendency to wander unguided, to follow chance turnings of a road, I ended up, quite lost, in the medieval quarter, a dense aggregation of whitewashed houses in a tangled skein of streets so narrow that only a burro could pass along. Red geraniums filled the window boxes. I was enchanted. I found the Plaza Mayor in the nineteenth century part of the city; the hours were marked not by church bells, but by chords, amplified by loudspeaker, on a flamenco guitar. That clinched it. After no more than an hour's acquaintance I decided that Cordoba was where I would spend the winter.

That very day I walked into a real estate office and by three that afternoon, I had rented a simple but roomy house in the middle of an orange grove. It was the summer home of a family in the city, but in the winter it was empty, unheated, and unfurnished. The owner, a middle-aged man with two attractive daughters, had never expected to rent the house, but after I'd signed the agreement, he came by in a small truck bringing four chairs, a large round table, and a bed that consisted of wire lattice attached by springs to an open frame. He also provided four white plates, two white soup bowls, two spoons, two forks, some glasses and cups, and a kitchen knife. A large pot and a frying pan completed the kitchen. I could make do with this. Finally two blankets and a pillow were added to the pile. While he and I unloaded all this domestic gear, his daughters sat quietly in the truck. I wished that they would somehow invite me to introduce myself. They never did. As the truck drove away, one of the girls glanced at me. In her dark eyes I saw a glimmer of recognition: I was a young male and an exotic one, an American. I waited for days for an invitation to my landlord's house for tea. It never came. I went into town the first of each month to pay my rent, always in cash to the realtor. I never saw the owner again, nor his daughters.

The weather was sunny by day and warm enough that I was able to sit outside at a little table and write. The nights were cold and the house also cold, as only stone houses can be. There was no heat at all except for a charcoal brazier under the table. A blanket, designed for the round table, hung down to the floor, so that if I sat there all evening, my legs stayed warm, but because of fumes from the brazier a window had to remain open. I wrapped my upper body in the other blanket.

Alone in the house, I imagined that ordinary noises were burglars or worse. I fought back by turning up the music on my little phonograph. I had three records: the Shostakovich Quartets, which seemed like a tortured argument about something theological, just my sort of thing; the Mozart Requiem, the anguished last thoughts of a dying Mozart; and Vivaldi's Gloria, the only uplifting music in the lot. On those winter nights, I wished I had brought some jazz with me, Duke Ellington or Louis Armstrong, but I hadn't; and so there I was, at the end of a dirt road in an unheated house, with music that either annoyed God or cracked the heart. The bed felt like a broken trampoline. I made a mattress out of a folded blanket and slept in my coat.

I had no neighbors. Three miles away was the city. At night I could see the lights twinkling. Solitude was to be my lot, at least in the short term. In that solitude, however, and by day, when the sun was up and my body warmed up, I had lots of time for reading and other forms of exploration. The history of the city of Cordoba became the focus of my attention, an interest that intensified as I knew more. Through my engagement with this particular history I came to understand, for the first time, what it was that my grandfather had wanted me to grasp. The past was not a static concept, a possession like a history text book; it was, rather, a living narrative, like an underground spring that fed rich material into the present and shaped it; we the living had the responsibility to keep this source alive, to keep it from being suppressed, polluted with propaganda and lies, or, by simple neglect, forgotten and lost. Truth was the important thing.

In Cordoba I discovered what amounted to a lost history, lost to me, at least, if not to the locals, *los Cordobeses,* or to scholars, but it was certainly to a large majority of people in the West. I began to dig into this hidden history. My brief stay in Cordoba was a time of exciting intellectual discoveries.

I had studied European history and Western cultural history in an excellent preparatory school, but I was quite sure that Cordoba had never been mentioned, not a single line in a textbook. A very important story about European civilization had been skipped over.

The facts I discovered were these: that in the eighth through eleventh centuries, the period justifiably called the "dark ages" in respect to Europe, the city of Cordoba was the largest, richest, and most cultured city on the continent. Population in 1000 C.E. is estimated to have been 200,000; Paris at the same time had 40,000 and London, 10,000; in Cordoba, they had indoor plumbing, libraries, and scientific medicine. Its university predated the founding of the Sorbonne by three hundred years. The great mosque of Cordoba had its cornerstone set in A.D. 785, four hundred years before breaking ground for the cathedral of Notre

Dame de Chartres. Yet, from my educational perspective, it was like Atlantis, the legendary city that sank into the sea. What made this story so very interesting was that it had been an Arab city, a Muslim city, and that almost the entire Iberian Peninsula had been under Arab rule for nearly seven hundred years. An Arab kingdom in Europe! I was shocked, not so much that it had happened, but that I never knew, that I had never been taught this fact. It seemed to me that an important chapter in the narrative that I was part of had had a devastating encounter with a censor, either cultural or religious, perhaps both.

The Iberian Caliphate, with Cordoba as its political and cultural center, had stretched from Toledo in the north to the Mediterranean and included Seville, Valencia, and Cadiz. This kingdom, called Al Andalus, was not just powerful; it was an enlightened and dynamic society. Cordoba's native sons include the Arab philosopher and polymath known by his Latinized name, Averroes (1126-1198) whose commentaries and translations of Aristotle introduced the west to the possibility of reasoning without reference to dogma or faith; the great flourishing of science and thought we know as the Renaissance was built on an intellectual foundation of Greek thought that had been transmitted in Arab translations. Furthermore, Cordoba, during the three hundred years of its heyday, roughly 750 to 1050, in stark contrast to the Christian states that bordered it and against which it warred, had been a tolerant society. Muslims were the ruling class, but Jews and Christians lived amongst them harmoniously, without fear.

Cordoba was the first of many adopted homelands that I would experiment with as my life progressed. Al Andalus and its history still occupies a considerable expanse of my mental landscape. It is, however, a sad place, for the reason that as a place of refined tastes and intellectual accomplishments it did not last. In the twelfth century, fundamentalist Muslim ideologues declared war on its open and cosmopolitan culture. The great palace was dismantled and burned by Berber armies of religious zealots. I went to see what remained; still unexcavated in 1960, there was little to see. Miraculously, the great mosque survived, and survives today as testimony to a civilization that had once flourished in the valley of the Guadalquivir. By 1100, the Caliphate had splintered into little Arab principalities, increasingly isolated and powerless. In 1492, the Christians from the northern principalities, Aragon and Leon, finished the job; the last Muslims and Jews were expelled from Spain the same year Columbus set sail for an undiscovered world.

This seven-hundred-year episode in European history had been pushed out of my high school history books by the exciting business of crusaders trying to recapture the Holy Land from the unbelievers, these same Muslims.

With evidence of a parallel history that was literally in front of me every day, I realized that what I had been taught—and what everyone is taught unless one digs deeper in university studies— is just a "version of history;" it is the Euro/Christian origin myth, the story that most in the west are familiar with. Roughly speaking, it is one that zigzags from Athens (birthplace of democracy) to Rome (the example of imperial glory that all nations thereafter will aspire to emulate); Rome, the pagan prelude, leads to Jerusalem (the appearance of a new God, the correct one, at last). From that point, things move in the "right" direction —Christianity is now the leitmotif—though the Middle Ages, where Christian piety is highlighted—while the six hundred years of internecine savagery, both Christian and secular, general squalor, and superstition are minimized—through the glorious Renaissance (Florence, Paris, and London,) to the industrial revolution and the rise of a proletariat work force (Manchester), to the pasteurizing of milk, to the steel beams and glass dome of the Crystal Palace, and so on. And, finally, in the version that I, as an American, received, it ends with what is called "the American century," the Wright Brothers, the cure for polio… It is a story with, to be sure, many true facts, but with so much left out that it is little better than a fable.

I began to understand that historical truths are regularly washed away and that the Soviet Union was not the only regime that airbrushed the disgraced, embarrassing, or inconvenient from of the pages of the history books. In the case of Al Andalus, I felt that I had discovered a much larger revision. Whether these acts of intellectual vandalism should be attributed to patriotism, willful amnesia, cultural aggrandizement, or voluntary ignorance, the effects are the same. A process had been set in motion that is as relentless as the blowing sands that buried those ancient cities of Mesopotamia,

I discovered that much of what is called "history" is only the victor's version, events that have been filtered through ideologies or that are shaped with the goal of legitimizing and preserving the power of a ruling clique. This filtering, this shaping of narrative, is true about whole peoples, periods, and cultures. This realization can apply equally to individuals and families. My family was no exception.

Now, when I looked down the valley, over the orange groves, at the city, slightly hazy during the day, its lights twinkling at night, I felt less alone. I felt a thrill, the sense that I had discovered a hidden treasure. The city itself took on great symbolic significance for me. Nearly every day I drove down the hill to the city.

On my walks through the old quarter, I usually returned to the Great Mosque. It was April now and already the days were hot. The orange trees in the patio had blossomed and filled the air with their perfume. The flapping of the wings of white doves and the gentle splash of the fountains were the only sounds. When the days got hotter, I moved into the shadowy sanctuary of the mosque. How different it was from Christian cathedrals---by this time I'd seen a great many—in which stern male saints stared down on us poor sinners and always the melodramatic depictions of torture reminded us that pain, not pleasure, was the path to paradise. In the mosque not a sculpted or painted figure was to be seen for Islam forbids figuration; there is no piling on of gold and architectural swirls of clouds, no soaring heights to strike awe in the hearts of the simple. The space is not hierarchical, having no focal point, neither elevated altar nor crucifix. The spiritual message of the mosque was everywhere, diffused in the forest of columns—some eight hundred and fifty of them—slender cool marble trunks that one can almost wrap one's arms around. The canopy of this gentle forest is of modest and uniform height, a rhythmic repetition of round arches in ochre and red brick. Light from skylights filters through the arches creating an amber ether that sweetens the silence, an almost luxurious calm. There is no place to sit in the mosque so one wanders through the forest. When sitting was needed, I went into the garden and sat beneath the orange trees and imagined a paradise that was quite different than that promised to Christians. It consisted of translucent skies and the clear sounds of falling water, not as a waterfall that would wake the caliph, but gentle sounds, an infinity of fountains.

A full size Christian cathedral, nave only, no crossing, was inserted into the mosque in the seventeenth century, but the mosque is so quietly overwhelming that one hardly notices the cathedral.

Outside the enclosure of the garden, great blazing sheets of sunlight lay on the valley of the Guadalquivir. From the bridge over the river, I could see the broad valley that had once sustained the city, providing it with olives, wheat, and sheep. There were always fishermen on the banks of the river, and always a man, a little way up river, who had the most incomprehensible of occupations. He rowed a little boat back and forth across the river, sometimes carrying a single human passenger, sometimes a single goat. He performed this operation daily, even though the bridge from which I observed him was barely 200 yards away and entire flocks of goats regularly crossed the bridge. There was something almost mythical about this scene—a ferry for solitary men and stray goats—yet for all that strangeness, I was comfortable as I had never felt before. I liked this place. Cordoba felt like home.

I made good use of my solitude—I read books and I wrote—but I was lonely. I had needs that were both romantic and sexual. Since the sexual part of my being was still a bit of a mystery, I convinced myself that my feelings were purely platonic, the source of romantic gestures that I would soon, I hoped, have the nerve to make toward some young woman. I was a confused mix of chivalry, loneliness, and frustration. My vow of leading a monk's life was weakening. In fact, I would have renounced it utterly if the opportunity had presented itself. How I hoped for a girl to come into my life! The young women of Andalusia, however, presented an odd problem for me. I found them *too* beautiful. Castilian bloodlines had long ago mixed with the Jewish of the Levant and the Arab of Morocco. With their bronze skin, dark eyes, and almond-shaped faces, they had a brooding quality that I took for a capacity for passionate emotions, the very quality that I had come to Spain to find, but was now afraid to reach for. The possibility that these *Cordobese* girls were little different from other girls, that they hoped to have a boyfriend who might become a husband, that they had bourgeois longings for family and security, never occurred to me. They seemed like mythical creatures. I was afraid of being overwhelmed by my attraction. I had a vague understanding of my conflict. I was trying to escape the pull of the superficial feminine that my mother represented; yet there I was, in mortal danger of losing myself to another version of feminine beauty, this one exotic and thus probably even more powerful than what my mother represented. I was at risk of succumbing, of giving myself away. "Mortal danger" sounds a bit melodramatic, but I was in that sort of state, dried out with longing, feverish with fantasies.

And I had reason to worry. I had a tendency toward reckless emotional plunging when it came to girls. Two years earlier, I had fallen in love with a girl from Sarah Lawrence College. We wrote and talked on the phone for two months, then rendezvoused in New York City over Thanksgiving vacation to take some sort of definitive step. I don't think the word "consummate" was in my vocabulary in this context, but at age eighteen, I thought myself ready for commitment to this girl. I was quite desperate. She was either more sensible or was conflicted because she had been going steady with a junior at Princeton who was on a career path for the law. He had better prospects than I did. I was the would-be poet, a young man who, however intriguing, must have seemed unstable, which I was. After an intense night of tears and touching, of approach and retreat, we were both still virgins. Ultimately, she chose him; after she wrote to tell me that they were getting married, my schoolwork fell apart.

This love affair, one that wasn't, was the catalyst for my breakdown. It wasn't the cause; but it was the last straw. I had, it is true, put myself back together—through the psychotherapy of the previous year—but my conflicts about love, sex, and women were unresolved. I was introverted and preferred solitude to casual encounters, but I was intensely attracted to women. Female beauty penetrated my heart too easily. I didn't trust myself; I had emotions that I didn't know how to manage.

There is no doubt, however, that I was becoming more resilient. The psychotherapy had helped and I had some good role models, Hamish Robertson being the most important. And I continued to find guidance among the characters in literature or in the writers who created those characters. One of the writers I especially admired during this period was a sixteenth century Spanish monk, a reformer, mystic, and poet, a man who was later canonized as San Juan de la Cruz. It was not the saint who interested me, but the poet. He is considered one of the greatest of Spanish lyric poets. He had come into my awareness during that most difficult year, 1958-59, in New York, the year of my breakdown. I had noticed a book while browsing in the Eighth Street Bookshop; the title was *The Dark Night of the Soul*. No surprise that I would notice this book, given the state of my soul at that juncture.

In his greatest poem, "The Spiritual Canticle," I found a counterpart to the yearning for love that I felt. I wanted to experience the ecstasies of love; Juan de la Cruz had known them. What he knew, however, was a mystical union with God, not sexual union, but this distinction, when one reads the poem, seems a rationalization or inconsequential.

I made a pilgrimage to Ubeda, some two hours from Cordoba, the town where Juan de la Cruz died. A monastery there had a relic, a finger bone from the poet's writing hand. I thought the business of relics to be superstitious nonsense and a bit ghoulish, but, inconsistently, I went off to see this odd relic.

A monk, a resident scholar, a man in his forties who spoke a refined Castilian that I could understand, set aside his work, took me into the catacombs and showed me the finger bone. (There are two now. I remember only one.) It was not the entire finger, just the first section of the first digit. It looked like a piece of blackboard chalk gone gray with age. The monk, impressed that a young American would even know of San Juan, spent an hour with me.

Juan de la Cruz interested me not only as a poet but also because he had been a dissident, a rebel. It was easy for me to identify with him. I knew nothing of the theological issues that concerned him, angels-on-the-head-of-a-pin sort of thing; it was the fact that despite harsh punishments imposed by his superiors, he stayed true to himself and his convictions. His superiors had responded to his reform efforts harshly. In addition to humiliations, he was required to sleep in a disciplinary cell that was smaller than his body.

The doctrinal rigidity that Juan de la Cruz resisted provoked thoughts about my childhood. My mother's requirements for conformity had nothing to do with religious beliefs, but *everything* to do with forms. I was required to believe that such things as how one held one's fork or tied a necktie contained some sort of important value, a moral value even, a marker of one's worth as a human being, or, at a minimum, proof of social class membership, an identity that she, for her part, could not do without and insisted that we, her children, should not either. These, and many more of her concerns, seem to me now so inconsequential that I would not notice them, but then they were experienced as oppressions. Some of the corrections that my mother imposed seemed almost superstitious. In my middle childhood, for instance, she taped my ears back with white adhesive tape as soon as I returned each day from school; she said my ears stuck out. For her being less than perfect was a sort of heresy. My mother's rigidity and narrowness had made my childhood a quiet misery. My mother's world was too small for me and I had escaped. Juan de la Cruz's ultimate appeal for me, after the glory of his lyrics, was that he was a man who escaped. He had made a rope of sheets and lowered himself from the window of his tiny cell. Friends had left a horse tied to a bush.

I wrote every day that I lived in Cordoba. I sat at a little table, no more than three feet square, in the bright sun and filled notebooks with hand-scrawl, very little of which I can decipher today. Only one poem has survived. It was published in my first book. The poem commemorates my last weeks in Cordoba, spring 1961. Summer had already come to the valley of the Guadalquivir.

> *So the summer river bent*
> *its brilliance to our plain,*
> *and beneath the bridges*
> *there was echo even*
> *of the glare,*
> *and sunlight glazed*
> *the flat and tropic stream:*
> *and so we were in our professions,*
> *through windless days, in heat*
> *and in illumination. . .*

I see in these lines, a fragment of the whole poem, that I had come to think of myself as a *Cordobese*. The pronoun in the poem, the "we," included myself. My profession was the poetry. In the fifty years that have followed I have returned to this ancient city five times. I have brought both of my daughters. It is, I have said to them, one of the places that I come from, a part of the explanation of how I became a citizen of the world.

9

A View of Toledo

Unscripted generosity played a very small part in my mother's behavior or personality. This was true in respect to herself, and, even more so, in respect to her children. Her interactions with us tended to be limited to improvement and correction. I say "tended" because there were exceptions, and in the summer of 1952, on a visit to New York City, she took me on a special sort of outing, just the two of us. to the Metropolitan Museum of Art. I think it was a gesture prompted by genuine maternal feelings: she wanted to give me something, show me something of herself. The mere fact of an outing with my mother for a purpose other than fitting me in new shoes made it very special. I was twelve years old. We went to see a particular painting, which made the experience all the more curious and interesting. It was El Greco's *The View of Toledo*.

I remember climbing the famous steps of the Metropolitan Museum, my mother in a tailored suit and sensible shoes and me in pressed khakis and a Brooks Brothers button-down collar shirt, white, junior size. We went straight to the El Greco, no stops in the Italian eighteenth century or the portraits of Bonaparte. I saw the painting, of course, but I also saw an aspect of my mother that I had never seen before. This was a woman who did not have emotions in the ordinary sense; she never cried, never hugged or caressed her children, was never passionate about anything, never showed joy or sadness. She was composure personified, always gracious, with perfect manners and the semblance of appropriate affect for every occasion. So why was she, the most self-controlled person imaginable, attracted to this particular painting? The gray buildings sit uneasily on the hillsides as if tensed, as if waiting for something. The sky behind seems to writhe in a sort of ecstasy. With El Greco, it is sometimes hard to distinguish content from style, his manner, but I have little doubt that it was *emotion* that my mother found in the painting, not mannerisms, and it was the sort of emotion that she would have suppressed in her real life. I understood nothing of this at age twelve, but I noted my mother's rapt attention; and I was very interested.

The visit to the Metropolitan and my mother's homage, if that accurately describes what was going on, to *The View of Toledo* created a desire in me to see the city. At the time I went to live there in 1961, my mother was the person from whom I was trying to escape, whose influences and attitudes I was trying to shake off. But my rebellions were not total or mindless. My rejection of my mother was nuanced. I rejected the conformity and superficiality that she required of me; I rejected her lifestyle and her worldview, but I kept what I think of as her best part.

That best part was a deep and genuine interest in the visual arts; she passed this on to me unencumbered. Without meaning to, she had given me the way to transcend the emotional limitations of her world and had started a process that could not be reversed. Art was the path she opened to me and *The View of Toledo* was the beginning of this process. And because it provided a brief glimpse into my mother's psyche, it planted a somewhat subversive idea, the feeling that I might someday understand her. *The View of Toledo,* like Citizen Kane's *Rosebud*, was a clue. But it was the clue to what? This was something I would spend a lifetime wondering about, not persistently or obsessively, but from time to time, when circumstances forced the issue on me. The underlying questions about my life are involved with the sphinx who was my mother. Where did her sorrow begin, what was she repressing? Whatever it was, I am sure that it stirred in her soul as she stood before El Greco's view of a Spanish city that she had never visited and never would.

* * *

My mother and I connected through art. It was what we talked about. I believe that art, more than her marriage, which ended in divorce when I was twenty-nine, or her children, was what mattered to her. Since my early adolescence, she had, with my father's money, been collecting and had accumulated some extraordinary paintings. All were quiet and tranquil, nothing like the El Greco. There were works by nearly every major nineteenth century European artist—a Cezanne watercolor of Mont Sainte Victoire, a Monet of the Japanese bridge that she bequeathed to the National Gallery in Washington D.C., a Van Gogh, a Gauguin, a Pissarro, a Braque that is also in the National Gallery, a Picasso, a Bonnard, a Watteau, and a Manet, just about everyone except Modigliani, who was too erotic for her, and Lautrec, who was a dwarf and whose brothel scenes offended her. And behind them all, I think almost like a Platonic archetype, was the El Greco. My father was indifferent to art. He was an "I know what I like" sort of man and left to his own devices he would have instructed some gallery in Beverly Hills to buy him some "art," not too expensive and not too large. But thanks to my mother, I grew up in a house surrounded by beauty. It made a great difference. And so it was that I ended up in Toledo in the spring of 1960.

I rented a stone farmhouse, plastered white, outside the city walls, on the other side of the Tagus River. Up the hill a short walk from the house was a concrete gun emplacement, and from this vantage point I could see the city, the cathedral spire and the Alcazar fortress. Rats inhabited the ceiling of the house. By daylight, I understood that rodents made the noises, but after dark, I imagined the unquiet spirits of men who died in the Civil War. I felt silly about the ghosts, knowing better, but there I was, alone and imaginative.

War had interested me for as long as I could remember. No doubt this preoccupation had its origins in my childhood experience of the Second World War. I experienced neither danger nor loss, but for me— aged two through five for the duration—it was a time of anxiety and dread. My father was in the Navy and often away, not in any danger but I could not have known that without convincing reassurance from my mother, something she apparently did not know how to give. From pictures in magazines, I knew ships were torpedoed and sunk. Through *Life*, which came every week to our house and, carelessly, was left where children could find it, I knew that war involved terrible things. The Korean War began when I was ten. I remember David Douglas Duncan's photographs, also in *Life Magazine*, pictures of exhausted young men huddling in the rain and pictures of bodies of Americans wrapped in tarps. It wasn't until Hamish began, very carefully and gently, to tell me about his war, that I started to get a picture of what it really meant to go to war. This aspect of my education began when I was about fourteen. "Don't believe anyone who tells you that war is a glorious experience," Hamish said. I became a student of The Great War and read much of the literature that came out of it, Robert Graves, Wilfred Owen, Ford Maddox Ford, Siegfried Sassoon, and more. The Spanish Civil War came into my awareness when I was eighteen through Picasso's *Guernica,* which, during the period of my psychological collapse and recovery, hung in the Museum of Modern Art in New York City. When I saw *Guernica* for the first time. I imagined that I could hear the screaming engines of the unseen Stukas as they swooped down, like harpies, on the little town, and the howls of terror and pain from horses, women, and children. Picasso's *Guernica,* to me, is full of terrible noise.

Despite a serious historical interest in war, my knowledge of the subject was limited to what I could extract from books and photographs. In Spain I had my first encounter with concrete evidence. On the walls of my little house there were hundreds of little craters made by the impact of bullets. I tried to imagine the sounds, the smacking of the bullets against the wall, and the emotions of the people, whether soldiers or civilians, who had been sheltering in the house. Whenever I walked in the hills behind the house, sharing the slopes by daylight with rabbits and with hunters with shotguns, I would pick up spent brass, not from the hunters' shotguns, but from machine guns and rifles, battles that had once raged among the boulders. I lined the brass casings up on my mantle. The old peasant woman who took care of things for its absentee owners thought that I played with the devil's trinkets and crossed herself whenever she entered the house.

I looked for books about the Spanish Civil War in the local bookstores. Nothing accurate about the war was available in Franco's Spain; there was only propaganda about the patriotic nationalists who saved the land and church from the godless Communists and the brutish workers. On one of my visits to Madrid, however, to collect my mail—I remember only receiving letters from Jim—I found in a secondhand bookshop a book that was banned in Spain, Pablo Neruda's *España en el Corazon* (*Spain in my Heart*). The man behind the counter pretended indifference to what I was buying, as if he was not responsible for what was on the jumbled shelves of his musty shop. Neruda, in Spain as Chile's ambassador to the Spanish Republic, recorded his response to the siege of Madrid by Franco's army. The experience, with thousands of civilian casualties, had turned Neruda into a writer who would remain political for the rest of his life.

I went back to the farmhouse with the Neruda wrapped in brown paper and sitting in the sun, translated a bit of it each day. This daily work with a dictionary, struggling with the difficulties of his language and surreal imagery, began a lifelong relationship with the life and work of Pablo Neruda. The life that I have lived follows, coincidentally, Neruda's residences on earth: the Americas—Mexico became an important part of my life— Spain and, finally, France. Neruda returned from France to his native Chile at the end of his life, only to become a casualty of the Pinochet coup.

Shortly after I returned from Madrid with this bit of literary contraband, I encountered a girl whom I wanted to meet. When I first saw her, she was sitting at a table behind the counter at the El Greco museum reading a book, completely absorbed. She did not appear to have noticed me. Pretending to browse, I observed her for quite a long spell, perhaps thirty minutes. There was something about her—which is often all one can say about matters of the heart. I was, of course, predisposed to find something about someone. In this case, however, my interest turned out to be justified.

She wore glasses. She was pretty, but less mysterious and exotic than the girls of Cordoba, so I was not scared off. She wore no makeup, her clothes were simple, her hair silky, loose, and combed, but not "done." Her fingers were slender, without rings or nail color. I watched as she turned the pages of her book; the graceful movements of her fingers stirred powerful feelings in me. She touched each page with a soft deliberateness, as if to indicate that the idea had been understood, sometimes pausing to touch a sentence or a word with her fingertip. Her fingers expressed intention and attention, a harmony of mind and tendons, of emotion and body; a complex loveliness. Standing in this bookstore, half-hidden behind racks of postcards with images of El Greco's saints with their elongated bodies and limbs, it occurred to me that it was her soul that I was watching, her soul expressing itself in her hands and fingers. I remembered reading about a Roman emperor who, with the help of his doctors, had dissected animals in search for some sort of physical evidence of the soul. Now I had it before me; I could see her body, her fingers, as they mirrored the totality of her being, her mind and her imagination. My feelings included romantic longing and an almost aesthetic admiration; they were also erotic, but, unsure and shy, I could not have acknowledged those feelings mostly because I would not have known how to sort the finer feelings from those less so and how to act upon any of it.

It took me several visits to the museum to get up the courage to approach her. I studied El Greco, pretending to like his work more than I really did. I bought some postcards. She took my money, solemnly, politely; I was still silent. It was like writer's block; I couldn't get the words out. Pablo Neruda came to my aid. I took a chance that Neruda was an acceptable writer for her. I couldn't imagine that any girl that I was so attracted to could possibly have fascist sympathies; I assumed also that because she was such an avid reader she would know who Neruda was. Both assumptions turned out to be true. One afternoon I carried my slender volume of *España en el Corazon* in my hand, with the title just visible—it was like the lure the fisherman casts out on the water—and, for the second time in a week, I bought a postcard and she, as I had hoped, acknowledged the book. A glance and a smile. I plunged and asked what she was reading. I don't remember the answer, but the result was that Maria Teresa Sanchez, Mari Teri as I called her, became, for a brief four months, my girlfriend. It was a formal sort of romance, very Spanish in the mode of 1960, or perhaps 1860, which meant next to no touching, but it was very meaningful to me. I had a friend.

Mari Teri spoke some English and my Spanish was improving, so we stumbled through conversations in the two languages. I would call on her at the bookshop near closing time and walk her home. She did not invite me in to meet her father because I was a foreigner, a fact that might raise suspicions with Franco's secret police. Her mother had died when she was very young. She was allowed to go out with me so long as our dates were controlled by the archaic courtship rules of the *paseo:* we strolled around the plaza with other young couples under the watchful eyes of black-clad old women. She said that her watcher was her grandmother but confessed later that her father had hired the "grandmother" and that most of these old women who sat around the plaza, perched on benches like crows on a wire, had been hired. After a time, though, the for-hire grandmother was withdrawn and Mari Teri and I had more normal dates, but limited in time and always in public places.

She was nineteen years old and though she was more protected than an American girl of the same age would have been, she was more mature and sophisticated. She was well informed about the outside world but knew little about contemporary Spain because the media was heavily censored. She was very curious about how dating and courtship worked in America. In the course of these conversations, I told her that my experience in this area had not been the normal one; my mother, reversing the usual need to protect girls from boys, had made every effort to protect me from girls. Mari Teri thought this a very odd notion and I found it embarrassing to admit that I had been brought up under such a strange regime. I feared that it made me seem unmanly, but since it explained a lot about my uncertainty around girls, I wanted to talk about it. I told her the story of my first girlfriend, Sue, the daughter of friends of my parents, who lived only four blocks away.

I was thirteen and went to see Sue nearly every day after I got home from school. My mother discovered these excursions and forbade me from going; it was too dangerous, she said, to cross the four lane street that lay between my house and Sue's. There was a traffic light, I argued, and Sue crossed that same street every day at that same light to get to her school. I begged, but my mother would not relent. Telling this story in Spanish tested the limits of my Spanish vocabulary. I didn't know the word for traffic light, for instance, or "defy," which is what I did; I went anyway. A month or so later, Sue's mother, encountering my mother at a cocktail party, had commented about what a well-mannered young man I was, saying that she saw me often. My mother was coldly furious. She chained up my bicycle and grounded me for three months. I was required to stay in my room after returning from school. Open rebellion was not yet possible, but the pressure was building. I had become like a dog that had been kept in a narrow yard. This dog would prowl the perimeter, waiting for the gate to be left open.

By talking about the different cultural ways that boys and girls behaved together, Mari Teri and I were talking, obliquely, about the fondness that was growing between us. But Spanish reserve was the rule, and talking about cultural differences was the closest we got to what was really on our minds, or my mind at least. Did she like me as much as I liked her? I wanted desperately to touch her, especially her hands, but since we weren't officially engaged, *novios*, even that was off limits. And we could not become *novios* because I was not staying in Spain forever. Indeed, by the time we met, I knew, and she knew, that I would be leaving in four months. Still, I threw myself into this odd cross-cultural courtship with all my energy. I saw her almost daily, often just for a coffee, sometimes for the *paseo* around the plaza. We laughed about the "grandmothers." I made a joke out of it. "I feel like an anthropologist who goes to an island to study primitive customs and falls in love with his native informant." This was the only time I ever used the word "love" with Mari Teri. She blushed. Native, but not primitive.

There were topics of conversation that were off limits. These included the Civil War and anything that touched on politics. She would, with a glance, indicate that someone at a nearby table might overhear the conversation and that this could lead to trouble.

After two months of these frustrating limitations, Mari Teri agreed to spend an entire day with me. We decided to go to Madrid, and, to give focus to our day of adventure, we decided to go to the Prado Museum. In the days running up to our excursion, as we plotted what she would tell her father and what route we would take out of town—we had to be secretive lest her father discover the plan and ground her—my fantasies became more and more agitated. I imagined that I would persuade her to elope with me. This fantasy advanced to the point that I actually packed a bag to take with me in the car; we could buy new clothes and a toothbrush for her when we got to where we were going, which could be anywhere where we could be in love. I saw us in a little hotel with geraniums in window boxes someplace across the French border, safe from General Franco's police. On the day of our excursion, however, I realized that I was being ridiculous and left the bag behind. I didn't share any of this with Mari Teri, even as self-deprecatory humor. I knew that I would look truly silly, perhaps even a little mad.

Perhaps I was a bit mad. When I was older and supposedly more mature, I acted on these sorts of impulses, often with inappropriate objects of my fantasies. Mari Teri, however, was not inappropriate. She was the right sort of girl for me, sober, thoughtful and intelligent, but the timing and circumstances were wrong. Mari Teri required that I bring to our friendship something more than fantasies and I managed to do so.

On the drive we talked about serious subjects, the things we could not talk about in public settings. She told me the story of her family, torn apart by political differences, her father of the left, and her father's brother a Franco supporter, and that there was no longer any contact between them. The brother, on the winning side, prospered. Her father, who had been a full professor in a prestigious university, got by as a translator of French scientific papers into Spanish. She sat quietly in the car with her hands clasped gently together on her lap. She showed no agitation. She accepted what had to be accepted. The experience of irreconcilable political opposites had given her a perspective on the human dilemma that I did not yet have. My country had not seen that level of inner conflict, of political division, of estrangement of American from American, since our Civil War.

In the privacy of the car, we could be more open. Her father, she told me, had a copy of *España en el Corazon* concealed in the dust jacket from some innocuous novel, and she had read it when she was seventeen. She described growing up in an authoritarian state that imposed on its citizens a single narrative of history, legend instead of facts, a childhood and adolescence in which the air was thick with propaganda, in textbooks, on posters, in songs on the radio. It could have smothered her, she said, but her father had inoculated her against dogma and propaganda by using such noncommittal phrases as "That's something we should think about" or "I'm not sure about that," all statements of resistance but that could be restated and made to seem innocuous. He couldn't be direct for fear that she, still too young to realize the seriousness of their situation, might have blurted out something like "My father says that that is a lie." Her father had encouraged critical thinking, the ability to think for herself and to ask questions.

My father's message to me was similar. The enemy for my father, however, had not been a political regime but dogma, all dogmas. Growing up, I heard the story, more than once, of Galileo's challenge to Catholic doctrine about man's position in the cosmos. The earth, Galileo had insisted, was not the center of the universe no matter what authority claimed otherwise. This opinion entailed great risk, for the Inquisition executed men for challenging the official version. The story of Galileo was a kind of parable for my father, a vehicle that he had used to convey values that he thought important. Truth seeking was his core value, mostly as it affected scientific thought, but it was a value that easily translated into the moral and political sphere. The oppressions and fears of Mari Teri's youth had been political, a childhood in an atmosphere in which opinions, the contents of one's mind had to be concealed. My oppressions had been of a different sort—emotional—but I saw parallel themes. My family was a public one; what we as a family represented was, for my mother certainly, more than who we were as individuals. In order to preserve this façade we had to keep our feelings hidden, not only from the world, but from ourselves as well. There was no private family, no intimate family life that we shared and which bound us together. This sense of suppression and secrecy, the hidden and denied, was the underlying tone of my childhood and early adolescence. My family's secrets were psychological, familial and personal, and hidden even from ourselves. Mari Teri's secrets were of the whole society and were of far greater magnitude. The Spanish of Mari Teri's generation lived with a terrible burden of not only the unspoken but also what for the older generation was unspeakable.

"It is strange," Mari Teri said, "to be talking about the Civil War. No one does. It is as if it didn't happen; we're supposed to believe that Spain has always been as it is now. And yet the war, now over for twenty years, overshadows everything in daily life, not just for those who lost family, but for all Spaniards. It affects the way the present is talked about, or *not* talked about. The real issues of the war, what it was about, what kind of country Spain was to be—secular or theocratic; the question of who should govern, working people and the middle class or the rich and the Church—those things are never talked about. We hear about the heroes and the defeated enemy, the communists, socialists, and unbelievers. The calm you see is not real. It is imposed. It is the calm of secrecy, of suppression. There were mass executions, the victors slaughtering the vanquished. My father was lucky. He was just purged, lost his job. Almost everyone of the war generation thinks they know where a mass grave is, but they would never tell you. Above all they would never tell their children."

Mari Teri's pent-up need to talk about the war and I, from a country that was not, or was not then, afraid of truth, had resulted in an out-pouring of feelings and stories about life under Franco. Her candor made a new sort of openness possible for me. I talked about my fear of dying, not from violence—for America at that time was remarkably safe and seemed even permanently sane, the war in Vietnam had not begun and the violence of the Civil Rights struggle lay ahead—my fear was cancer. Our conversation had evolved from the circumstantial to the personal. It was a beginning of intimacy. I told her about the jagged scar on my back. I knew that it was unlikely that she would ever see it, but wishing at the same time that she could, that she would be able to love me as disfigured as I imagined that I was. I talked about what I had fled from—an upper-class family with suffocating restrictions and inflexible and rather banal expectations. "Like Franco's Spain," she said.

The kilometers went by. There were no motorways then, it was just the road to Madrid. We went through little towns where the bottom four feet of all the trees were painted white and where we saw the ubiquitous pairs of the Guardia Civil, the Civil Guard soldiers, with their machine guns across their chests and with their patent leather hats. Lorca's *Ballad of the Spanish Civil Guard* has images of spilled ink and wax staining their uniforms, of their skulls as heavy as lead so they are incapable of grief or guilt, so they do not cry about the things they do.

I shared feelings as I never had with anyone except my psychiatrist. Intimacy, the doctor had said, is only real where there are risks. For me to be open with a girl, a woman, was the most difficult of tests. Now I was trying. Mari Teri didn't comment on any of it, but she was listening; that was response enough.

We spent the better part of that day wandering through the Prado Museum. The marble and granite halls were lined with portraits of royalty and field marshals from epochs long past. Viceroy this, Count that, men whose relevance to the present was only that their images, on larger than life canvasses covered wall surfaces that might otherwise have seemed too empty. There were enormous paintings depicting the life of

Christ, from his birth to death, countless saints and martyrs, scenes of torture and mutilation. Such a strange preoccupation, I thought, sadism glorified, gruesome but mannered images of bodies, usually near-naked, in terrible pain. It seemed to me to be a kind of pornography. In a side gallery we found the great Goya etchings, *The Disasters of War*, all 80 of them lined around a room. I had the insight that through art one could "think" about the worst things and not be overwhelmed by one's knowledge. With Goya one is forced to look and to acknowledge the unspeakable, the unthinkable, the ever reoccurring unthinkable. I sensed the moral rage that animates Goya. He finishes one drawing, then moves on the next.

"How could such things be?" he asks.

Mari Teri and I were unsettled by the Goya etchings. On our drive from Toledo we had talked in candid terms about the Civil War. Our viewing of the *Disasters* was in that context. Nevertheless, we were in our bubble of youth and we acknowledged our feelings for each other. We were now holding hands—at last—and in a somewhat euphoric state, we moved on. The signs on the walls pointed to what the museum thought visitors should see: the *Salas Velazquez*.

Diego Velazquez was a seventeenth century painter whose works I'd seen in reproduction in my mother's art books. I remembered a standing portrait of the painter's patron, the King of Spain, Philip IV, a man with a long Hapsburg face and a protruding lower lip. There was another image of his little daughter in a formal gown; the child, ten perhaps, looks uncomfortable. I remember thinking, rather idly, about this child, hoping that she would not inherit her father's looks. Generally, I thought Velazquez and his subjects boring, because as an American I was predisposed to be dismissive of royal portraits. Velazquez, I had decided, was a genre painter, better technically than most, but still just a high-class court recorder.

With those preconceptions and prejudices in place, Mari Teri and I entered a large oval room in which hung some twenty portraits of the clowns, dwarfs, and actors who would have waited interminably in corridors and anterooms to perform for the king or the ordinary men, not the aristocrats who were the painter's usual patrons. I immediately sensed that these portraits were quite exceptional, that they somehow transcended the "realism" to which an art history book would have assigned them. I had the sensation that these long dead human beings were outside of time, suspended in a sort of hologram, something that the artist's feeling *for them* had made possible. It was not that Velazquez had replicated their appearances, for that was an expected skill for a seventeenth century master; it was more. He had understood the humanity of his subjects so deeply that I could feel each of them as they had been. "We were human beings," the paintings proclaimed. My hair literally stood up on my head, prickling. From the red velvet walls they watched us, staring out of their time into ours. And they introduced me to the most extraordinary aspect of Diego Velazquez, his profound democratic insistence that all humans had an inalienable dignity; the king and court dwarf were, in the mirror of Velazquez' canvas, equals.

In the next room, we encountered the king that I'd seen in my mother's books. He was still homely. But now, seeing him life-size, he became a presence not just a picture. I understood that the king too had been a human being. And Velazquez had painted the man, not the office, and had shown him as vulnerable and insecure, yet dignified and trying his best to be a king. I saw, or felt—for with Velazquez one *sees*, as with no other painter except, perhaps, Rembrandt, with one's emotions—Philip's dilemma. It was similar to one of mine: how to be worthy, how to define one's self, when feeling overshadowed by one's more successful and powerful ancestors. In Philip's case it was especially difficult: his paternal grandfather was Philip II, the great, if ruthless, monarch of the expanding Spanish empire; it must have been a hard act to follow. My solution had been to distance myself from family. Philip IV had stayed at home and had attempted to find his place in the family business. As it turned out, hiring Diego Velazquez was his greatest contribution to civilization.

Near the portrait of the king was a portrait of his son, Balthazar Carlos, at ten years old. The little boy, feeling proud and very grown up, is posed with his own hunting rifle and two of his dogs. I saw myself in him, as I was at ten. I would have liked to have my own rifle. The prince died at age sixteen of smallpox.

The next room was the Prado's inner sanctum, where it keeps its greatest treasure, Velazquez' *Las Meninas, The Maids of Honor*. When I saw it in 1961, it occupied a room of its own, now it is more "democratically" displayed with the other Velazquez in the Prado collection. A mistake, I think, for if there is a work of art anywhere that is so complex or more moving I can't think of it.

Velazquez has put himself in the picture. It is not a self-portrait though; it is himself as the painter, the artist at his *metier*. His face is a bit hazy and poorly lit because he is not the real subject of the painting, but there he is, unavoidable, his brush loaded with paint, his hand in motion. We don't see the painting that he is working on, only the back of it, the blank canvas and the stretchers. His gaze is not on his canvas but on his subject, but we don't see his subject. We infer that it is the king and queen because their images are reflected in a mirror that hangs on a wall behind the painter; and, extrapolating from the mirror and from the painter's gaze, we know that the subjects can only be in the room where we, the viewers, some three hundred years later, are standing. Involuntarily, one looks around. It is an uncanny sensation.

Much is happening in the frame. At the back of the room, on the same wall as the mirror, a door has opened to a stairway. A man is silhouetted in the doorway, an event in progress. The important action of *Las Meninas,* however, is in the foreground, in good light.

We see a large dozing dog that is about to be poked by the foot of a little boy who has appeared from somewhere out of the frame. The little boy's foot has not yet touched the dog but in less than a second the dog will startle, but only startle, for we can see it is a gentle creature, quite comfortable with active humans and the silliness of children.

Velazquez has painted a moment in time. That he could imagine and portray such a thing two hundred and fifty years before the invention of the camera seems quite remarkable. This is not the melodramatically posed "action" canvases of the Renaissance, the battle scenes, mythical rapes and flights; this is a snapshot. And we, the observers, I at least, are not so much looking as watching. An intimate moment in a royal household is unfolding and the uncanniness of Velazquez' painting is deepening. As our eyes move closer to the true center of the scene, we pause at the figure of a female dwarf, who is looking directly at us, at our moment in time. "Who are those people?" her look says, "and what are they doing here?"

And then, in full light, the central figure in the composition is the king and queen's little daughter, the *infanta* Margarita. The little girl, perhaps eight years old, is dressed in her best, ready, we think, to join her parents, to pose with them, to join them in the immortality that art gives its subjects. She too, like the dwarf, looks out of the canvas, but not at her parents, who are behind us, but at us. And finally, there are the two young women who give the painting its name, the Maids of Honor. These are aristocratic girls of twenty or so who attend the princess. They too are in motion. The manner of both these young women is affectionate and supportive. One is speaking to the princess, an intimate communication, close to the little girl's right ear. Perhaps she is saying that she should not be alarmed by our presence, that we are far away, in an unimaginable future.

Meninas is a glimpse into the transitory dream that is our lives, the reality that falls behind us as we try to seize it. In a moment, the dog in the foreground will wake, the painter's hand will apply the pigment to the canvas, the man in the background will close the door. In another moment, the little princess will grow old and die, and the Spanish Empire will collapse.

As I write these passages, I realize that Maria Teresa Sanchez, if she is still alive, would be seventy-five years old. But I can still see her as she was then. Mari Teri, delicate and lovely, in her light cotton dress, seems about to step across three centuries and into a fictional world where she will share a moment of time with a little girl who was the daughter of a king.

10

The Middle East

In the early summer I sent a carton containing my books and winter clothes back to the United States and set out for the Middle East.

My destination was Mesopotamia, the place that my grandfather had introduced me to a decade earlier, stories that had whispered in my imagination for all those years. Even the names of the places had excited me. I liked the way the syllables divided and recombined. "Ur of the Chaldees" had a mantra-like quality to me when I was younger, and the almost mystical people too, a great king called Ashurbanipal who had built the world's first great library. Libraries, books, and I were compatibles. Now I could locate Mesopotamia as a region in the real world, as the modern nations of Syria and Iraq, and that was where I was headed. I bought an airplane ticket with flexible dates that would take me to Athens, Istanbul, Ankara, then to Cyprus and Beirut. From Beirut, I would improvise. I carried only a backpack. I had provided no way for my family to reach me. I had not even told them that I was going.

America was generally regarded well in the Middle East in 1961. It had no colonial footprint in the region and so was seen as a champion of human rights. Furthermore, the United States had declined to participate in the Anglo-French invasion of the Suez Canal in 1956. Those facts generated goodwill, and that, plus the allure of American popular culture, served me well as I traveled, young and solitary, through a region that I wouldn't think of visiting today.

I made no display of my American identity, but when asked, I always replied, American, but being American was beginning to have less importance to me. I was coming to the conclusion that, of all the varied identities that are either inescapable—skin color—or that people attach to themselves— religion, nation, political party—the one that mattered most was simply Human Being. At least there could be no disagreement about what that label meant. We would be right or wrong together. True, "American" was one of my possible identities but this, I realized, didn't make me better than anyone else. "Caucasian" didn't either, though there is no doubt that both of those identities made the road a bit smoother. Neither was an accomplishment of mine. It was purely a matter of luck, the accidents of birth.

Greece was the first stop. In Athens I climbed to the top of the Acropolis and saw where soldiers, first Turkish, then German, then twenty-five years later, British, had scratched their names into the soft stone of the steps and walls. I sat in the shade of the Parthenon and listened to the muffled din of traffic in the city below and to the buzzing of flies. I found the desiccated body of a dog half-hidden under a fragment of a marble column, the animal's fur ruffling in a hot breeze. I descended from the Acropolis satisfied. I'd visited the place my schoolbooks had called the birthplace of democracy. It wasn't until I read Thucydides, probably thirty years later, that I understood what an inconsistent and morally ambiguous polity Athens had been, democratic at home but ruthless, violent, and grasping in respect to its neighbors, and how fragile its democracy had turned out to be.

I took a rickety bus to the port of Piraeus. With my head full of Homer, I walked along a sea wall and tried to imagine the Greek triremes setting out for Troy. I heard the whisper of cadenced strokes in the water, thousands of oars dipping in unison into the wine dark sea.

At Piraeus, I went to an open-air cafe by the water's edge. A three-man band played traditional *taverna* music. The owner of the cafe was a handsome woman in her early forties. She had a strongly defined nose, a few streaks of gray in thick black hair that was tied up in a bun, and an easy smile for each of her customers. I ate grilled squid and drank two glasses of *retsina*. A string of naked light bulbs hung along the quay and bobbed and swayed in the soft breeze. She cleared my plates, then returned to a little table covered with a blue and white oilcloth where there was a stack of white slips of paper, the evening's receipts, that she was tallying on a mechanical calculator. She entered a number and pulled a lever. Her forearms were bare, the sleeves pushed up above her elbow. As I watched her, I remembered my fascination with Mari Teri's fingers and my rather tentative approach to erotic feelings. Now I was less uncertain. I was expanding my emotional range. The music swirled. A portly man in his fifties got up and danced with his companion. Other customers watched and smiled. A large cat ambled through the restaurant and into the kitchen. I felt a strange excitement. It occurred to me that I should stop worrying about feeling unformed. One always is to some degree; what matters is that the process of shaping one's self continues. And, I thought, I should not let myself be debilitated by the fear that the cancer would return. I was going forward; it had occurred to me that I should try to imagine the sort of person that I wanted to be and that if I were to act as if I were already that person, the reality of it might emerge, be born out of what might have begun as a bluff. It was a realization that action would do more for me than thinking. I thought too much. I knew that I wanted to be confident and comfortable with women, and so, with that image of myself as an inspiration, I got up, made my way through the tables, and, with gestures, asked the proprietress to dance. She laughed, stood up, smoothed down the front of her dress, and joined me. The band gave a little surge for the boss lady. Inside, I trembled. Outside, I suspect I was just the right mix of boldness and politeness.

I held her close. We smiled at each other and talked, neither understanding a word the other said. I felt the fullness of her body. With my hand on her back I could feel the roll of plumpness that bulged out from under the bra strap; she smelled sweetly, faintly, of sweat and garlic. She was a beautiful, desirable woman. The cook, her husband, I presumed, watched from the door of the kitchen, amused, or so I hoped, and we danced. I returned to Athens on the last bus of the night, pleased with myself; I thought that I had been quite brave.

Istanbul was next. My three days there were a blur of wanderings, labyrinths of narrow streets, markets and cafés, but the meaning of Istanbul was sharply defined in my mind. I had come to the end of one civilization and stood at the beginning of another. Beyond was *The East*, the steppes that had given birth to the great Khan, the Scythian horsemen, and the ancient empires of Persia. Istanbul was the terminus of the Silk Road from China. All of this was historical, but it was more than that; it was part of a great epic, the city where some of the most diverse narratives in the world's story had come together, to be knotted, entangled, frayed.

I had a cinematic sense of my time in Istanbul, as if seeing myself in scenes. In one, a boy of fourteen, who wanted to practice his English, approaches me on the street and offers to introduce me to his family, to meet his father, an army colonel, and his mother and younger siblings. The boy seemed to think that he had captured me, an American. I remember that triumphant look on his face when he introduced me. His house, with generic pictures on the wall of snow-capped mountains, photographs of an older generation, a TV in the corner, could have been a house almost anywhere. We sat at a long table and ate a meal. The whole encounter, the boy, the father in his uniform, the family with quiet children who stared at me discreetly, the communal meal with no common language except for the boy's handful of textbook phrases, had a dreamlike quality. It dissolved as soon as the meal was over and became an almost indistinguishable part of the mélange of sensations that Istanbul became for me.

In another of these scenes, I have crossed the Bosporus on a ferry and am leaning on a low wall looking back at the city, its domes, minarets, and plumes of smoke. I imagined that the moment was a clip out of a spy story by Graham Greene. A wind flowed out of central Asia, pushed at my back, tugged at my hair and clothes. I imagined that I could see the wind spinning, like strands of silk, around the spindles of the minarets. The ferries moving back and forth were the shuttles in the loom. I stole the secrets and saved some part of the world.

From Istanbul, I took a short flight in a prop plane to Ankara, the capital of Turkey. I arrived in the midafternoon. In keeping with my practice of trusting to chance, I got off the airport bus before reaching the center of the city. It was a working-class residential area of relatively new apartment blocks, cold. There were few people about, but everywhere I heard music, the drumming, the repetitive strings, the Middle Eastern singsong of the vocals. The music came drifting out of windows with white curtains or pouring from little transistor radios sitting on windowsills. Perhaps the music had enchanted the place and put everyone to sleep. I found few cafes and no hotels, so I walked on, carrying my backpack. I walked for an hour, without a map, with no destination in mind. Finally, I came upon an open field as large as two football fields that sloped upward and at the top of the slope I saw a building with the promising words, in large block letters, in English, "Plaza Hotel." I crossed the rocky field and approached a substantial two-story stucco building with a large balcony on the second floor. It was very rundown, but I was tired. Inside, there were more signs of dilapidation, but it was a working hotel, and I decided to risk it. Using sign language—head to palm and eyes closed—I got a room on the second floor, the room with the balcony. It was very inexpensive, perhaps fifty cents, and when I entered the room, I immediately saw why. The toilet no longer flushed and was full and repulsive. Many others had slept in the bed and the sheets were filthy. But there was a bedspread that I pulled up, covering the sheets. I figured I'd sleep a couple of hours in my clothes and then move on. I locked the door and closed the louvered shutters on the silent and empty field below and fell fast asleep.

When I awoke, it was night. I had slept a good six hours or more. The night was full of strange noises, animal sounds, tinkling of bells, discordant music, a distant cacophony of voices. I jumped off the bed and

opened the shutters to an amazing sight. There were campfires everywhere with women in bright costumes cooking over open flames. There
were horses and donkeys. The donkeys brayed, shaking their harnesses.
Great bundles of wool were stacked on the ground. There were little
flocks of sheep and goats. A trading caravan had come from the great
emptiness beyond the city and had set up shop. I had stumbled into a
scene from another century.

Fascinated, but unwilling to spend the night in the hotel, I put on my
shoes, shouldered my backpack, and opened the door of the room. As I
did, I encountered a wave of men's voices. I started down the stairs, and
as I appeared, the room below went silent. I descended to a room full
of fierce looking men with black mustaches, most wearing bandoliers of
bullets across their chests. Some had rifles strapped over their shoulders
and all had large knives stuck in their belts. They wore sheepskin vests
and, despite the warm temperatures, some had sheepskin caps. There
were at least twenty-five of them and all were looking at me.

I couldn't retreat. It would have been cowardly, and besides, they
had done nothing to make me afraid other than looking fiercer than
any group of men I'd ever seen. I noticed, too, that they were drinking
only coffee. I descended. As I approached, they began to talk to me. I
understood nothing, but it was clear that they were asking where I was
from, words that sounded like "English" and "Russian" as they pointed
at me. I answered. "America." And with that they all broke into smiles
and brought me into the crush of them, passing me around as if I were
a pet. I was talked at and touched by every man in the room. Someone
handed me a bowl of meat, probably mutton, richly spiced, in dark
sauce, and a large spoon. I drank many tiny cups of strong coffee before
I could finally escape. I was pointed in the right direction and eventually
found the center of the city and a less interesting hotel.

I flew on to the island of Cyprus. The birthplace of Aphrodite and
the birthplace of the Mudd fortune, the beginning of a civic-minded
and respected family. My paternal ancestors had found a rich mine on
the island, not gold, but another bright metal: copper. My father was the
president of the company that grew out of that discovery. The Cyprus

Mines Corporation was to become a diversified minerals company that was substantial enough to be traded on the New York Stock Exchange. A chunk of raw copper, gleaming orange, nearly twelve inches tall and weighing fifty pounds, sat on my father's desk. Its surface was twisted and furrowed by the geological process of its creation. It had aura; it was like a meteorite, but not one that had fallen from the sky; this had burst, hot and glowing, from the depths of the earth. It was very beautiful. When I was a child, I imagined I could still feel warmth, an afterglow. It was my family's talisman, the bringer of luck. It was not only luck, however, that had done it—though luck played a part in the story—it involved entrepreneurial daring and hard work.

My great-grandfather and my grandfather, both trained as mining engineers, had, in the search for opportunity, turned to their knowledge of the ancient world. The Romans had manufactured a great many things out of bronze, the principal ingredient of which is copper, and had refined it for 600 years. My grandsires reasoned that the Romans must have had a rich source of the raw material and so they went looking for it. They did some preliminary prospecting in the New York Public Library, reading nineteenth century travel accounts written by those eccentric Englishmen who ventured out in the midday sun. These men were usually missionaries, but were often amateur naturalists and anthropologists too. In their books about their adventures as evangelists in faraway lands, they often described natural features, hills of greenish dirt for instance, in which the family geologists saw the possibility of an abandoned mine works. A field geologist named C. Godfrey Gunther had had a role in the development of this original idea and so it was he whom they hired to go to the Arabian Peninsula, the Sinai, and the island of Cyprus to investigate. My ancestors had not been at risk of heat stroke or Bedouin bandits, but they had risked their money; it took vision.

The mine was in the western part of the island. I knew that if I managed to get there, by bus presumably, I would be treated as a visiting dignitary, and since this was contrary to my overall purpose of breaking free of privilege, I decided not to go. When later I told my father about the trip, I left out the fact that I'd stopped in Cyprus. That I had not gone to the mine and introduced myself would have hurt his feelings. I knew, too, by my twentieth year that I was not destined to be part of the company and saw no need to emphasize that fact.

I went on to Beirut by air; it would be the last airport that I would see for at least a month. I had an open-ended return ticket from Tel Aviv, but since that ticket was without a date certain, I was at the edge of an unknown of my own choosing. Poetry was my guidebook. I could recite from memory poems from Lord Byron's "Hebrew Songs."

> *The Assyrian came down like the wolf on the fold,*
> *And his cohorts were gleaming in purple and gold;*
> *And the sheen of his spears was like stars on the sea*
> *When the blue wave rolls nightly on deep Galilee.*

The language, the cadences, the images so seduced me that I lost sight of the facts in the case, what must have been a season of horrors for the people of Judea. But I was looking to the past not so much then for help in understanding anything, but for inspiration and pleasure in the present. The past was still more fable than the cautionary tale that it is for me today. The thought of what lay ahead in the immediate future thrilled me. Damascus, the oldest continuously inhabited city on the planet; Ur, the birthplace of Abraham; Nineveh, the city whose kings hunted lions from horseback; Babylon, the city of gardens by a river called Euphrates. If I were to fully experience these places, some no more than outlines in the sand, it would require some sort of trial, an admission fee—I never assumed that anything was included with the silver spoon of my birth. It would require inconvenience and discomfort. Buses were air-conditioned, but I, following these odd requirements, chose to travel to Damascus by collective taxi. I waited in the sun until there were enough passengers. There were five other men, of varied ages, none of whom spoke a word of English. I was the youngest so was crammed between the driver and the lucky fellow who had the window. I retreated, for the five hour drive, into a private world. I remembered, almost as an aural hallucination, lines and images from the Old Testament: "By the rivers of Babylon, there we sat down, yea, we wept ..." Mesopotamia was shaped in my emotions by the King James Bible, rather in the way that Andalucía had been shaped by Garcia Lorca.

In Damascus, I walked along the ancient "Street Called Straight," threading my way among the sellers of grains and vegetables, of copper pots and textiles, of spices, listening to the cries of the merchants hawking their specialties. I thought of Saint Paul, Saul as he was then, blinded by the Lord as punishment for his cruelties. I pictured him praying his blighted heart out in a house on that street.

I took a bus to a little restaurant on the top of a hill overlooking the city. I sat outside beneath a canvas awning. Below me was a vast and sprawling mosaic of buildings, a jumble held together by a green band of trees that followed a stream of underground water. The sun was so bright that the waiter wore dark glasses. Feeling lucky, I ordered my lunch by pointing at an unknown item from the Arabic menu. The waiter reappeared shortly with a white ceramic plate upon which were two gray hemispheres that I recognized as brain. By their size, I deduced them to be calf's. The plate was ice cold and beads of condensation appeared on its bright surface. The convoluted medallions, like slippery coral, were flanked by bright yellow sections of lemon. It seemed sacramental, like the Christian Eucharist, something ineffable expressed as something edible. I felt that I would be eating the soul of an animal.

Heat, blinding sunlight, and the clamoring souks of Damascus. It is little wonder Saul got himself turned inside out in such a place. He said that God had done it. For me, it was an exotic meal and the strangeness of things. I hadn't found God and had not expected to. What I did find confirmed that I was on the right track. Open engagement with the world was what I wanted. Experience was valuable for itself. Some risks were worth taking.

Of all the meals I've ever eaten, including the dinner at *la Tour d'Argent* in Paris, none is as fixed in my memory as this modest meal on that veranda overlooking Damascus: the glistening hemispheres of the calf's brain, the yellow of the lemon, the cold white plate. And beyond, in the bright clear air, was the desert. Mesopotamia, the place I'd come to see. The place where man first learned to cultivate grain, the birthplace of bread. I felt that I was in the care of angels. Such clarity.

But then, in a rush, as if a dust storm had come from nowhere and blocked out the sun, the clarity was gone. I was, suddenly, quite sick, gut sick, beset by agonizing cramps and not able to be more than one hundred feet from a toilet. After two days of it, holed up in my hotel, I could tell it was getting worse. I fought this knowledge, for, if true, it meant Mesopotamia was no longer possible.

Through the hotel I located a doctor who spoke some English. He gave me some pills that eased the symptoms but insisted that I should get to a place with more modern medicine. There were French doctors in Amman, Jordan, one hundred miles south. It was the wrong direction. Babylon was to the east, but now, I didn't care. I knew that it was something more than ordinary traveler's discomfort. I took a bus to Amman, found the French doctors, and, because of my dehydrated state, was admitted to a hospital. I was diagnosed as having amoebic dysentery. I spent three days in the hospital on a drip, in a shared room with a man whom I never saw because of the curtain, and I improved. The doctor urged me to go to Israel where I'd get better care. He gave me some medications but insisted that I was still sick and should expect a relapse.

I did feel better for a while, so, still in pursuit of the mythical, I made another pilgrimage, this time to the Jordan River. A taxi took me for a ridiculously small sum, mostly I think because the driver wanted to talk to an American. In minimal English he asked about the movie stars I had seen. Coming from Los Angeles, I had actually seen a few, including Humphrey Bogart and Lauren Bacall. He told me that he would tell his friends that he had given a ride to a man who knew Humphrey Bogart. I took a swim in the Jordan River, taking off my shirt, shoes, and trousers and then, in my boxers, I immersed myself in the slow green waters. I was running a fever and the water was wonderfully soothing. I hung on to a branch of a tamarisk tree and let the current pull at me. "I will hang my harp on the willows," I said to myself. In the cool wash of the river, listening to the whisper of its current among the rushes. I was self-baptizing.

In 1961, the Israeli/Jordanian border was a wide no-man's land, cleared of habitation, tangled with razor wire, and patrolled by UN soldiers. There was no vehicular connection; to go to Israel, one had to walk. With a 103 fever, under the blazing August sun, I managed it. I moved in fifty-foot increments before I'd have to sit on my backpack to rest. A Swedish UN soldier about my age watched me from his observation post. The muzzle of his rifle followed me, casually, without menace, but I knew he could have changed attitude in an instant.

It took an hour or more to cross fifty yards. Finally, I passed through Israeli border security and was in Israel. Even in my weakened state, I could sense the vitality of the country. The girl soldiers, with tan legs and their shorts rolled up, were exciting. That I could see and appreciate the beauty and vitality of these young women was reassuring. I would probably live, but there was recuperating to do. I found a taxi and asked the driver to take me to a boarding house. I had not the strength to shop for something pleasant. All I said to him was cheap, clean, and safe. He said that he knew a place.

I settled into a tiny room with one transom window that opened onto an alley and another above the door that opened to an interior courtyard about fifty feet square in which were some bedraggled flowers in pots and three metal chairs. The windows provided light and ventilation but no view. The medical expenses had depleted my funds, so I wired Hamish in London and he forwarded enough money to get me through a convalescence of several weeks. That I turned to Hamish, my grandfather's friend, rather than to my parents was an indication of how far from family I had drifted. Hamish became my lifeline. All he asked was that I come to see him when I made it back to London.

I found a doctor, started a course of treatment, and retired to my dreary room to rest. The proprietor brought me water and saltine crackers. After four or five days, I felt strong enough to take a meal with the other lodgers.

There were only men at the communal table. All were gaunt, pale, and slow moving. They talked among themselves in a language I didn't recognize. On the second day, one of the men addressed me in German. From travels with Hamish, I had heard enough German to recognize it and I knew how to say that I didn't speak the language. I assumed that this quashed the possibility of all but the simplest communication, pointing at the saltshaker, for instance, but I added, probably wanting nothing more than to make myself appear a little less provincial, that I spoke a little Spanish. The entire company at the table turned toward me with great curiosity, and all began speaking to me in a Spanish dialect I'd never heard and had difficulty understanding, but which I recognized to be Spanish. Gradually, I came to understand that they were descendants' of the Sephardic Jews who had been expelled from Spain in 1492, and that they were, by nationality, Romanians. Their Spanish was a fifteenth-century variant called Ladino, full of words no longer spoken, and with stresses and rhythms of another age. Among a persecuted people, Ladino, as secret language, had been useful, so they had kept it. And I got used to its sounds and began to fill in vocabulary blanks.

Now, at the midday meal that we took together, usually little more than soup and bread, I engaged with my tablemates more actively, conversing in faulty Spanish about various things, mostly about America, which was a subject of great interest to them. The man who always sat next to me was in his middle fifties, white-haired, arms very lean, skin very pale. He wore a short-sleeved shirt with an open collar, lapels spread to the side. He was a sober man, reserved, but not standoffish. He, like the Palestinian taxi driver, wanted to know if I knew any movie stars. I sensed that he felt somewhat sheepish in asking, as if it was a childish interest. But, as I was discovering, America, as creator of fantasy worlds, was everywhere. He told me that as a child he had liked going to the cinema and had especially liked The Keystone Cops. One subject led to another. I was curious about his country. He described both high mountains and beaches too. Like California, I remarked. He described holidays with his parents at the seashore, on the Black Sea. His holiday sounded as ordinary as an American holiday, the umbrella, the tin sand bucket and shovel, father swimming, mother relaxing with a book. I knew nothing of the history of Romania other than the fact that it had been allied with Nazis during the Second World War. Remembering the sensitivities about war and political divisions that I encountered in Spain, I didn't touch these subjects. If he opened the door, I would follow, but I didn't want to seem accusatory or to open old wounds. I assumed, because he was in Israel, that he was a Jew. Even with these limitations, for about a week, while I still took my meals in the boarding house, we had interesting, if clumsy, chats. That my tablemate and I, separated in years by nearly three decades and culturally by even more, were bridging those gaps in an ancient language, Ladino, struck me as a wonderful thing.

One day, for some reason, my table mate and I switched places which changed my physical perspective: I now saw his arm as I had not been able to before. There, imprinted just above his wrist, was a tattooed sequence of seven blue numbers. I understood immediately what the numbers meant. He noticed my glance and said simply, "Auschwitz."

I trembled inside myself at this moment. I felt as if, by looking, I had opened the door, but one that I shouldn't have. I knew there had been horrors, but at this point I had no idea of their extent or gravity. In the years to come I would learn more, but that year, when I was twenty one, I was probably not ready to know more. And I thought that to inquire about this man's experience would be an invasion. He never offered anything more. Over the next few weeks, I observed carefully, and sure enough, all the men had similar tattoos.

When I first learned about the Holocaust, the simplest knowledge, just what happened, the emotion I felt was not shock. It was a kind of nausea, not of the stomach but of the heart, of the soul. I was thirteen years old, an eighth grader in a private military school in Los Angeles. They taught us boys not just how to march in step and carry a rifle but infantry tactics too, enfilade, fields of fire, and other skills for which I could not imagine that I would ever have any use. It was also an Episcopal school where I took confirmation classes. "Onward Christian Soldiers" was sung in chapel; the inconsistency was apparent to me even at this green age. In religion classes, I memorized the 23rd Psalm. "The Lord is my shepherd…"

When it rained, religious instruction went on uninterrupted. The military instruction, however, drilling and marching, was curtailed by inclement weather, so they showed us movies. These were usually patriotic morale-boosting films, exciting scenes of soldiers and war machines, but without any American bodies lying on beaches. On one of those weather days, a mistake had been made at an ROTC supply facility and the wrong film had been sent.

It started with the usual graphics, then numbers counting down, then there were images of an American army detachment moving through a gate into a wired compound. It was clear that they had entered a prison camp, but almost immediately it became clear that it was no POW camp but something quite different. The camera panned along rows of dilapidated wooden bunkhouses in front of which were ranks of dead bodies in striped uniforms. The steady voice used in all the Signal Corp films identified it as a place called Buchenwald.

I could hear the sergeant whispering in the back of the room about how to handle a situation that seemed to be slipping beyond the boundaries of what was appropriate for boys as sheltered as we were. The images became even more horrifying. A bulldozer was pushing a mound of forty or fifty emaciated corpses of both men and women toward a pit. They tumbled into it like logs where they sprawled out, naked and appallingly immodest in death. Someone put his hand over the projector's lens. The lights came on. We students sat in stunned silence. The silence among the faculty, both the ROTC instructors and the clergy, was excruciating, an awkwardness that revealed their utter inadequacy as teachers and guides; there was no attempt to explain what we had seen. Somewhere in the following days, I encountered the word "holocaust," but having a word for it didn't drain any of the power from the event itself, the images, those terrible images. The silence in classrooms, even in the religious instruction classes, the avoidance of any mention of the occurrence at the school's morning assembly, increased, rather than diminished, its significance. It was as if something had happened that was too embarrassing to acknowledge, a moral nakedness, a terrible truth about human beings had been exposed, and in a way that was irrefutable. We had seen the pictures. The curtain had been pulled away, and there Man was. The event changed me permanently; it produced a lasting interest that became something of an obsession.

In the same school context in which I learned about the Holocaust, I learned about anti-Semitism. There was one Jewish student in my class, a curly-haired boy named Altman; I believe that he was the only Jew in the whole school. And as Altman's friend I observed the sickness that nourished the roots of the Holocaust.

The Latin teacher, whom we knew as Mr. Solon, referred to Altman in class as a "kike," sometimes as "our little kike." He piled on punitive and demeaning homework—a 500 word history of a cream puff in the Trojan War was one such assignment—for the slightest error of conjugation. Mr. Solon was a vile creature. The displays of sadism so angered me that my stomach hurt. It was through the experience of this Latin class that the idea of injustice first entered my consciousness: injustice, as distinct from the many forms of unfairness that one encounters in the course of one's childhood. Apparently, like many young children, I had a natural intuition of what justice meant and that inborn quality allowed me to recognize its opposite.

I felt profoundly distressed for Altman and told him so, but I was thirteen and in no position to defend him. I reported these things to my parents, thinking that they would do something about it, but they apparently thought I was exaggerating and did nothing. My father's inaction seriously troubled me. Feeling depressed and powerless, I endured an agonizing semester in a classroom with the hateful Mr. Solon. Altman did not last the school year. Two years later, my brother John had the same teacher, was equally distressed, and also told our parents. This time, with my story corroborated, my father acted. He called on the headmaster and complained. My father told me that he had done this and he actually apologized for not taking my reports seriously. It was my father who explained anti-Semitism to me.

I don't know what became of Altman. One day he was not in school and never came back. I felt guilty that I had not been able to help him. We had met in the valley of the shadow—with Biblical references everywhere the metaphors came easily— and I felt that this had created a bond between us. I went on to become a card-carrying Episcopalian which, however, turned out to have no significant effect on me. "Confirmation" meant memorizing things and declaring beliefs that I did not have. Why was it necessary to kneel at a rail and pretend to eat the body and blood of Christ? I didn't understand. It struck me as weirdly cannibalistic. My mother had insisted that I be confirmed as a Christian, more, I suspect, as a mark of class identity than from any strong religious feeling on her part. Nevertheless, I think that being exposed to the fables of the dominant religion was useful. I know what Italian paintings depict and those fables provided powerful metaphors. "The valley of the shadow of death" was one such. I had encountered evil and I recognized it for what it was, as evil, not just badness. However, unlike the Psalmist, I was uneasy, even afraid; these feeling would grow stronger over the years, as I learned more.

And there, in Jerusalem, I had broken bread with a handful of men who had encountered the worst of that evil and survived. Much later, I returned to the subject as a serious student and finally as a writer.

After three weeks of convalescing, I flew to London. Hamish treated me to the Hotel Russell in Bloomsbury where I slept on clean and ironed sheets and had long hot showers. I stayed four days. Hamish took me to Simpson's on the Strand for the traditional roast beef dinner. We talked about everything: his friendship with my grandfather, God, and history.

He had amusing anecdotes about my father, whom he had nicknamed "Socky" because in post-war European hotels the beds were short, and since my tall father's feet stuck out, he wore socks to bed.

Hamish told me about the company's efforts to help Jewish colleagues get out of Germany after 1936, when the pogroms began. He had been the third party in a series of letter exchanges between my grandfather, himself, and Bernard Baruch, who had been the company's initial stockholder. Baruch, a Jew, was a prominent philanthropist, financier, and advisor to President Roosevelt on economic matters. After *Kristallnacht*, in 1938, Mr. Baruch had wanted Cyprus Mines to cease doing business with the Germans.

"Your grandfather argued that to do so would put hundreds of miners out of work. Mr. Baruch accepted this argument. But less than a year later, when Germany invaded Poland, your grandfather, without any prodding from Baruch, cancelled all his contracts with German smelters. He even ordered an ore carrier that was on the sea to turn back to Cyprus."

This story provided the missing piece to another puzzle. I had not known what Baruch's role had been in the family story. I had met him when I was four. My mother had bought long pants for me because we were going to meet someone my mother called "a great man." We met in Lafayette Park in front of the White House. The great man was sitting on a park bench. He wore wool gloves with the fingers exposed, so it must have been cold, but not terribly, the fall. He shook my hand and said, "I like your grandfather, young man." I didn't know who he was or why I'd been taken to meet him.

Hamish continued with his history of the company. The decision to stop doing business with Germany was not something that was required by law. As an American company, the Trading with the Enemy Act did not apply until the United States declared war on Germany in 1941.

"Harvey Mudd was a very principled man. He did the right thing because he could see that there was a single and unambiguous right thing. It was not legally prohibited for an American company to do business with Germany, but he severed relations immediately. He didn't consult lawyers. He put the company into mothballs for the duration of the war and managed to keep the miners busy. They built docks and a hospital. Your grandfather was optimistic by nature. He thought we, the British, would win the war. He thought we would win because we, unequivocally, were the better people. We were on the side of civilization. The Nazis were evil, the barbarian, and there was no ambiguity in that. We wouldn't have won if you Americans had not joined the struggle." The good had prevailed, at least for the moment. I heard in Hamish's tone something that I'd heard before, that sense that the peace and civilization were fragile.

Later in the evening, we managed to get to the theological.

"I don't think God created the world," I said. "I know too much geology and evolutionary theory to think that."

"Science is in your blood, young Harvey," Hamish replied. "You can't un-know what you know."

"But could God have created himself?" I asked. I had no particular beliefs of my own. I just wanted to know what Hamish thought. "And if that were so, then everything else could be an after-effect. Like ripples in a pond." Had I heard somewhere of the Big Bang theory? I must have, but have no memory of it.

"If it is," said Hamish, "it was an unintended after-effect. This world we live in contains no evidence of divine thought and damned few traces of human thoughtfulness." There was that dark undercurrent again.

"What has happened," he continued, "what goes on happening, is mostly accidents. Paths fork, empires rise and fall. Violence, ignorance, and hate are as much a part of the human condition as the virtues that stand in opposition."

I asked him if he thought there was such a thing as progress, not in technology, but in human affairs generally.

"I've lived through two wars, young Harvey. I think mankind is failing the most fundamental tests: rationality and decency. I think the majority of human beings are inherently irrational, greedy, and violent. Mercy, charity, and justice are qualities that are found in many of us, but not in enough. And the people who have those qualities are almost universally reluctant to use force, which gives the barbarian, the tyrant, and the thug the advantage."

* * *

Twelve months earlier, I had purchased a return ticket to Los Angeles, which I now used. I wired my parents about my return, hoping to be met at the airport, but I suspected that by being so uncommunicative for so long, I might have forfeited the traditional welcoming of the prodigal son. And that was how it was. My father told me that he could not get away from the office. My mother was shopping. I was disappointed. In the weeks that followed, I shared some of my experiences with my father, but only when we had time alone. My mother had made it clear that she was not interested. At cocktails on my second day back in Los Angeles, when I started to talk about my discovery of Arab Spain, she found an excuse to leave the room to consult with the cook about dinner.

HM and Jim in Italy, 1960

Mildred Esterbrook Mudd,
my paternal grandmother

My paternal grandfather as a
young man, circa 1920

My parents, 1940

My father, as Stanford student,
circa 1935

Hamish Robertson and my father,
on our way to Germany, 1956.

El Greco's View of Toledo

Part II

Falling, but Forward

Every time he was x-rayed, doctors vainly tried to puzzle out what they termed "a shadow behind the heart." "Good title for a bad novel," remarked Chateau.

Vladimir Nabokov, *Pnin*

11

Teetering

A claim of having "fragile" health, a condition that would have been called hypochondria in another family was, in respect to my mother, taken as a sign of her sensitive nature. Her health issues were often presented as signs of her refinement. She needed the very best; the medical care in Los Angeles was not good enough, so her primary doctors were in New York. She had chronic back pain, but had had no injury and the doctors could find no physical deformity. A fusion of several of her vertebrae was seen as the solution. Not too many years later I read Edmund Wilson's novella "The Princess with the Golden Hair" about a beautiful socialite who had a neurotic need to present herself as fragile, with an injured back that required a steel brace which she even wore to bed. Because of the back pain and the brace, the character in the novel was sexually and romantically unavailable. It occurred to me that my mother's story might be similar. My mother had worn a brace for a while, but said it did no good, so she elected surgery.

She was in traction for several months. My father took me to New York to see her. There was a long, noisy flight, at least seven hours, sitting in first class next to my father. The propellers pounded away at the air, everything vibrated, and the bourbon in my father's glass rippled. While my father read business papers, I read Sigmund Freud's treatise on religion, *The Future of an Illusion*. It was my first exposure to Freud. Two years later, I discovered his concept of the unconscious, a place in the psyche that stored traumatic experiences and past emotions. The idea that I had an unconscious was an important discovery for me; it was like finding a hidden valley or the headwaters of a river.

In 1956, the notion of an unconscious was a radical idea for some. It came with the implication of disorder, of illness, and of some sort of dirtiness. Unhealthy thoughts originated in the unconscious and since our family, of course, did not have unhealthy thoughts... denial took strange routes. As long as everything looked fine, there was no need to speculate about something that did not exist; this was my mother's position. Psychological problems could be expected in less fortunate people, but for those who had every advantage and who had been well brought up, it was out of the question. Indeed, two years later when I insisted that I needed psychiatric help because I had emotional problems—to my mind quite serious ones—my mother adamantly refused to consider the idea.

I had no resistance to the idea of the unconscious. I was sure it was real because I had seen it at work. During my eighth and ninth years, for instance, I had had recurring infections called boils; they had a name but defied explanation as to cause. Boils were abscesses, pockets of pus, that appeared on my thighs, sometimes both at once and were so severe and potentially dangerous—a risk of blood poisoning— that I was kept out of school sometimes for as long as a week. The boils came and went, following their own rules. The family doctor came to the house occasionally to lance a boil or to consult, but usually the treatment was hot compresses. The infection came to the surface, a slow and very painful process, and finally erupted and drained. When I discovered Freud on the subject of repressed emotion, I remembered that I had identified the boils as being "angry." I could remember feeling, despite the pain they caused, a kind of malicious glee in that they forced my mother to deal with the unpleasantness. I was, it seems clear to me now, opposing her, expressing anger in the only way that was permitted. One did not, in our house, express anger, or much of anything else.

* * *

It would be 1959 before my unconscious erupted again, not as boils this time, but in a more serious way, as a general convulsion of my whole being. On that 1957 trip to New York, however, it was under control.

My father and I went uptown to see my mother every morning; in the afternoon, we became tourists, visiting places like the Natural History Museum. In the evenings, we went to jazz clubs; I loved jazz and still do. My father was curious and surprisingly open-minded about it. We heard the Jimmy Giuffre trio and Lionel Hampton, and my father liked both.

On this 1957 trip I had a life changing exposure to the theater. My father took me to see Eugene O'Neill's *Long Day's Journey into Night*. I had read a review in *Time* magazine and wanted very much to see it. My father preferred musicals; we saw *Damn Yankees* on that same visit, his kind of theater. The 1956 production of *Long Day's Journey* was the premiere; the play, never performed during O'Neill's lifetime because he considered it too personal, is now considered one of the great moments in American theater. It is a four-act dissection of a tormented American family, a play about things that no one in that fictional family would talk about. The play was instrumental in forcing me to think about my own family and my feelings about it, to talk about it, at first only with myself and then with a psychiatrist.

At that time, aged seventeen, I had a driver's license and felt, as all teens do, that a great freedom had been bestowed on me. I explored Los Angeles from one end of the basin to the other, Watts, Redondo, El Segundo, Tarzana; there was virtually no part of the city that I didn't prowl. I did it always at night, a reprise of the night wandering I'd done as a little boy. The deeper part of my emancipation, however, the emotional and spiritual part of it, was a task that would have to be for the future, but the degree of freedom that came with access to a car made me think that I was in fact free. I imagined that I had left all the torments and unhappiness of my childhood behind, that the process had been as simple as going to the stern of the ship and dumping the garbage overboard. In keeping with this mood shift, I had done a sort of whitewash of my childhood. I argued to myself that no childhood was completely happy. I imagined that few children feel that they are loved enough. I didn't feel that I had been loved at all by my mother, or at best, loved strangely, but I tried to convince myself that I exaggerated my unhappiness. Get over it. Turn the key in the ignition and off you go. To Pasadena where there was a girl. To Santa Monica where there were white beaches and the ocean. Besides, worse things could have happened. Indeed, from the perspective of what a great many children experience, nothing terribly serious, other than the cancer scare, had happened. I had never been beaten or terrorized by a drunken parent, as Huckleberry Finn had been, nor had I been abandoned, or poor, or gone hungry, or lived through bomb attacks, or been a refugee. But there was no denying that I had been very unhappy. Was something wrong with me for feeling that? I had begun to feel guilty about my perceptions, my interpretations, and about what I felt about my family, especially about my mother.

The O'Neill play straightened everything out for me. I saw many similarities between the obviously tormented Tyrones and the discreetly, politely, tormented Mudds. The focal point of the O'Neill story was the heroin-addicted mother, in denial about her condition, about the secrets of her life and heart. When she speaks the line, "Fog hides you from the world and the world from you," the words jumped at me. I saw that I had lived in a similar world. It wasn't fog though; it was the "special family" narrative with which we had surrounded ourselves. It was perfect appearance, perfect manners. But like the Tyrones, we too, collectively, were faking it. We were all surface and what was beneath was neither orderly nor happy. Indeed, there was a dark side to us, though what it was I could not have said then. More important, there was a dark side to me. I could feel it stirring, though at the time I had no idea where it would lead me.

The play was very long and exhausting. My very literal father, whose benign view of family had not yet been shaken, slept through the final act. It was very late when we returned to the apartment that my parents kept on Madison Avenue. The night was hot and humid, but the air was soft. The sound of strolling people laughing and talking and the rattle of taxis surging along the avenue gave a comforting human presence to the hot New York night. The lateness of the hour and noises of the city, the flow of lights, combined with the emotional agitation provoked by the play, put me in a heightened, strangely euphoric state.

My father retired to the bedroom and continued his sleep. The air-conditioned room seemed sterile, so I opened a sitting room window onto the warm night, and with the sounds of taxis echoing up the urban canyon, I wrote my first poems. They are lost, but it was the beginning. The psyche, that complex geography of moods and experiences, the darkest region of the self, became the place where I would, thereafter, do my most purposeful wandering. O'Neill had shown me that one could write one's way into the unconscious and by the same route find one's way out of it.

The next two years, 1957 and 1958, my junior and senior years in prep school, went well enough, without outward signs of trouble or rebellion. Jim and I were appointed prefects and were put in charge of the dormitory for ninth graders, the young ones. Jim was the star athlete in the school, and I was seen as somewhat eccentric, a proto-bohemian perhaps, but still a good citizen. During school vacations, however, I was developing into a different sort of person. I gave up living with my family and was taken in by Jim's parents. This was a subtle transition, a departure without melodrama, that my parents seemed to understand, so they did not object. I did not engage in risky behavior, no drugs or alcohol. I had discovered a universe of literature that explained my feelings and perceptions to me. I felt alienated from the society around me—no doubt a common affliction of late adolescence— and I found explanations for these feelings in books. I read Camus, Dostoyevsky, Colin Wilson, Allen Ginsburg, and Jack Kerouac. And I read Freud. The unconscious became more than an idea: it was a reality that I began to explore. I wrote down my dreams. I wrote poems. I felt that I was drifting further and further away from the society that I was expected to become a part of, but I suppressed those feelings. I was, however, beginning to worry about myself.

I was accepted at prestigious Amherst College. It quickly became clear that I did not fit in at Amherst. Coming from the West Coast, I was on the defensive from the beginning. I compensated by being "laid back"; I had attitude and I insisted on finding causes. Mandatory chapel, even if God was never mentioned, was one such. Anything having to do with college tradition was another. I declared my outsider status, that I was a Californian, by going barefoot to classes even into the late fall when the walkways were wet with rain and splatted with sodden leaves. A love affair that wasn't—the girl from Sarah Lawrence College—put my time as an Amherst student into a slow-motion collapse. Across the next five months, my emotional state disintegrated. I jumped out of a third story window, not to kill myself, but to prove something, that I was fearless perhaps? Or that I could fly? The alcohol content in my brain had made this seem important. The same alcohol had kept my joints loose and a shrub below that I had deliberately jumped into had helped. A branch cut a groove in my back but I broke nothing.

I had come to the attention of an upper classman, a senior who had spent two years in the Navy and was then twenty-five years old. He, Charles Wells, saw in my growing misery something that perhaps he had known when he was my age. His empathy and friendship kept me together. A sculptor and print maker, he was the first real artist I had ever known. Without him, my implosion would have happened sooner.

For the first time in my life, I failed an academic course, calculus. I was judged to be an unsuitable student for Amherst unless I got rid of the attitude and could pass calculus. Officially suspended, I returned to California. I told my parents that I needed help.

"Dear," my mother said, "there is nothing wrong with you."

They were having their martinis on the veranda. Golfers, on the course below the house, played through. I heard the occasional crack of a club hitting a ball. I was in such a state that I was almost hallucinating.

My father's size thirteen shoes seemed too far from his head to belong to him. I was vividly, excruciatingly, aware of my mother's ankles, the only part of her body where flesh showed. She was wearing one of her elegant at-home gowns, a peignoir with layers of lace and a feather collar.

"I am afraid I'm going crazy," I said.

"Don't you think that's a bit overly dramatic, dear?" my mother said. Desperation came to my rescue. Adrenaline flooded my system and I picked up the Baccarat crystal cocktail pitcher, martini and ice sloshing down my arm, and threw it with all my strength against the brick wall of the house. Point made. My father overrode my mother. He told her that anger over what I had done was not the right response and agreed that I could enter treatment. I'd never seen him take charge quite like this before. Within a week, through connections at Columbia Presbyterian, he had found a psychiatrist for me. Dr. Shervert Frazier was head of the department. Sending me to New York spared my mother from having to explain why her son was not in school and from having to admit that she had a troubled child. And putting a continent between us was the smart thing to do.

12

Into the Thicket

When I moved to New York City in the late summer of 1958, it was to begin psychiatric treatment. Choosing a voluntary out-patient way was clearly better than having a complete collapse and having someone check me into the psych ward. I knew I needed help. I had read enough Freud and others in the field to understand where the problems had originated. I knew that I needed to acknowledge my emotions and to recover things I'd forgotten or suppressed. I needed to have someone with whom I could talk without fear of disapproval or betrayal. But, fresh off the airplane, I had no idea how bad things were. I persuaded myself that I was under the protective spirit of Jack Kerouac and headed for Greenwich Village to find an apartment. Beyond naïve, I was clueless about big cities and so found myself in a menacing world for which I was completely unprepared.

Homosexuality was still illegal in 1958, a decade before the Stonewall riots and the changes in societal attitudes that evolved in the years that followed. The little I knew about homosexuality was generally neutral. I had heard the schoolyard slurs about "faggots," but didn't associate the term with homosexuality. I thought the term meant sissy.

I knew a homosexual man. He was my father's administrative assistant; a slender man, in his fifties when I knew him, was "out of the closet" with people he trusted, which included my father, his boss. He was not in the least bit ostentatious about his orientation. Evan was always in the background of my late childhood and early adolescence. He was important in my father's business life; they addressed each other by their first names. Evan's duties occasionally crossed over into our family life, as, for instance, on occasions when I needed to be driven somewhere when my mother was unavailable. He was trusted with me.

I liked Evan. I had noticed slightly effeminate gestures, but thought little about it; these perceptions, however, led to my becoming aware of this aspect of his being. Sometime in my middle teens, during a conversation with my father about marriage, I had asked if Evan was married. My father had explained about Evan's sexual orientation, including the facts about the prejudices and fears about homosexuality. I was not to gossip about it. My father was not gossiping either; he was conveying important information about the world, and at the same time demonstrating something about himself. I feel certain that my father had cleared this disclosure with Evan himself. It was the first time I'd heard the word "homosexual." The term "gay" did not yet exist. Because Evan's life or way of being didn't seem to shock or offend my father, it didn't shock me.

I went from a tolerant environment, in which an admitted homosexual was considered almost a family member, to the culture of Greenwich Village ten years before Stonewall, where, indeed, I had a shock.

Suppression and closeting produced some ugly consequences. The Village in those days was full of sexual predators who saw a green boy from the provinces like me—6'1", 170 lbs. and, I suppose, pretty—as easy prey, a lamb that had strayed from the safety of his flock. I was followed down dark streets, hit on in public places, and touched often on my thighs and buttocks. It was quite frightening, both in the sense of the invasion of my personal space and in terms of threatening my sense of self. I was still a virgin, very unsure with girls, and it was inevitable that I would wonder if the men who followed me at night or who stared unblinking into my eyes in invitation knew something about me that I didn't. Was I homosexual? I could offer little evidence to the contrary.

I believed that I was heterosexual, but I had no way of knowing this for sure. My mother had disparaged and suppressed my interest in the opposite sex. At age eleven, for instance, I had pasted a color photograph from *Silver Screen Magazine* of an actress, Anne Francis, in the style of gown she would have worn to a movie premiere, on my bedroom wall. My mother demanded that I remove it. I argued. My mother said that she would allow the picture if I cut off the image at the collarbone, removing even the suggestion of breasts. I cheated by folding the lower third of the picture under. I unfolded it from time to time and admired this beautiful woman. About this same time, in the sixth grade at Wilton Place Grammar School, I had traded a handful of my best marbles for a torn fragment of a pornographic photograph. It was black and white, showing neither the male's face nor the female's, but showing penetration, which was the information that I had needed. My father, very repressed in sexual matters, had told me nothing. He and I talked about God, geology, and evolution, but never once did we have the customary father and son chat about sex.

The next year, seventh grade, when I had defied my mother to see my first girlfriend, my mother had searched my room. She found the well-hidden pornographic picture and discovered my subterfuge concerning the Anne Francis photograph. I came home from school to find just bits of scotch tape on the wall. She had confiscated both pictures. She said nothing. Her knowledge about the contents of my mind combined with the fact that she had searched my room and therefore could again, convinced me that not only was greater secrecy required but that I should escape at my earliest opportunity. I began then to work toward that goal. It was freedom that I wanted, not just for my physical presence and a sense of privacy, but, even more important, for my mind and my feelings, my being. I wanted girls in my life.

My mother's innuendos, however, had managed to plant so many poisonous ideas about women that I feared that I was destined for a life of tormented solitude. Sex was dirty, improper, a source of infection, *and* it was a tool that unscrupulous women would use to ensnare me. Most women, she told me explicitly, would be interested only in my money, money that I didn't know I had. The daughters of her friends fell into a different category. I could pick from among them, except, apparently, for the girl down the street. In my heart, however, I held on to a belief that there were good women of all sorts and that I would one day find one. At the core of my being, or so I wanted to believe, there was a capacity for love and that somehow sexuality was a part of this story. For the moment, however, I was so unformed in that respect, that it is little wonder I was poorly equipped to deal with the attentions of assertive homosexuals. I was, for my first four or five months in New York, constantly in flight. I'd hurry back from the market and up the steps of my brownstone apartment, hurrying so that no one would get the idea that I was loitering and thus available.

I made it through those anxiety-filled first months in New York because I now had a lifeline, my appointments with Dr. Frazier on 168th street. For fifty minutes a day, five days a week, I would crawl out of the waters that swarmed with menace and rest on a patch of dry land. The sun, however, on that little island was harsh. I was required to explore myself.

I knew I had little chance of understanding what was happening to me if I didn't understand where I had come from. Woven into my being was not just my parents' DNA but the threads of their lives and their personalities. Since these were influences I would feel for the rest of my life, it seemed necessary to understand them. Thus in my early sessions with Dr. Frazier there was a great deal of back-tracking. I started with what I knew about my parents' courtship and their relationship before I was born.

My mother, at eighteen years old, was popular with good-looking boys who dressed well and had access to sailboats belonging to their parents, and who took my mother on overnight sails to Catalina Island. Among these young men, my mother had a boyfriend whose name she never told me, but I'd seen his picture in an album she had kept from her younger days, days of tennis, the Santa Monica Beach Club, and the

Cotillion. My mother was considered beautiful—a round face, perfectly symmetrical and balanced features, none too prominent, and a well-proportioned figure. My father, on the other hand, was not endowed with the standard-model good looks; he had a long face, was six-foot-four-inches tall and lanky. As a boy, he had been teased because he looked like Ichabod Crane. He was a serious student, a senior at Stanford, from one of the richest families in the city and had the best of expectations, both in terms of career and inheritance.

As a suitor, my father was, in his own words, "awkward," probably as easily rattled by a girl's beauty as I was at the same age. He was apparently utterly ignorant about sexuality, handicapped by attitudes that were probably typical of his background.

The keystone of my parents' story, their courtship and marriage, came to me after my parents' divorce in 1969, some ten years after I had sketched out what little I knew of it in Dr. Frazier's office. My mother's best friend, someone with whom I was close because her son, Dan, had been my best friend in childhood, was my source. My mother, according to her old friend, had not been interested in my father. My mother's mother, however, saw in my father a perfect fit. My mother's family was comfortable, but nothing next to my father's family. My mother's mother, therefore, pushed her daughter, her only child, at my father. She pushed physically, and they fought. My grandmother ended up dragging my mother out of her bedroom and along the carpeted hallway toward the staircase. Below, in the sitting room, sat my very nervous father, with a ring in a velvet box and a proposal of marriage. My mother, clinging to the carpet, broke a fingernail, a detail that had firmly planted the entire incident in the mind of my informant.

My mother surrendered to parental authority. She was no rebel and it is likely that she eventually came around to her mother's way of seeing things, that wealth and connection were worth a sacrifice. The sacrifice, I deduced from my mother's description of her youth, was romantic love. Romance left behind, my future parents went along the proper path, a yearlong engagement. My father told me, indirectly, that there was no sexual contact before marriage. When he went off to graduate school at

M.I.T. in Cambridge, Massachusetts, my mother followed, enrolling in secretarial school in Boston just across the Charles River. My mother told me that she wanted to be able to support herself. One could just as easily learn to type and take shorthand in Los Angeles, but, on her mother's instruction, she was to keep my father on a short leash. In the early spring of 1939, they were married in an extravagant Episcopal wedding covered generously by the Los Angeles Times.

I suspect that this loveless beginning set the tone for the marriage generally. I do, however, have a photograph of the young couple taken in 1940 in which they seem happy enough, but from my father I knew that the marriage had been without passion. I had long suspected this because I never once saw them kiss, except for a peck on the cheek. My father had implied, in the conversation alluded to above, that the kind of woman that one would want to marry was not expected to have sexual desires. What my mother felt about my father I cannot say because she never, in the fifty-five years that I knew her, said anything about how she felt about him. No expressions of fondness or irritation, neither complaints nor compliments. But that, perhaps, means little, for my mother never expressed feelings about anything or anyone. She said that I was attractive. "Attractive" was her highest compliment. But even that approbation was always qualified: I could be *even more* attractive, she would say, "if only…"

"My mother's words were empty," I said to Dr. Frazier in one of the early sessions. "And I had always felt that I was empty. There is nothing real, nothing substantial inside me. No self, no identity, just guts."

I recounted a recurring dream that I began to have in the late 1940s after the family had left Washington D.C., where my father had had war-related work, and returned to California. It cropped up over and over, with slight variations, until I was fifteen or so. In the backyard garden of the Washington house in the dream setting, there is an arched arbor, painted white and covered with roses. The roses look dry. A clump of hollyhocks is positioned around the arbor, tall plants with dusty, tattered leaves; they seem like sentinels, inattentive but still vaguely menacing. Seated on a bench in the arbor is a woman in a black robe; a black hood conceals her face. By her sitting position, I associate her with Mary, the mother of Jesus, but in the dream there is no infant on her lap. I want to be the infant on her lap, replicating the countless Mary and baby Jesus images one sees in Christian countries. In the dream, however, I know this woman is not Mary; she is my mother, but I want *us* to be like that idealized mother and child. I approach the arbor and reach out, touching the woman in black on her knee. She raises her head and I see, with utter horror, that inside the black cowl there is no one, no face.

I spent the last two years of the Second World War in the care of an emotionally inadequate (or distracted) mother. The dream image captures that aspect of my world. Would I have even noticed the war had my mother been attentive and comforting? I cannot say. But since I experienced the atmospheric changes that the war produced, there is no question that war shaped my understanding of everything. I lived in a state of low-level anxiety. I wasn't sure where the war was happening and was never convinced that I was not in actual danger. After 1944 my father was in the Navy and away often, and I feared for him. He was never in combat, so not in danger, but, for whatever reason, I was never reassured.

I have real memories that date from this period. Some of the memories are unspecific, like cold and snow, novelties to a California child, or like the sight of fireflies blinking on and off in the warm summer nights. Some memories are specific, like the time I thought I'd killed my brother. We were quarreling in the sandbox in the backyard. The quarrel escalated to the point where I hit him on the head with a sand bucket. (Better the sand bucket than Cain's jawbone of an ass.) The sight, in the first seconds, of a half-moon of crimson suddenly appearing on his forehead is burned into my memory. The injury was minor; the blood came from the tiny capillaries that run shallowly across the forehead. My father, who was home from one of his frequent trips on Navy business, decided that making much of it would traumatize me further. His calm intervention inspired confidence in him.

* * *

"I think your father loved you," Dr. Frazier said. This was the first time that this idea had occurred to me. Most men of his generation didn't express that sort of feeling easily. Perhaps he did love me; he had tried to demonstrate what he could not say. He would periodically engage us boys in major projects. When I was ten, for instance, he, my two little brothers, and I, had built a shed for a pig that we would eventually eat. We designed the roof so it could be lifted off to facilitate the changing of straw. "The pig should be comfortable," my father said. We all participated. He measured, sawed, and hammered, the hard parts, while we carried boards, held a coffee tin full of nails, and painted.

My father's hobby was wild flowers. I helped him collect the flowers and together we dried them between sheets of blotting paper. I watched him press them into albums. His fingers had a slight tremor. He would then write both the Latin and common name for the flower beneath it. I would look over his shoulder as he performed these operations.

His respect for curiosity, for investigations of any sort, was a great help during the year and some months that I was in therapy. I was attempting to dismantle and inspect the workings of one of the most complex of human inventions, the family, and beneath that was an even more complex entity, my psyche, my unconscious. For the process to work, I had to be actively, aggressively curious. What had happened to me? How did I get this way? My father, through the lens of scientific curiosity, thought that therapy, though it was exclusively concerned with the emotions, was a rational activity. To my mother, however, psychotherapy was worse than unnecessary; it was subversive. Its implications conflicted with her world view. I am not sure that my father recognized the power of the unconscious in human affairs, but this was of no consequence; what mattered was his respect for any investigative process. He never asked what I was discovering about the family, about him, or about myself; but he always paid the bill. I saw him three or four times during my therapy, when he came to New York on business. He always asked if the process was interesting. And that was all he asked.

* * *

Home was much talked about in the early therapy sessions. For most children, home is a place where love is first experienced, but for many, it is where neglect is experienced and trauma occurs. An American's house is, as we like to say, his castle, but for an abused child, it is prison; and for an emotionally neglected child, it is a sterile white room with controlled temperatures. From a very early age, perhaps as young as eight years old, I had one idea: escape. And once I had escaped and made it to New York, my apartment became home. My first apartment in New York was on the same block of West Fifteenth where Thomas Wolfe had lived. *You Can't Go Home Again* had had a profound effect on me. When I finished the novel, I cried and cried. I revered Thomas Wolfe. I would imagine that I saw his ghost walking up the block, always in a big overcoat that billowed in the autumn winds. We would walk together, past the Catholic home for unwed mothers, as far as the Seventh Avenue subway entrance at Fourteenth Street. I would disappear down the stairs to the subway platform and Thomas Wolfe's ghost, having escorted me safely to the subway, went back to the block we shared. I imagined that he looked after me.

I had real protectors in my childhood. They were the people who worked for my mother, "the help," and they made a great difference in how I got by in those years, ages four through fourteen. Indeed, this larger community may have been the crucial factor that protected me from the fate of so many people who have had unhappy childhoods, consequences that run the range from general failures caused by lack of self-esteem to alcoholism and drug addiction. To my mother's credit, she treated the people who worked for her with courtesy and respect; they appeared to respect and even like her. Once established in our household, they became almost permanent. She managed the house, but she did not micromanage, letting each have considerable autonomy. My mother managed family and household as a micro-corporation, and it often felt that impersonal to me, except, as I said above, for the very real personalities of the employees of the enterprise.

My mother's cook of twenty years, Eleanora White, was stout, very dark-skinned, and was always dressed in an immaculate starched uniform. She was a commanding and graceful presence in the kitchen. There was never any question that it was *her* kitchen. She was one of the few people to whom my mother ever deferred. By way of establishing her bona fides with a seven-year-old white child, she told me that she was the *very one* who had cut off the tails of the three blind mice. Brandishing an enormous kitchen knife, she pantomimed this event. Around the kitchen table she went. And I, delighted, objected.

"But, Eleanora, the mice were blind. Not fair."

"No matter, honey," she said, "they can scoot under the furniture and they is quick. And they see with their whiskers."

She was always kind to me. When I graduated at about age eleven from the children's dinner table to the big table, I was always expected to help Eleanora clear the plates after the meal. I often reported my school day experiences to Eleanora over milk and crackers at the kitchen table.

Then there was Eleanora's nephew, Andrew, who was my maternal grandmother's driver, cook, caretaker, personal secretary, and, in her final years, caregiver. Andrew was a handsome man, lean and athletic. He had a beautiful voice that he used in a Gospel quartet in South Central Los Angeles. He always had Sunday as his day off. Occasionally, when I visited my grandmother, he sang for me. "Go Down Moses" was my favorite. Once, while at my grandmother's beach house, Andrew went swimming in the Pacific with my brothers and me. A neighbor called my grandmother to complain about the black man in the surf. My grandmother capitulated, but left to my mother the unpleasant task of telling Andrew that he could no longer swim in that portion of the vast ocean that faced this gated enclave of rich white Americans. I overheard the conversation. My mother apologized, quite sincerely, to Andrew for the behavior of our white neighbors. She suggested that he swim in the evening, when most had retired for cocktails or dinner; he did sometimes, when he could get away from his cocktail duties, and I sometimes went with him. This incident was my first exposure to

America's endemic racism. My mother, for all her limitations, was not infected with it.

There were other influential adults in the village of my childhood. Louise Hanneman, the cleaning lady who came daily, had complete authority over the appearance of every room of the house; she set the position of ashtrays on the tables. She was a north German who had fled Germany in 1934. She was not Jewish; she had simply refused to live under the Nazis. She told me all this in bits and pieces over the years, but I only understood what she had done and why when I was much older. Carlos Muñoz, the gardener, was a distinguished looking older man with a salt and pepper mustache. He was a native of Chihuahua state in Mexico and spoke very bad English. I can remember following him around the garden as he watered, and feeling that I liked him and that he reciprocated.

From 1946-1954, while I still lived at home and before I went away to boarding school, a wiry little English spinster, Kathleen Clifford, was at the heart of my childhood. She was my nanny, responsible for everything, for getting me up in the morning, getting me dressed, helping with homework. She was stability and affection. She lived in the house with us and ate with us children at the children's table. She had a small apartment somewhere in the city that was her retreat on her days off. She took me there once or twice. It was full of snapshots in little frames, pictures of her father in his deacon's collar, of her soldier brother who was killed in France in 1917, of little dogs and a cottage. There was a rebellious side to her. She smoked covertly in the laundry room or in the utility yard; I thought that her willingness to conceal something from my mother was quite daring and, in fact, admirable.

It was she, "Cliff" as I called her, who read to me. I have no recollection of ever being read to by my mother. Cliff read *Winnie the Pooh* and laughed out loud at the antics of Pooh Bear and friends. Having lived through the Blitz in London, she had a visceral fear of dictatorship, so when she read me *The Adventures of Alice in Wonderland*, she made sure that I appreciated the scenes near the end of book in which the Queen of Hearts, in an irrational rage, yells, "Off with his head."

"Can you imagine cutting off someone's head because the roses were the wrong color?" she asked rhetorically. "Kings used to do that," she said, "cut off the heads of people who disagreed with them." These exchanges contained my introduction to political science.

"Or," she went on, "feeling that you had to paint the roses to get them the color that the Queen wanted." The story of the Queen of Hearts and the roses resonated especially with me because of the emphasis my mother put on appearance. I was a bloom of the wrong color.

I like to think that Cliff understood the emotional emptiness in my world and, above all, its mysteriousness. She made a conscious effort to help me deal with it. She didn't just read books to me; she discussed and interpreted them. My mother, I came to see, was like the Cheshire Cat, whose body, whose very self, dematerialized if one got too close, leaving only the smile.

As I described these people —cook, chauffeur, cleaning lady, gardener, and nanny—and my feelings for them to Dr. Frazier, I began to cry. I had not, until that moment, realized how much I owed to them, how much their warmth, dignity, and humanity had given me. They had provided some protection from my mother's criticisms and an antidote to her remoteness. What I learned from them, by their example, were rules for living and that one's value as a person had little to do with money or status.

My paternal grandfather had given me another version of those same rules.

"A gentleman," he had said, "is someone who treats a king and a bootblack in the same way."

13

The Worst of Times

In my first months in New York I had established a daily routine that kept me from falling into an abyss. As I walked to the subway, I seldom looked up. I watched the pavement. I was invisible. I took the #1 Express train from Fourteenth Street to 168th Street for my appointment with Dr. Frazier. I negotiated the halls of the medical offices building with their polished linoleum floors to Dr. Frazier's office, then the famous fifty-minute hour. Then back to 14th Street, where I cooked some rice and a sausage. I bought ropes of linked sausages so I only needed to go to the store once a week. I read a lot. Then sleep, if I was lucky. I have no sense of where the rest of the time went. I had no TV and never went out. Five days a week, for the first six months, on the subway, I sat on the bench, almost catatonic, my mind clenched against the fear that I was so insubstantial that I would not survive the psychological jostling of the New York subways. The dark tunnels between stations seemed endless; I kept my eyes shut. The people standing on the platforms as the Express careened through the local stations sometimes seemed like guardians, my protectors, making sure that I made it safely. Other times, they seemed isolated and miserable creatures like me, lost and bewildered in an indifferent metropolis; on their faces I saw what Blake saw in London, "marks of weal, marks of woe." I absorbed their woes, the loneliness and failures, adding them to my own. I had no defenses; it was a sort of dispersed and general vulnerability, a condition of too much empathy.

I was afraid of a general sort of madness and this intensified my sense of isolation. Sane people don't want crazy friends. Once, I was sure the worst had happened, that I had gone mad. At the end of several sleepless nights, I was walking along Seventh Avenue and, abruptly, someone came into my line of sight who looked exactly like me, down to the shirt and shoes. It was me! It was as if I had stepped away from or out of myself, and was walking away. I followed this doppelganger, terrified that if I lost sight of him, the now tenuous thread that connected me to sanity would be severed and I would disintegrate. I would become little more than the trace of a being that no longer existed, like a faint odor, neither pleasant nor noxious, that anyone who encountered it would wave away without a thought. I was on the edge of panic. "We" managed to get ourselves, me, the version of myself that I was still in control of, and my escaping alter-self, up to 168th Street. It was a Sunday and I was reluctant to call Doctor Frazier. I went up to the neighborhood of the hospital in case I needed to check myself into the psychiatric ward. I wandered along upper Broadway and watched people's reactions to me. Did they see my double, the escapee? Did they see me disintegrating? There was no sign that anyone noticed anything, but New Yorkers are used to seeing just about everything, the lunatics and the lost, so their failure to notice was not reassuring. Nevertheless, my façade seemed to be holding up. Apparently I looked normal. Appearance, as my mother always insisted, was everything.

Finally, I overcame my shame, and, from a phone booth, I called Dr. Frazier at home. He answered and quietly questioned me about what I was experiencing. And then, calmly and lucidly as if he had diagnosed that my car had run out of gas, he said, "You are having a depersonalization episode. It is a stress symptom. It will pass."

The fear dispersed; such was the power of a few words from someone I trusted. "Depersonalization," like a hiccup of the soul. He called in a prescription for a few doses of Valium. I went back to the Village and to my tiny apartment. I was not disappearing and that was a comfort.

But I was not getting any larger. The four walls of the apartment and the New York City subway made up my world; my time was measured in therapy sessions. I was very much alone. I was reading Franz Kafka in those desolate days. Kafka wrote that his loneliness was all that he had, that he would not use drugs or alcohol to deaden his pain because then he would not even have the familiar loneliness. I maintained the same discipline: no drugs, no alcohol. Loneliness defined me in that period; it was, at least, an emotion that I could identify.

Eventually the loneliness became unendurable, but I was so fearful and the girls of Manhattan seemed so worldly and tough that I was sure I would never meet one who would like me, as shy as I was. Believing that I would never be able to meet a girl practically guaranteed that I wouldn't. I had, however, met a girl the previous summer, in Berkeley where I'd gone hoping to pass Calculus, a precondition for returning to Amherst, should I want to. Judy was literally the only girl I knew. I invited her to join me in New York; she could stay with me in my apartment. Though we hardly knew each other, we could, I thought, form a relationship. When she arrived in New York, it was clear that a relationship was not likely: she had come for New York, not to be with me. She slept on the floor wrapped in a blanket. After a week, she moved across the hall to sleep with its occupant, a man in his thirties who said he was an actor and could get her into TV. Even though by this time I had no feelings for her, the situation was a torment. I should have said good riddance, but I was literally eaten alive by jealousy. Feeling an emotion that I didn't actually feel was neurotic agony in its purest form, a state of self-induced and self-reinforcing misery, a circular hell that one could not escape. I didn't like or love this girl. Why was I jealous? This was a transformative moment; I decided consciously that I didn't want to live this way, and that I would redouble my efforts in therapy.

In the meantime, there was still Judy. She sometimes came back to me, contrite and apologetic, but still slept curled up on the floor. One afternoon, the man came over when Judy had gone out, ostensibly to apologize, but actually to invite me, not Judy, to spend the night with him. It seems that he had seduced her as a way to get to me. Every time I came home, he opened his door and invited me in. Apparently he sat by his window to watch for me coming up the steps. Did he have a job or a life? New York was a strange place indeed. Because of his constant attention, I felt like I was being stalked. My home no longer felt safe. Finally, when he realized that I was not available, he stopped inviting me to spend the night, and he no longer expressed any interest in Judy.

"He lied," she wailed. "He doesn't know anyone in television." She was very distraught. I offered to send her back to California. She declined the offer and refused to leave my apartment. She had become my problem. One day, when I had gone to my therapy session—where I talked about my unwanted roommate and about how I had gotten myself into the situation—she took an overdose of sleeping pills. On my return, when she did not answer the doorbell and would not undo the security chain on the door, I managed to get out on the windowsill—my apartment was on the first floor so this was not especially dangerous. I could see her, on the floor, in her white cotton underwear, unconscious. I had a moment of panic, sure that she was dead. But the window was not locked, so I got in, got her up and walking, and called an ambulance. When she came back from the hospital the next day, stomach pumped and, I presume, psychiatrically evaluated and declared normal, I had changed the locks and had put her things outside the door. It was a matter of self-preservation. I knew she had enough money to take care of immediate needs, even to get back to California. I never saw her again.

Gradually I learned to take advantage of the process of psychotherapy. I learned how to listen to myself and how to recognize my own evasions. The work—and psychotherapy is work—became easier as the content became harder. I began to approach the heart of my problem: my mother. I had to acknowledge how very angry I was. Composure, which I had inherited from my mother as a required and necessary value, actually meant denial and suppression of emotion. In her world, strong emotion of any kind was taboo. We were a bridled people, good to look at, like show horses. I would never have described myself as an angry person, but now, in my psychiatrist's office, anger became the focus. I realized that I had been angry even before I had the word for the feeling.

My earliest memory of a willful act was certainly an expression of anger. I was five years old. The incident started innocently enough. I was recovering from a minor cold and had been allowed to spend the day in my mother's bed. I liked being sick because it brought out more active caring from my mother— managing might better describe it—but that was better than nothing; it was attention.

My parents, as in the movies of the period, slept in separate beds with a bedside table between. On this particular day, I lay beneath the pink satin bedspread that had my mother's monogram, VNM, rendered in lace in the center. The spring air was floating in through the window and I could hear the clunking of glass bottles as the milkman deposited them on the kitchen stoop. The kitchen door opened and someone came out. I heard a voice that was unmistakably my mother's, not the cook's, so I knew that the coast was clear.

I lowered myself from the bed and went to my father's dressing room. I pulled the bottom drawer partially out to use as a step, climbed on it, reached the top of his dresser and captured the dish of fudge that he kept there. I then went in search of my mother's sewing basket. I took her scissors, climbed back onto the bed and, while I devoured my father's entire stash of fudge, I destroyed the satin bedspread with the scissors. I picked up a pinch of the spread with my fingers and with the other hand snipped off the piece. Over and over, I did this until the spread was covered with little diamond shaped holes, like shell holes on a battlefield. My face was smeared with fudge.

I knew what I had done. It was an act of rebellion, a puny and futile rebellion to be sure; perhaps it was also a cry for attention, a declaration of unspoken needs. But I had no words to go with the act, neither a list of demands nor a manifesto; it was just a ruined bedspread. My mother did not see what I had done as something that indicated some inner distress in me; she saw badness, a character trait that needed to be crushed.

No beating resulted. But the consequences were severe: I was required to wear diapers for three days. I had to appear before the cook wearing diapers and have her verbally acknowledge that I was in diapers. I had to appear before my brothers, themselves long out of diapers, and my father too, in diapers. For three days, I was not allowed to wear pants, which would at least have hidden my shame. My father had looked but had said nothing. The children were not his department. My father's disengagement in this incident was terribly upsetting. I felt utterly abandoned. I did not know why I had done what I did and no one cared enough to find out.

There were many things that went on in our house about which my father either knew nothing or said nothing. The disciplined bowel movements were one of these. Our mother wanted my brothers and me to have a bowel movement at the same time every day, in the morning before we left for school. This was a daily expectation. It could not be something that we did at school because she would not accept an uncorroborated report. And so, every morning for fifteen minutes—an enormously long time for a child—we were required to sit on the toilet until we produced. It was a big house and there were lots of toilets.

When one of us was successful, the cry would ring out, "Mom, I'm done." The boy would stand and she would inspect. I stood each morning, pants around my ankles, while my mother inspected. I sometimes resisted. If, when I was finally allowed to leave for school, there was nothing in the toilet, on an unconscious level I considered myself to be the victor. On returning from school, I would find a glass of prune juice on the enameled table in the kitchen. If by the next morning I had produced no results, that afternoon there would be on the kitchen table a blue glass bottle, Milk of Magnesia, with a spoon beside it. These laxative drinks were always for me, never for my brothers, who were more compliant. The cook, Eleanora, administered these "medications" on instruction from my mother. My mother was never present. She was either shopping or taking a nap, her beauty rest.

My mother would inspect the next morning. When she discovered that mild laxatives had not dissolved my stubbornness, she advanced the matter to the next step, castor oil; then, when all else had failed, the enema.

The enemas gave a sort of ritualistic rhythm to my life between the ages of eight and eleven. I have no recollection of how many times it happened, but would guess three or four times a year. Always the same procedures, and always carried out in my father's bedroom, a room that was referred to as the "guest room," as if his banishment from the master bedroom suite—for snoring, we were told—was temporary. There were never any guests, so my father became its permanent occupant. The enemas only occurred when my father was at the office, never on weekends. I remember this detail because I was always aware that there could be no appeal.

My mother would lay me face down on the extra bed. The fingers of her right hand would press down on the back of my neck, just at the base below the skull in order to interdict any resistance that might arise. I cried in the first couple of incidents, but learned to be stoic in subsequent episodes. My brothers sometimes stood at the doorway and watched. Having intoned a liturgy about why this was good for me, she would raise her left arm with the red rubber bag filled with soapy water. I would have filled the bag myself. This seemed to have been part of the ritual; I was both the sacrificial victim and the acolyte.

"Anger," I said to Dr. Frazier, "was not an option." Nor was open defiance. I could not run away. I didn't know then what to call these events but now I would be tempted to say rape. What made it all so psychologically confusing was that there was an element of pleasure, a kind, I suppose, of sexual pleasure that came from being touched intimately by my mother. I was not conscious of those feelings, but I am pretty sure that I felt them. I did know one thing very clearly though: I feared and hated my mother.

My anger was like a fire in an underground coal seam that, as it worked its way toward the surface, produced dangerous side effects, the boils for example. The anger itself was frightening, especially since it involved my mother. To the psyche, to the soul even, one's mother, even a bad one, is somehow sacred. Thou shalt not hate thy Mother. If one does, one has no mother. And if one has no mother, perhaps one has no right to exist. These cross currents produced the most perilous period in my therapy. There was the risk of suicide.

I was healthy enough, however, to be terrified of these feelings. I sometimes felt as if I was standing on a crag of rock watching a raging, storm-driven sea and a great wave was building that would sweep me away. The turbulent sea was, of course, within me. Sometimes I found myself being drawn toward the edge of the rock, as if wishing it to happen. I was terrified of heights, especially bridges. The falling-jumping fear was also present when I rode the subway. Coming to the edge of the platform and allowing myself to fall in front of a subway train became the idea that most terrified me. Once, I was so afraid of these self-destructive impulses that I called Dr. Frazier at eleven o'clock at night. He was home in bed in New Jersey. He heard my tone of voice and said he'd meet me at his office in half an hour. To get to his office, I had to take the subway. I couldn't take a taxi because I would have to speak to the driver, and I was afraid that I would not be able to find my voice. As the train approached the station, I clung to a steel girder on the platform, a desperate grip, as one might cling to a tree in a hurricane. The wave of suicidal impulse passed over me. The train screeched into the station and I darted into the car. When the train arrived at 168th Street, I bolted up the stairs before the train had even left the station.

We talked until one in the morning. I was calmed. Dr. Frazier asked if I wanted to be admitted to the psychiatric ward. I had a lonely subway ride ahead of me, the train likely to be carrying drunks and possibly worse. I thought about it and said no, that I thought I could make it. He trusted me. It was an extraordinary therapeutic decision that told me that I was, in fact, going to make it.

My mother, I don't doubt, wanted me to make it, but only on her terms. I, her firstborn, who bore the name of a distinguished man, was to be a proper son, a man who was attractive and who behaved appropriately in company, and who had chosen a career fitting his family's reputation and social station. She had in mind a version of "my son the lawyer," that I would become the head of the company, my father's successor. Her efforts, however, to assure some sort of success for me never took the form of encouragement; it was always criticism. I needed improving. It mostly had to do with how I looked and behaved. Her greatest compliment was that I was "attractive" and the most cutting criticism was couched as "You would be more attractive, dear, if you would sit straighter, not chew your nails, comb your hair…" There was never any affirmation of character traits that demonstrated individuality, things like curiosity or creativity. When I was in my late teens, she approved of my interest in art, but she would have been appalled if I had shown any interest in becoming an artist. Artists were unruly and painting was a messy activity. Sometimes her interest in me took painfully negative turns, became humiliation or cruelty inflicted, or so it seemed, for its own sake.

Once, for instance, when I was eleven, at the beach, she told me that because I had rather broad hipbones, I had a perfect body for childbearing. This remark hit me like a slap in the face. Coming at a time when becoming a man was my main psychological project, it cut to the most secret and sensitive place in my being. When she said it, we were sitting on towels on the sand; I was in my swimming suit and shirtless. Girls my own age, girls who were my friends, were nearby. If they heard the remark, they had the kindness not to say. Nevertheless, for days afterwards, I went into self-imposed house arrest, pretending that I preferred to stay home. Inside I was cringing, afraid that one of the girls whom I liked would mention my hips. They never did.

Age thirteen was a disturbing year. The Holocaust, discussion of which was mostly suppressed in the polite world that I lived in, had escaped from its confinement, however briefly, and I knew about it. It was a knowledge I could not reverse and it changed me permanently.

And I had cancer. My brother Tom noticed a lump about the size of a small grape under the skin on my back. I reported this to my mother, which resulted in an out-patient visit to a doctor, a general surgeon who was a social friend of my parents. He removed the little lump—a shot of Novocain, two stitches—and sent it off to four laboratories to be biopsied. My mother reported to my father that one out of the four results found cells that were "atypical"—I remember that word being used— and the finding suggested, as she informed my father, that I had a life-threatening cancer called "fibrosarcoma." The conversation occurred at cocktails and they had called me in to inform me that surgery would be required, and soon. With cancer, one had to act quickly; that point was made clearly. My father looked grave; my mother seemed capable and in command of the situation. The surgery happened quickly. Less than a week later I was admitted to the Good Samaritan Hospital and wheeled on a rubber-tired gurney into a cold operating room. It was a terrifying experience. I experienced it far more vividly than is generally thought possible while under anesthesia. Not pain, but awareness of things happening, sounds of metal instruments dropped into trays, voices, the feeling of the flesh on my back being stretched. All the muscle tissue in a band on my upper back was removed, the tissue layer that the cancer was believed to inhabit. I stayed in the hospital for five days. My father visited on his way to and from work. My mother never visited.

"She would be too upset to see you like this," he told me. It was axiomatic in the family that our mother, who never showed emotion, was especially emotional. My father apparently believed it and was always very solicitous.

I went home in an ambulance. When my mother met the ambulance at the door, she was dressed in black, a message that my brothers, who witnessed this portentous homecoming, were sure meant that I was going to die very soon. I interpreted it the same way. In the midst of this fear, there were the mixed messages that my mother always managed to generate; she smiled her beautiful smile, was friendly and gracious to the ambulance attendants, and appeared to be in an almost festive mood, as if my homecoming on a stretcher was a birthday party. Would I make it to my next birthday?

The consequences of all this would last the rest of my life. In addition to the trauma of the surgery—which took years to get over and had lasting effects on my posture and how I walk—I had seen the end of my life before I'd started it. I knew that cancer was often fatal and the speed with which things had happened, from diagnosis to surgery in a week, told me that my kind of cancer was serious.

"I am afraid of dying," I said to Dr. Frazier. "And this makes me afraid of living. Why would anyone invest in something that might soon be taken away?"

When I went away to prep school the next year, I was so embarrassed by the nine inch scar, red, jagged, and lumpy, that I would not shower with the other boys. My body was now even more imperfect, hips and now the wound. The only consolation was that I couldn't see the scar when I looked at myself in the mirror.

14

Sexuality

In therapy, I remembered an incident that occurred when I was seven or eight. I had been put to bed by my mother, "tucked in" as she always said. I was young enough that I still said my prayers, the "now I lay me down to sleep." My dog, a springer spaniel named Cockie, lay on the floor beside my bed; she would always stay until I fell asleep. I would put my hand in her fur and she no doubt could sense when my hand went still. Her presence usually comforted me, but this evening was different. I was overcome with a terrible sadness. I left my room and went down the hall, Cockie following behind, to the master bedroom suite where my mother slept, where my father didn't sleep but where he had his reading chair. My parents were both awake, my father reading business papers and my mother, on the sofa, reading a magazine. What did I want? I said nothing, but standing in front of my mother, I began to cry, great uncontrollable sobs, no words, just grief. There was no specific reason or cause. I wanted my mother's love. My father looked bewildered. As the sobs continued, my mother became angry, as if my anguish was a sort of misbehavior. She took me brusquely back to the children's quarters, ran a tepid bath, took off my pajamas, and picking me up, plunged me into it. She sat by the tub, saying nothing, until I, shivering, stopped crying. I got out of the tub. She dried me off, put my pajamas back on, and put me back to bed. What made this incident especially memorable was the physical contact with my mother, the undressing and dressing, the drying off. It happened so rarely.

My memories about being touched by my mother are somewhat confused. I am sure that I was never cuddled, held, or stroked. I have another set of memories, however, that appear to contradict this impression. These are not memories of events, but of sensations that I associate with being two and three years old. It is neurological memory of being handled and fussed over, of scrambling about, naked, in the beds of both my mother and her mother with whom we lived for a time in 1942, while my father was in Washington D.C. establishing himself in war-related work. I suspect that for a period of time, during the war, I was treated as a sort of adorable toy. Included in this memory are smells of perfume and powders, the feel of sheets and powder puffs, and awareness of the soft skin and pliant flesh of both these women. Memories like these, whether real memory or blends with fantasy, support a theory of personality development that recognizes infantile sexuality. I cannot comment on whether there is such a thing, but I retain in my nervous system the sense of over-excitement, a free-floating arousal that produced as much anxiety as it produced pleasure. Notably absent, however, is any memory of being held quietly on my mother's lap. I am sure that by the time we moved to Washington D.C. in 1943, all physical contact other than the necessities of getting me dressed had stopped.

Receiving little or no tenderness or physical affection, I became a remote little boy. Every impulse and every feeling that might have led to relaxed intimacy was suppressed. Yet I think of my childhood as a time when sexuality, but ambivalent sexuality, secret and dangerous, was always present as an undertone, or perhaps, as an undertow.

When I was eleven or twelve, a man came to the house with a movie projector and, in the middle of the afternoon in the darkened library, showed a scratchy film about venereal disease; only my mother and I were present. The film showed men with their noses falling off; an image of a decaying penis appeared briefly on screen but the man quickly blocked it with his hand. The message from this grotesque film and things my mother said and did was unmistakable: sex, which meant women, was dangerous. Women, therefore, especially beautiful women, were dangerous. It was a confusing message, because my mother was beautiful and she used her femininity to please and manipulate my father. She was a subtle master at it. I had watched her in action. I had observed his apparently happy submission. He pulled out her chair at the dinner table and seated her, for instance, as I was expected to do when I was tall enough.

There was still another message about feminine attractiveness, a crosscurrent. When I was eight and nine, my mother gave me privileged access to her secret world, the places she went when she "went out," her shopping expeditions. Since there was always someone in the house and thus never any problem about leaving me home alone, her motives had to do with me. She wanted me to watch her as she shopped. As we walked along the shopping streets of Beverly Hills, I looked in the street-level display windows and saw the beautiful mannequins with their composed faces, their graceful poses, and lovely clothes, and I thought that my mother was like the mannequins, always composed and beautifully dressed. I watched the reflection of my mother as she watched herself reflected in the windows. She never passed a reflective surface without looking at herself. In the fitting rooms there were mirrors on every wall and she watched herself again, and always, it seemed to me, approvingly. I approved too. I sat on a chair, feet barely touching the ground, and watched. The saleswomen, all of whom seemed to know her, were like the priestesses conducting a service.

"Perhaps she brought you along to admire her," Dr. Frazier suggested. "A living mirror. Or a devotee." And in some part of my conflicted being I was a devotee.

As a child, I observed that much power lay with female beauty. I saw its effects on my father. No matter how exhausted my father might be after a day at the office—he never came home before seven p.m.—he always brought my mother her nightly cocktail, and she always sat on the sofa in the living room, in her elegant peignoir, and said, "Thank you, dear." When I was ten or eleven, I experimented with the idea of being a woman. I would stand before a mirror, tuck my genitals between my legs, and try to imagine myself as a grown woman, beautiful and pampered, and as powerful as I believed my mother was. That my mother had no power except that which beauty bestowed, and nowhere except in the home, did not occur to me. Feminism had not yet brought those issues to my attention. But where power matters most to a child, the home, it was my mother who appeared to have most of it.

When I was in the fourth grade, I was enrolled in an after-school program in which I was to build muscles and acquire the aggressive masculine traits that might be lacking in my character. The program focused on gymnastics and boxing. I loathed every bit of it, loathed the competitive spirit that the operators of this little Sparta insisted that boys have; I dreaded the parallel bars and the vaulting horse. I was mortified by my inability to land an effective blow in the boxing ring; I didn't want to hit anyone, nor be hit. The story of Ferdinand, the little bull who refused to fight in the ring in Madrid, was to me a sensible attitude. Fight bravely and then be killed, that or smell flowers; to me this was a pretty easy choice.

On the days when I went to this schoolboy boot camp, I arrived home later than if I'd come straight from school. My mother's beauty sleep would be over and she would have retired to her boudoir and begun what she called her *toilette,* a word she carefully pronounced in the French way. This involved bathing and creaming her body, makeup, selection of the right peignoir and slippers, in short, making herself attractive for my father. In the midst of this rather mysterious two-hour procedure, I still had to present myself. Sometimes my mother was still in the bathtub.

Her bathtub was walled with mirrors on three of its sides creating such a multiplication of her body that I, trying to concentrate on my report about school work, mastering multiplication tables for instance, could hardly avoid seeing her nakedness. No matter which way I looked, there she was. This ritual of presenting myself to my mother while she bathed persisted through the sixth grade. The display of my mother's body, large breasts barely concealed by the froth of bubble bath, a washcloth carefully placed (for modesty) and drifting over her pubic region, was, I now think, the real subject and purpose of these encounters: she wanted to be looked at. I wanted to look, but was ashamed of my curiosity. I looked and pretended that I was not looking. There she was, naked and languid, wherever I looked, directly, or indirectly in the mirrors where she was repeated over and over, disappearing into an infinite corridor of reflected images. I always felt profoundly uncomfortable, trying to look at her body while trying not to be caught doing it.

The atmosphere of sexual tension, of veiled seduction combined with the opposing message that sex was dangerous, permeated those years. She, not my father, provided my brothers and me with a facts-of-life book that contained a few anatomically correct drawings, that described puberty and where babies came from. Well and good. But at the same time she was opposed to my having actual knowledge of girls, hence her interference with my attempts to have a girlfriend. Even fantasy was to be suppressed, hence her search of my room, mutilating, then destroying, the picture of the movie starlet in an evening dress. I didn't dare ask why she had taken it because to do so would have opened the issue of the pornographic picture.

By the time I found my way to Dr. Frazier's office, I had read enough Freud to have an understanding of the Oedipus complex, the story of a tabooed mother-son relationship: the son, Oedipus, with no conscious awareness of his relationship with the man he meets on the road, his father, kills him and marries his own mother. I explored the Oedipus story with Dr. Frazier.

"Was my mother actually opposed to my forming a relationship with a girl of my own age?" I asked him. "Was there something she wanted of me, to keep me for herself perhaps, or am I projecting something that I wanted?"

Dr. Frazier waited, listening. By this time in the therapy process he had trained me to ask the most embarrassing questions without being prompted.

"What do you think?" his silence said.

"Perhaps when I was four or five, in the war years, when my father was away on Navy business, I didn't just *want* to possess my mother, I *did* possess her. But I didn't possess her in any meaningful emotional way. Even when I was little, she was remote, physically absent often during the day and often at night too. My mother was the opposite of the smothering mother. She was seductive, yes, but always in retreat. So my story doesn't fit the classic pattern. Besides, I remember feeling enormously relieved when my father was released from the Navy and came home to stay. I even remember the day that he came home."

"How was that?" the doctor asked. "What happened that you would remember?"

"He did something dramatic, something we little boys thought positively heroic. Before he had even unpacked his suitcase, he announced to my brothers and me that he could throw a tennis ball over the tall palm trees that lined the street. I think he was trying to make his homecoming as dramatic as possible, so we would know for sure that he was back and, indirectly, that the war was over. We all went out on the front lawn and watched. He wound up and threw the ball over the palm tree. I recovered it and ran it back to him. He did it again. Later that week he threw the ball over the house. I remember standing in the back yard watching the roofline, and then the ball appeared, like moon rise. It landed in a hedge; I recovered it and scampered around the house with it in my hand, a little boy retriever. He did it again. I'm surprised my father didn't injure his arm.

"My point is that I was glad my father was home. Life could return to normal, though what *normal* meant I could not have said. During the war, my mother was seldom home. That was wartime normal. I waited up for her if I could stay awake. Sometimes she brought friends home in the evening. After they left, I prowled around the house in the dark. I was like the little boy in the A.A. Milne poem, James James Morrison Morrison Weatherby George Dupree, who took great care of his mother though he was only three. But by the time I was five that had changed.

I was not trying to hold on to my mother; I was trying to get away from her. The opposite of the Oedipus complex."

"But you felt that your relationship with your mother was somehow sexualized. A mood…" Dr. Frazier said.

"It became even more so as I got older. When I was sixteen and had the freedom that the car provided, my relationship with her improved. Being freed from her strictures—and she really let most of her strict rules go—I was happier and therefore more open. She became graciously inviting, often asking me to have a special evening with her, for supper and a chat. These always occurred when my father was out of town; and she made it explicit that our conversations, a suggestion of special intimacy, were easier to fall into when my father, the businessman, was absent. The implication was that he was insensitive to the finer things. I could not decline these invitations graciously. She referred to me, on these occasions, as her "beau," as if we were a couple on a date. I was uncomfortable, but at the same time I liked the uncritical attention. She seemed, for the first time, to accept me the way I was. So, for a brief period, I enjoyed being with my mother. The conversations that seemed to deprecate my father, however, made me uncomfortable.

"And having made my escape, I felt that it was safe to come a little closer. Our relationship during those two years, before I went to college, was probably the best it had ever been and would ever be again. It was somewhat circumscribed though, almost ritualized—we talked about art almost exclusively—but compared to what had come before, it was welcome. It made me realize that I did, like most children, want a loving relationship with my mother. But art was a limited subject. I could not, would not, and did not ever talk to my mother about what interested me most—girls and my feelings for them."

Sex, of course, is the current that runs through adolescence. It was in mine certainly. I found ways of working around my mother's negativity about it. I had to work around my father too, not because he opposed knowledge about sex, but because he was too repressed and conflicted himself to approach the subject. Hamish Robertson had stepped in where my father failed. There was a specific incident on that first trip to Europe, in 1955, that I especially remember.

My father, Hamish, and I went to Italy. Hamish had asked me what I wanted to see. I had read *The Last Days of Pompeii* in school and had wanted to see the ruins, and so we went. On the day of our visit, a hot day in August, we were the only tourists. Hamish and my father threw their jackets over their shoulders, an uncommon informality for these men, but both still wore their ties.

Hamish led the way into the archaeological site, gently tapping the rutted cobbles with the walking stick that he usually carried. There were signs of ongoing excavations everywhere, shovels and picks leaning up against barriers, holes in the ground with protective ropes around them, lest we, the tourists, get too close and fall in. My father followed behind a dozen yards or so. I walked with Hamish because he had more information and was always entertaining.

My father, as a geologist and mining engineer, was more interested in distant Vesuvius than in the city that it had buried. "Sixty feet of ash in three days," I remember him saying with a tone of wonder, as if calculating how many ore haulers it might have taken as an engineering project. He eyed the distant mountain, secretly hoping for a rumble or a puff of smoke. Hamish approached Pompeii as a historian would; he was interested in what the ruin could tell us about human beings and it was he who discovered the phallus carved in a paving stone.

"Young Harvey," he said, "this points to the brothels. Do you understand what a brothel is?"

I must have, a little, probably from looking at the Toulouse Lautrec lithographs in my mother's art books. What men did with those strange women in the drawings, women partially clad in voluminous underwear, sitting with their knees open, I did not fully understand. But I knew it had to do with sex. That Hamish, the most cultivated man I knew, knew about brothels was a surprise. Our night in Paris, with the street walkers of Pigalle, came back to me; that experience had added to my little bit of knowledge, but now there was to be more.

Hamish and I went down a narrow street, following the direction suggested by the stone phallus. My father was far behind, so I was entirely in Hamish's orbit. We came to a double wooden door that had a sign on it saying, "entrance forbidden" in Italian. The door was ajar, suggesting that someone was inside. Hamish knocked loudly on the unpainted panels and an old man with a leathery face appeared. He wagged his finger at us, explaining that there was no admission. But Hamish was not deterred. They negotiated in Italian, some money changed hands, and we went in.

It was cool and dark. The room, as best as I can remember, was lit by a transom above the door and a single light bulb that hung over a little table and chair where the old man, an unofficial concierge, sat.

The room was about twenty by forty feet. There were rectangular cubicles off this main room, each of these perhaps five by seven feet. The old man switched on a light in the cubicles, again a naked bulb suspended from the ceiling. On the walls were the notorious erotic paintings the existence of which had been, at one period or another, either denied or plastered over. There was an image of a little Pan figure with hairy legs and an engorged phallus about the size of his arm. I thought this very funny. There was also a painting of a woman riding on top of a man on a bed. The painting was instructive for, except for the tiny scrap of pornography that my mother had confiscated, I had had nothing to guide my erotic imagination.

My father by this time had reached the doorway. I saw him, hesitant, silhouetted against the blazing summer light. He had allowed himself to come part way into the room and he pretended that he was looking. He was clearly uncomfortable. I had a vague feeling that my father's impulse was to retreat, taking me with him. But Hamish's unflustered masculinity combined with the fact that he was older, of my grandfather's generation, kept my father and his prudishness at bay.

As a child I had been a night wanderer. I liked darkness. I could hide in it. As early as age three or four, I would climb out of my crib and creep quietly through the house. I would listen at my mother's bedroom door, stop in the kitchen to listen to the hum of the refrigerator, and to the cook snoring in her bedroom. Sometimes, after we returned to Los Angeles, I would quietly open the back door to the driveway and listen to the night in the city, crickets and the murmur of cars. I would look. I would go to the door of the library or living room and simply look. I was fearless. What I was listening for or looking for I could not have said. It was probably information about the unspoken, the unknown, and even, I suppose, about sex, though I could not have conceived of this as the project at age four. I was, then, just looking. This behavior was intermittent but habitual. It came and went.

As my therapy continued, I became a night wanderer in the city of New York, continuing with my sexual education, now looking for and finding subversive lessons. For three or four months, I was a regular nighttime visitor to one of the seediest places in the city at the time, Forty-Second Street between Seventh and Eighth Avenues. In those days, before it became a tourist zone, it was a solid block of porn shops and rundown movie theaters, a block inhabited at night by whores, their pimps, drug dealers, and little clusters of police whose presence kept physical violence suppressed.

I went to see what there was to see. I endured the shaming inspection of my driver's license to check my birth date before I could enter the pornography shops, the racks of magazines and VHS tapes. I sat in cramped video booths that delivered movies of sexual acts in grainy images at twenty-five cents a minute. On the street, I watched the bantering and boasting of the pimps, black men in velvet hats and wearing gold chains and big watches. I watched the whores, both white and black, tough women who were no doubt submissive to their pimps but who seemed contemptuous of the bright world and of innocents like me. I thought of the visit I had made with Hamish to Pompeii. He had given me the freedom to know about such things, but this was a different sort of knowing, one not dignified by any sort of scientific purpose like history or archaeology. I was beginning to understand that behind the façade of respectability that had been my upbringing, there was this other world, a secret place that the better people didn't talk about, a world of just sex, a tabooed place. Sex, I realized, was *the* secret, no matter where or who one was.

That sex need not be only in the noble cause of procreation or sanctioned by marriage was a discovery of some moment for me. I wondered if the thing that differentiated the worlds of the respectable and Forty-Second Street, worlds which on the surface were so far apart, was little more than the price of admission. Was sex just sex, no matter what one wore in the antechamber?

My preoccupation with sex had had a long history in my psyche. As a ten-year-old, for instance, during our annual summer vacation at my maternal grandmother's beach house, I would gaze at my mother and her friends as they lay on beach towels sunbathing. They all pulled the straps of their bathing suits—one piece in those days—aside so there would be no tan lines when they wore off-the-shoulder gowns for their husbands when they, the workers in offices, came down from the city on weekends. These were beautiful women in their thirties, their bodies glistening with tanning oils. In my cloak of invisibility—the fact that I was only a child—I walked among them unnoticed and fantasized. My fantasies had no content as yet, no narrative, but, as if in the hands of ancient gods, I was following a well-worn path.

And now, here I was, age eighteen, wandering through the mean streets of New York, again watching, feeling the sexual charge of the scene. I was there not just because I was curious, but also as a kind of rebellion. Since my mother had implied that sex was ugly, I would go and see for myself. Ugly, I could see that, but some of the women on the street were not. Some were, in fact, very pretty. I felt guilt, desire, and fear. For many years afterward, I had a kind of addiction to the dark side of cities and have explored them from Los Angeles to Hamburg and many in between. But I always managed to put down the "intoxicant" before doing myself any lasting harm.

There were some side benefits that came from my adventures in night-town. First, I lost all fear of cities, learned how to read them and their streets, and how to be safe without being paranoid. Second, I learned, by looking at pictures and grainy films, what sex amounted to anatomically; it surprises me how ignorant my upbringing had kept me.

In my fascination with the night world, I could see how conflicted my feelings about women were. There were on the one hand the idealized and self-idealizing women, the respectable women that my mother represented, and on the other, the despised and possibly self-despising street girls. These were stereotypes, extremes that over time I learned to demystify. There could be respectable women who were sexual, and escorts who even enjoyed their work and who made an honest living at it, even if such work was illegal. Between the poles of the cold lady and the whore was the emotional and societal space where, I suspected, real women lived, but at this stage of my life, it was only a suspicion. I knew no such women. I was so timid that the possibility of a mature relationship was theoretical. In this, Dr. Frazier was no help. I would have to get there on my own.

15

Getting Better

My sessions with Dr. Frazier tapered down to three times a week, then two. I had more time and more self-confidence; I discovered the New School for Social Research on West Twelfth Street and took evening courses in a variety of subjects such as primitive religion, Chinese art, and the nineteenth century English novel. I found a job as a salesman at the venerable, now defunct, Brentano's Bookstore on Fifth Avenue at Forty-Seventh Street; at nineteen years old I was put in charge, both as buyer and seller, of the poetry and theater sections. Greta Garbo, whom I did not recognize until one of the older men identified her for me, was one of my customers. I selected a book of poetry for her twice a month. We had short conversations about the authors I selected. She had especially liked Saint-John Perse's *Anabasis,* which she could read in the French and which I knew through T.S. Eliot's translation. Ms. Garbo was quiet and reserved. In the winter months she always wore a brown wool coat and a beret. This legendary beauty, wearing no makeup and always appearing in the same coat, made an interesting contrast with my mother, whose outfits, from shoes to jewelry, were changed several times daily and who never appeared anywhere, even to family, without makeup.

Around the corner on Forty-Seventh Street was the Gotham Book Mart, now also gone. There I encountered a much wider world of books than at Brentano's. With guidance from a friendly clerk I discovered

James Joyce, Samuel Beckett, Ezra Pound, and many others. In this same period, I discovered film as an art form and became a regular at the Bleecker Street Cinema. Alain Resnais' *Hiroshima, Mon Amour* and Bergman's *Seventh Seal* brought me to the limits of art; that death and the fear of it, that the horrors and sorrows of the war, could be so powerfully rendered was a wonder to me. I saw both films several times, and each time I walked out of the theater, into the afternoon sun or the neon evening, in a changed state. It would take hours to settle my emotions.

I was already deeply engaged with literature. T.S. Eliot's *The Love Song of J. Alfred Prufrock,* which I read at age seventeen, stood out. I understood it, not just in a classroom way, but inside myself. Images in the poem had risen off the page and had stung me; the itch has never gone away. I wanted, as Eliot wrote, "to have squeezed the universe into a ball / to roll it toward an overwhelming question." And now, as I write these words, in 2017, with my life entering its last phase, the images from *Prufrock* still speak to me. "I grow old. I grow old. I shall wear the bottoms of my trousers rolled and walk upon the beach." The poem was a sort of measuring device for me, like the weathered mile markers on English country roads. And by those measurements, I have not, as Mr. Prufrock fears for himself, failed myself. I never found the overwhelming question, but I have never stopped looking.

It was more than poetry that influenced me. In prep school, I read Thoreau's "On Civil Disobedience" and had been powerfully moved by it. Thanks to Thoreau, the obligation to dissent, to resist an unjust law or an illegitimate command, was solidly installed in the operating manual for living that I carry around in my head. The ideas contained in Thoreau's famous essay, his response to slavery and the Mexican War, have contributed to the political and life decisions that I made much later in my life. Also in school, I read Emerson's "Self Reliance"; the idea that "a foolish consistency is the hobgoblin of little minds" has stayed with me too, a reminder to look at all options, to try things out. It led eventually to my love for the *Essays* of Michel de Montaigne. In the politics of the present moment, I see many who have great ambitions but who have very little minds, minds bedeviled with hobgoblins.

What more foolish consistency could there be than to submit one's mind and integrity to the hobgoblins of party loyalty, to "talking points."

Literature—poetry, essays, fiction— provided me with contexts, with maps to the heart and to life. Much of what I know of myself, even today, comes from filtering my experiences through books. The influence of books on my life has been one of the few constants. What more felicitous employment could I have found than Brentano's? I was surrounded by books (in the age before the books for "Dummies") and I could even read on the job. Brentano's allowed us to take books home. I lost my shyness and my social discomforts through interactions with customers. When pretty girls were my customers, however, I still got rattled.

Eventually, I had a girlfriend. Liz was twenty-five, English, with a delightful accent. I lost my virginity with her. I've never understood why one says "lost." I had "found" something surely more important than ignorance and fearfulness, namely the possibility of manhood. Liz was a pretty brunette with a gap between her front teeth. She worked at one of the cosmetics counters on the main floor of Bloomingdale's applying lipstick and mascara on the faces of middle-aged women or, when there were no customers, on other salesgirls. There was a childlike quality about her, a bit sad, but sweet. She told me that she had had an imaginary childhood friend named Geoffrey Duck, a gentle downy companion for a lonely little girl who had grown up without siblings. I became her little duck, part younger sibling, part shy young boyfriend. We liked to go to the carousel in Central Park to watch the laughing children riding on wooden horses. She announced one day that she had met a man in his forties who had offered to take her to Bermuda. She was very excited. She thought that she had found what she really wanted, a man who would love her and take care of her. She had told me stories of similar romances; it was a pattern she didn't recognize. I knew she would leave me for this man, this fantasy. And she did. I was sad, but I was no longer susceptible to having my heart broken. I would get over it.

* * *

Little by little I was working free of my mother. I discovered that I had a capacity for loving in spite of the possibility of loss. I had managed to preserve a trace of innocence, a belief that "the impossible"—as Marcel Proust had called true love—might actually be possible. I knew where this hope, this faithfulness, came from.

"I had an experience when I was twelve," I told Dr. Frazier, midway through my time with him, when I was sure the crisis—the possibility of suicide and disintegration—had passed, "that inoculated enough of me against my mother's influence. It was such a strange experience that I've almost suppressed the memory of it, as if something so wonderful could not have happened."

"Tell me," he said. I did, reluctantly at first, afraid this wise and rational man would find my experience bizarre.

"My family always went to a dude ranch in Palm Springs for the Christmas holidays. One day there was an organized trail ride that my father insisted we go on. At the stable, I heard my name called by a female voice. A girl, probably eighteen years old, appeared, leading the horse I was to ride. She was slender, with narrow hips, small breasts, boyish. She had laugh lines around her eyes and wore her hair in a ponytail.

"But as she approached, leading the horse, something quite extraordinary happened. I felt—the feeling came on suddenly, almost instantaneously, like a blush or a fainting spell—as if a sort of cloud had enveloped me. It was a cloud that was even less material than vapor, a cloud of light or, perhaps, a magnetic field. It is impossible to describe because it was not of the world that I usually lived in. But it was *something*, and because I was enveloped in this cloud, I could see nothing, *nothing*, except her. The rest of the stable, the other horses, the smells of hay and manure, had disappeared. I ended up sitting on the horse, in the saddle—she had helped me, putting her hands together for a boost up— and now she was settling the reins in my hands. My heart was pounding so loudly I thought she must hear it. Perhaps she did. I think that she intuited what was happening inside this kid, this twelve-year-old. She took my hands and positioned the fingers of my left hand around the leather reins just so.

"Then she gave me her hand to shake. I reached across the saddle and shook her hand. 'My name is Pru,' she said. I think that not only had she understood, but that she felt strangely honored by the emotion she had stirred in me, and in return, for the next ten days, she treated me and my emotions with great care. She did not mock me or dismiss me. In fact, she seemed to like me. I pretended that I liked horses and went on every ride I could, just to be around her, to see her, to exchange a word or two with her. She always accepted me, she smiled, she talked to me. Yes, she knew."

"What a wonderful experience," interjected Dr. Frazier. "The light or whatever it was that you experienced suggests the sort of sensation of changed reality that religious mystics report. One doesn't have to believe in God to understand that such things happen."

"So I'm not just making it up?"

"Not at all. It seems that certain intense emotions can so flood the nervous system that all the senses get knocked out of their routines. That sounds scientific. I don't mean to take anything away from what you felt."

"I saw her every day. I had never, in my whole life, been happier. In fact, I lived in a state of rapturous happiness for those ten days, even though—and this is the oddest part—even though I knew that eighteen-year-old girls didn't have twelve-year-old boyfriends, even though I knew that I would leave at the end of the holiday and that I would never see her again. She would go back to college. She was studying to be a vet.

"When the time came, the day before my family went back to Los Angeles, I was filled with so much sadness that I hid myself in the forest of smoke trees and cactus and walked about, sobbing. On the last evening, there was a campfire and singing, a typical dude ranch thing. 'From this valley they say you are going...' I don't know if you know the song about the Red River Valley. If you grew up in the west you would.

Pru walked me back to our bungalow. She said she had enjoyed my company. Then she kissed me on the cheek."

I knew then and I know today that I had experienced love. Capital letter Love. It had nothing to do with sexual attraction or anything that fits in our ordinary understanding of relationships. It was a transformative experience. Literature, that I discovered years later, helped me understand it. It was similar to what Dante experienced when he saw Beatrice for the first time. In college, I wrote a paper about Dante's *Vita Nuova* in which the poet describes the experience. The professor gave me a failing grade on the paper because I had not understood that the whole thing was allegory. I was sure that it wasn't. I'd been there, the sweats, the heart palpitations, the temporary blindness.

Dr. Frazier was quiet. I knew he wouldn't take it from me.

"It was like I had been visited by something sacred," I said, "I had been led into an extraordinary place of the heart and then had been guided safely out. It was an anomaly, a stepping out of the normality, a blessing. I don't know how else to describe it. It didn't last long, just ten days. But it was so real, so intense, that my understanding of life and of myself was forever changed."

One day, Dr. Frazier informed me that he had received a letter from my mother asking if she could see him on her next trip to New York to see her doctors. She wanted to talk about my progress. He said that he could only meet with her with my consent, and since I had complete trust in him, I assented. After this meeting occurred, I asked Dr. Frazier what she had wanted.

"She wanted to know what you talked about and what you had said about her, both subjects that I would not divulge."

Then he expressed an opinion that rather startled me.

"Your mother is a very disturbed person. But it is so deeply rooted that any attempt to 'get at it' would probably destroy her. She is a beautiful, well-dressed screen that conceals a great deal of emotional chaos. She is very frightened by this chaos. Containing it, concealing it, uses most of her emotional energy."

Should he have told me this? Was it ethical to do so? And how could he know all this after just a one hour visit? I can't answer these questions, but I am glad that he did tell me. What was amiss with me was now more understandable, both to him and to me. It was a comforting thought, for it proved that I had not invented my troubles.

Looking back, I can evaluate my experience with Dr. Frazier. He was a humane and compassionate man who worked with me as an individual, not as a member of a diagnostic category. He had no hobgoblins. My sense of gratitude to him cannot be overstated. I think he saved my life. Literally, in that I didn't kill myself, and virtually, in that I went on and had a life. He had a genius for knowing when to intervene and when to sit back and let me muddle forward on my own.

I owe my life, literally, to another man. He was a Los Angeles police officer who might have been justified in shooting me, but, because he was rational and professional, didn't. Jim and I, aged sixteen, had been driving in Los Angeles in the middle of the afternoon. Jim, in the passenger seat, was playing with a realistic-looking toy pistol that a younger sibling had left in the car. He poked it out the car window, aiming at nothing particular. The officer saw us and thought, quite reasonably, that we might be teenagers on some sort of rampage. He pulled in behind us and waved us over. What had I done? As the car slowed down, the officer's revolver appeared over the windscreen of his motorcycle and I knew exactly what we had done and I knew that if I made a mistake or the officer did, one or two idiotic teenagers would be dead. Frightened as I was, I noticed how very calm and careful the policeman was, and this calmed me. I watched him in the rear view mirror first then the side mirror. He was close enough that I could see the brass jackets on the bullets in his revolver. His aim was somewhere between Jim and me. He ordered us out of the car, told us to take the leaning position, arms outstretched, hands against the wall of a nearby house; I could feel the heat emanating from the wall of the house. Then, never taking his eyes or revolver off us, he reached back into the car for the gun. He held it in his hand, shook his head, and dropped it on the grass.

"You kids have just had a very close call," he said. He holstered his gun, returned to his motorcycle, and rode away. Like the Lone Ranger. I never had the chance to thank him. At the time, it never occurred to me that the outcome might have been very different had I been a black or Hispanic teenager. I was that innocent.

I continued to work at the bookstore until the time came for Jim and me to depart for Europe. In August I gave up my apartment and put my few pieces of furniture out on the curb. They probably disappeared before I had crossed the George Washington Bridge. With my books and clothes in my car, I drove back to Los Angeles. This was a trip I took many times between 1959 and 1962. There was no Interstate Highway system. It was US 40 to Joplin, Missouri, then US 66 to LA. It usually took me three days. I ate on the move. I slept in the car or, in hot weather, would pull off onto a side road and throw a blanket on the ground. I enjoyed the drive. On this trip it was to say goodbye to my parents, to my father principally because he had made the trip possible, and to stash my books in their basement. I still find books on my shelves, tattered paperbacks, that I know, from copyright dates, or from the notes in the margins and the passages underlined, came from my original library.

HM, aged five, wartime

The family with our mother, father behind the camera. HM in the center,
John on the left, Tom, right, Virginia and Victoria, circa 1951

Supervisors Approve Two
More Steps on Smog War

HARVEY S. MUDD, CIVIC LEADER, DIES

Mining Engineer Stricken Suddenly at Home; Funeral Services to Be Conducted Friday

Harvey Seeley Mudd, 66, mining engineer and Los Angeles civic leader, died suddenly at his home at 1240 Benedict Canyon Drive, Beverly Hills, at 4 a.m. yesterday.

He leaves his widow, the former Mildred Esterbrook; a son, Henry T. Mudd, a daughter, Mrs. Norman F. Sprague Jr., Beverly Hills, and a brother, Dr. Seeley Mudd, Pasadena.

Funeral services will be conducted at 2 p.m. Friday in St. John's Episcopal Church, 512 W Adams Blvd., with Bishop Francis Eric Bloy officiating. Forest Lawn Memorial-Park is handling funeral arrangements.

Active in Many Fields

Mr. Mudd was active in numerous phases of the life and development of Los Angeles and Southern California, his services covering cultural, charitable, educational, governmental and business fields. For his contributions to the upbuilding of the area, he received many honors, including an award as the citizen considered to have performed the most valuable and unselfish service to the community.

Likewise, he was honored in his profession. He was given the Egleston Columbia (University) Engineering Medal for 1948, the award being the highest granted in the engineering field. He was the first Californian to be so honored. He was also chosen to be president of the American Institute of Mining and Metallurgical Engineers and was given a scroll by the Engineers and Architects Association for his outstanding achievements in engineering.

Helped Found Symphony

Los Angeles music lovers hold themselves in debt to him for his part in founding the Southern California Symphony Association in 1934 to support the Los Angeles Philharmonic Orchestra after the death of W. A. Clark, who had sponsored the orchestra theretofore.

For 12 years, from 1934 to 1946, Mr. Mudd served as president of the symphony association, relinquishing the post because his business interests took him out of the country. He continued to serve as chairman of the board of the association until his death.

Chief among his business interests was the Cyprus

DIES — Harvey S. Mudd, mining engineer and civic leader, dies suddenly.

Mines Corp., which mines copper on the island of Cyprus in the Mediterranean, an age-old source of the metal. He was president and managing director of the concern for many years and was chairman of the board at his death.

Claremont Chairman

For many years he had been chairman of the board of fellows of Claremont College and trustee of the California Institute of Technology. He was a director of the Southern Pacific Co., Texas Gulf Sulphur Co., Founders Fire & Marine Insurance Co. and a voting trustee of the Pacific Mutual Life Insurance Co. He was a director of the Hospital of the Good Samaritan and chairman of the board of directors of the Welfare Federation of the Los Angeles Area.

In 1943, he was president of the Los Angeles Area War Chest. In February, 1948, he was named to the board of directors of Greater Los Angeles Plans, Inc.

Other posts which he held included trustee of the Southwest Museum and of the American Heritage Foundation and member of the advisory committee of the Henry E. Huntington Library and Art Gallery and of the California Community Foundation.

Besides having been a

Technical Staff Enlarged; Ban on Incinerators Set

County smog control officials loosed a two-gun attack upon air pollution in proposals which won the unanimous approval of the Board of Supervisors.

In one action, Chief Smith Griswold of the Air Pollution Control District will establish 55 new technical jobs in forming an augmented force which will "bring about greater control of pollutants from industrial and commercial sources."

Second, County Manager Arthur J. Will sought new laws for the restriction of incinerator operations through-

LA Times, April 13, 1955. The death of my grandfather and the dawning of awareness of air pollution.

Dr. Shervert Frazier

Part III

The Journey Resumes

16

Love in a Dark Time

I came back from Europe much changed. I felt that I was ready to set a life's course for myself. I knew where I was going and saw no reason why I would not get there. I could not precisely say where that place was. It was a psychological condition or plateau of awareness rather than anything specific. It was less about ends and more about the journey. How soon the illusion that my destiny was in my own hands would be dispelled!

For the moment, however, for the first weeks after my return from Europe, I lay about my parents' house, recuperating. I got my books out of the cartons in their basement and I read. I still experienced bouts of severe intestinal distress, some nausea, and was quite weak. I was told that the parasite could cause liver damage if not knocked out completely, so I took medical advice seriously. During this convalescent sojourn, I had talks with my father about my trip and about my visit with Hamish. I had polite talks with my mother, though never about any of the more adventurous aspects of the experience. She and I talked about museums. Generally, however, she was unreceptive and wanted to know next to nothing about what I'd done or experienced. She had not approved of the trip, possibly because it represented my final breaking away from home and from her.

In the late fall, I returned to New York City and committed myself to getting a college education. I enrolled in the New School. Since I had the luxury of not needing to find a proper career path, I became a generalist, or what has sometimes been called a "secular humanist." I concentrated on literature and anthropology; the latter interest came from a desire to know how other cultures structured family, the relations between parent and child, what sorts of obligations were imposed. The family part of American culture had not, in my particular experience, worked terribly well. I wanted to know when infants in different societies were weaned, when they were turned loose, who raised the child, an aunt (a version of the nanny) or the mother. I read ethnographic literature on the Crow of Montana, the Inuit of Canada and Alaska, and the Hopi and Navajo of Arizona. In a very few years I would be having frequent interactions with both the Hopi and the Navajo, and my studies, though academic, had prepared me to encounter them without the bias of "primitive" or similarly dismissive prejudice. The Navajo name for themselves is *Dineh*, which means "the people."

I did not have a serious girlfriend for the first year that I was back in New York. The wariness about intense feelings was still with me and I developed a protective persona, the moody bohemian. I could be intimate with my muse when I was writing— but with a real woman, I wasn't there yet. I focused on school. I had a close woman friend though, a good pal and confidant named Sylvia Bloch. Sylvia and I had worked together at Brentano's. Sylvia fell in love with an aspiring writer named Leonard Michaels. It was the stormiest of relationships and I often found myself in the role of intermediary, peace maker and message carrier, sometimes sitting in their tiny apartment over the Fat Black Pussy Cat on MacDougal Street listening for hours to Sylvia's neurotic anguish about Leonard's imagined infidelities. I could never dissuade her. She was the most miserable of souls, a person who lived on the edge of the abyss, always one step away from falling, but because she was my real friend, my only one, I would sit up with her. Later the same day Leonard would tell me his version of the event that had created the storm. Because I was not romantically involved with anyone, I was seen as somehow special, the innocent, and thus wise in the affairs of the heart. I wasn't at all, just available.

Leonard and Sylvia married in 1962. They went to Ann Arbor where Leonard earned a Ph.D. and then on to UC Berkeley where he had a distinguished career both as writer and teacher. I lost sight of them until, in 1992, Leonard published a book called *Sylvia*. She had committed suicide and Leonard felt guilty. I don't think he should have; he couldn't have saved her. Suicide was in her destiny. I remember her with great fondness. With me, for me, she was happy, never possessive, anxious, or suspicious. We had avoided romance and sex and so we remained friends. I mourned her. Sylvia Bloch was not the first person whom I had loved who had died, but she was among the most significant. I wrote Leonard but heard nothing back. This hurt me. I had thought that he and I were friends. Thinking about it though, I realized that he, eight years older than I, had never quite seen me as a peer. As Sylvia's friend, I was just tolerated. He may even have seen me as a romantic rival. But up until the time they departed for Ann Arbor in 1962 we remained in close contact. I had been part of their scene and had been present when Leonard's career took off.

I remember the excitement the three of us felt when a short story was accepted by *Playboy*. Leonard's euphoria evaporated when he became convinced that the University of Michigan would now take note of him and would remember that he had borrowed a number of books from the University Library and had not returned them. They were now overdue some eight years. He was sure that they would bring criminal charges. He showed up at my apartment one afternoon with a carton of books, all tattered and worn, with Dewey Decimal System numbers in white ink on their spines, and a University of Michigan stamp on the title page. Would I keep them for him, in case his apartment was searched? I thought his fear unreasonable, bordering on paranoia, but I agreed. My library now had a wide selection of the New Criticism: William Empson, Northrup Fry, I. A. Richards and others. I had my own copy of *The Meaning of Meaning*, which was a notion that I took seriously at the time, the idea that meaning itself had a meta-meaning (whatever that phrase might actually mean). Now, I am unsure if anything has meaning beyond what works for each of us individually. I kept the books

for Leonard for many years. He never came back for them. I still have
several; most fell apart and were left by the wayside.

I liked being a student and wondered what I might do to prolong a life
that consisted mostly of reading books and thinking about them. Fairly
early, however, perhaps because of the obsessive focus on minutiae that
I noted in Leonard Michaels, I had decided that I would not go on to
graduate school. I didn't need to. I could continue to be what might be
called an intellectual, but freelance. If I wasn't going to be a college professor—and I was sure I wasn't—what then? I needed to do something
useful with my life; it was in my family's tradition, but what? I would
wait and see. Since I no longer had periods of anxiety or depression and
no longer thought about suicide, it seemed that the wounds of childhood had healed. I was not suffering; therefore, I must then be happy.
Or happy enough. Then events, the unexpected, took me, and indeed
the country, by surprise. My life swerved.

On 22 November 1963, a little before two in the afternoon, as I exited
the elevator on the ground floor at the New School, preparing to walk
to my apartment, the school's PA system announced the assassination
of President John F. Kennedy. The disembodied voice broke into sobs.

It was a day when America changed. The nation came to a fork
in the road and instead of pausing to consider which path to take, it
rushed, or was pushed by the passions of the moment, onto a path that
led, through Vietnam and Nixon and through the financial catastrophe
of forty years later, to the chaos and darkness of the present, when the
democracy itself seems is on the edge of failure. The unravelling of
values and the promise that was present in the beginning may have
begun with the assassination. America had been a society that was, in
the Beatles uplifting tones, "getting better all the time," but then, to
employ another image from popular culture, "the music died." The
country's unconscious, its *Id,* if one thinks in Freudian metaphors, took

over and a dark national spirit, a death wish perhaps, has been gaining strength ever since.

With the assassination, the quality that I think of as civic virtue, in the ancient Roman sense of virtue, not of moral purity but as integrity and responsibility, evaporated. America, the warrior for just causes, became America the confused and arrogant aggressor. Vietnam might not have happened had Kennedy lived—I like to think that he would have seen the error and withdrawn—and the republic, spared that trauma and the divisiveness that ensued, would be a different country than the one it is today.

The tragedy plowed through America like a truck that had lost its brakes and steering; it struck every one of us, deflecting our trajectories, upending our assumptions, requiring a rethinking of goals and expectations. I cannot imagine that there is an American who lived through that trauma who was not in some way changed, even if only briefly, by the events of that terrible day. They knocked me out of the course I had been on. I became an entirely unexpected person.

At two in the afternoon, the lobby at the New School was a scene of stunned pandemonium. Men and women were crying; people were staring at the loudspeaker as if expecting the news to change, that it was a mistake. I turned to the only person I knew in the room, a woman from my Renaissance literature class. I knew her only as Mrs. Foster. We shared our sense of shock and of disbelief. Grief had not yet had time to form. We went out into the sun and walked, without clear purpose, along Sixth Avenue. We introduced ourselves. Her name was Elizabeth.

The city, for the next hour or so, entered a dreamlike state, a nightmare in which everything seemed to move very slowly, as if caught in some sort of malevolent ether. Cabs stopped in the middle of the avenue as drivers tuned their radios to find news, talked with other cabbies or with their passengers. Even the raucous and raunchy sidewalk displays by boyfriends and pimps that usually went on below the women's house of detention on Greenwich Avenue were stilled.

Later in the afternoon, we went back to Elizabeth's apartment, a little red building on the corner of Perry Street and Greenwich Avenue, and watched the TV coverage. Elizabeth's daughter was four. The baby sitter sat with us and watched, crying.

Elizabeth was a widow aged thirty-six; I was twenty-three. She was a good looking woman; she wore no makeup and left her hair alone, un-styled and free. A New Englander, I remember thinking when I first saw her in class, which she turned out to be. I had noticed her but, since she was so much older, it never occurred to me that we might have a romantic liaison. In class, she was thoughtful and reserved. She participated actively in class discussions so I knew the sound of her voice and the quality of her mind.

Together, sitting on her sofa, we followed the aftermath of this national tragedy—Johnson's swearing in, the First Lady's bloody dress, the silencing of the essential witness, Lee Harvey Oswald—all filtered through the measured intelligences of Walter Cronkite and Eric Sevareid. Elizabeth's little girl played quietly on the carpet.

Four days later, Elizabeth and I became lovers. It was a coming together that was tender and passionate and at the same time strangely sober, almost dignified. We took what was happening seriously. School reopened and we returned. We sat in class together and, as before, discussed great books— Rabelais, Cervantes, Shakespeare—but we were now in possession of an enriching secret. In the midst of the sorrow and uncertainty, in the midst of national tragedy, we were in love. I was deliriously happy.

The infatuations I had experienced before, the painful longings, the fantasies—the girl from Sarah Lawrence whose name I no longer remember, the idea that I might elope with Mari Teri—the memory of all those sorrows and enthusiasms dissolved in this new reality. Elizabeth filled my heart. I loved the streaks of gray in her silky hair, the down on her cheeks. The difference in our ages had no effect. Elizabeth's daughter, Leslie, who could not remember her father, took me into her heart too.

I moved into Elizabeth's tiny apartment. There was no bedroom for us—her little girl had the bedroom—and we slept on the sofa bed in the living room. We walked to school together. On weekends we explored New York, eating in delicatessens or watching dogs play in Central Park. We picnicked, all three of us, at the Cloisters, bundled against the November cold, sitting among fallen leaves. There was, however, a cloud on the horizon. Responding to the call made by President Kennedy in his inaugural address of 1961, "Ask not what your country can do for you, ask what you can do for your country," I had enlisted in the army and was contractually obligated to report when I finished my degree.

I had made no effort to duck military service. There was a draft in 1963, which I probably could have escaped through family connections or by extending my education. I had no desire to be a soldier nor did I have any fascination with guns; I was, nevertheless, patriotic. I believed that service of some kind was consistent with my values: if young men less well-off and less well connected than I were required to serve, I should as well. As to the military generally, I was not a pacifist. Knowledge of the Second World War and the Holocaust made doctrinaire pacifism untenable for me.

There was also pragmatism in my decision. Since I had a 1A draft category, it was possible that I would be called up anyway. The idea of living for two years in a barracks as an enlisted man, of pounding a typewriter, pushing a broom, or lugging a rifle, filled me with dread. Instead, I enlisted. I would serve three years, but in exchange, I would have some choice as to what sort of work I would do. I had some Spanish language skills and a good education. I requested the Intelligence Corps. My year abroad presented an obstacle in terms of getting a security clearance—what had I done overseas and whom had I met?—but after several months, I was approved and given a Top Secret security clearance. I signed the contract in August of 1963.

Meeting Elizabeth shortly after I had enlisted changed everything. I had fantasies of flight: Elizabeth, her little girl, and I disappearing, going to Mexico perhaps. I went through a period of intense agonizing over the situation. But a sense of duty was too much a part of my heritage to be overcome. If I had ideas and values that I took seriously, surely "duty" was among them. Besides I had made a deal. There were practical considerations about living on the run. I couldn't imagine hiding for the rest of my life. There was never a real question: I would be a soldier for as long as I had agreed

In late January, Elizabeth accompanied me on the subway to the Army Induction Center on Whitehall Street in lower Manhattan. It was a tearful parting. She looked stricken. I felt stricken but pretended not to be.

I climbed the steps into the old stone customs building, was examined by an Army doctor and found fit, took an oath to defend the Constitution, and boarded the bus. I carried a regular army service number on my dog tags, a number that fifty years later I can still remember.

17

Basic Training

The bus carried fifty young men, forty-nine of them covering up anxiety with noisy bravado. I, pretending nonchalance, read a book.

Most of my fellow recruits, some just boys of eighteen or nineteen, had never left their familiar corners of the Bronx, Queens, or Staten Island and were already homesick. I was homesick too, for Elizabeth, but I felt no anxiety. At nearly twenty-four, having traveled widely and having been on my own for several years, I was the mature man in the crowd and felt confident. My confidence would not last.

When the bus turned into the main gate at Fort Dix, the army's basic training post, there was a larger-than-life sculpture of a soldier in WWII combat gear, rifle, with bayonet affixed, charging the front lines of enemies that lay in the nation's future. The figure looked like the little green plastic GIs that I played with at age eight. The words below the figure read "Fort Dix, Home of the Ultimate Weapon." In the age of thermonuclear bombs and intercontinental delivery capabilities, this struck me as rather absurd.

From the moment I had left home at age eighteen up until the moment I stepped onto that army bus, I had had nearly complete control over my daily life. I could quit a job I didn't like, move to another city, or change schools. Now, as if passing through the looking glass, I was entering a world that was opposite, upside down. It was a system that had complete control over my daily activities, and over my life too, a system that could use my body in any way it chose, even waste it, though in that year, 1963, with Vietnam barely visible, just below the horizon, I didn't give that extreme outcome much thought. But the upending of my sense of myself as an autonomous actor was so complete that it took a considerable effort to get used to. As an infantryman, all that mattered was my physical abilities, my bodily presence, and unquestioning obedience. Neither intelligence nor education mattered. Indeed, on day one, after my hair had been shorn, the Sergeant Major asked for a show of hands of those with a college education. I raised mine. There were only a few of us. The declaration of higher education turned out to be a mistake; it resulted in an assignment to scrub out some garbage cans. Lesson learned. The brain was to be emptied. The drill instructors' often repeated mantra was, "Everything you need to know we will teach you." They meant everything. There were young men from the mountains of West Virginia who had never experienced dental care of any sort. The army replaced their teeth.

The basics of military training covered close order drilling, throwing a live grenade, digging foxholes, putting on one's gas mask—I remembered that Hamish had told me about a chemical attack in France in 1917.

"Life is unpredictable, young Harvey," he had said, with his characteristic sardonic chuckle. "The wind shifted and blew our own gas back on us." Chemical weapons training took place in a wooden shed with no windows. We, the recruits, stood with our gas masks in a pouch on the hip. Tear gas was pumped into the space and we fumbled to get our masks out and onto our faces. Much cursing, a feeling of panic, the damn snap doesn't yield, some of us forgetting what we've practiced in open air. We were not allowed to leave until we could stand calmly in the cloud of the chemical agent. One boy just couldn't get it right and had to be carried out, crying and choking. If it had been nerve gas or chlorine, the boy would be dead. The training sergeant made sure that we knew this.

There was training in field first aid—how to staunch a bleeding wound being the most relevant for an infantryman. Tourniquets and pressure were things I knew from the Boy Scouts. A "sucking chest wound" was another thing altogether; one seals a hole in the lung with a piece of plastic from the rain slicker that we were all issued, the piece held to the wounded man's body with tape. Medics apparently carried duct tape in their packs. There was an elementary course, two hours of instruction on those ideas which, on the day of our enlistment, we had sworn to defend, the Constitution. Most of the young men I trained with had never heard of it. The elementary school Pledge of Allegiance was, I suspect, their only exposure to the idea that they were Americans. Most got their sense of identity from their favorite football or baseball team. The demands of communal living were difficult for me; there was no privacy about anything: about dressing, bathing, even toilets. The care of an M-14 rifle was the center of infantry basic training. It is significant that when one goes to the rifle range, a counted number of rounds are given out and empty brass in equal number must be returned at the end of the session. They don't want a live round brought back to the barracks; the concern was for an accident, an act of revenge against a hated drill instructor, or, I suppose, suicide.

I was initially assigned to a training company staffed by drill instructors who were all African American and who, while tough and demanding, were fair and supportive. My D.I. was Sergeant First Class Simmons. I never knew his first name. He made it clear that he was not our friend, but that he was not our enemy either. He was in his early 50s, a career soldier. He would wake us every morning, in the dark of winter, at 5:45 a.m. He was always fully dressed, boots polished, fatigues pressed to razor seam. I never heard him curse a recruit, never saw a gesture or heard a word that was even remotely threatening or humiliating. He worked us hard and never asked of us anything that he didn't do himself. When we ran in the snow, he ran in the snow. More accustomed to poetry than push-ups, I was not as physically capable as many of the younger men, but managed. We had to be able to run a mile wearing combat boots in under seven minutes. I was sure that I could not, but Sergeant Simmons got me through with a touch on the elbow and a supportive word. We, his recruits, worked hard for him; by that I mean that we did our best. Through him, I came to an understanding of the meaning of leadership. In school I had been *guided* by teachers; being *led* is different.

Midway through the training cycle, I got sick. February in the New Jersey pinewoods was a grim experience: wet, cold, and dark. In a drizzle of freezing mist that turned into sleety rain, I stood in the sick call line outside the medic's office. Twenty shivering recruits lined up in the gray dawn. It took me an hour to reach the warmth of the medic's office where it was discovered that I was running a 103-degree fever. I had pneumonia. It was my twenty-fourth birthday.

I was confined to a ward with fifteen other recruits for six weeks. The television went on at eight a.m. and stayed tuned to cartoons and game shows until lights out. I tried living under my blankets in order to read but could not escape the voices of Tweety Bird, Puddy Tat, and the room full of boisterous American eighteen-year-olds. I volunteered for medical tests and experiments—I walked on a treadmill and breathed into a mask—just to get away from the ward for an hour a day. I thought of writing my parents, asking for what I had no idea. I knew better. My mother became maternal only when her children were sick; the idea that she might show up at Fort Dix or phone the hospital commandant killed that idea. I spoke with Elizabeth every evening from a pay phone. Standing in the glass booth, clad in a military-issue blue bathrobe, I was often teary. I was becoming depressed and beaten down. To make matters worse, I had to restart basic training from the beginning.

The non-commissioned officers who ran my new company were corrupt and sadistic and, in one case, openly anti-Semitic. The company commander, a second lieutenant just out of ROTC, visible only when strutting about in starched combat gear, was a joke, intimidated by the rogue non-commissioned officers he was supposed to control. He smoked a corncob pipe, imitating General Douglas MacArthur.

Once a week, around three a.m., my platoon's drill instructor would wake us up with a bellow. We would scramble out of our bunks and stand at attention in our boxers and white T-shirts, blinking in the lights. The sergeant would shout out the accusation that fifty dollars were missing from his footlocker and that one of us was a thief. The fact that his room, at the end of the barracks, was kept locked at all times did not deter him from making this absurd accusation. But if we wanted to go back to sleep we would have to come up with the money, a dollar from each of us—we always complied. Sleep was more important than the money, dignity, or justice. He extorted the money either on Thursday, before the weekend's drinking, or on Sunday, to recover his expenses.

Worse than sleep deprivation were the arbitrary and capricious trials that seemed to have no purpose other than to demonstrate the NCO's power over us. We were theirs in all respects. They enforced their power through our bodies, knowing the soul would soon enough capitulate. They ordered us, without reason or pattern, to take stress positions. There were a variety of them. We were required, for instance, to hold our arms straight out in front of us until we couldn't hold them out any longer. If we did not hold them out long enough to suit, further punishment resulted. It is remarkable how heavy one's own arms become and how demoralizing the experience can be: when the arms fall, it feels as if the self has betrayed the self. There was also the squat position, which we had to hold despite great pain in the knees. If you fell over or stood up without permission, you repeated the exercise.

The worst of these positions was called "front lean and rest." This is the push-up position—plank when done voluntarily in yoga—held interminably, trembling and shaking, until we were released or fell face down into the mud. They would walk on our hands while we were in this position. On one occasion a sergeant put a bayonet, point up, beneath my chest. I was terrified that I would fall on it and seriously injure myself. He squatted down, taunting, asking if I was afraid; he removed it before I fell. I had not been singled out; this particular refinement was applied broadly. Having experienced the rigors of training under Sergeant Simmons, I came to see that these practices had neither instructive purpose nor any physical toughening goal. The method was humiliation and exhaustion; the goal was to break us down, to diminish us, and thus to inflate themselves.

The sergeants ran us around the company area. They sat on a bench in the middle of the compound and ordered us to run. Around we went. They ran us until some of us were sick or had collapsed. Both happened to me. I would fall to my knees, in complete exhaustion, vomiting down the front of my shirt, feeling a mix of shame, fear, and hatred. Those who had not made it through this ordeal were lined up and ridiculed; they called us girls or pussies.

There were Jewish draftees in the training company. They took the worst of it: name-calling, *kike* being the one I heard used most often, and that threat of being circumcised again with a bayonet. A boy named Esch was in my squad. He was a clumsy young man from Brooklyn, a draftee who had been training to be an accountant. Once, on a forced march through the woods, one of the sergeants pounded on Esch's helmet with a stick because he was not walking fast enough. As he stumbled along, frightened, humiliated, and in tears, I did the only brave thing I did during this whole experience. I told him to hold onto my belt and I gave him enough of a pull so that he did not fall behind.

There were a few of our number who were probably tougher than the sergeants. One was a nineteen-year-old African American from Cleveland named Willie Stokes. He never fell, never collapsed, and, consequently, they left him alone. He became our recruit platoon leader. He was fully aware of the character of the sergeants, but did not complain. Stoic acceptance was the message his manner sent to the rest of us. I was the college man who had thought that decency and reasonableness were forces that operated everywhere. Stokes had probably come to the army knowing otherwise and thus, by natural selection, he became our leader.

The things I learned from these men were not a soldier's skills but a prisoner's: how to make oneself invisible, how to avoid being noticed. The effect on me was the opposite of what the military might have wanted. Notions I had had when I had joined the army, that I had some qualities that might be of use to my country, qualities such as courage or initiative or even patriotism, were ground out of me. The only thing I needed was the ability to finish each day without collapsing physically or descending into robotic deadness; any better qualities were so little valued that I gave up trying to hang on to them. It was a miniature totalitarianism where the only reality was the barracks, the fear of what each day would bring, and the certainty of irrationality and unfairness. I was beginning to lose my trust in my country. The black members of our group, like Willie Stokes, had probably never had much trust, but for me, it was a beginning of a profound disillusionment, a loss of faith. My intellect, my creativity, my love of country, parts of myself that I most valued, had no place in this reality. They were not just ignored; they were declared useless.

I don't think the Army as an institution wanted any of this negation to happen; I feel certain that it would not have happened had I continued under the guidance of Sergeant Simmons. I would have graduated from basic training with the knowledge that I was tougher than I thought I was—not meaner or more prone to violence, just tougher—and that I had learned worthwhile things about myself. The Army, however, is an institution in which the boundary between discipline and sadism, between building up and tearing down, between appropriate use of authority and unbridled use of power, is somewhat hazy. In this case, legitimate authority became a perversion, the application of power for its own sake. We were fodder for their essential emptiness. I came away feeling I'd been trained, out of fear of punishment, to surrender my will, trained to be servile, afraid, and obedient; and for someone who valued freedom, both personal and political, and in the abstract, the ideals that came to me through the Declaration of Independence, this was a steep price to have paid for nothing.

I was saved from doing something that would have been seriously self-defeating, like running away, going AWOL, by the certainty that they were not likely to physically harm me—their torments left no bruises—or kill me. What made the real difference, however, was the knowledge that it would end. I could count the days.

Ultimately, there was rescue. An Italian kid, more practical and less proud than I was, from tough Bayonne, New Jersey, wrote his father about the drill instructors, the extortion of money, and the sadistic treatment; his father, apparently a man with some influence, wrote his congressman. One morning, we woke to find that a Judge Advocate General's investigation of our little Devil's Island was underway. While our training continued, some of us, a selection among the recruits, were called in, one by one, and interviewed by a colonel from the JAG division. We finished our training, doing poorly on every test, but not enough to be held back. I believe that our collective near-failure was an unconscious act of passive sabotage. We shamed our instructors.

As the investigation wound down, nine recruits and I were chosen randomly to be witnesses in a court-martial of several of our tormentors. We ten—a couple of black soldiers, but not the tough Stokes, and a group of South Boston Irish—were gathered in the Battalion Commander's office. He, the military version of middle management, a balding man in his fifties, sat behind a desk while we, in fatigues, stood at ease. There was another soldier in the room, an enlisted man who took notes. I understood the Commanding Officer's dilemma. Bad things had happened in a training company under his command and this was career-threatening situation for him. Concerned mostly about himself, he set out to talk us out of pressing charges. If we insisted, he said, we would remain under the control of the very men who would be brought to trial, but, he assured us, we would not be harmed, harassed, or pressured. We knew this was nonsense and he knew that we understood this. He told us that, even without a court martial, administrative discipline would ruin the careers of these men. In this, I suspect, he was being truthful, because he had every reason to avenge himself on a group of sergeants who had potentially done so much damage to his own career. But by telling us this, he was also giving us a way out. "Now, go and talk it over amongst yourselves, men," he said, his tone avuncular. He even called us "men." With the stenographer in the room, he had it on record that he had exerted no pressure.

It was April. Pansies grew in pots along the sidewalk that led to the battalion offices. The breeze was cold. We ten, privates, stood on the sidewalk looking at each other, feeling like a bunch of peasants being bamboozled by the nobleman. We talked, everyone at once, loosely, roughly, emotionally stating our positions. We wanted justice. No, truthfully, we wanted revenge. We wanted these sadists to be punished. But more than anything, we wanted to leave, to get away from Fort Dix, to be anywhere but there. By virtue of my age, I was the jury foreman, and that responsibility made me think that we should see it through. But I knew that I could not have persuaded them to stay because I could not persuade myself either.

We voted not to press charges. The battalion commander asked us each if we agreed with the decision. To save face, I asked again about the Army's assurances of administrative punishment. Whether it happened, I cannot say. Perhaps the incident was reported up the chain of command that it was all a mistake, a trumped-up charge by a bunch of malcontents.

I felt that I had been a coward. There will be those who will say that what I experienced was ordinary military training. I do not believe this. Soldiers shaped by fear and abuse would repeat the pattern with others. As an army, they would be unreliable, tempted to mutiny, and they would be without the values of duty, honor, or patriotism that make for an effective army, an army that thinks of itself as projecting values rather than simply killing, bringing destruction and suffering.

18

Soldiering On

During the miserable eight weeks of "training" that followed my six weeks in the hospital, I had lived on the edge: I feared some sort of personal failure. I didn't know exactly what form my collapse would be but I knew I was close to it. It would be worse than embarrassing. Only my nightly phone calls with Elizabeth, sometimes no longer than two minutes because there was always a line of other recruits standing outside the phone booth, waiting their turns, kept me from slipping over. I was physically exhausted, in the hands of bad people, doing things that made no sense to me. The patriotic feelings that had led me to enlist in the first place were gone. I was in fact depressed and just hanging on.

But I made it. No one but me knew how close I had come.

I finally escaped Fort Dix; I had two week's leave. I went straight to New York. My self-esteem was very low, but by ignoring that fact, Elizabeth helped. She loved me better than I did myself.

We talked about the future of our relationship. We were, we thought, realistic about ourselves as a couple. We recognized that if my next army assignment led to a distant place, Korea, for instance, or Germany, we would be forced to separate. I, as a private, would not have had any sort of family allowance, and besides, we weren't legally a family. We would have to wait. But for the moment, the important thing was to do well at my next assignment: Army Intelligence School. Fort Holabird,

Baltimore, Maryland, would be home for the next six months. I usually had weekend leave, which I always took.

The training covered the various aspects of military counter intelligence, essentially defensive security. Our brief was to catch the spy or the mole before he'd done much damage, or better yet, keep him out of the garden altogether. Much of the training was interesting, but would seem quaint and useless in today's electronic environment. I learned, for instance, how one makes a microdot for transmitting information concealed as a period in a page of text. We studied the case of the Soviet spy, Colonel Rudolph Abel, and how the hollow nickel led to his capture. We practiced surveillance in downtown Baltimore. There was an excellent course on the Constitution and a photography course that was as good technically as any that a private photography school could offer. No one was abused and nothing was arbitrary. It was like college except that I could not cut classes, was required to live in barracks, and to keep my bunk area to military standards: a nickel must bounce on the made bed and the T-shirts in the footlocker had to be folded just so. None of that suited my personality, but since these requirements did not ask me to suspend a moral value or to believe something that wasn't true—the sun revolving around the earth for instance—I did as was required. After I separated from the army, I promptly forgot how to fold a T-shirt.

My weekends, Friday night until Sunday late afternoon, were with Elizabeth. A slow healing process had begun. Back in Baltimore, I learned typing and darkroom photography. The lack of privacy was something I found difficult so I rented a cheap furnished room, $40 per month, in a rundown neighborhood that I could reach by bus; I would go in the late afternoon, when classes were over, turn on a floor lamp by the only chair, a lumpy thing covered with frayed burgundy-colored velvet, and read. The tiny room was my secret, my safe-house; I felt a bit subversive.

Midway through the course, my orders came. My next assignment was not to be in one of America's foreign outposts, but in El Paso, Texas, a city with a large Mexican-American population. My Spanish language abilities had turned into a military asset. This posting, Fort Bliss, would be home for the duration of my army time, the next twenty-eight months. I called Elizabeth. We could stay together, but there was a catch. We could only live together if we were a family. We didn't hesitate. We married in the late fall of 1964.

We chose an Episcopal ceremony at the old Saint John's Church in the Village. Only Elizabeth's mother and daughter attended. In this fact I could see that my distance from my own family was more than just in miles. I didn't even tell them that I was marrying until after the fact. My estrangement from my mother had settled into a predictable rut. If I had introduced Elizabeth to her, she would have been, as she always was, gracious, polite, and at the same time transparently insincere. I knew how my mother would view the situation: she would see a lowly private in the army and not an officer, marriage to an older woman from an undistinguished family, and a simple wedding. I knew from my father that she disapproved of the fact that I was in the army at all and not embarking on a career in law or business. I was sure that she would not have come to my wedding even if I had asked her.

With my father there was less of an issue. He too had served voluntarily in the military. He liked Elizabeth. I had introduced her to him on one of his business trips to New York. He had invited us to his apartment on Madison Avenue for cocktails. Because our relationship was so unconventional, Elizabeth and I had been quite nervous about this meeting. She wondered if she should dress for the occasion. Looking foxy wasn't her style. She had only one pair of high heeled shoes. We decided that she wouldn't. She wore a skirt and sweater and a string of pearls, her customary shoes, and only minimal makeup. After we'd gone through the introductions, Elizabeth engaged easily in conversation with my father. She looked almost prim and I felt a secret pride in knowing that she wasn't. And I was pleased that she had not felt the need to look younger than she was. My father had been genuinely friendly, but I couldn't have invited him to the wedding without including my mother, so neither was invited.

* * *

In El Paso, we rented a ranch-style house in a subdivision on the west side of the city. The development was new; there was no landscaping, not a single tree. The house was as far from the post as I could get; the half-hour morning commute was a price I was willing to pay to keep my personal life separate from my military life. I was in love with my wife. I was surprisingly happy and I wanted to protect that feeling.

Our house was the last on the street and beyond it there was nothing but desert. Today tract developments advance, sometimes in squares, sometimes with curves, for five miles further to the north and west. From the satellite, they look like military formations as they are rendered on battle maps. The advance of cities into the undeveloped lands has always seemed to me, perhaps because I came from Southern California, an attempt to vanquish emptiness, the battle of the beyond. The "beyond" does not exist in America as a permanent condition. In the East one cuts down the trees to get at it. In the desert one adds water. During the two years that I lived in El Paso, I always expected the bulldozers to arrive and begin to tear up the desert behind our house.

I liked the desert. By day it was inhospitable, a place of rocks, spiny plants, where nothing grew tall enough to provide shade. At night it was different. I would often walk after the sun went down in the arroyos behind our house. In a matter of minutes, I could be past the reach of the street lights, beyond even the street noises. If the moon was full I could pick up the occasional paw print of a coyote in the sand. The coyotes sang. I wanted to believe that it was for the sheer joy of hearing their voices. When the night was quiet, it was so quiet that I could hear the whispery sound of the little desert rodents as they scampered about searching for food. These two creatures, hunter and prey, coyote and rodent, shared the nocturnal desert. I, the interloper, heard them, but I never saw them.

By day, on weekends, I occasionally took my motorcycle, one designed for that sort of environment, knobby tires and robust shock absorbers, into these same arroyos. I rode as fast as I could, venting the frustrations associated with a boring job. Young and male, I was seduced by the power of the machine and I admit that I even liked the noise. Not too long after this, however, I had a revelation—a gradual evolution actually— about the relationship of man to the natural world. I look back on my motorcycle days with embarrassment. It was a behavior—the noise, the tires chewing up terrain, the stink of exhaust fumes—that I would not engage in again. "The beyond" had become more important than my amusement. I became, or would become, five years later, an environmentalist.

Home life settled into a comfortable routine. I was just another young husband who left the house every morning at seven and returned by six in the evening. I wore a suit, even in the worst of the summer. We were a family with one child and a dog, a Basset Hound that we named Charlie. There was nothing to evoke my previous bohemian tendencies. On longer holidays we often drove north to Taos, New Mexico.

These trips were not purely touristic. I already had tentative roots in the region. My friend Jim had spent family vacations in Taos; he had told wonderful stories about riding bareback on the mesas and skinny-dipping in a hot spring. He and I had spent the summer after graduating from high school in Taos. I fell in love with the clear light, the limit-less space, and the silent mountains. Elizabeth and I were following an already marked trail. We began to make friends and acquire some local knowledge. I purchased some land that had a simple adobe house on it. The house had no plumbing and needed repairs to roof and floors. This was the start.

El Paso still was home. In the late winter into spring of 1966, we watched our local college basketball team, Texas Western (now University of Texas, El Paso,) rise to prominence and finally to the national championship. In the March Madness of that year they defeated the reigning champion of college basketball, Kentucky. It was a major upset. It was especially meaningful because Texas Western was the first ever college team with a starting lineup of all African American athletes. The Kentucky team was all white. I felt I had witnessed a landmark in America's struggle with its demons.

The victory celebration that followed was surprisingly moving for me. I tended to be wary about collective events. The people of El Paso poured out onto the streets; happy crowds filled parking lots and honking cars clogged the streets. There was some firing of pistols into the air; we could hear the pops and cracks. Someone in our subdivision had fireworks left over from the previous Fourth of July. Elizabeth and I went out to watch the rockets. A neighbor had set up a laundry tub with ice and beer and we joined the little group. The night was crisp. The sky, between bursts of roman candles, was splendid with stars, millions of them. I talked to people from down the street with whom I'd never spoken. We all acted as if we'd known each other for years. There was much back slapping among the men. There was an aura of illogical self-congratulation, a happiness, unearned, for none of us had done anything other than be spectators and live in the same city, but still happiness; it mattered; psychologically, emotionally. A championship for the home team brought generalized feelings of goodwill that were hardly typical under ordinary circumstances.

During this period, photography was my sole artistic outlet. Sometimes, I went to Ciudad Juarez (the city was relatively safe in those days), and explored its poorer neighborhoods. I was attracted to its municipal cemetery, a place of broken stones and plastic flowers in coffee cans. It was a dry, bleak place, a field of death, but it had a curiously calming effect on me. I saw in the dust and plastic flowers a sort of tenderness, a profound acceptance of the inevitable. Taking artistic photographs in a cemetery, I was struggling with my fear of an early death.

My job was almost entirely in the area of personnel security, conducting background checks to determine if a soldier or a civilian employee of the Department of Defense might be a security risk. I discovered that most of my fellow citizens were churchgoers and that few had strong political opinions. Most seemed to have inherited their political ideas and affiliations from their parents. The Army, at least officially, was concerned only with anti-American views, not with partisan issues. I uncovered no Communist cells, no Maoists carrying little red books of the chairman's sayings. Islamists did not yet exist.

There was one bit of minor excitement. Fort Bliss was a missile training base, mostly defensive surface to air missiles, but also ground to ground offensive weapons. On one occasion, one of the long-range missiles went off course shortly after launch and instead of heading north toward a designated impact range in Utah, it lurched toward Mexico. The abort button had been pushed and the missile was destroyed midair, at a high altitude. Most of the pieces landed on the launch areas of the base, but the day was windy and the wind was blowing south. It was thought that some lighter pieces might have been carried as far as Juarez. I and another Spanish speaker in our unit were sent to Mexico, in plain clothes, without the credentials that would have made our visit official, to determine if this was the case. The other agent, Mr. Soto, a portly man of fifty, was from the Dominican Republic so his Spanish was heard by the Mexicans as a bizarre dialect. He went to the commercial street, the bars and night clubs, to ask around, to listen to the gossip. I went into the barrios. When I came to the municipal cemetery, a place I knew well from my photography expeditions, there was a man carrying a piece of shiny metal about three feet long and two feet wide. It didn't seem to be heavy and he had it tucked under his arm. A woman told me that it had fallen out of the sky. "A piece of an airplane, perhaps." But since no complete airplane had fallen from the sky and since no one was hurt, there was no fuss, no press, no police. The man was taking it away, useful, perhaps, to patch a roof. Without any official reason to be in Mexico, I could not approach him and demand the return of a piece of a US Army missile. In fact, that seemed the least advisable thing to do. The incident would have immediately been turned into a "missile incident." I could imagine the headlines. I asked around further, showing only the most casual interest. A little boy, maybe nine years old, ragged and dirty, came up to me and showed me a piece of torn aluminum, about five inches by nine inches, that he said had also fallen out of the sky. It had no markings on it. I offered him $2.00 and he accepted. For all I knew it had come from the dump and I had been conned. I rendezvoused with the genial Mr. Soto. He smelled of beer. He told me that some people had observed a puff of smoke in the sky, which must have been the destruction of the missile. We returned to our office on the base. I gave my scrap of aluminum to the operations officer, a major, who said he would give it to the colonel who commanded our unit. The major ordered me to put in a reimbursement request for the $2.00. It took over a month for the request to be processed through finance at Fort Sam Houston in San Antonio, but I got my money back.

The Vietnam War was not much in my mind during the first year of my enlistment. I knew that there were bases, housing and warehouses, being built and that American helicopters, carrying officers and advisors, went scooting across the sky like dragonflies over a pond; but my impression was that there was not a war, or at least one in which Americans were involved. The administration had tried hard to convey that impression; it was a Vietnamese war and we Americans were just helping, never interfering, not acting like overlords or typical colonials. I didn't think much about it. I had not yet developed the habit of reading newspapers and, indeed, in El Paso to have come by the New York Times I would have had to go to the city's library. I was not alarmed so was not terribly curious. How little I knew. The TV images of Americans in combat, of body bags and helicopters, did not begin, in my recollection of the period, until 1966. But knowledge was creeping up on me, the engine of war cranking up, sputtering, like a long neglected lawnmower motor, producing more exhaust than power. But by early 1966 the fumes were detectable and I began to think about Vietnam mostly in terms of my own potential exposure to it. I didn't want to go to Vietnam for no other reason than an aversion to danger and the discomforts that would come from living in barracks or worse, a muddy trench. My brother John had in this period declared himself a conscientious objector and was involved in the legalities that came with that position. I knew in my case, however, that even though my opinion of the adventure in Vietnam was becoming more and more negative, I would not have qualified as a pacifist on moral principles.

My understanding of the moral issues had been shaped by the Second World War. The circumstances of 1933 onward had persuaded me that some wars were necessary. Nothing, however, about Vietnam seemed to satisfy the requirements of necessity. The so-called domino theory, that all of Southeast Asia would fall if North Vietnam prevailed, seemed doubtful. A little reading satisfied me that the underlying conflict was not part of a communist-inspired conspiracy against America, but was simply a continuation of the anti-colonial struggle, part of an historical shift toward self-determination that had its roots in the proclamations of the American president Woodrow Wilson in 1918. The Vietnamese wanted to govern themselves, to be rid of the artificial borders and proxy governments that the Western powers had imposed on them.

I could not, however, give voice to these views while still in the service. The constitutional guarantee of free speech is qualified for an active duty soldier. With speech curtailed, so is thought; my outrage about the war came later. While I was still subject to military rules and sanctions, the best I could do was feel uneasy. Besides, until 1966 the level of US involvement was not so great that I could confidently declare that the war was either criminal or folly. We were not yet "all in" and could, presumably, disengage.

But unease had activated interest, an interest that was supported and encouraged by an Air Force colonel stationed at Holloman AFB in Alamogordo, New Mexico. I had met him on official business; now he became an informal mentor.

Because I wore civilian clothes, the colonel assumed I was a lieutenant, a distinction that made some socializing possible. I had noticed a copy of *The Iliad* on his office bookshelf, and that book, which I considered the ultimate war story, opened the door to a wide range of conversational subjects, including the war in Vietnam. I began to come out of intellectual hibernation. Once a week, I drove the seventy-five miles from Fort Bliss to Holloman in my green unmarked Plymouth.

Because of the possibility of intelligent conversation with someone who had such a very different perspective on the world than I had, the perspective of a career military man, I looked forward to these trips. There was a picnic area on the base set among ancient cottonwood trees that provided an oasis of shade. After I'd finished my work, the colonel and I sat at a picnic table and talked for an hour or so about wars generally, from the siege of Troy through the Second World War, and about Vietnam specifically. We didn't discuss Vietnam in terms of the political issues, which he, as a serving military officer, was required to stay clear of, but we could examine it as history in the making, a war that would eventually take a place in the American narrative. The books he loaned me became my introduction to the formal study of history. I was thrilled by Barbara Tuchman's *The Guns of August*, about the miscalculations that led to the outbreak of the First World War; Bernard B. Fall's *Street Without Joy*, about the French experience in Indochina, provided the prelude to America's Vietnam story.

More important to me, however, than factual history were the philosophical discussions that the colonel and I had. They reprised the sorts of free-ranging conversations that I had had with my father when I was a teen. The colonel introduced me to the idea that there were different kinds of war. Some of these distinctions were fairly obvious, such as a defensive war or a war of conquest. We talked about the concept of preemptive war. The more interesting discussions were around the moral dimensions of war. I remember a particularly striking observation that the colonel made.

"There is," he had said, "no such thing as a *good* war. When all the reasons and justifications are put in the balance against the horrors and violence, the destruction and waste, the idea of a good war simply does not hold up. But that does not change the fact that some wars are unavoidable simply *because the alternative, declining to go to war, would be worse than the sufferings caused by the war itself.* Life under the Nazis would have been such a situation. Such a war is *necessary.*"

A war that was necessary for one's survival is a simple enough idea. But he saw that there was also such a thing as a *just* war, one that must be fought for moral reasons. It might be a response to unprovoked aggression, the invasion of a friend's territory, or your own, or to prevent a heinous crime like genocide. The American participation in the Second World War was *both* necessary and just.

The question of the just and the necessary opened the issue of the atomic bomb. The subject came up naturally enough because the location of the original atomic test, called Trinity Site, was only eighty miles away. Shortly before my discharge, I paid a visit to Trinity, a sort of pilgrimage. I went in my government Plymouth, rattling along miles and miles of gravel road, kicking up a plume of dust behind me. I don't remember whether the site was officially open to the public yet, but the road was marked and my Intelligence Corps credentials would serve me if I were stopped. I encountered no interference. At the site, I saw only a primitive pyramidal monument of volcanic stone and a work crew building a chain link fence. Not much to see.

Was it a war crime to have incinerated two non-military targets, killing more than 130,000 civilians? It met the standard definitions of war crime: a terror attack on a non-combatant population. Through conversations with the colonel, however, I moved into an awkward sort of understanding, one in which I was required to hold conflicting ideas. He made me see the question in a wider context: the confluence of military and political considerations in the summer of 1945 was so particular that an absolute moral judgment would be hard to form. To win the war had been seen as absolutely *necessary*. The Japanese showed no signs of surrendering, and with the terrible American losses that had already resulted as US forces advanced, island by island, on the way to the Japanese home islands, it would have been, *from the American perspective*, a dereliction of a moral responsibility to the American people at home and to American soldiers not to have used a weapon that could end the war quickly. The bomb, framed by those circumstances, had been *circumstantially justified*. After reflection and much reading over the years, I have come to accept that this way of framing the issue had been inescapable. The alternative, if the bomb had not been used, an invasion of the Japanese home islands that would have been enormously costly in American lives, was worse than the guilt that would inevitably follow if the weapon was used. It was a matter of choosing which guilt to accept.

Nevertheless, the thought that such a terrible act could be circumstantially necessary and, indeed, justified opened up an intellectual abyss for me. I had until this time thought that there could always be found some cluster of moral absolutes that would stand up, like granite monoliths, impervious to all arguments and in all circumstances. This certainty had come from my vaguely Christian upbringing or from Plato perhaps. But these notions dissolved in the corrosive realities of the Second World War. Those certainties were dispersed, never to reassemble. That there could be different moralities, that moral judgment was relative to where one stood when making it, was a difficult idea for me to accept. I was and am still of two minds about the bombing of Hiroshima and Nagasaki; I accept that the two minds cannot be reconciled. The idea of the *good* war no longer had a place in my thinking. But to the ideas of a *just* war and of a *necessary* war, I added *circumstantially justified.* The difficulty involves the question of who, what sort of man or woman, makes these sorts of decisions. Does one turn the task over to a representative legislative body, for instance, the voice and mind of a democracy? From Thucydides we learn that the *demos* of Athens, the voters, regularly approved evil acts. And in my time and in America, legislative bodies have devolved into partisan factions which have not the moral compass, the maturity, or the intelligence to make judgments such as these. What then? A conundrum to be tackled by philosophers, not politicians. And where does one find real philosophers?

It was through these reflections that I came to the conclusion that there is a level of reality in which moral principles do not apply. War is that reality. Bringing war into the great calculation, as part of the overwhelming question, is like imagining a universe parallel to ours, but one in which there is no gravity.

At Trinity site, some vegetation, low and meager, had reestablished itself. The wind blew. I could hear snatches of the workmen's conversation between sighs of desert air. I picked up a little glob of what was called bomb-glass, the greenish droplets of melted sand that the blast had produced. Several years later, I read that these were still radioactive and should not be handled. I gave mine a ceremonial disposal in the Taos, New Mexico landfill, where, along with empty pop bottles and road kill, it was eventually covered up with dirt.

I ended my three years of military service as a buck sergeant (three stripes) with an honorable discharge. I had fulfilled an obligation. As a taxpayer, I was shocked by the financial waste that I observed. I had found pleasures: getting to know the Mexican border and exploring the abandoned mining towns of New Mexico; amateur archaeology, digging broken bits of pottery out of the yellow dirt, hoping to find some small treasure; photography, which was the Army's lasting gift to me; and playing in the arroyos with my motorcycle. There was, however, nothing in the work that was interesting and if it hadn't been for my occasional conversations with the Air Force colonel, my intellectual life would have dried up completely. Emotionally, I was kept alive and green by Elizabeth, her daughter, and the comical dog. Despite all of that, it was a slack time. I ate my lunches at fast food joints, and gained weight. I had allowed myself, like the hibernating desert toads, to settle into a lifeless state, a state of limbo, wanting above all not to be noticed by the system and sent somewhere else. I felt dissatisfied with myself and vaguely ashamed.

19

Interlude

It was January; the desert nights were cold, clear, and filled with stars.
The mornings were so bright that even Juarez, across the river, seemed
almost beautiful, not poor and grim, but exotic, like a city in North
Africa. My mood was good. I signed some papers and sold my uniforms.
I was a civilian again, a free man. Because I had decided to serve three
years instead of two, I was not eligible to be recalled, a decision, given
the buildup in Vietnam, that turned out to have been the better one.

We moved to the village of Arroyo Hondo. The little adobe house that
I had purchased a year before was livable. We moved in and began the
improvements: a poured concrete floor, polished and stained earth colors, a
kitchen area in the living space, a sink. Elizabeth painted the pine kitchen
shelves white and the window frames blue. We had only a fireplace for heat,
but in February that proved inadequate so a gas space heater was installed.
Slowly I came back to life. It was as if the rains had come and I, the hibernating toad, had emerged from his motionless state. With this sense of
greater control over my life came a greater degree of self-knowledge.

I have, as everyone has, what Andre Malraux called *un misérable petit tas
de secrets,* a miserable little pile of secrets, and these I will keep to myself

and will no doubt die with them. From a writer's perspective, to do so seems a waste of good material, but it is a precaution against irreparable loss of something important: reputation, perhaps, something intangible we pass on to our children. But since having a reputation for valuing truth is part of the legacy that I would pass on, describing myself *en plein air* seems necessary. The history of my relationship with Elizabeth fits into that category.

Elizabeth and I lived together for nearly eighteen months after I left the army, but it was a strange time, because we had decided to separate and knew that it would be our last time together. We loved and liked each other, but we had looked as far as we could into the future and we recognized that it was possible that the difference in our ages might and, probably would, eventually become an issue. I found Elizabeth desirable and was tempted to hold her while that lasted. But if I had, and then in fifteen years, I lost "interest" in her—those seem cruel words to write, even now, so many years after Elizabeth's death—I would have used up some of the best of her remaining years. At forty, as she was then, she had every possibility of finding a new relationship. These were issues that we should have given more thought to in the beginning of our relationship, at least before we married. When I say "we decided" to separate, I mean I decided. The guilt is mine.

Our relationship had been distorted by the basic training phase of my military experiences. Depressed, I'd gone from loving freely to needing. The need contaminated the love. I had been unable to admit that I was wounded, that I needed her. Masculinity, as a role, required that I deny that need had entered into my relationship with Elizabeth. The result was that we married; the wiser thing would have been to have let things evolve and see where we ended up. It turned out to be a painfully difficult place. After some time in New Mexico, we returned to New York and rented an apartment in the west Village. We did this as a conscious effort to make the transition to living separately as painless as possible.

* * *

During that New York City sojourn, the summer of 1967 to May of the following year, I became political, increasingly aware of the consequences of politics and more engaged. The war in Vietnam was the most important issue for me. Soldiers and journalists who had been there and who had seen through the Pentagon's lies were telling tales of violence and destruction on an unprecedented scale. Napalm. Chemical defoliation. Helicopter gunships that were allowed to kill anything that moved, human or animal. The many thousands of tons of bombs dropped on jungles, rice paddies and villages. The scale of the violence, the greatest military machine in the world savaging a peasant society, appalled me.

The American military proclaimed that things were going well. The politicians fell back on their talking points. Some probably believed what they were saying on camera, all certainly needed to, but for most it was ego and face-saving: they had already invested so much of the public treasure and so much of their own reputations in the project that they could not admit that they had made a mistake. They'd been wrong in their understanding of the historical background and wrong in their conception of a remedy. The U.S. could not provide a remedy; the U.S., like France before, was the problem. Unable to admit their error, they doubled down on the bad bet and made a conscious effort to deceive the American people. And worse, they deceived themselves. "Whom the gods would destroy, they first make mad," wrote Sophocles.

I no longer had any doubts. I saw the war as a perversion of the strength that America had shown in the Second World War. I participated in a number of anti-war demonstrations. On the steps of the Battleship Maine Memorial at Columbus Circle, I joined a peaceful crowd and carried a sign. There were thuggish hecklers; police, one could tell, wouldn't have provided much protection. The Maine monument was an appropriate venue because it memorialized something that didn't happen but had been used to justify a war, just as the Tonkin Gulf incident had been used. The Air Force colonel, my mentor in Alamogordo, a man caught between three hard places—career, duty, and conscience—had said he thought the

Tonkin incident had been exaggerated in order to justify expanding the air war to North Vietnam. He could not go further than say "exaggerated," but I understood him. The Maine incident, the blowing up of an American battleship in Havana Harbor, now understood to have been a boiler accident, was the justification for the Spanish-American War, the war that marked the beginning of American expansionism. Fanned by Hearst's right-wing press— the pre-cable equivalent of Fox News—the public demanded revenge; and the war party in America, with empire in mind, got what they called "a splendid little war." Guantanamo Bay Naval Base, today's infamous Gitmo prison, was among the spoils of that war. The Philippines were the big prize. Deception as an excuse for a war of choice was becoming an American habit.

My window into the war in Vietnam came from in the field reporters in *The New York Times*, which I read carefully. There was also a small circulation political newsletter called *I.F. Stone's Weekly* that I bought at the news kiosk at Sheridan Square. I also bought the *Baltimore Sun* to follow the war through the reporting by Peter Arnett. I was so eager to read these periodicals that I would sit on a bench in the little park as soon as I had them in my hands. The poet E. E. Cummings lived in the neighborhood and I would see him on a neighboring bench, sitting in the spring sun, reading. I admired his poetry. A poem about Buffalo Bill might easily be about America.

> *Jesus*
> *he was a handsome man*
> *and what i want to know is*
> *how do you like your blueeyed boy*
> *Mister Death.*

* * *

Izzy Stone (1907-1989) remains one of my heroes. He guided me through the thickets of political corruption, corporate greed, and government propaganda. I began to see things in the contexts of political ambition and financial interests. Most importantly, I began to see things through the lens of what I would call rational skepticism: little is as it appears and very little is what they say it is. That is how I saw both the Johnson and Nixon presidencies. I was now certain that my government lied regularly. I saw, too, that the American military, the institution that I had thought noble because of what it had accomplished in the Second World War, now behaved very badly. Thus, when an American commander said of the little Vietnamese city of Ben Tre, "It became necessary to destroy the town in order to save it," (a Peter Arnett dispatch from 1968) I understood that, morally and intellectually, America had stepped over the line that separates the just from the unjust, the sane from the mad. America, indeed, had become quite mad.

The country was starkly divided on the issue of Vietnam, with the opposition passionate and coherent, but those in power, from Johnson to Nixon, chose to hear nothing but their own propaganda. The Vietnamese, the American leadership believed, would someday welcome our gift of democracy, but they were, in the present moment, a people too ignorant to understand, and, more to the point, they were too short, too poor, and too skinny to stand up to the might of the American war machine. Might makes right seemed the underlying logic of American politicians—except for William Fulbright, Frank Church, Mike Mansfield, Gene McCarthy and a handful of others who resisted. But the Vietnamese did stand up and because their cause was the better one, they prevailed. The Tet Offensive of January 1968, a year after I separated from the Army, shook even the most committed American hawks. We watched all this unraveling on television. The My Lai Massacre, in March of the same year, though it did not become public knowledge until late 1969, was in the political and societal air, a nameless toxic leak out of a corrupt government, a leak that eventually became information and photographs. With My Lai, the American people's sense that they were involved in a righteous cause began to fall apart.

As the military version of events looked increasingly like delusion— "light at the end of the tunnel" was a favorite phrase—the government's version of the larger issues, the justification for the war, was unraveling. I could not see how a unified Vietnam, even if under Communist Ho

Chi Minh, posed even the smallest threat to the United States. Ho Chi Minh was a great admirer of the American Constitution and initially thought Americans would understand his cause. Failure to defeat the North Vietnamese was a threat only to military vanity, but nothing more. Since I could find no justification for the war, I could finally say, at the end of 1967, that I was of one mind about it.

I went looking for a way to do something more meaningful than carrying a sign at a rally. Inspired by *I.F. Stone's Weekly*, I started my own newsletter, a three-page mimeographed broadside that, oblivious to copyright issues, I called *Commentary*. I researched and wrote the newsletter in a little room at the top of a fifth floor walkup on Bleecker Street. This effort was so unlikely to have had any effect whatsoever that I am almost embarrassed to recount it. I actually thought that I could "liberate" minds captured by the ideologies and delusions that had led to the war. The minds I had selected were my parents' friends, an audience that would have shared few, if any, of my views. Why this unlikely audience? The *Southern California Blue Book*, the society register, was the only mailing list I could get my hands on. Since several of my pamphlets were in support of Senator Eugene McCarthy's 1968 presidential campaign, it is little wonder that my target audience was not interested. McCarthy was resolutely anti-war and thought it had created a grave moral crisis in America, not a position even the moderate Republicans of my parents' circle would have openly agreed with. My pamphlets were pretentiously over-written, because I was trying to sound older than I was, but they were not polemical or intemperate; nevertheless, I am sure they were tossed, unread, into the trash. I never heard a word of response from anyone on my mailing list. This effort no doubt contributed to my mother's view that I was an embarrassment. She never mentioned my quixotic newsletters.

These mini-broadsides changed nothing, certainly not the course of history, and probably not a single mind, but they were important because they were the first sign that my life would, from time to time, become politically active. Initially, the activism was the anti-war movement; later, in much more depth, it focused on environmental and social justice issues. Vietnam was a watershed event for me and, I remain convinced, for the American republic. Nothing, since the Civil War and the battle over slavery, had so divided the nation. These divisions remain, now hardened into intractable partisan positions, class warfare of rich vs poor with the poor falling ever further behind, that have made the United States almost ungovernable. For me, it was a profound disillusionment. Our elected leaders, our generals, would lie to the country and to save face would waste the lives of thousands of my fellow countrymen, fifty-five thousand by the end of it. For no justifiable reason. For delusions of military glory. Both Johnson and Nixon declared that they would not be the first American president to lose a war. I wanted to believe John F. Kennedy would have had the courage to admit the mistake and put an end to the suffering, but this is, of course, unknowable. I am firm in my conviction, however, that the suffering inflicted on the Vietnamese people is unpardonable.

When I left the military in January 1967, the antiwar effort shared the public space, politically and emotionally, with the civil rights movement. They seemed related, but how I could not have said until Martin Luther King Jr.'s extraordinary speech about the war in April of that same year. From the pulpit at Riverside Church in New York, he called the war "unjust, evil and futile," and by describing its toxic effects on American society and America's spirit, he showed us that ending an unjust war and ending the unjust treatment of black people could be understood as part of a related struggle, a struggle against attitudes about America's supremacy on the world's stage and white supremacy at home. Eventually I would come to see that environmental issues could be understood in a similar frame. Societies always favor a notional *superior self* that has the right to lord it over, to dominate and exploit, the "other." The "other" in one context can be people of color, or the poor, or a foreign nation. And to this superior self, *nature is always other*, always not-self. It is just rocks, trees, rivers, and creatures. It has no value until it can be monetized. Surely something better can be done with such things, the thinking goes, than just letting them be.

During this period of fledgling activism, Charles Wells, my protector during the unhappy Amherst College days, came by the apartment. He brought a 33 RPM record with him.

"Mudd," he said, with a wild sort of urgency, as if I might die if I ignored his message, "you must hear this."

The album was Bob Dylan's *Bringing It All Back Home*. I had heard Bob Dylan's name but knew nothing more. Wells was right about it being necessary. Listening to that album, which he, Elizabeth, and I did on the spot, was electrifying. It was as if the tongue of flame had descended. In the swirl of unexpected and illogical images, the shamanistic rhyming and rhythms, I experienced something that has influenced me ever since. It was as if previously unknown aspects of my being, quarks of the soul, popped into existence. Dylan changed forever the way I would *feel* the world. Not see it or interpret it, for that came through knowledge and study, but feel it. The music was part esoteric intoxicant, like absinthe, and part raw America, like backcountry moonshine. It was what I needed. Dylan, America's Baudelaire, adrift in a leaky boat on the bayous of the national narrative, its dark places.

The last issue of my newsletter, May of 1968, was a reflection on the assassination of Martin Luther King Jr. When, in June, Robert F. Kennedy was assassinated, I was too disheartened to put out another issue. The assassination within a five-year period of three Americans whose lives and messages represented the America that I believed in struck me as more than the republic could endure. It was more than I could.

The car, a silver mustang with red vinyl seats, was loaded with virtually everything I owned. Only my books would follow, in cartons by truck. Charlie the Basset Hound sat on the passenger seat. Elizabeth came down in the elevator with me. We stood on the sidewalk, West Twelfth Street, barely a block from the New School where we had met four years earlier. It was early afternoon. We'd had lunch together. We looked at each other, both determined not to cry. When I got into the car, she reached in and patted Charlie for a moment, then said, "take care."

"You, too," I replied. These were the last words we ever exchanged.

And so, in May 1968, I was heading back to New Mexico, a place that seemed not quite the United States, more Hispanic and Native American than white America. I listened to Dylan on tape. *Like A Rolling Stone* was the mantra that made those two thousand miles go by. "With no direction home," the song says. I felt that I already had a home and was on my way to claim it, to settle into it. But the Dylan poetry in that iconic song travelled along with me. "With no direction home" has been a part of my entire life history, the history of my soul as I've wandered in the world. I must have known it at the time.

As I crossed the state line at Tucumcari, I felt a surge of joy. I had made it. At the same time, I felt a great sadness. I stopped the car in a rest area and got out to walk Charlie. We walked out in the sagebrush, Charlie discovering all sorts of wonderful new scents. I began to sob. I had lost Elizabeth. I had left her. In that act, I lost what remained of childhood innocence. To this day, there is a thorn in my heart that will not come out, and I think that it should not.

HM in the army, 1963

Elizabeth, El Paso, 1965

Part IV

The Pursuit of Happiness

The effect of liberty is to let individuals do what they please: we ought to see what it will please them to do, before we risk congratulations.

Edmund Burke, *Reflections on the Revolution in France*

20
New Mexico

On Army business one late November day, near the end of my enlistment, I had found myself stranded in the little town of Silver City, New Mexico. I had expected to be back in El Paso by suppertime, but an unexpected snowstorm had closed the roads and I was forced to spend the night. Having brought nothing to read, I went to the public library, and there, guided by nothing more than curiosity, I picked from the shelves Virgil's *Georgics*, a description of rural life in Italy circa 35 BCE. And so, on a winter night in 1966, lying on a motel bed, I read the poem. I read it as a bucolic idyll, a paean to the life of the farmer, hardly noticing that Virgil made it clear that farming was hard work and that things can go badly wrong. But the opening lines gave me hints of what a life close to the soil and ruled by the seasons might be like.

> *What tickles the corn to laugh out loud,*
> *and by what star to steer the plough,*
> *and how to train the vine to elms,*
> *good management of flocks and herds . . .*

I stayed up late that night reading. From time to time I went to the window and watched the snow fall, a silent blanketing of parked cars, halos around the street lights. In the morning I returned the book to the library; by noon, the snowplows had cleared the roads and I drove home. On that drive, I decided that when I got out of the Army I would become a farmer. The summer jobs on my father's ranch had planted the seed in me. I liked that sort of life. But it was the line in Virgil, "by what star to steer the plough," that had closed the deal.

I was fourteen when I made my first visit to the American Southwest. I had been walking in the desert and came upon an anthill, a symmetrical pile of tiny stones that looked like a miniature pyramid, and there on the surface was a spot of bright, blue-green turquoise, but not a chip; it was clearly something made by the human hand, a bead. It was perhaps 3/16 of an inch in diameter with a little hole bored in the center. I was told later that its presence on the anthill indicated that an ancient burial lay somewhere nearby and the excavating ants had brought it up from a burial chamber. The ants were red, the sort that bit, so one usually gave these anthills a wide berth; I plucked the bead from the anthill, disturbing their operation as little as possible, and brushed the warriors that had already detected an intruder from my boots. I managed to keep the bead for many years. Somewhere in a lifetime of many moves, it was lost, but that tiny turquoise bead remains in my consciousness as oddly large and important: it reinforced and reactivated the vision of the past, Mesopotamia, that my grandfather had shown me when I was ten. There developed a personal and mysteriously emotional aspect to my interest in the past. I wanted there to be some sort of historical foundation to my life.

I had a memory of an idyllic California. It was so long ago that it seems almost ancient history. When I was growing up, before the freeways, the smog, and the sprawl, I thought Southern California was Eden. Who would ever want to leave such a gentle and benign place? But I did.

Northern New Mexico, where I ended up, has a deep past, but in the present it is a harsh place. There is little rain; the summers are hot and the winters long and cold. The land is either flat and arid or steep and uninhabitable for five months of the year because of deep snow. There is a thin crust of soil on the mesas and even less on the mountains. The mesas are ancient lava flows, black basalt, 600 feet thick; nothing grows on them but some cactus and a woody shrub called sagebrush, a sturdy weed that survives where nothing else can. This is a man-made landscape: thousands of square miles of native grassland had been ruined by vast herds of sheep in the nineteenth and early twentieth centuries. Manuel Ortiz, who was to become one of my neighbors—who lived to be 102—told me that he remembered grass as high as the step on his grandfather's buckboard. Streams from the mountains have cut narrow valleys into the basalt and only in those valleys does anything grow.

In a winter with inadequate snowfall, which happens often, there is not enough water to irrigate the summer fields. If the mountains are dry, there are no berries, so the bears come down to rummage in the apple orchards. But, it seems, there has always been enough to maintain a delicate balance between human needs and deprivation. Subsistence, perhaps, is the name that best describes that balance. After living for a while in this world, I came to think that "enough" is a profound philosophical concept, a counter value to those of the consumerist dominant culture.

The little farming communities are poor. I settled in Arroyo Hondo, north of the town of Taos some ten miles. Fences are patched and re-patched with pieces of baling wire. Rusting pickup trucks sit in people's yards, indicators not of indifference or carelessness, but of frugality, the possibility that some part can be salvaged, a replacement that might keep the successor pickup truck on the road for another year. The people of the villages don't have the resources to vanquish scarcity, to build a dam, for instance, or to defeat winter with greenhouses, but they resist. I saw a sort of heroism in the lives of the Hispanic people who accepted me as their neighbor. It was a generous thing to do. I was an Anglo outsider, too young at twenty-eight to be taken terribly seriously. I knew nothing about the kind of life I seemed determined to have and there was no other place on earth where I wanted to be.

The spaces are vast. The horizons are empty and distant, like the sea. When the snow melts in the spring and the water comes down into the valleys from the mountains, the fields of alfalfa turn green; the sweet corn, squash, and chili peppers grow; the little apple orchards flower and bear fruit.

The town of Taos has its own sort of beauty, not clean and white like the orderly little towns of New England, but more in the way of a medieval village in Morocco: mud-colored houses, a haphazard network of lanes that radiate from the central plaza as if searching for the little farms that surround the town, roads like the roots of a plant seeking water. Today, the roads are paved and the original settlement is adulterated, with typical American carelessness, by strip malls, fast food restaurants, motels, and gas stations. But the four-hundred-year-old soul of the town remains; still dusty and slightly off kilter. It is an old town, older even than Plymouth Plantation in Massachusetts.

Older still is Taos Pueblo, the town of the Taos Indians, just two miles north. It has been inhabited continuously for perhaps one thousand years. But exactly how long, no one knows because the Taos tribal government will not allow archaeological digging. They are a farming people, always have been, and require no affirmation of what they already know, that they were the first people to settle in the valley. Whether they were the same people as the hunter-gatherers who made up the earliest human presence is unknown. Their village is a gentle sort of castle made of adobe mud which they restore each year lest it wash away. It has protected them as a people and a culture through vicissitudes that would have demoralized and dispersed a less resilient people. First there was the settlement in 1615 by the Spanish, with their demanding religion, which they adopted to avoid the harsh methods of conversion that the Spanish practiced in other parts of the New World. They survived the raids, two hundred years of them, by Comanches riding horses stolen from the Spanish. They survived the occupation in the 1840s by the Americans who had stolen the territory from the Mexicans. And they have endured the artists—there have been many over the years— who found them picturesque and painted them, who might have stolen their souls, but weren't allowed to. And finally, there are the tourists who come year after year to see what hardly exists anymore in the United States, a glimpse of the original America, a people that has not been assimilated into oblivion.

Part of Taos' appeal for me was its foreignness. The state of New Mexico is itself a bit foreign and Taos county is out on *its* margins. It is "The North," underpopulated and underdeveloped. But its relative irrelevance in the grand schemes of the United States, and its distance from the concerns and ambitions of the modern world, have protected its unique character: Hispanic Catholic, Native American with spiritual practices rooted in nature, and Anglo-Americans with Bohemian eccentricities that they themselves see as a kind of superior normality. There is an unresolvable friction of races and cultures that usually doesn't much matter. Assimilation doesn't happen because no one wants it. A rich disharmony: a diversity of peoples and interpretations of life given unity by the extraordinary beauty of the land and sky, a sense of the sacred, though each group has a different way of describing that quality.

Pueblo Peak, 12,300 feet high, dominates the landscape. To many of us who have lived near it, beneath it, the mountain seems to live, as if it has a heartbeat. This expansion and contraction is that of time itself, and it is very slow, perhaps one pulse each one hundred years. The birds, bears, pines, aspens, deer, beaver, chokecherries, are all carried along in a great slow current. The Mountain is like an eternal thought. It was, I sometimes felt, the only thought that I would ever need.

My little farm had eleven acres of irrigable land in the valley of the Rio Hondo. The community of Arroyo Hondo consists of houses, some adobe and some cinder block, a few mobile homes, each has a little strip of farmland, strung out along a single road. There is a post office, a bar, and a church that was built in the early nineteenth century. The Rio Hondo, really more of a stream, comes down from the mountains, runs the length of the valley, and empties into the Rio Grande two miles to the west.

The little adobe house where I lived when I first settled in the valley was probably eighty years old, had a pounded-earth floor, and only two windows. I learned, sometimes by trial and error, more often under tutelage from my neighbors, some basic building skills, plastering, carpentry, and plumbing. It had no indoor plumbing except for a sink. I built an outhouse some fifty feet away, an inconvenience in a snowstorm. In a similar learning mode, I worked the land. I bought a used tractor, John Deere green but the paint faded and chipped, and turned fields, long neglected, into pasture and alfalfa. A crop of stones, glacial rubble from an ancient geological age, emerged from the fields after each plowing. I piled them on the sides of the field; they looked like petrified potatoes. The roots of the sagebrush resisted the plow, so I had to dig them out by hand, one by one. I made little piles of these gnarled and twisted creatures, aliens almost, and I burned them. At the end of each day, I was physically exhausted, but I felt strong. My hands were calloused. I worked until the sun dropped below the San Juan range to the west. The Sangre de Cristos, less than three miles away, remained luminous long after the sun set. In May there was still snow on the peaks; in June, the Hondo was full of the spring melt; by August, it is too modest a stream to be called a *rio*. It snowed sometimes in May and sometimes it didn't. Yet it always seemed the same. Time seemed circular; it encompassed the course of a day and nothing more. It was not historical, not a part of any larger narrative, neither Spain's, nor America's.

The irrigation ditches, the *acequias*, early 19th century marvels of folk engineering, are the artery that brings lifeblood to every farm and family in the valley. The men of the village come together each spring and clean the ditch with shovels and machetes. I was one of the men of the village; many who joined were teenagers so I didn't feel quite so much the greenhorn. We shared the water through the summer. We had conflicts with the village upstream, but among ourselves, few. Each took from the ditch only as much water as the *mayordomo,* the ditchmaster, an elected officer, allowed. Linked by the water and the responsibilities that came with it, I became a member of the community. This was the first experience of community that I had ever had. The drama of water in these valleys is wonderfully told in John Nichols' novel called *The Milagro Beanfield War.*

Irrigating the fields was hard work. When my fields were dry and the alfalfa wilting, I would open the gate in the ditch on my designated day, and, wearing rubber boots, with a shovel as my only tool, I would guide the water across the top of the field, directing it, rivulet by rivulet, making sure every square foot of the field was soaked by the end of the day. I began to think of the cycle of the farmer's year as being a sequence of sacramental acts. The plants drank the clean cool water and returned to life; the shriveled leaves plumped up and the stems straightened. They were comforted. I thought of the goddess of the Americas, the Virgin of Guadalupe, who brings fecundity and comfort to a hard place and to hard lives. Her image is ubiquitous in New Mexico. By July, the alfalfa would have reached maturity and it would be time to bring in what I had sowed; my seeds had fallen on ground that was indeed rocky, but they had taken root and had rewarded my efforts.

Mowing was a meditation: hours on a tractor moving slowly through fields of alfalfa. I had one of the few tractors in the valley so I mowed fields other than my own. The sky became more than atmosphere or weather; it was the roof of Heaven— or it was Heaven's floor—but no matter how I envisioned this architecture, it was a sky infinitely more beautiful than the sky in every other place that I knew. The skies over Los Angeles were now gray with smog and scarred with contrails. Ours was a sky like Giotto's, dark lapis at night and jeweled with stars, pure *azul* and transparent by day. It may have lacked Giotto's angels, but it seemed, to me who had no religion, to be a holy sky. The earth below was exceptionally lovely and, in its own stubborn and unyielding way, was good.

I watched the plants fall. The sound of the reciprocating blades, the smooth scissoring of steel through the alfalfa, an unvarying rhythm that suggested the running of a stream over rocks, was as calming as the cloudless sky. The smell of new mowed hay was an incense that was integral to the ritual of those harvest days. Then the alfalfa, lying as the blade had left it, would stay on the ground for a week, drying. During that week we prayed, not for rain as we usually did, but for sun. Then, when the moisture content was right, additional appliances in this service were hooked to my tractor. First was an elegantly simple assemblage of moving tines called a "side-delivery rake" (I especially liked the name of this device) and then a wire-tie baler. The hay bales, each weighing fifty or more pounds, had to be picked up with hooks, bounced on the knee into the back of a pickup, and finally unloaded and stacked. Fodder for cattle in the lean months of winter. By this time I had four steers.

Clodoveo Chacon, my closest neighbor, helped me with my unmanageable livestock. Mrs. Chacon kept a small store in the front room of their house, where she sold matches, loaves of Wonder Bread, and bottles of ketchup. Manuel Ortiz explained how things worked politically in the village and told me when to plant and when to harvest. Manuel, then fifty years old, his face sun-worn and lined, was tall and handsome with some gold dental work that showed when he smiled. His hair was black still. He had served in the Second World War, had landed in France on D Day, and had been in the first contingent of Americans to enter Paris in August of 1944. He showed me the tunic of his dress uniform hanging in his closet encased in drycleaner's plastic, the corporal's two yellow stripes unfaded. After the war, he returned to the valley where he was born and had left only one other time, to go to Albuquerque one hundred and thirty miles away, to pick up his son at the airport.

The lessons I learned came in the simplest forms. I regarded my hay baler as a sort of mechanical Zen master. The machine had its own set of rules—work, then stop. So, with pliers in hand, I would have to squirm into its innards, hay down my shirt, to tease out broken bits of wire from the machine's blades and pistons. My farming efforts were similarly frustrating. Half my little herd, two of the four, died in that first year. The remaining two, when they came to market, did not cover the cost of the original four.

21

Alarms and Excursions

I felt completely comfortable with the life I was making for myself. I was in the process of shedding my old skin, of becoming a different sort of person. I thought differently. At the same time, I no longer felt it necessary to deny where and from the kind of family I'd come from. That had seemed a necessary posture for a time. Now I could acknowledge California's place in my psyche. It was my inner version of having an "Old Country," my Ireland, my Italy. I was also able to acknowledge my debt to my family, recognizing that their histories had been honorable. I no longer thought of myself as rejecting my family but as writing a new chapter in our story. In that positive frame of mind, then, I planned a trip to Los Angeles. It was December.

My parents had divorced recently and I was curious to see how they fared. Their marriage had seemed a formal one, of another age almost, my father gallant, my mother a bit removed, accepting his attention as her due, but without reciprocating in the same vein; but then a lady, of the sort that my mother thought herself to be, wasn't expected to show strong emotions about anything, even her husband. There had been little physical affection, at least none I ever saw. I took this to be characteristic of the age rather than a sign of trouble. Since they never fought or argued or were openly critical of each other, when divorce came I was a bit surprised. My sympathies were with my father, but I wanted to treat them both fairly. At this point in time, I knew nothing of the specifics, only that my mother had initiated it.

I first visited my father. He lived in a luxurious apartment in Westwood. He offered me his guest room and I accepted. From him I learned the details of the dissolution of his thirty-year marriage. My mother, Vicky, as he always called her, had accused him of adultery, which he admitted was technically true. He had had a single encounter with an escort who had come to his hotel room at Claridge's in London. The elevator operator had asked him if he would like a woman and he, as nervous, he told me, as he had been on his wedding night, had said yes. It was the only time he had done this. He had felt so guilty that, on his return, he had confessed his indiscretion to his wife. He had hoped, he said, that confessing might nudge her into going into marriage counseling and that would allow him to address what he then told me was the most significant thing missing in their marriage, a sexual life.

My mother had filed for divorce within days of his confession. My sister Victoria revealed a few months later that our mother had told her that the divorce was already on her mind on the grounds of incompatibility. The incident with the escort was not the cause, but was rather a serendipitous excuse for a course of action upon which my mother had already decided. Given the speed with which things happened, I was sure that divorce proceedings were already in the works. My mother was not hurt by what he had done; insulted perhaps, but hurt, no. Being the betrayed wife enhanced her chances of a substantial settlement, which, as I found out from my father, she received. The house, all the art, and many millions of dollars.

My father and I, sipping bourbon, sat on his terrace overlooking the river of headlights along Wilshire Boulevard and talked well into the early morning. I told him about my divorce, my sorrow over it, and he expressed condolences, for he said that he had liked Elizabeth. I was eager to tell him how my life was turning out. Farming, after all, was a taste that I had acquired through him, from his love for his ranch.

As the night went on and whiskey eased his tongue, my father talked about his marriage to my mother. He had idolized her, but had been quietly unhappy for many years. He had not wanted to end the marriage and had thought that its principal shortcoming was perhaps inevitable given what we all had been taught to think of as our mother's delicate constitution. He had struggled for years, he said, to minimize the issue, telling himself that it was inconsequential in the big picture and that he was being selfish by wanting a sexual relationship with her. After all, he said, she'd given him five children, kept a beautiful house, and was beautiful herself. But that had not been enough, and so when the elevator operator opened the door to temptation, he saw his unhappiness, and he went through the door. I did not judge him. I understood. I mentioned the fact of his sleeping, for as long as I could remember, in the "guest room."

He nodded and looked unhappy. "I always felt humiliated by that," he said. "I never knew how it would appear to my children, but I guessed it looked just like what it was."

"I never once saw you kiss Mom on the mouth," I said, feeling embarrassed as I said it, for it acknowledged that I had paid attention to such things, "except for a little peck."

My father, with a surge of emotion I'd never seen in him before, said, "The woman in London was the first woman who ever really kissed me." He choked up. "And she didn't even pretend to love me." This was one of the most revealing things my father ever said to me. Memory of his awkwardness in the fossilized brothel of Pompeii came back to me. Sexuality must have always been frozen in him. This woman in London had opened something in his heart, awakened a part of himself that he had never known.

I asked him how my mother had gone about requesting the divorce. "She said nothing to me. She went to her mother's at the beach, something she often did. There had been no scene. This was on Friday. I received a letter from her lawyer on Monday at my office. It spelled out the grounds for divorce and instructed me to remove my personal effects, but to take nothing else. Vicky would be out of town for a few days."

Now I was shocked. I was having difficulty with the several versions of my mother that were emerging. I saw how sudden and even savage her action had been. There had been no discussion, no attempt at reconciliation. Virtually overnight, a subject that had never been discussed previously, divorce, became a fact, an irreversible course of action. I saw how threatening her lawyer had been: "Hoping to spare Mrs. Mudd the pain of scandal and protracted litigation" was the weapon the attorney had used. My father quoted it to me. I felt that my mother had dealt my father an undeserved blow. He had been a good husband, a good provider, always respectful, and had, for thirty years, given her everything she had ever wanted. Her response had a legalistic violence to it that seemed completely out of character for my mother. I was at this point unaware that she had already decided on divorce.

In this conversation, my father mentioned that he had had the impression that my mother had had an affair with my psychoanalyst, Dr. Frazier. My father had not accompanied her on that particular trip to New York. I asked him if he wasn't self-justifying by hinting at a possible similar transgression by his wife. But he felt sure that my mother had wanted him to have this suspicion. I could imagine the conversation that would leave him with that thought. I knew her ways. It would have been vague and elliptical allusions over cocktails, suggestions in tone, which might have produced this feeling of unease in my father. She, skillful always in such areas, would never have said anything that would have justified either a direct question or accusation. I could imagine that she might have hinted that Dr. Frazier had made a pass at her, thus proving that she was desirable. This, as a fantasy, seemed possible; I knew that she had a penchant for father-figure doctors. The story did not distress me because I could not imagine Dr. Frazier committing such a flagrant violation of professional ethics. And I remembered the comment that Dr. Frazier had made about my mother being a disturbed woman. Perhaps she had tried to seduce him, or at a minimum, flirted with him, hoping, through the promise of sex, to find out what I had actually said about her.

At about three in the morning my father and I turned in. I gave him a hug. He teared up. I slept with the window open, enjoying, in the minutes before sleep, the nocturnal murmur of Los Angeles, distant automobiles, thousands and thousands of them, singing with the crickets. It was a comforting sound, one that I remembered from my childhood.

Knowing how my mother had gone about the divorce made me angry, but I understood that I could not know everything about their relationship, and that it would be inappropriate to probe further. Perhaps keeping up appearances for all those years had been harder for her than I imagined. So I decided to let the matter go. We were living in the present, with new rules and new domestic arrangements, and since I had decided to keep my relationship with my mother alive, I approached our upcoming dinner with a degree of pleasurable anticipation. I didn't want to go feeling angry.

She was forty-seven years old, and, as I could not help noting when she opened the door, still beautiful. She was wearing an elegant full length robe, one of her at-home evening garments. It was white and cut fully so it flowed gracefully as she walked. She wore nylons and high heeled slippers with white puffs of feathers on them. Her hair, with only a few streaks of gray, was perfectly in place. Her wedding rings were gone.

I had dressed for the evening, wearing a corduroy sports jacket and tie and jeans that were clean. She told me that I looked attractive, the highest compliment she ever paid anyone.

As she led me into the house, she informed me that she'd given the cook the night off and had herself prepared one of my favorite meals, poached salmon with fresh peas. This was a significant gesture, one that said we were starting a new chapter in our relationship. We ate on trays in the living room, under Monet's *Japanese Bridge*.

Little had changed in the house. The Van Gogh sunflowers still hung over the little Georgian table in the entry where my father had always left his hat. I felt a moment of sadness, but it passed. It was time to move on. A fresh start for each of them seemed a good idea. I saw them as two adults making an adjustment.

My mother and I talked briefly, but only in platitudes, about the divorce. At one point, as if she thought that it was necessary to reassure me, she said, "I am your mother still." Then, as we inevitably did, we talked about art. I expressed my gratitude for having been taken to see the El Greco *View of Toledo* in the Metropolitan Museum. This opened the way to talking a little about my trip ten years earlier, the trip that had included Toledo, which, at the time, she had pointedly not wanted to hear about. Now she listened. I kept it brief, tailoring my narrative to conform to her requirement that life be without ugliness. I described the year, from the ocean crossing to the Middle East, in lyrical terms. In an effort to keep her attention, I invented things. I described, for instance, the elegant dining rooms of the great ship, which, in fact, Jim and I, eating in the second-class cafeteria, never saw except in brochures.

I described the landscape of the land of Canaan, a cleaned-up narrative, stripped of soldiers and barbed wire, that left an idyllic scene of fig trees in the courtyards of farmhouses. I said nothing about my illness or about anything remotely adventurous, moments in which she might have seen me as a whole person. My mother had always presented to me a façade and, quite consciously, I presented myself to her similarly, someone presentable whose story she could talk about with her friends. It was hypocrisy on my part, but, because it was temporary and so trivial, I didn't hesitate.

Nothing was said about the army years. Nothing asked, nothing offered. I mentioned my divorce and my mother did not pursue the subject. It was as if aspects of my life, from my emotional breakdown to the army to living in New Mexico, a state that her sort of people would never have any reason to visit, had been stuffed into a drawer that had been closed and locked. Yet, despite the disconnect with the realities of the last fifteen or so years, the conversation moved along. I understood that if I wanted to have any relationship at all with my mother, I would have to play by her rules. And, apparently, I did want some sort of relationship, even if it had to be shallow and formal. If I was to see her for dinner once or twice a year, it would cost me little to appear to be more like her than I was for a few short hours.

She suggested that we go to her upstairs sitting room for an after dinner drink and dessert. The sitting area was a part of her bedroom, separated from her king sized bed by a waist high bookshelf wall. I took this removal to the upstairs as her signal that she was preparing to retire for the night and that I should be ready to leave soon.

Two silver trays, each with caramel custard in a glass dish along with a snifter of fine cognac had already been prepared. We climbed the stairs. I took off my jacket and lay it over the arm of the sofa. We sat side by side, our trays on the coffee table, and continued our conversation, about art, her collection, her friends, her mother, about nothing, but it was nothing done so graciously one hardly noticed. Out of the window was the familiar view of the "Hollywood" sign.

I suddenly felt awkward. Out of the corner of my eye, I had noticed that my mother had kicked off one of her slippers and then the other.

"We used to watch *Ozzie and Harriet*," I said, "sitting on this same sofa, all of us, sometimes you and Dad too."

My mother did not respond to this evocation of an old family ritual. Conversation seemed to have ended.

She then raised her stocking-clad right leg, the one nearest me, and pulled up the folds of her gown as far as her hip. This exposed the ribbon and little wire and rubber clasps that held up her stocking. She reached down, unhooked the outer one, then the other, on the inside of her thigh. With her toe pointed outward, a gesture that emphasized the shapeliness of her leg, she rolled down her stocking. I watched, but didn't watch, just as I had done when, at age ten, I stood by her bathtub and mumbled my multiplication tables. I was frozen in fascination, as if in the presence of a dangerous animal. She bunched up the stocking and, without a word, handed it to me. The wad of sheer nylon seemed to retain a trace of body warmth. She then unhooked the other stocking and peeled it off. Now barefooted, she stood, smoothed down the folds of her gown, and put out her hand for the stocking that I held.

"I'll be back in a minute," she said, and disappeared into her dressing room.

This had all taken less than a minute to unfold. I sat, stunned.

Something inconceivable, yet utterly unmistakable, was happening. I was in a state that bordered on panic.

I moved to protect myself. I slid to the far end of the sofa. To occupy the space immediately next to me, so that my mother could not sit close enough to touch me, I took some magazines from the coffee table and piled them on the sofa, as if I had been reading them while she was in her dressing room. I constructed a dam, a levee, of magazines, *House Beautiful*, *Vogue* and *Ladies Home Journal*.

My mother returned to the sitting area. I had been right. No mistake. She was now wearing a beautifully layered sheer nightgown. I could just make out the areola around her nipples and could see, silhouetted against the urban glow through the window, her wide hips, and as she approached the sofa, the dark delta of her pubic region. I stood abruptly, before she had a chance to sit or speak, and said, "I see you are ready to retire. I'll be off."

In the midst of panic and confusion, I had the presence of mind not to use the word "bed." My mother put her hand on my arm and held me back.

I had to wrench my arm free. If she had not released me, I would have done whatever was necessary to free myself. As I reached the door, I turned back. I saw her standing in the middle of the room. The diaphanous nightgown revealed the curves of her body. Her face turned my heart to ice and at the same time it nearly melted. She was clearly in great distress, anguished, ashamed, rejected. I almost turned back, an impulse of compassion, to comfort her, but I knew how dangerous that would be. As I left, I hazarded a last glance and saw that her expression had turned to one of hate.

In a state of shock, I drove back to my father's apartment. I said nothing about the incident to him, thinking it would rob him of any last remnants of good feeling that he might have about the woman who had been his wife for thirty years. The next day as I flew back to New Mexico, with my emotions still roiled, an odd memory came back to me, a fragment from my twelfth year.

Before dawn on July 21, 1952, I was awakened by a rumbling sound, like a distant train, more felt than heard, but still a noise, and then, almost simultaneously, my bed, which was on coasters, darted out from under me, a lateral motion of at least three feet that dropped me to the floor. The bed then reversed and charged back at me, rolling over my head. I was not harmed, but I was certainly frightened. I jumped up and ran to the hallway to see the chandelier swaying, making at least a four-foot arc. The lights went on and my parents appeared at the doors of their respective bedrooms, my father in pajamas, my mother in a sheer nightdress, through which I could see her breasts and pubic shadow.

Two days after the quake, which was the most powerful earthquake California had experienced since 1906, my mother took me on the train to San Francisco to visit my godfather, Colbert Coldwell, my "Uncle" Colbert who was to the rest of the world the president of Coldwell Banker Real Estate. It was a trip that had been long scheduled, and since San Francisco had experienced no damage, we went ahead with it.

Landslides had closed the customary coastal route, so that evening the train went through Tehachapi, the little town near Bakersfield that had been the epicenter and by whose name the earthquake is still known. The summer days were long, so it was still light when we reached the town. There was damage to the roadbed, so the train slowed to a crawl as we passed through. I sat at the window, transfixed by the sight of such devastation. Buildings had collapsed; cars were buried under piles of brick. The fear I felt during the quake itself, the physical sense of panic, came back to me. As I stared out the train window, watching people picking through piles of brick, tugging at boards, looking for bodies or their property, my heart pounded.

My mother had another reason to go to San Francisco, as I learned after we got there. She went to visit an old friend who lived in Berkeley, a man who had often taken my mother out to dinner during the last year of war after we had returned to Los Angeles. This man had had a snappy yellow car that had a rumble seat, which is why I remembered him so clearly. When he came to call for my mother at my godfather's penthouse in Pacific Heights, he asked if I remembered the rides in his car during the war. I told him that I did. My mother and he went out for the evening.

Seeing the devastation caused by the earthquake and seeing a person from the war years, the period through which I lived with so much anxiety, was what made this trip so memorable. The confluence of these incidents—being tossed out of my bed, seeing the chandelier swaying, seeing my father come from his separate room, seeing my mother in flimsy bed clothes, seeing the ruins of Tehachapi, meeting the man whom I associated with the war—became, in my psyche, a single event.

What brought it to mind in the present circumstance, as I tried to process what my mother had just done, was the sight of my mother and father emerging from their separate bedrooms. The sexual implications were clear to me even then. Sex, the lack of it, had been the cause of my father's lapse in London and the subsequent divorce. I saw, or perhaps more accurately, I felt that there was an entire story inside my family's narrative that was unified by sex, sexual frustration, repression, and sexual secrets.

In the weeks after my mother's attempt to seduce me, I tried to talk myself out of it, to think that it hadn't happened. Ultimately, however, I was certain that I had not misinterpreted the incident. A confirmation came two years later when I mentioned it to my brother, John. He told me that he too had experienced an inappropriately sexualized encounter with our mother in the months immediately following the divorce, not as direct as my experience, but a conversation with her that he thought remarkably inappropriate. A disturbing incident, he said. By the time we spoke of it, he was a practicing psychoanalyst.

"I had," he told me, wryly, in that conversation, "lots of incentives to become a shrink." Several years later, he had written a letter to a fellow psychoanalyst about our brother, his twin, who was at that time experiencing significant difficulties—he copied me with this letter—in which he referred to the "severe psychopathology" of his birth family.

The "seduction incident" overturned every hope I'd had about my

trip to Los Angeles. I saw that my mother was an emotionally dangerous person. I was not sure the word "crazy" applied, but the conclusion
that there was something seriously wrong in her was unavoidable. The
incident reinforced my conviction that putting considerable distance,
psychological and geographical, between my mother and me had been a
good idea. It would be three years, before I would approach my mother
again. During this interval, I never wrote or called her and she never
contacted me. Whether I could preserve something of our relationship,
I was not sure, and for a time, I did not care.

I had more pressing things to think about. I returned home, to Taos.
And there, as Bob Dylan sang, things were a changing.

22

A Long, Strange Trip Begins

For the Hippies, Taos County was Shangri La, the magic kingdom in the mountains. By 1968 they had established communes at each end of the Arroyo Hondo valley. In the beginning I was amused and bemused. Plymouth Plantation, the first commune on the continent, the foothold of the Puritans in the new world, had morphed, across four hundred years, into ragtag assemblages of makeshift shelters and tipis called New Buffalo Ranch, Morning Star, and The Reality Construction Company, none of which were the least bit puritanical. Everyone was stoned most of the time and that condition was considered to be enlightened. These pilgrims were mostly young people in their late teens and early twenties. They came in broken-down buses and Volkswagens and on their thumbs, a progress on the roads that resembled the migration of displaced farmers during the Great Depression. They were not, however, fleeing either poverty or religious repression but from prosperity and the conformity of middle class life in America. They were not fleeing hardship either, but seeking it, and they found plenty: cold winters, little water, no plumbing, hostility from the "natives," and little appreciation for the ideals of communalism and the benefits of stimulants. They came also to escape the war in Vietnam and the draft. I would guess that most of the young men that I knew had discarded their draft cards; some were fugitives. The times in America, especially after May of 1968, when university campuses across America and Europe were convulsed by protests, were strange and tense.

Many, the true believers, came not in protest but as social pioneers. They intended to transform the whole of America by their example: sexual liberation, return to the land, to domestic essentials, a society of goodwill and good vibes. The Grateful Dead and Jimi Hendrix were the Pied Pipers, leading the children into the mountains; Bob Dylan was the philosopher king. Many accounts have described the period as a long Dionysian high. Few, however, if any, have examined the unsettling collateral effects on the Hispanic communities that, without being asked, played host to the newcomers; all was not happy. There was a great deal of friction, for along with the visionaries and sincere communalists came the dopers, fakers, runaways, criminals, mentally ill, the arrogant and rude.

Arroyo Hondo, "Hondo" as we called it, experienced an influx of perhaps one hundred permanent new residents in a matter of months. Behind them came hundreds more, drifters who appeared, stayed a while, then moved on to places like Drop City, Colorado, but who were always followed by more drifters. For several years Hondo was the most densely populated among all the gatherings of the tribe. It was a "scene" and I, at first, was swept up in it.

Marijuana was readily available and inexpensive. I liked the herb. It was a relaxant; it opened the door to a broad range of pleasures, some simple-minded; I remember watching a bird on a bough and thinking that I had solved one of the great questions. My attraction to marijuana faded after a few years, but I had found it liberating and psychologically health giving; it relaxed some of the inhibitions that my conservative background had pounded into me, relaxed them and ultimately dispensed with them.

I took up with a hippie girl. She, Paloma, lived at Morningstar commune on the mesa above the valley. She was an earth-mother type who had come to Taos with young children, all under six, the youngest still nursing. She was a big-breasted woman of Mexican heritage, a Los Angeleno like me. Exuberant, always cheerful, and utterly certain that life was unfolding as it should—and thus that there was nothing to worry about—she lived in a Plains Indian type tipi with the children. I had the impression that she received remittances from one or more of the fathers of her children, and so, by hippie standards, she was well off. She may have collected food stamps, but I am not sure.

She liked having a man around and she enjoyed mothering. I was the man of the moment. I often spent the night with her in the tipi, sleeping under a buffalo robe. The children crawled over the bed on their way to their piles of blankets and the infant shared the bed with us. After the children fell asleep, we enveloped ourselves in the buffalo robe. It wasn't love, but was friendly and fun; we were always modest and covered, conscious of the sleeping children. Besides, it was cold. I often stayed awake late into the night and, through the smoke hole at the peak of the tipi, I watched the stars. Sometimes, while all slept, I would sit cross-legged at the door of the tipi and, wrapped in the buffalo robe, listen to the silence of the mountain; only three miles away. It towered over us, over our little world of passions, pleasures, and resentments, over our petty but pressing concerns, such as where to score some good hashish for the morrow. Paloma's little children, each not much more than ten months apart in age, breathed quietly under their blankets; Paloma, her breasts leaking milk, slept the sleep of the innocent. I felt fondness for them, for all of them, but in the presence of the mountain I saw us as we truly were: of no real consequence. I felt even greater fondness for the sleepers because of this awareness. The Mountain, its stillness, its unchanging presence, put me, a most rational and scientific sort of person, in touch with something I can only think of as unknowable.

Change, contingency, and accident, however, were the laws of the daylight world, the only certainty. And so it was that when, one day, Paloma came down to my little house by the river and announced that she was going to make me a special meal, I felt uneasy. Even more cheerful than usual, she bustled around my simple kitchen; hers on the mesa was an open fire, while I, at least, had a four-burner stove. The meal, a traditional New

Mexican chili, was delicious, but, as it turned out, she had laced it with a hallucinogenic drug. She thought she was liberating my uptight self and thus doing me a favor. I thought she had poisoned me. I was sure I was going mad and was scared out of my wits. I was, in fact, for a number of hours, out of my wits. When I came down, I was furious. Trust broken, the relationship was over. It had lasted several months.

After this, I got my bearings and settled down. I had attempted to write poetry during my "stoner" period, hoping to approach Coleridge's flashes of opium genius. Most of it was gibberish. Only one remains, "A Song for the Angel," which appears in my fifth collection of poems.

In the beginning, as the communes were being built and populated, there was an authentic communal spirit. In a letter to a friend of mine, Laird Grant, the Grateful Dead's first roadie, I found this description of the moment. The writer is Max Finstein, a man who was to become a close friend and important figure in my life.

> …things very groovy, here. Chuck back from the Apple, feisty as ever and with a new old lady and we've decided to build a new pueblo. M. D. is going to let us have some territory and there's about 20 or more adults and kids and I feel very good about it. Between us and the Buffalo, there'll be 60 or 70 acres of land planted and that's a gob of food. We're going to build a big house. Randy and Anita, too, with us. We'll be near game also and have some decent guns among us. Tomorrow, we're going to go up and try to choose a house sight (sic) and, so, should be at work within the coming week. I've even managed to dig up a grand to help us on our way, but it ain't 50 and we'll be doing most of it by hand, as they say. All kinds of shit going down in town. Lots of heat and narks and hippies by the droves. But it don't get out here, where everybody is working… Dope scene clean here, excepting for the wanderers and that is a drag.

And it was groovy for a while. But there was trouble on the horizon. One summer afternoon, as an example, when I was in Mrs. Chacon's store buying a quart of milk, a rattling pickup truck pulled up in front. The driver, a shirtless young man with a wispy beard, earrings, and hair pulled into a ponytail, sat in the truck while a young woman got out. In the back of the truck were two dogs and three rather dirty children aged about four to seven. The screen door swung open, and the young Anglo woman entered. She wore the loose, long, skirt of flower-patterned cotton that was the informal uniform among the hippie girls. Her blond hair was matted into accidental dreadlocks, her hands were dirty, her feet bare, legs unshaved, and her halter top nearly nonexistent. She wanted to buy a box of matches. She might have been pretty, but, unwashed and her hair in tangles, she had done everything possible to obliterate any signs of it. Mrs. Chacon, with courtesy, sold her the matches. Her teenaged son, Albert, was behind the counter staring at the girl's breasts, but trying not to be caught doing it. After the girl left, Mrs. Chacon looked at me with an expression of indignation and apprehension. The scene encapsulates much of the tension and cross currents of those days and the years that followed. I knew something about the young hippie male in the truck. He had torn up his draft card and given himself a new name, something natural like "pine-top." Albert Chacon would be drafted several years later. I tried to help him get Conscientious Objector status, but failed. He went to Vietnam, survived, and came home, returned to the valley.

The communes on the mesa, half a mile from my house, were reached by a narrow and steep dirt track that crossed my land at the southern edge. One day, while eating my lunch under the little portico at the front of my house, I watched a white van creeping up the hill, and then, in an almost comical pantomime of catastrophe, it slid off the road and down into the ravine. I went to help.

No one was injured. I climbed down into the ravine and got down on my belly to inspect for damage to axles or frame. Across from me, on the other side of the vehicle, was another man making the same inspection. He was older, in his fifties, with a grizzled white beard. I knew him by reputation but had never met him. He was the "Godfather" of the Reality Construction Company, the closest thing that the commune would acknowledge as an authority. Under the van, he reached his arm across to shake my hand.

"Max Finstein," he said.

I can date this incident to the spring of 1969, because the van belonged to Chuck, who was "back from The Apple." Thus began an important relationship in my life.

I came to consider Max a close friend. He was a non-practicing Jew with leftist political sympathies. He was small and wiry, perhaps 5'6" with thinning white hair combed straight back over the top of his head. He smoked, holding the cigarette between two fingers and his thumb, and his fingers were stained with nicotine. Max had lots of friends in the American literary world, from Lawrence Ferlinghetti to Robert Creeley and Ed Dorn. Max was a poet and had published several books of poetry, but he was by emotional inclination an activist committed to social justice. To the poor, the black, and the immigrant, those marginalized in American society, Max had added the hippie. He was attracted to the utopian socialism of the movement: everyone was welcome; from each according to his ability; to each according to his needs.

But Max was also a realist. While the hippie youth believed "like, man, change will just happen" Max knew otherwise and was willing to engage with the local power structure. He was a natural mediator and networker; he did as much as anyone to cool off the social tension in Taos County. He'd been poor and he'd gone to jail for labor organizing in California. He had also been a heroin user and was a convincing spokesman against the use of hard drugs. Above all he had no dogmatic beliefs about either religion or politics; he cared about practical results. The village of Arroyo Hondo, for example, was able to buy a fire truck because Max raised the money and organized a legal entity that could accept it. I donated the land for the fire station and for a baseball diamond behind it.

Max and I forged our friendship cautiously; I came from a background that from his socialist perspective was "the wrong side of the tracks." But through our conversations about poetry and through simple cooperative projects, like getting the van out of the ravine, we forged a relationship that lasted until his death some thirteen years later.

One day a new Ford sedan appeared on my road. Such visits had happened before, usually government agents looking for someone thought to be living in the communes. Out of it stepped a man in his fifties, slight and balding, not a government agent, but an occasional guest of my parents at dinner parties. He had a pinkish complexion, skin that looked soft and very clean, and manicured nails. He explained that he had flown into Taos in his personal airplane expressly to see me.

"I've asked your mother to marry me," he said. Standing in the blazing sun, dust covering his polished black shoes, nervously eyeing the ocotillo cactus, he looked very vulnerable. "And I have come to ask your blessing."

William Coberly, my future stepfather, was a widower, a wealthy cotton broker, and I knew, from a conversation with my father, a member of the John Birch Society, the ultraconservative group that my father thought somewhat loony. As I got to know him, I discovered that he had political views that I could not believe any rational person could hold. He was also courteous and seemed quite decent. He told me that he had adored my mother for years.

I asked if he'd like to come in for a meal or a drink. No, he said, he needed to visit another of his wife-to-be's children. The gesture, flying all the way from Los Angeles to ask me for my mother's hand, was a piece of nineteenth century gallantry, and while it seemed mildly ridiculous, I admired him for it. He was marrying a woman with some "issues;" but by this time I had classified the attempted seduction incident as a moment of temporary insanity and since I had no desire to destroy my mother's chance for happiness, I said that I was delighted for them both. Perhaps this polite and proper man could work miracles. Off he went in his rented car, back to the Taos airstrip and into the clear desert air, a knight carrying his lady's favor on his sleeve.

23

The Trip Continues

Much had happened in the previous year: my parents' divorce, the interesting trip to Los Angeles and the bizarre encounter with my mother, the arrival of the hippie tribes, and with my mother's remarriage, her rehabilitation as a matron of society. I had begun the construction of a modern house. I needed to do a reset. I needed an adventure.

So, in January, 1969, I entrusted the house project to a contractor and after I had serviced my farm equipment, made necessary repairs to fence and ditch, I threw a sleeping bag in the front seat of my pickup truck and set out for Mexico City. I had no agenda. I went, as I had once before, to change perspectives and to test myself. The road, the unknown, was the metaphor for this process.

Down through the northern Mexican states, Chihuahua, Durango, Zacatecas, through Jalisco, with its endless rows of agave cactus, a regularity that flowed and curved over the hills like some obscure mathematical theorem. Arid beauty. I dodged burros, alive and dead, on the side of the road. Juggernaut trucks crowded me toward nonexistent shoulders. But the Aztec Lord of the Roads, a deity whose name I could not pronounce, kept me safe.

I pushed south into the state of Michoacán. I was drawn by a fascination with volcanoes, first kindled by the sight of Vesuvius and the visit to Pompeii. And I remembered seeing pictures, at age seven or eight, of a Mexican volcano that had appeared in a cornfield. The volcano was Paricutin, now extinct; I wanted to see it.

Ten miles from the dead volcano, I drove off the paved road to look for a concealed place to cook my dinner and spend the night. One hundred or so feet from the road, I got stuck. The ground was not earth; it was ash. The tires were spinning their way deeper and deeper into the powder. I got out shovel and axe and began to dig and cut branches from the sparse vegetation to place under the tires. Night began to fall and I lit a Coleman lantern.

In the last minutes before it was completely dark, I happened to look beyond the circle of lantern light and saw a little column of ten burros laden with firewood emerging from the spindly forest that had established itself in the ash. The burros were accompanied by a group of five men in white trousers and blouses. The men walked behind the burros, making it seem that the burros led the men. The burros' feet made little fluffing sounds in the gray ash. The men were Tarascan Indians; they had coppery skin and strong noses. They passed within one hundred feet of me, yet not one man looked at me or at my stranded truck. There was a dog with them and it, too, acted as if I did not exist. The scene was dreamlike: the volcanic moonscape, the patient little beasts of burden with their huge cargoes of sticks for the cook fire, the dark-skinned men with machetes in their belts, and me, the stranger who seemed to exist in some other dimension. I could almost believe that they were ghosts, or that I was. They disappeared into the night.

I resumed digging. An hour later, dripping with sweat and despairing of getting the truck out, I looked up to see an Indian man in loose white clothes standing beside me. He had been one of the woodcutters. His dark face was utterly serious; his eyes, black. He had in one hand a shovel and in the other a gourd full of water. I greeted him in Spanish. He replied in Tarascan. He spoke barely twenty words of Spanish. We began to work together, silently, surrounded by the yellow halo of light from the Coleman lantern.

By midnight, after nearly four hours of labor, we could move the truck backward a few feet at a time, but it would not climb out of its rut. The man, his shovel over his shoulder, made signs to indicate that he would be back after some sleep, when the sun returned. He disappeared into the night. I, forlorn, filthy, and exhausted, went to sleep in the back of the truck.

Before the sun was over the horizon, I heard a knock on the side of the truck. I awoke. There was my friend, looking fresh and alert. He gestured back toward the road. He had brought a man with an ancient dump truck that had a winch attached to it. He attached the cable to my rear axle and after a few tugs, my truck climbed out of its rut and sailed across the sea of ash to the roadway. I took out my wallet and gave the man with the truck the peso equivalent of ten American dollars. I then turned to my rescuer and began to count out some more pesos. He raised his hand and shook his head in a way that indicated he would not accept any money. I insisted, but he declined firmly. He remained the same quiet, serious man that I'd worked with through the night. He shook my hand and turned away, walking toward the truck. I looked around and noticed my Coleman lantern. I picked it up, called to him, and offered it. He gave me a slight, shy smile and accepted it. I remembered that I had a red metal can of fuel and this too he accepted. A few words in Tarascan, again thanks in Spanish, and they climbed into the old truck and were gone.

I walked back into the ash field and sat on the edge of the hole we'd made. Out of both exhaustion and a sort of joy I'd never before experienced, I began to weep. In this blasted landscape, I had encountered the simple grace and generosity that distinguish the best among us.

As I drove into Mexico City and joined the traffic on the Paseo de la Reforma, I was carried along the swollen stream of cars and taxis like a stick in a flood. Neither Los Angeles nor New York had prepared me for Mexico City. It was a feast of color, cheerful crowds, and mariachi, exotic smells from restaurant kitchens, an exciting place, and yet I saw it as an environmental disaster, the mega city nightmare. The air was so polluted that I never caught even a glimpse of the great volcano that rises above the city.

I stayed in the Polanco neighborhood, a random choice that renewed my interest in the war. The owner of the simple hotel was an elderly Jewish man who had fled Germany in 1934. Mexico had been hospitable to the fleeing Jews and the neighborhood was full of his co-religionists, all Germans. I took notice and, indeed, the older couples that I saw strolling in the park reminded me of old Jewish couples I was accustomed to seeing on upper Broadway in New York. For a week, I went to the museums and wandered. I felt at ease and was not lonely. I was content to be on my own and was looking for neither companionship nor excitement.

One evening in the Zona Rosa, I came upon an outdoor book fair; the woman who tended one of the stalls caught my attention. She had black hair and opaque dark eyes that indicated Indian blood, mestizo, as are most Mexicans. Her face, too, reflected the mixed lineage, traces of the high cheekbones, her nose not aquiline, but not flat either, a face beautiful, yet not conventionally so. She was different, arresting.

The bookstall specialized in poetry. There was a copy of Pablo Neruda's *España en el Corazon*, the book I knew so well from Spain, on a wire rack, so I had a ready topic of conversation. The first words that I exchanged with this woman were about that book and Neruda. Years later, after Neruda's death, she, Alicia, had a dream in which the poet had appeared to her and had given her a fountain pen that she was to give to me.

Alicia came from a middle class family, with socially conservative Catholic values, that was ruled, gently, by her widowed mother. Her father had been killed in a traffic accident when she was six. She had no education beyond high school. Her three brothers had gone to college, but the four girls went only to vocational schools to train for jobs considered suitable for women in the Mexico of the 1960s. She was then thirty-five years old, almost five years older than I was. She still lived with her family, had never married, and had had just one relationship with a man, but that had been brief, secretive, and unsatisfying.

As we talked, I sensed that this was a woman primed for life, needing to break free, and that she wanted me to see this quality in her. After thirty minutes of conversation, standing in the warm night, she had managed to sketch a picture of her previous life: a suffocating existence in a conservative but loving family, with no outlet for her energies, for her spirit. She knew that she had spirit.

"I was a kid of the city," she said, "I grew up playing on the streets. They called me *la callejera*, street urchin."

She was still that. She conveyed the idea that she could become a rebel given half a chance. She saw in me a man who might lead her into a wider, freer world.

We'd known each other all of four days when she took a leave from her secretarial job and we set off in my pickup for Acapulco. The hotels were full, so we slept in the back of the truck, swam in the ocean, and washed the salt off our bodies in the pools of hotels, sometimes having to evade hotel security staff. Tanned and happy, we ate all our meals on the beach under palm thatched roofs. Our conversations were in Spanish—she spoke no English—and although my Spanish was entirely functional, it was not nuanced, so the level of our emotional intimacy was limited, and, unhappily, would ever remain so. Nevertheless, at the end of two weeks, we felt we knew each other well enough to take a next step. She would join me in the United States.

Despite our cultural differences—and there were many including language and a deeply ingrained Catholicism—we were kindred spirits. She was certainly the most adventurous woman I'd ever encountered. I never doubted that we had fallen in love, but we had other reasons to move toward each other. She had found in me a path to liberation and personal growth, and I had found in her qualities that fed my tendency to rebel against my background. Her mixed blood, as well as her mixed cultural ancestry, the Indian and the European, were exotic and attractive. But those aspects were secondary; Alicia was courageous, beautiful, and desirable. Part of her charm, her appeal, was that she was an innocent, inexperienced in almost everything. I imagined that I would, in an image from one of Neruda's love poems, do for her what the spring does to the cherry tree.

In March I was back in the United States. Alicia would join me later.

She had made it clear from the beginning that she did not want to be my mistress. Nor did she want to end up being my housekeeper in an isolated farming valley in the United States. She insisted that she would come to the United States only if she could go to school. She wanted a college degree. I rented a small house in the Roosevelt Park section of the city of Albuquerque and she enrolled in the adult education program at the University of New Mexico, courses in English and Native American history. Our situation was a compromise between the life I lived in Arroyo Hondo and her desire for an education. About the possibility of something more permanent, living together, we would have to see. I came to see her on the weekends. I didn't go every weekend. Sometimes, when she had extra homework, she preferred to concentrate. She was a serious student.

In May of 1969 my oldest friend Jim showed up in Arroyo Hondo. He came with his wife, Deirdre, and her two children. I was glad for the company, but most of my energy still went to my farm. A black piglet had joined us. She was Jim's pig but she had the run of the farm and spent a great deal of time at my house. We were so impressed by the pig's intelligence; she was at least as smart as a dog. "The pig" became "she," and became a pet, running loose around our respective yards, gaining access to the house on her own, coming to eat when called. She was housebroken and quite clean. We called her *Mariposa*, "butterfly" in Spanish. Neither Jim nor I could bear the thought of eating her; and because of this unlikely fondness for a pig, I could see that I was not cut out to be a real farmer. Eventually she got too big. A 200 lb. animal putting hooved feet on one's lap, expecting an ear scratch, was actually hazardous. So Jim sold her to one of our neighbors for what he had initially paid for the piglet, just five dollars. By weight she was now worth over one hundred dollars, but she had given us more than that in pleasure, and much more in a lesson about the animal kingdom, about the souls of animals. Both Jim and I felt guilty about this betrayal of her and vowed to never again cross the social boundaries that separate farm animals from farmers. Years later when I read *Charlotte's Web* to my children, I would tell them about Mariposa. She too had been "SOME PIG!"

Generally, this was a quiet period. There was détente between the hippies and the village. The unrest over Vietnam and civil rights seemed remote. I practiced a sort of short term amnesia, a Zen of ignoring, something rather easy to do in a place like Northern New Mexico. Nothing clamored for attention, a condition that allowed me to think about something I'd always wanted to do, to step out of the world, not forever, but long enough and actually enough to experience something of my soul.

Heading west from Taos, then north from Tres Piedras, there is an extinct volcano, San Antonio Mountain, rising some 11,000 feet above sea level. Standing alone on the mesa, it may have been the source of much of the lava that makes up the plateau. It was to the geologist a "shield" volcano, because it looks like a shield laid concave side down; its profile thus is a broad, gentle curve. The mountain is named for Saint Anthony, the holy man who had retreated into the wilderness to escape the temptations of the flesh. Being tempted by the flesh was one of my weaknesses and, I suppose, Saint Anthony's retreat into his cave in the wilderness was vaguely in my mind. He was fed by the crows. I would take food with me.

The previous summer, I had discovered an abandoned fire lookout cabin on the top of the mountain. I was able to reach the peak in a four-wheel drive truck along a rutted track through the aspens. So I took some books, food and water enough for Charlie and me. I went to commune with sky and distance, with myself. It was a sort of exile, an experiment in total separation.

In the mornings, I cooked a proper breakfast of eggs on an open fire.

After this quiet and solitary meal, taken as the sun rose, I had chores. I'd brought a bundle of shingles and a bag of nails with me. I parked the truck on the side of the cabin, climbed from the roof of the truck to the roof of the cabin and worked on repairing the roof. When it rained, which it did every July afternoon, Charlie and I needed to stay dry. I'd brought a folding garden chair with me and after the chores were done, I read. Charlie wandered about, reading rocks and grass.

The afternoon was a time for what I considered the grandest show on earth. I sat in my chair and watched the skies spawn clouds. I could see hundreds of square miles of sky. I imagined the clouds as flotillas of ships, white sails above, with gray, water-laden bottoms. I imagined them as Achaean triremes crossing the Aegean bearing wine and olive oil in great clay amphorae. I imagined that the distant thunder was the sound of the amphorae bumping against one another in the turbulent passage. Sometimes the flotillas came close to the mountain. One afternoon, as I watched, a cloud approached that was clearly full of rain and, I suddenly realized, it also contained a great deal of energy. I could see lights, a gathering of electrical charge, flickering inside the cloud.

It came on fast. I scooped up Charlie, all gawky forty pounds of him, and ran to the lowest place in the rocks I could find. I put my arms around him. He seemed to understand and stayed very still. The cloud enveloped the mountaintop, and then the lightning. A burst of white light more brilliant than anything I had ever seen before or have since, a light that was neurologically beyond the brain's capacity to process. It was as if we puny creatures, man and dog, had been taken up into the palm of the powerful deity whose hand, hot still, had thrown the lightning bolt. The sensation of being lifted was real, perhaps caused by the electrical charge that surged through the mountain. I experienced a moment of perfect terror, and at the same time I was filled with a sort of ecstatic knowledge. There we were, man and dog, in our odd and ancient society, held in this god's hand for a fraction of a second that felt as long as eternity. Then, almost simultaneously, there came the thunder clap, a rending of silence that was beyond comprehension or description as mere decibels, a crack experienced in the depth of my bones, a slamming against the heart's rhythm that made the mindless, wordless body think "I am dead." Then rain pounded the mountain and soaked me through.

In the next second, the terror was over. We had survived. The cloud sailed away. The whole affair, from the cloud's approach to its departure, had lasted no more than fifteen seconds. Somewhere below us, in an aspen tree, a bird gave a mighty chirp. The raindrops sparkled on the leaves. Charlie, still in my arms, was trembling.

For those two weeks I had known nothing about the dramas that roil the world, the assassinations, earthquakes, the posturing of politicians, nor anything about the teases and temptations that fill shopping malls and move markets. I had been outside of time, living, literally, above it. The experience taught me that I could live without the popular enthusiasms and America's ever-renewing cornucopia of products and sensations. My shelter had been, for that short time, a one room cabin with no plumbing and a leaking roof, and I preferred it to a four star resort. It lacked some comforts to be sure, but the only thing I really missed was a hot shower. On a thin foam mattress on a hard wood floor I slept well. I had been content and, indeed, happy. The birds sang in the forest, the stars arched over us at night. The little cabin was snug and dry when it rained. I read long Russian novels, Nikolai Gogol's *Dead Souls* was the most memorable.

At the end of the time that I had allowed myself, I came down from the mountain. I came down with my books, my companionable hound, and the trash I had not been able to burn. I brought no commandments down from the mountain. Just a peaceful spirit and the sense that I'd had a close encounter and survived the experience.

San Antonio Mt. elevation 11,000 ft, an extinct volcano, is the
highest free-standing peak in the United States.

24

Things Fall Apart

The peace between the Taoseños and the long haired newcomers turned out to be shaky. It had been the result of good manners rather than any real spirit of welcoming. There were incidents of hippie males being beaten up and rumors of hippie girls being raped by Hispanic men. The Taos police began arresting hippies for trivial, and usually absurd, offenses, jaywalking for instance. The harassment did not have the effect the police and the hardliners in the town had hoped for, that the tribes of uncouth youth would pack up and flee. Instead, the hippies, who believed that they were on a virtuous path and so expected to suffer a little along the way, were, like the early Christians, strengthened in their commitment to their communal living arrangements and sacramental stimulants. The government began a crackdown on food stamps, but this inevitably affected poor Hispanics who had not taken voluntary vows of poverty. Hispanic wives and mothers feared that the availability of what they imagined as easy women would tempt their husbands and corrupt their sons.

One night, gunmen attacked a parked school bus in which a number of hippies, including their children, were sleeping. Some twenty shots were fired. Fortunately, the bullets went through the windows and everyone inside the bus had stayed down. The official response highlighted how much the situation had deteriorated. The police chief issued a statement that treated the incident as a minor case of vandalism. Rumor in town was that this was not a prank by drunken teens, but that older men, including local businessmen, had been involved.

I went to see the bus the day after the incident. The longhaired, bearded man in his thirties who owned it, his children, in torn and dirty clothes, stood around and stared at it. The man was badly shaken. He had come from somewhere back east to start a new life in what had been billed as paradise. He had decided not to stay, but the bus, with its bald tires, frayed wiper blades, and with most of its windows shot out, was unsafe to drive. Besides, it had been impounded as evidence.

I had a general abhorrence of violence, but most especially violence by or tolerated by the state, the sort of thing that was happening in the American south. The images of police terrorism, Bull Connors' dogs and mounted, baton-swinging white cops against peaceful marchers in Selma, Alabama (1965) had fermented into a bitter knowledge.

The undercurrents that were tearing at our already somewhat factional community were clearly building, so I decided that something had to be done and pushing back against police abuses seemed a place to start. I made a trip to the ACLU affiliate in Albuquerque where I received a crash course in criminal procedures; under what circumstances could police hold a prisoner, and how to get someone out of jail. I was not motivated by what might be called political advocacy or identification with the hippies. On the contrary I fully understood the Hispanic community's unease, but I thought the abuses of constitutional protections, especially by officers of the law, were unacceptable. Without wanting to be, I became the unofficial advocate for a persecuted minority. The word spread among the communes. Hippies who were jailed for carrying a concealed weapon, usually a pocketknife or even a nail clipper, or littering or spitting, eventually got a visit either from me or a like-minded local attorney with whom I worked. I bailed them out and by so doing served notice to the police that their actions were being monitored. The Taos police, to their credit, were always cooperative as long as I followed the correct procedures. If the young person, usually a male, had been arrested while hitching into town and had no connection with any of the established communes, I would urge him to leave town. Many did. Taos had become an unfriendly place.

I saw Alicia on the weekends. Under the protective dome of higher education, the violence and tensions that deviled Taos County seemed far away. I never talked about it. Eventually, however, the stresses that came with dramatic changes in society caught up with us.

One Saturday evening in Albuquerque, I answered a knock on the door to find a red faced middle-aged man pointing a loaded .357 magnum revolver at me, the muzzle six inches from my forehead. I knew it was loaded because I could see the brass jackets on the bullets. The man was full of fury and was very drunk.

"Fucking longhairs" was his expletive; he shoved the gun closer to my face. The muzzle, for a second, touched my forehead.

He spewed a stream of invective and spittle; I'd never encountered anything like it and was very frightened. I made out the outlines of a story. The previous tenants had been hippies and the man's teenage daughter had run away with them. He wanted his daughter and he said that he would kill the people who took her. He shoved open the door and was at the threshold of our living room. I began talking, nonstop, explaining who we were, literally surrounding him with domestic details about us—our dog's name, Alicia's street address in Mexico City—anything I could think of to convince him that we were not the people he was looking for. I was sure that if I tried to push him back out the door he would shoot me. He was fifty pounds heavier than I was and was fueled with rage. I was fueled by adrenaline, but neither fight nor flight was an available choice. The third choice was to stay calm, or at least pretend that I was.

Another man, the same age, the same look of booze fueled belligerence, appeared in the doorway. He was carrying a shotgun. I thought we were going to be murdered. Through the open door, I could see the lights of passing cars on the street. I thought again, for a second or two—if "thought" is the correct word—about a physical response, but I had no martial arts skills, no experience with fighting. I'd never hit anyone in my life. If I'd had a weapon in the house, I'd have been shot dead before I could reach it. So I kept talking.

"Tell your friend that we aren't who he thinks we are. We know nothing about them." I repeated my litany of biographical detail.

The second man appeared to listen. Then he said, "They ain't here, Bob. Let's go."

"I'm going to search the place," the first man, Bob, said. He crashed around the little house, into every room, opening every closet, with the enormous pistol in his right hand. Alicia stood against the wall, terrified. I kept talking, a controlled panic. "I am from Los Angeles. I am thirty years old, we have a dog..."

As abruptly as the incident had begun, it ended. They left.

Alicia was trembling. But after several hours of talk and decompressing, Alicia seemed to have purged it from her nervous system. We decided that we would not call the police because we could tell them nothing that would lead them to the men. They'd come from out of town, a fact I had deduced from something that had been said. Besides, Alicia was on a short term tourist visa, and by being in school, she was in violation. She feared deportation. We decided to go back to Arroyo Hondo together. She would stay a couple of weeks and see how she felt. I had finished my new house and was in the process of moving in.

In May my friend Jim and his wife and her children showed up and moved into the little house. They had spent a year in the English-speaking community of American expats in Ajijic, Mexico. It had been a wild year, and they wanted to settle down. Jim and Deirdre were welcoming and warm toward Alicia, but neither spoke much Spanish, so real friendship was not likely. After a month or so, Alicia decided that she was ready to go back to school.

In the middle of that following month, around eight in the evening I received a phone call from a very shaken, sobbing, Alicia. She told me that she had been attacked while walking in the park that was just across the street from the house. She said she was not hurt badly but was very frightened. She had made it to the house, had locked all windows and doors. Would I come? I left immediately.

I drove like a madman. A drive that should have taken three hours was accomplished in just over two. My worst fear was that she had been injured more seriously than she had said. I imagined her battered and bleeding in a fetal curl, clinging to the telephone. Along with these thoughts and images, I was tormented by self-recrimination and guilt. The first incident was unforeseeable in that we had no knowledge of the history of the house. This second was different in character and was, perhaps, something I could have and should have foreseen. Should I have asked the police about crime rates in the area? It had never occurred to me. We had chosen the house because of the trees and shade in the park. A modern apartment building, with a pool and underground parking, did not appeal to either of us. Clearly, it would have been safer.

I arrived at 10:30 that night. Alicia opened the door for me. She was clearly traumatized, but in command of her feelings and not seriously injured in any physical sense. She had a bruised and cut lip where she had been hit. She told me that three young men, teenagers, had attacked her as she walked through the park and taken her wallet. Since it was summer and not yet dark, she had thought it would be safe. As she told me later, she had spent her childhood darting among the cars and crowds of Mexico City and had never felt the slightest fear. America had shown her its violent face, and now she was afraid. The saddest part was that she was ashamed of being afraid. Her injuries had been psychological. Without saying explicitly, she conceded that she was defeated. I recognized such feelings. Basic training at Fort Dix had defeated a significant part of me. I could not judge her.

Indeed, I could imagine what a woman, essentially on her own, in a strange country and not speaking the language, would be feeling under these circumstances. So there was no question about what to do. We packed her personal things and left for Arroyo Hondo that night. With that decision, her life sustaining dream, a college education, died. She had come to America as much for that opportunity as to be with me. Now she was forcibly retired to Arroyo Hondo and became what she had not wanted to be, just my girlfriend.

The dynamics of our relationship changed. We were pushed closer together in reaction, but it was not by choice. Alicia's dependency on me became absolute. Despite both of our best intentions, an accident had intervened and shifted the ground under us and upset a balance of independence and dependency, of gender roles that we had thought we could maintain. I felt uneasy with the change. But Alicia felt as she did and I felt responsible for her; I had, after all, invited her to come the United States with me. So we made an honest attempt to make it work.

I urged her to talk about it, if not with me, with a professional with better Spanish than mine. She declined. I think she was afraid that her emotions would be so strong that she would want to return to the cultural safety of Mexico, an outcome that another part of her did not want. As time went by, she communicated less and less. We'd never been especially good at deep conversation, not because we did not want to, but because my Spanish was not nuanced or spontaneous enough. I think, too, that at that stage of my development, I wasn't terribly good at emotional intimacy in any language. As she withdrew into herself, I retreated too, behind rationality, which was my default form of masculinity.

The beauty of the valley would sooth her, heal the trauma—or so I wanted to believe. But Taos was not free of violence in that period either. These were tense times. And except for me, Alicia was alone. Arroyo Hondo, though Spanish-speaking, was almost more foreign than modern Anglophone America. Mexico City was modern; Arroyo Hondo, by contrast, seemed the old world, a cluster of Spanish settlers that had been forgotten long ago by one distant government after another. Alicia, feeling ever more isolated, was slipping into depression. I was slow to notice, thinking that her silence was cultural or even deeper, something in the Aztec part of her ancestry.

And I was involved with community issues, hippies and Hispanics. The troubles continued. There were undesirable people who took to hiding out in these anarchic micro-states, the communes. One late afternoon, after the garden work had been done, without a knock on the door, three young men with bandoliers of bullets across their chests and rifles in their hands, burst into our house. They were members of a Puerto Rican gang from New York City who called themselves "The Up-Against-the-Wall-Mother-Fuckers." Now, they were in my kitchen. They had come, they told me, to liberate their sister, *la hermana*, Alicia, the *chicana* who, they were certain, had no desire to live with a honky. Whether they were just a raiding party looking for a woman to carry off or ideological revolutionaries I could not tell, but I was thoroughly alarmed. Alicia, frightened, stood behind me, as I, as if invoking some sort of ecclesiastical authority, said that no one was ever allowed to enter my house carrying guns. And I added that if they did not leave, I'd have the sheriff there in five minutes. It was sheer bluff. In New York City, the law might appear in five minutes, in Taos County it could take an hour. The bluff worked. They left, but I was afraid they'd return. So, taking Alicia with me in the truck, I drove up to the Reality commune to consult with Max. They had taken up residence in the commune and he had already decided that these were bad actors and wanted them gone. He had a political problem, however, for deliberately calling in the police ran counter to the ideals that commune society espoused, of being out of the bourgeois system; furthermore, police presence always put the community at risk of being "busted" for something unrelated. We decided that he would tell the hoodlums that I was well connected with the FBI and that I was, if anyone was, a truly ruthless "motherfucker." They left that night, for Colorado or California, but exactly where no one knew. No trace of them remains in our narrative, no names. Wikipedia, however, memorializes them as an anarchist gang from the Lower East Side of New York.

There were many interesting stories that flickered briefly into life in those years of the Hippie revolution in Taos County. We who were part of those stories hardly considered them stories and seldom wrote anything down. This was surprising, because Taos, in addition to being a place for painters, was writer's country. D.H. Lawrence had lived in Taos between 1920 and 1922; he was much in Jim's mind and in mine too in those years, and had had something to do with why we had come in the first place. Lawrence's ashes are said to be in a little shrine of fieldstone and whitewashed cement in the piñon forest three miles north of Arroyo Hondo. Some believe that his ashes were lost during a wake in Santa Fe; someone, possibly Frieda, Lawrence's widow, wandering drunk up Canyon Road, had set the urn down on a wall and forgotten them. In the morning, the urn couldn't be found. The shrine, however, is the official repository.

Lawrence's passionate commitment to the art of writing was inspirational to both Jim and me as young men. Lawrence's famously stormy love affair with Frieda was reflected in Jim and Deirdre's story. They had plunged into life with the sort of headlong élan that Lawrence would have approved but that was more than I could have mustered in those days. I saw myself as very conservative and was envious of Jim's romantic freedom.

As if following Frieda's example, Deirdre had forsaken a comfortable life with a lawyer husband to run off with an impoverished poet with limited prospects. Jim had a teaching certificate that he showed no inclination to use. Their leap into the unknown was the more impressive because they had children in tow. Frieda had abandoned her children, but Deirdre brought hers along. Jim, less self-involved than Lawrence, took step-parenting in stride. They, all four, had come through a turbulent year in Ajijic, where they, the adults at least, had gone in search of experience. For Jim, experience involved hallucinogens and another woman. But now, back in New Mexico, Jim was settling down to be a good father and husband, and as a writer to make use of the experiential material he had gathered in Mexico. There was good material for writers in Taos too. The "up against the wall" gang had passed this way.

Jim, Deidre, Alicia, and I combined our energies in a large vegetable garden, perhaps 50 feet square, in which we grew sweet corn, several squash varieties, peas, pole beans, and rows and rows of leaf vegetables. We froze enough to last until the next growing season. Raccoons and porcupines took advantage of our abundance and our good will. I had, and still have, great respect for wild animals. I thought we could share our space in the valley with the creatures. Jim shared this value and so, apparently did Deirdre. Alicia, the city kid, had never seen any sort of wild animal and was fascinated. Without our being consciously aware of it, to allow all creatures a place at the table is a Zen Buddhist posture of the soul. Nevertheless, as we harvested the corn, we griped, complaining that the porcupine was so inefficient; this odd and ungainly creature would gnaw on an ear of corn here, then gnaw a little on another over there. Then it would go off and gnaw on the shovel handle because it contained salt from our hands.

Jim and Deirdre's marriage, however, had been stressed by the excesses of the year in Mexico. Like so much that year, it fell apart. Deirdre became a much loved Buddhist nun and teacher. She is now Pema Chödrön.

Disillusionment with the hippie movement came as a steady drizzle of unpleasant encounters. A single event finished off any illusions I might still have had.

The Hog Farm commune was located in Rodarte, about forty-five miles from Taos. Under the leadership of a man named Hugh Romney, the "Wavy Gravy" of hippie folk legend, the Hog Farmers were considered the anarchistic purists, rejecting everything of the bourgeois world. Romney was considered a guru; he was, at a minimum, a great self promoter.

One day, a group of Hog Farmers had been arrested. It was a typically phony charge, so I bailed them out. They came to my house later that afternoon, along with others from their community, to thank me. Some wine was drunk, some food shared. The next day, while Alicia and I were in Santa Fe for a doctor's appointment, the house was burglarized. Everything of value, which consisted primarily of some good quality Navajo rugs, was taken. The car the thieves had come in was recognized as having been at my house the day before. They had apparently sized up the house while we broke bread. They'd come to the communal supper and had stolen the silverware.

Since I knew where to find the perpetrators, I called the State Police. The case was assigned to a trooper, an officer named Ben Salazar. He and I became paired for a day of pursuit, waiting, and negotiating. I got my first ride in a patrol car and saw the world from the other side of a policeman's windscreen.

We drove first to the Hog Farm itself and strolled among the tipis and shelters dug into the sides of a hill. An old school bus perched on blocks served as a communal dormitory for the children. I identified the faces I knew from the day before. Officer Salazar questioned them. No one knew anything about a burglary. We encountered a wall of unblinking innocence and expressions of shock. How could I think that they were capable of such ingratitude? Salazar and I were unconvinced but since I had no hard evidence, we left. As we drove back toward Taos we spotted a car that matched the description of the car seen at my house; it was heading up the mountain toward the commune. Officer Salazar snapped on his flashing lights, did a U turn, and we went in pursuit. The driver was one of the men whom I had bailed out. He, too, was offended that I would suspect him of such a thing. Salazar stood by the car and parlayed with this young man, who, after a time, asked if he could leave. Officer Salazar asked if he could look in the trunk of the car. The young man said no. The cards had been played. And we began a waiting game.

Officer Salazar said that he would radio to Taos for a warrant and that we would all have to wait until it arrived. Back in the patrol car, he told me that he could only hold him for a limited time. He had not been caught in the act and the make and color of his car was common. There was, therefore, no cause to hold the young man except for my suspicion. There might not be a judge available or willing to issue a search warrant or an officer available to deliver it.

"So, in effect," he said, "we are bluffing. The next step, if there is one, will have to come from him."

Officer Salazar and I sat for nearly two hours in the patrol car. I learned about the dangers of the job, the hours, his family life, his background, and his views about hippies—they were none of his concern until they broke the law. He was a good police officer. We were chatting about where to eat in the town of Española, where he lived, when the door to the other car opened and the young man approached us.

"The parley has started," Salazar said. "You have to decide which is more important, sticking to principles or getting your things back. I think that in order to get your things back, you might have to give up on the principles, which means no prosecution."

"Why not both?" I asked. I wanted them prosecuted.

"Because if we don't get the warrant soon, by tomorrow morning everything that was taken will have disappeared and then you would have neither a conviction nor your things." He gestured toward the radio. "We've heard nothing."

Officer Salazar got out of the car and stood in the sun.

"You stay in the car," he said. "You are emotionally involved and I have more authority here. He is a little afraid of me, but judging by what they did, he isn't of you."

They talked. He got back into the patrol car.

"He will persuade his fellows to return your possessions if you agree not to prosecute. I cannot charge them on the state's account if your goods are back in your possession. And I believe you are an honorable man and would not go back on your word."

"If," I said, "he will open the trunk of his car right now, and if each member of the commune who has something brings it to me in person, I will agree."

That was how it was resolved. The trunk of his car was opened and in it was one of my rugs. We drove back to the Hog Farm and sat in the car while the young man went into the encampment and explained the situation. One by one, both women and men brought my rugs and other items to the police car and placed them in the trunk. The Hog Farmers, true to their values, had divided the spoils among other members of the community. There was no embarrassment and no guilt. I asked one of the men whom I'd gotten out of jail why he stole from me.

"You are rich," he said. "You don't need it. It all belongs to God anyway."

His girlfriend, or his "old lady" as hippies called their women, was standing beside him, and she added, almost by way of correcting him on a doctrinal point, "It all belongs to the universe."

One incident captures the period and the social atmosphere so completely that I've wished I could make a short film of it. It cheers me because it was funny and not traumatic, odd and yet typical. One hot summer afternoon, I was driving down a winding dirt road to the Rio Grande to take a swim. As I came around a sharp turn, I met a pickup truck with three young Hispanic men in the cab. As they passed me, the driver shouted, "Pig!"

"Not again," I thought. There had been so much trouble, so much tension between native Hispanics and Anglo newcomers. Cops were "pigs" and now, apparently, so was I. Around the next corner, however, I almost hit a three-hundred-pound sow. The pig, her dugs flopping, was sauntering along the road; she too, no doubt, was going down to the river to cool off.

In retrospect, I think of the hippie movement as a Rube Goldberg contraption of wishes and defiance, of pleasures and voluntary discomforts, nostalgia for a freedom that had never really existed. There were ideals, of anarchism without violence, for instance, or of a society with self generating infrastructures—roads, hospitals, and order— that would appear as if by magic, like Jack's beanstalk, ideas that were actually little better than notions. The rhetoric about the dawning of a new age was hype. The first part of the revolution—the personal liberation, which included a shedding of sexual inhibitions, the "letting it all hang out"—went off well enough. American society, generally, became sexually and perhaps emotionally freer. It seems to me that women picked up a momentum of sorts from the period and improved their place in American society; I am not sure women would agree with this analysis. The idea that a new sort of society was in the making was stillborn; this, I think, was because the hippies had only daily behavior and their feelings in mind—no philosophy, no ethical sense, no politics, and no historical awareness. They had no ideas that were mature or solid enough to have nudged America in a positive direction or any direction at all.

"Do your own thing" was the mantra, but that is not a philosophy. Permissiveness, by emphasizing the individual, one's personal liberty, degrades quickly into appetites. By the decade of the eighties, liberty for the dominant culture had come to mean not much more than greed. Its popular manifestation, consumerism, is the shallowest and most destructive form of liberty.

The idea that there was something called "love power" that was going to change America is ludicrous. There was love, perhaps, and lots of dancing in the streets, but as a source of power, never. Those with the real power in America were not about to surrender it, especially not to love or to the young. The ethos of the hippie movement lives on only in the music. I listen to the music still. The Grateful Dead, Creedence Clearwater Revival, Steppenwolf, The Stones, The Beatles, Jefferson Airplane, Janis, Jimi, Joe Cocker, and so many others; especially Bob Dylan. If any part of the experience belonged to the Universe, perhaps the music did.

In that period, the troubles in my immediate neighborhood—worried natives, insensitive newcomers, an unhappy partner, my friend's divorce—left me little time for thinking about global issues. But then, late summer, something happened that brought the dysfunctions of modern America, its appetites and agendas, into my world of sky and light, the majesty that I had lived with and within on San Antonio Mountain the year before.

It was evening, but only a month or so after the solstice, so that days were still long. I had finished irrigating my pasture and was trudging back to my house, shovel on my shoulder, when I noticed that the sun, as it slid down toward the western horizon, seemed blurred and discolored. It was as if I were seeing it through a veil of gauze, a fabric stained a nicotine reddish brown. It was so noticeable that I walked over to the Chacons' store and asked Clodoveo to take a look. He was just sitting down to supper, but he came out and we stood on the road together, looking west, toward San Antonio Mountain.

"Must be a forest fire," he said. But we had heard of no fires, and a search in the next day's newspaper turned up none.

It had appeared so suddenly and the change in our previously pristine skies was so noticeable that I felt a sort of emotional nausea. Something I valued deeply had been attacked, soiled, and desecrated. What had happened? We were too far from Los Angeles for it to have been exported smog and our only city, then less than 350,000 people, was too small. For days I searched the newspapers for a story about a fire. I paid a visit to the regional offices of the Forest Service to enquire about distant fires, in Colorado, perhaps, or even Utah, but there was nothing. And no one seemed to have noticed the change. Was I crazy?

Clodoveo had noticed. He wasn't indifferent, but he was resigned. What could one do? He came from a culture accustomed to having things taken away by distant forces.

I, however, was not resigned. I'd come to New Mexico in part because of its air and skies. I had fled Los Angeles as I saw its beauty eroded away by progress. Desecration was a word that kept coming to me. A sacred space had been invaded by vandals, its glorious windows smudged and smeared with obscene graffiti. I was profoundly distressed.

It was anguish that only eased when I understood what had happened and when I began to take some sort of action.

I had already started a business in Taos: I had renovated the town's movie theater and owned a bar. But as it became clear that the issue that truly engaged me was the air pollution, I began to lose interest in these projects. A slow evolution was in process. The idyll was over, Arcadia was over. I learned to channel my anger and dismay into constructive activity. I was becoming an activist.

I began to divide my time between home and the state capital, Santa Fe, seventy miles to the south. At the same time, I wanted my relationship with Alicia to find its footing. Alicia wanted us to be a proper family. I did too. I had doubts, mostly around the state of Alicia's spirits, but since I believed, or wanted to believe, that a child might give her life a new sense of purpose, I agreed. In April 1970, our daughter was conceived. Our own little commune, the family in the making, was a fortress against the world. I was optimistic. I believed I could be several beings at the same time: husband, father, adult, farmer, businessman, and involved citizen. It was quite a trick, this juggling; some of the things that I intended to keep in the air were sharp and some breakable.

Our daughter, Mariana, was born in January of 1971. Mariana's infancy should have been blissful for her parents, and indeed was at times, but there was a shadow over us, a sense of impending unhappiness, of mortality even. I know this not so much from memory, but because a number of the poems I wrote in this period speak of this quiet sort of dread. Perhaps it was because my relationship with Alicia was not on a solid footing at all. Or perhaps it was because family life was in conflict with activism and my need to fight back against the invader.

I was not lost to a life of the heart though. Alicia and I dangled our daughter, age seven months, in the cold, clear waters of the Hondo as they came down from the mountain, and each of us said what we thought necessary. It was an improvised baptism: pure water and good feelings. I still considered Arroyo Hondo to be my home, but I was spending less time in the valley, less and less as the months went by.

The three years of working the earth in Arroyo Hondo changed me in profound ways. During this period, I began to integrate myself, to understand that mind, emotions, and external realities were not separate components of self and experience. Together, like a sort of alloy, they made up a gradually more harmonious consciousness. I began to see the spiritual and the body as parts of a unified whole person.

And I had found elements of happiness. It came from the work itself, work with stubborn earth and with dumb machines, work beneath an open sky, in all weather, winter and summer. It was honest labor, meaningful work. I remembered the Virgil that I'd read four years earlier about the life of the farmer. He had not led me astray.

Pueblo Peak has an elevation of 12,300 feet.

Max Finstein, 1977

Jim and Deirdre, the future Pema Chodron

Part V

The World as it Is

"I cannot praise a fugitive and cloistered virtue, unexercised and unbreathed, that never sallies out and sees her adversary, but slinks out of the race where that immortal garland is to be run for, not without dust and heat... That which purifies us is trial, and trial is by what is contrary."

John Milton, *Areopagitica*

25

"Into the Breach, Dear Friends"

It turned out that I wasn't the only one upset by the change in our skies. Two scientists from Los Alamos National Laboratory were so distressed that they hired a private plane and, from an elevation of ten thousand feet, they saw that the pollution was not something dispersed like smog, but was a discrete plume that could be followed, which they did, tracing it back to a single source, a coal-burning power plant in the northwestern corner of the state, a region called The Four Corners, where the states of Arizona, Utah, Colorado, and New Mexico share a common boundary point. The burning of coal for the generating of electricity was the problem. The gasses and particle pollution from the plant spread across a wide area, from the valley of the Hondo two hundred miles to the east and to Grand Canyon two hundred fifty miles to the west. Grand Canyon National Park and all the other national parks and monuments that lay in between cover an area half the size of France. All of it was affected, visibility reduced dramatically. During the Reagan administration, Park Service employees at Grand Canyon National Park were instructed to tell tourists that the severely degraded visibility—sometimes one could not even see from rim to rim, just six miles—was from natural causes.

I, along with a band of committed activists and many volunteers, decided to set the record straight, to tell the truth, and then, with citizen concern awakened, to change it. The two men from Los Alamos, John

Bartlett and Mike Williams, had performed the role of Paul Revere—
they awakened us to the fact that the enemy was not just coming, but
had already arrived. And they told us who the enemy was. A power
company, a coal company, and the appetite for electricity in the big cities
of the west: Los Angeles had, in a sense, come to us.

The story of how this happened is almost surreal in its simplicity: by
locating on Navajo Indian land neither notification nor consultation
with the state of New Mexico or its citizens had been required. The
Navajo Reservation, like all Indian reservations, is, by treaty, a separate
nation, legally not a part of the state of New Mexico or fully of the
United States. This created a loophole of enormous convenience. The
Arizona Public Service Company had not applied for even the most
rudimentary sort of building permit, something the county requires to
add a garage to one's house.

At the time, little could have been done. The state had no environmental agency, so no part of state government had jurisdiction. And
the federal Environmental Protection Agency (EPA) did not yet exist.
The Bureau of Indian Affairs had no environmental mandate; it kept
a drawer full of rubber stamps with which it approved every paper
the power company had put before it. In effect, the project could go
unnoticed—except in the local area, some 250 miles from the state capital—until something happened. And now, something had happened.
Someone threw a switch and The Four Corners Generating Station
had come fully on stream, all its stacks belching thousands of tons a
year of toxic chemistry and ash. It was for a time, when all its boilers
became operational, the largest coal-burning power plant in the world.
Its waste plume was the only manmade object visible from the Apollo
space mission.

Bartlett and Williams wrote letters to the editors of the major papers
and those letters saved me from a dispiriting sense of helplessness.
Knowledge pointed the way to action. I no longer felt alone: I found
that there were many who felt as I did and I joined with them. At first I

was one in the crowd, but over a rather short time, I emerged as a leader. This happened quite by accident; it was not something that I'd sought; but I had the free time, money independent of job, and a passion. At the core of this leadership group were the two careful men of science. I was a generalist. The poet became the writer of pamphlets and ad copy.

The Four Corners Plant and the Black Mesa coal mine, located on lands sacred to the Navajo People, became the symbols of a fight that I was deeply involved with in a critical period of my early adulthood, a time when more traditional career paths might have been found and taken.

I became, in every sense of the word, an "activist." It was an occupation. I took an apartment in Santa Fe and saw my family on weekends. I had an office, wore a tie, drank too much coffee, read scientific journals, and gave speeches and interviews. I have enough stories about politics and power, corruption and powerlessness, about economic theories and political ideologies, complex technical issues as well, to fill a book, but I recount here only enough to provide a sense of what it was like to be in the trenches in the early days of the environmental movement.

I assumed the leadership of a preexisting organization called the Central Clearing House (CCH). It had been started by two men whose primary interest was Native American issues, and they, Jack Loeffler and Jimmy Hopper, continued with their focus on the effects of the energy development projects on the Navajo and Hopi people while I, with a co-director, Sally Rodgers, turned CCH into an umbrella organization that would support, through lobbying and organizational assistance, a variety of environmental and social causes. Sally was the political brains of our operation. Brant Calkin, who, like Bartlett and Williams, came from the labs at Los Alamos, translated the science for us and lobbied tirelessly. Grove Burnett, a lawyer, showed up one day and offered to craft crucial lawsuits.

I bought a building in Santa Fe, the use of which I donated to activist citizen's groups. There was a library and meeting space where environmentalists could interact with poverty activists, with people involved with women's issues. I provided the operating funds; it had a paid staff of four, telephones, advertising expenses, etc. In addition to the staff, there was an army of competent volunteers, people who ranged from young people with long hair to grandmothers. Both Brant and Sally were philosophically as committed to the cause as I was. None of us had training in anything relevant to the political tasks that lay ahead—public relations, public speaking, organizing, nor any formal study of political science—but we would learn. The first lesson was that logical argument and common sense had little value in this marketplace. Success would boil down to gaining the attention and support of the public and, through pressure from an involved citizenry, winning the votes of politicians.

We were involved with just about every major environmental issue of the period: energy policy, which included coal mining and Native Americans; land use policy; and subdivision regulation. Our adversaries were major corporations, corrupt politicians, and even the Mafia.

Air pollution was our initial concern. In 1969 there were virtually no air quality standards in the United States. Few regulations, state or federal, addressed airborne particulate matter, sulfur dioxide, carbon dioxide, or nitrogen oxides. SO_2 is the cause of acid rain, NOX the cause of smog; CO_2, as a greenhouse gas, was not yet on the radar screen. The particle pollution was what had caught our attention initially because it so dramatically affected visibility. The health issues connected with air pollution had received little attention. Scientific information about acid rain and its effects on forests, soils, and lakes, was just beginning to filter into the public awareness. As our efforts continued, we discovered that it was not just coal burning that affected our air. New Mexico had a significant copper mining industry; a smelter operated by Kennecott Copper in the south of the state was a major source of air pollution. At one point I went to the smelter town of Hurley in an effort to organize a citizen's group. The air was so bad that my eyes burned and I could taste the sulfur. I asked a man what he thought about it. "This is a company town," he told me, "and if you want to work, you breath what they offered you and say nothing." Another man told me that a paint job on a car lasted about two years in Hurley. I imagined the lungs.

The copper smelter experience defined our basic objective. We would push to establish emissions standards that would protect human health. These standards would also protect what virtually every citizen in the Southwest considered a public good, an essential element of their birthright as human beings: clean air, air that one could not see or taste.

There were legislative committee hearings to attend, scientific evidence to marshal and present, and legislation to craft. The arena was the state legislature. We proposed the creation of a state environmental department with adequate funding and powers to set standards and impose regulation. We wanted the legislature to require the installation of technologies that would chemically scrub the gases from the smelters and capture the ash from the power plant. The copper refiners and power companies opposed every proposal that we advanced.

In both these efforts we would eventually prevail, but it was a long slog, interminable and infuriating, Sisyphean. Industry would claim that there was no evidence of harm to human health or to the environment, or if suspected, it could not be proved absolutely. When we presented evidence that reduced the margin of uncertainty to statistical inconsequence, they invariably introduced a second objection, claiming that no technology existed to address the problem. We would present engineering reports from more progressive countries, like Sweden and Germany, that established beyond a doubt that the technology existed and that there were competent American firms that could do the job. For their next evasion, they claimed that they could not afford it and that the cost would outweigh the benefits. And besides, any regulation, they insisted, would curtail economic growth. They would not accept the argument that installation and maintenance of pollution controls would have a positive economic impact in terms of new jobs.

The overarching method of industry's attack was to confuse the public, to foment doubt and worry, doubt about negative health effects and worry about economic consequences. They always found a scientist whom they could pay to introduce these doubts. The tactics were not new. Recall the cigarette ads from the fifties that showed doctors in white coats with stethoscopes around their necks claiming that cigarettes were not harmful, the endless claims that the tobacco issue was still open to question and that the science was flawed.

The counter arguments that we presented in the first years of our efforts were met with skepticism, indifference, or outright hostility. Advocacy groups like ours were a relatively new element in the political process, and legislators didn't know quite how to deal with us. Our legislative proposals were usually defeated. Some legislators were swayed by the attention of corporate lobbyists, the attention being lavish meals, campaign contributions, and flattery. Some, indeed many, were unfamiliar with the complexity of these issues. Fortunately, however, the state of New Mexico has an important science industry, all supported by the Departments of Defense and Energy. The legislators who came from those districts were usually politically conservative, but were scientifically literate.

Learning how to relate to the public, how to persuade voters to reach out to their legislators was our principal task. We needed to lobby with the voices of an engaged and aware public. We had to persuade the public to be more than just our partners in a political fight, but to see themselves as believers in a similar value system, the environmental ethic that, in a sense, we had to create.

The challenge to the environmental argument in the hard world of politics is that nature, in its unprocessed state, not yet a product with a price tag, has no inherent value and therefore no voice of its own. The lack of verifiable numbers in dollars makes environmental politics more difficult than, say, the defense budget. We had to give reality to an issue that seemed to many to be just philosophical. And we found it. In January 1970, we embarked on a campaign to protect the rarest of the wild animals in the Southwest, the mountain lion. We were convinced that the mountain lion would appeal to the noblest part of the public imagination. We could talk about intangible environmental values by narrowing the focus of the discussion to a specific creature that the public could visualize, four foot tail, tawny coat, and clearly not a house cat.

The opposition to giving the mountain lion protected status came from the state's cattle industry. The cattlemen always lost a few head of cattle every year to mountain lions, but the financial losses were relatively small. More important was an issue of values, the belief that the natural world was for the sole use of the human species. We strongly disagreed. The mountain lion fight was a significant one, a defense of ideas that touched all aspects of man's life on the planet. It was a fight to which we gave all the imagination and energy that we could muster.

The cowboy families are seen as an important part of the state's tradition, cattle raising the old way, before feedlots came to dominate the beef business. If we were to win the fight, we needed to be seen as practical and reasonable, and above all, we had to be respectful of their part in the state's history. We would not be dismissive of their concerns. We wanted only to change the mountain lion's legal status, to give it "game animal" status so its breeding season would be protected and its numbers monitored. To achieve our goal, we needed to present a story that would engage the urban populations that had no issues about predation on cattle. We located an old trapper in Colorado who had a tamed cougar, an animal he'd found as an abandoned cub and raised. We persuaded him to bring his one-hundred-pound cat to a public hearing in the state capital. We also invited the media and grade school children from local schools. This large tawny cat, eight feet long nose to tip of tail, stretched out on the carpet in the hearing room in front of the raised desks behind which sat the legislators, most still wearing their cowboy hats. It was an unprecedented sort of testimony to a legislative body. The children, fifty or sixty of them, watched spellbound. The tip of the cougar's tail drifted up and down. "She's relaxed," the old trapper explained to the children. The TV cameras gathered a good piece of political theater, and we got the result we wanted. The legislators could hardly have given the thumbs down to the cat in front of all those school children and TV cameras.

Through the cougar campaign, we acquired a level of political credibility that served us well in the years to come. From that day forward, the politicians paid attention. There were more complex issues in the future, energy and land use principally, but none of those campaigns were as emotionally satisfying as the mountain lion effort.

When the annual one month long legislative session was over, Sally, Brant, and I spent our time building networks, organizing citizens' groups, and working with volunteer leaders. There was a movement to be shaped, encouraged, and above all, we had to keep them optimistic about our chances of success. Sally and I covered most of the state by car, living in motels and eating in diners. There were groups of people, often very small groups, in every corner of a very large state that supported our objectives and we had to support them. And they had to see who we were.

There was a disturbing emotional and intellectual dissonance in those times. We were building our movement at the same time that the country was ramping up its military involvement in Vietnam. The environmental message, with its emphasis on careful behavior in respect to the planet, clashed with the reality of the war. The level of violence that the American military inflicted on Vietnam presented a picture of America that was incompatible with any sort of environmental value system. Brutal indifference to human beings and their suffering, deliberate large scale environmental destructiveness, carpet bombing and defoliation, and such staggering waste did not suggest a society that would understand, much less adopt, the basic changes that an environmental ethic required. The disconnection between America's behavior in a faraway place and the idea of an environmentally sane America was more than just disconcerting. It took a kind of creative intellectual immunization to keep the war from infecting the environmental movement. Unconsciously, we compartmentalized and ignored our discomfort.

* * *

Our organization played a pivotal role in the fight over the Super Sonic Transport (SST). The SST was to be the American answer to the Anglo-French Concorde. A very fast passenger airplane that only the very rich could use answered no real transportation need; it was a national vanity project. The environmental concerns were our interest. It was thought that the aircraft's exhaust at high altitudes would harm the ozone layer that protects the earth from UV radiation. The public had only recently become aware that the depletion of this protective layer was a threat to human health. Sonic boom was also an issue.

The SST was not a project that could be supported by the free market. It would require massive federal subsidies, which meant the Congress was involved. One day in 1971, with the vote in the Senate to fund the SST coming up in a matter of days, I received a phone call from the Sierra Club's congressional lobbyist; he told me that New Mexico's senior senator, Clinton Anderson, appeared to be wavering. This was a surprise because Anderson had generally looked favorably on anything connected with aerospace and, probably more important, he was a personal friend of Senator Henry Jackson of Washington, whose state was the headquarters of the Boeing Corporation, which would be the major contractor. The final vote was going to be very close, he said, so it was worth an effort.

We established a phone bank in our Santa Fe office and contacted as many people on our lists as we could, urging them to contact Senator Anderson's office, and if our supporters felt that they would not have the time for that task, we asked if we could compose and send a telegram in their name. We put in two long exhausting days. On the day of the vote, we had a live radio feed from the Senate Gallery.

"Mr. Aiken." George Aiken, Republican of Vermont, was one of my political heroes, the man who told President Nixon that the war in Vietnam was lost and he should "just declare victory and get out."

"No."

"Mr. Aiken, no," the clerk said.

"Mr. Anderson."

"Pass."

Senator Anderson had passed! This was an extraordinary thing to have happened. It meant he wanted to see if his vote would be needed, crucially, at the final tally, but we had no idea why he wanted this sort of flexibility. At the end of the roll call, the vote was tied. And only Clinton Anderson had not voted. It returned to him. Our phone bank volunteers—grandmothers and college students—were all glued to the radio.

"Mr. Anderson."

"No."

There was pandemonium in our little office. People were hugging one another, crying, laughing.

"Mr. Anderson, no."

The measure did not pass. There would be no SST funded by the American taxpayer. Senator Anderson was the focus of attention in the corridors outside the Senate chambers. He had gone to the quorum call in a wheelchair, for he was unwell and near the end of his life. As he left the Senate floor, the press surrounded him. Asked why he had voted as he had, he answered, "Because my constituent mail was running 4 to 1 against."

26

Tales of Corruption

Along all the highways leading into New Mexico one saw enormous billboards advertising the newest residential paradise. The state was undergoing an epidemic of sprawl, of aggressively-hyped subdivisions scattered around the two largest cities, Albuquerque and Santa Fe. Counties were being overwhelmed by development proposals; and commissioners, seduced by promises of an expanded tax base, had little understanding of the potential negative effects, both environmental and economic. CCH's position was that only uniform statewide regulations could prevent the new developments from adding to the existing community's financial burdens in respect to infrastructure and services. Availability of water in the desert was the major environmental concern. The developers were promising municipalities virtually unlimited growth—more and more houses, pools and lawns, more jobs building those houses—promises that were essentially fraudulent because the water simply wasn't there. The developers' position was that water was someone else's problem, to be solved after they had sold the lots and decamped. We framed the whole issue in consumer protection terms.

We targeted specific subdivision projects whose practices we thought were especially egregious. One development in Tesuque, called Colonias de Santa Fe, was important because it was on Indian land, and thus, the company claimed, it was not subject to local or state regulation, the same tactic Arizona Public Service Company had used to get around regulation at Four Corners. We began a series of "consumer beware" ads concerning the water issue. These ads infuriated legislators who were either secret investors in the project or had taken "contributions" from other hidden investors. Though at the time we had no firm proof, we were certain that Mafia money from the Tucson mob was involved in the New Mexico land developments. There were comical moments. The younger brother of U.S. Senator Joe Montoya, a powerful state legislator, rose on the floor of the senate chamber and gave an irrational speech, sputtering with rage, in which he accused me of having "small hands;" the implication was that I wasn't manly, and therefore, I suppose the smear went, one could assume worse things. Another senator accused me of being a closet developer and demanded that I reveal all my land holdings in the state, which I did, most of it piñon and cactus covered hillside, waterless and worthless. All this was duly reported in the papers as a feud between certain politicians and me. This ongoing fuss provided a platform through which we could discuss real issues. The subdivision industry and their legislative flunkies looked like fools. They lashed out and in their fury they went beyond insults about my small hands.

They struck again, this time in the courts: Colonias sued me for what they called "interference with business opportunity." They asked for thirty-five million dollars in damages. Although the claim was legally fanciful, an intimidation tactic, it was potentially devastating because even the cost of defending such a charge would have destroyed me financially. My inheritance, a significant part of which I had already plunged into these efforts, was never more than two million dollars, but for all they knew I had 135 million dollars. So I bluffed. I answered, in the press, "They are trying to nickel and dime me to death." The quip made good copy. The national media picked up the story. Calvin Trillin wrote about it in The New Yorker in December of 1971.

Their suit was ultimately dismissed as frivolous. But, neither chastised nor embarrassed, their intimidation campaign found new avenues. Because CCH was the lead organization in the campaign to force Colonias to come clean about their water resources, the developers stepped up their attacks.

One evening, midway through the 1972 legislative session, with some of our proposals and questions generating positive interest among conservative legislators (often the same cowboys we had confronted over the mountain lion,) New Mexico's attorney general accosted me in a restaurant. As the state's chief law enforcement officer, he was a joke, a man whose corruption was well known to anyone with knowledge of how the state worked. He had a potbelly hanging over a white belt, a florid face, and wisps of thin hair with which he attempted a comb-over. He stalked over to my table, lowered his head so that it was within eighteen inches of mine and snarled, spittle flying, "We are going to get you, blood, guts, feathers and all." I laughed at him and said something dismissive. Whether the "blood, guts, and feathers" part of the threat was sanctioned by his masters or not, I didn't know. My response, defiant and unshaken, sprang in part from a certain fatalism that having had a cancer had instilled. I often thought that the cancer cells might still be ticking away in me. But it was not just fatalism. After my encounter with bullies during basic training in the army, I had vowed that I would never again allow myself to be intimidated. I had started down this path freely. I was discovering that it led to places more difficult than legislative hearing rooms where I jousted with well-mannered utility company lawyers. My two closest associates, Sally Rodgers and Brant Calkin, were also subjected to intimidation. If there were real risks to our well-being, we all faced them. We did not back down. We ran more consumer education ads and intensified our lobbying for uniform statewide regulations. We developed a print media ad campaign that highlighted the social and environmental costs of unregulated development. In one of those advertisements, a bulldozer comes over a ridge in a cloud of dust; the text reads "Los Angeles doesn't work, so they are sending it here." We coined a word for these ads that later had all sorts of other uses: "Californication" was the noun, "Californicate" the verb. Print media advertising was our biggest expense in the years 1972 to 1975.

The developers escalated. One night, a small bomb was exploded outside the Colonias sales office. After the bombing, the developers, through their lawyers, pretended to be aggrieved and claimed that our ads had created the "inflammatory atmosphere" that provoked this "act of terrorism." I, they charged, as the chief ad writer and director of the organization responsible for the ads, was a provocateur. And, they hinted darkly, an "eco-terrorist," the term having only recently been put into circulation. On the day after the bombing, they went before a judge and requested an injunction against any further speech on the subject, no more ads.

We were sure that the developers had planted the bomb themselves but there was no way to prove it. Meanwhile, we had to address the request for what amounted to a gag order. Our defense stood on three legs: there was no evidence of any connection between the ads and the bombing or between me and the bombing; diminishing water resources was a matter in the public interest; and most importantly, the first amendment protected our right to speak. I sat in the courtroom and listened as our young attorney made these arguments. It was the first time I had ever been in a courtroom as a defendant. That the Constitution provided the foundation of our defense gave me a sense of proud identity with the United States. Our attorney was named Seth Montgomery, a young man who went on to become the chief justice of the New Mexico Supreme Court. We prevailed. The judge agreed. No prior restraint. Injunction denied.

In the aftermath of our success in court, however, the developers became even more threatening. By this time, we were convinced that Mafia interests in Tucson and Las Vegas were using some of the subdivisions to launder money. My co-director, Sally, whose children still lived at home, began receiving late night heavy-breather phone calls. The threats grew more serious. Her son was followed home from school by a car with four men in it, the car so close that it tapped the back fender of his bicycle. The boy was terrified. Sally's babysitter was also followed and run off the road when she had Sally's daughter in the car. The babysitter became so frightened that she quit. Sally received a phone call in which her children were directly threatened. Ultimately, Sally and I decided that the threat to her children was so serious that she sent them to Kansas to live with her parents until the situation cooled off. We informed the FBI about these threats. This may have had some effect; more effective, however, was calling them out. We told many legislators, those who were our friends, knowing that the word would filter through the system to those who weren't our friends, but who may not have wanted to be associated with Mafia tactics.

There was an attempt to discredit me, assassination in the modern way, by painting me as a drug dealer. I learned of this scheme when two hippies appeared in my office one day. I'd never met them before but they knew of me and approved of what I was doing. They told me that they had been paid $250 each to plant drugs in my office. A brave friend volunteered to infiltrate this operation. He was successful. The plan was to blackmail me into leaving the state. Another friend in Taos recalls that there were men known as undercover narcotics agents snooping around town asking questions. "Some heavy people are after you," he told me.

At the same time, a senior state police officer was sent around to numerous legislators and businessmen to discreetly "investigate" me, a ploy that allowed the policeman to imply that I was a drug dealer. The interviewees were instructed not to inform me that I was being investigated. Several people, both politicians and business leaders, who knew the charge was ridiculous, violated the prohibitions and informed me. I called the lead political columnist at the Albuquerque Journal, whom I knew well, and told him everything I knew about the threats, the attempts to plant drugs, the bogus investigations, and my certainty about mob involvement. In March 1972, the paper ran the story. "State Police Check Mudd" read the headline. The story gave me the platform that I needed to explain the connections between political corruption, the mob, and the land developers. Nothing so effectively kills vermin as fresh air and sunshine, as the expression has it, and by going public, I had called them out again. And I had experienced firsthand the value of a free and courageous press. In 1975, when Mafia interests began pushing for legalized gambling in New Mexico, I wrote an opinion piece that made explicit the charges of political corruption and the connection between gambling, subdivisions, and the mob. Gambling, except as it has cropped up on Indian reservations across America, did not come to New Mexico.

The bogus investigations ceased. I let it be known that I had assembled a dossier of information about various kinds of corruption, both in the political sphere and in certain business cliques, which would be turned over to the FBI and the press if anything happened to me. My file didn't consist of much, but nothing physical was attempted or threatened thereafter. The timing of our challenge to the hidden Mafia interests was fortunate. We had defeated them in New Mexico, but they remained active in neighboring Arizona. In 1976, an investigative reporter for the Arizona Republic, Don Bolles, was killed by a bomb planted in his car. Bolles was investigating the connections between the Mafia, politicians, and land deals; he had been an invaluable source of information for us. The men who planted the bomb were caught and convicted. Those who had ordered the hit were never named.

The Clearing House victories continued. In response to a CCH lawsuit a federal judge ordered construction at Colonias de Santa Fe to cease until the water question was effectively and transparently addressed. Since there never could be enough water for the projected population of the development, the project was effectively dead. Our lawsuit established the applicability to Indian reservations of a regulation that required an Environmental Impact evaluation of any major project in which there was a claim of federal interest. Indian reservations, because of the stewardship role played by the Bureau of Indian Affairs, now fell under this definition.

These encounters—with developers and builders, with promoters and mortgage bankers, with hucksters and mobsters—were skirmishes in the larger effort to fashion a uniform statewide subdivision law regulating all aspects of the process, from standards about sewage and dust control to provisions for funding the public infrastructure to marketing and truth in advertising. Eventually, the other side requested a conference with the goal of coming to a compromise. We reasoned that something was better than nothing and that we would be able to tighten an existing law in future legislative sessions. We agreed to accept a bill that, in retrospect, was too loose. In years to come, the developers argued the fact that since there was something on the books, nothing more was needed. We had been working on the statewide issue for several years by this time, but without meaningful progress. We were buoyed by having successfully faced down the Mafia threats, so we thought we negotiated from strength. But we were few and were exhausted; the developers had unlimited resources and lots of lawyers.

Sally, Brant, and I lived on a steady drip of adrenaline. Disappointments were mixed with successes. I would kick-start the morning with too much coffee and bring myself to a halt in the evening with alcohol, often consumed while talking into the night with some tipsy legislator about energy policy. I would try to explain why the practice of externalizing costs—the electric utilities pocketed the profits while sending their waste out into the air—amounted to an unjust subsidy. I argued that it was hypocrisy to claim that this was a free market solution. One doesn't dump one's household garbage over the neighbor's fence or in a public park. These arguments, to the extent they were even understood, made little headway with legislators who lived on the short election cycle, always under pressure to bring even a few jobs to their constituents. With many legislators, discussion was pointless because they voted as the corporations and lobbyists who funded their campaigns instructed. Some venality was so petty that it was comical. One representative said that he would vote for our bill if I brought him a hippie girl.

The Native Americans of the Southwest, especially the Navajos and the Hopi, have become very much a part of the struggles around energy policy. They are painfully entangled in America's energy dilemma because, in one of the great ironies of history, some of the reservations, the fragments of their ancestral lands, have turned out to be rich in valuable resources, coal and water. Times have changed, though. It is no longer politically feasible to send in the cavalry. Lawyers now do the appropriating. Money has replaced bullets.

The case of the Hopi is instructive. Today the Hopi number nearly 19,000 souls. They live in stone villages perched like medieval castles on the tops of mesas in northern Arizona; they are poor by our general standards, but they are still lords of a land that is vast, empty, and breathtakingly beautiful. The Hopi have lived in these villages for an estimated 800 years. The sun is brilliant. The winter brings heavy snows. The water they drink, wash in, and cook with, and which irrigates their crops comes from springs that are fed by an ancient aquifer.

The aquifer is at risk. A coal company is emptying it for the sole purpose of transporting coal. The coal mixed with water becomes slurry that is then pumped to a power plant on the California border, the Mojave Generating Station. The water, then too toxic for any further use, is discarded through evaporation. The destruction of the aquifer would mean the destruction of the Hopi as a culture, a concern that continues to this day. There is controversy, however, within the Native American communities because the mines have provided jobs for nearly forty years, jobs that did not exist before the development of the coal. The mine has undoubtedly provided a better material standard of living for some Hopi and Navajo. Royalties from Hopi water and coal pay most tribal government salaries, creating a form of social organization and employment that is foreign to the Hopi, but upon which many are now dependent. These economic improvements have been, some think, a devil's bargain. The benefits will disappear when either the water or the coal has been depleted. If it is the water that goes first, the Hopi would be forced to abandon the ancestral villages and their traditional culture, move to the cities of the white man and, if they are lucky, to get government-funded retraining. Americans have always moved on when a boom ends. It is in the white American tradition to uproot. For Native Americans, the land, not a house, not a job, is home.

I witnessed a moving encounter between the Hopi and the other America in 1972. By the summer of that year, the environmental movement had generated national interest in the energy issues generally and of the Colorado Plateau in particular. The Mojave plant was already operational and the Kaiparowits Generating Station was in the planning stage. Kaiparowits, if built, would be even larger than Four Corners. A congressional fact finding delegation was sent west to hold hearings. Everyone with a stake in the outcome, the power company representatives, Native Americans, and environmentalists, converged on Page, Arizona, on a day in August. Before the formal hearings began, a strange scene unfolded on the airstrip.

The heat shimmered on the macadam, creating the mirage of water. The desert sun reflected off the cowlings and wings of the chartered twin-engine airplanes of the Washington attendees and the utility company lawyers. The men from the corporate and government worlds stood in the sun in their dark suits while a small group of Hopi elders explained their view of the world. A tribal leader in his seventies named Thomas Banyayca, a man known and respected by all of us in the environmental movement, was the center of attention. Thomas was barrel-chested, with a deep melodious voice; he wore a starched white shirt and the traditional Hopi red headband. Helped by another Hopi chief, a wiry old man with a furrowed face and wearing Ray-Bans against the mind-stunning glare, Thomas unrolled a discolored muslin cloth about six feet long. It was an ancient text, probably copied over and over as earlier versions of it disintegrated, a document that only he and other old men could interpret. The text was pictographic, little glyphs laid out linearly. Whether Thomas read from left to right, or globally, interpreting the whole, I do not know. Thomas explained, in the clipped English characteristic of Native Americans, that the scroll was a warning about the end of the world.

This catastrophe, he said, would come through mankind's refusal to recognize the laws that govern the planet. He used the word "laws." These laws were, in his understanding of the world, sacred principles, but as I listened to him, I realized that they could be translated into the language of science. He was describing such things as the carbon cycle, photosynthesis, and rates of aquifer recharge. Climate change was not yet an issue, but by implication, Thomas was talking about catastrophes of that magnitude.

The Hopis had brought to the conference their most persuasive argument. The other Americans, because of their worldview and the agendas that they pursued, their certainties about the inevitability of progress and the virtue in profit, were simply incapable of hearing it. I could see in their faces what they thought of the presentation. It was little more than a roadside attraction, something to entertain the tourists.

But in this case our efforts and the combined efforts of other groups paid off. California, the state with the highest level of sensitivity to environmental issues, had noted that activities that California prohibited, like coal-burning power plants, were locating just across the state line to get around that law. Now, through the regulatory process, California was moving to address the air pollution concerns raised by the Kaiparowits project; the state was involved because the electricity would be sold to California utilities. In the end, the California Public Utilities Commission killed Kaiparowits on environmental grounds.

But the problem was, and still is, that when we chopped off one giant's head, we found that there was another giant right behind it. There were other power plants planned. Las Vegas, which doesn't turn its lights off even in the middle of the day, was growing rapidly, as was Los Angeles. The growth rate of Phoenix was exponential and Arizona politics were decidedly anti-environment. The operator and co-owner of these plants, the Arizona Public Service Company, opposed regulation of any kind at every stage of development and permitting, a tactic that required fights already won to be fought again. And again. Furthermore, they habitually cheated to get around existing regulations. As recently as June of 2015, for instance, the owners of the Four Corners Plant signed a consent decree with the EPA that acknowledges that they had circumvented a regulation that mandated upgrading anti-pollution technology when a plant was significantly expanded or reconfigured. By pleading no contest, they were admitting that they had broken the law. The fine was a slap on the wrist, but the cost of upgrading their equipment would be significant.

The air quality got better. Then it got worse. Then better. Automobile pollution controls have made a big difference. Coal is another matter.

Because of the power of the corporations in the energy sector, cleaning up coal-burning power plants is a Sisyphean task. The root problem is American consumption. At the 1992 Earth Summit in Rio, President George H.W. Bush declared that "the American Way of Life" was not negotiable.

I saw our efforts as vital, urgent, and honorable, even then, before the far more serious threats of climate change that we face today. I thought it the best thing I could do with my life and with the money I had inherited from my grandfather. I did occasionally wonder if I might be slightly mad. I could have done almost anything else.

I often tried to see these questions and struggles from the perspective of my paternal ancestors. For three generations they had been in the natural resource business. They were miners. How would they have responded to the shifting of environmental consequences to someone far away either in place or time, or to the destruction of a native culture to satisfy the appetites of another? I couldn't say. My father had no particular affinity for intangibles like a culture, like traditional societies, and certainly not the idea that the land itself could be viewed as sacred. If a landscape contained useful minerals, that would be and should be considered its best use. And he believed that relentless change was in itself a good thing. As to the Hopis, I am sure that he would have thought that jobs, especially those that paid more than farming, would be adequate compensation. My father's blind spot was his nearly religious faith in an American model in which free markets ruled and should outweigh considerations that he thought were purely sentimental. I was so sure that his opinions were unshakable that I decided there was nothing to be gained by discussing these matters with him. I knew I would not change his mind, so I kept my focus on the practical level. I worked on changing laws. The more ambitious goal of changing attitudes in the American polity would, I hoped, follow. My father did, in fact, come along part way. After he retired from business and no longer had obligations to the shareholders, his views became less rigid, more sympathetic.

Toward the end of my father's life, as our relationship improved, we revisited these subjects often. I remembered his more progressive ideas. He favored a progressive income tax, arguing that since the rich had more they could, and in fact should, pay a higher rate of taxation. He once told me that he had so many loopholes available to him that his tax rate was lower than his own secretary's and he thought this wrong and that it did not make good sense from the perspective of promoting a healthy society. As to regulating business and restraining capitalism, I argued that Capitalism was a belief system, a dogma, like many others. "Free markets, like Popes, are neither infallible nor always virtuous." He allowed that I might have a point. His most radical idea was that the rich have more than enough and that, *nothing else,* was what defined "rich." Rich did not necessarily mean morally better or smarter. In this, his opinions had not changed. His behavior had, however, and in ways that revealed some conflict between his values. But we dropped the subject. We were not, either of us, trying to score points.

27

Lovers, Mothers, Fathers, Daughters and Terrible Pain

My weeks were full of meetings and interviews, strategizing and writing. Weekends I returned to Arroyo Hondo to be with Alicia and the baby. These relatively quiet times were a welcome respite from my involvement with the complexities of environmental politics. Alicia and I had an amusing menagerie of animals: Charlie, our dog, had made friends with Mariposa, the pig. They slept together on a mattress in the garage. We also had a white rat, called Fortunata, that had the run of the bedroom until lights out, when she went back into her cage. I think, though, that we were both unhappy. I knew I was. But neither of us would have said so. Because of her limited English, she could not participate in my political activities so she was left out of a good part of my life.

But if I could not bring Alicia into my public life, I felt that I could, at least, introduce her and our baby to my birth family. It was time, I thought, after three years of estrangement from my mother to try again and I thought that a first grandchild might be a gift she would welcome. I hoped that the passage of time had blurred the outlines of the event in bedroom and erased her shame, or even better, perhaps, that she had managed to suppress the memory of the incident entirely. Temporary insanity was the way I now explained it to myself and this permitted me to think that some relationship with my mother was still possible.

I felt, apparently, that having a mother, even one who was as disturbed as mine, was better than having no mother at all. "I am," she had said that night, "still your mother."

In preparation for a trip to Los Angeles, I sent pictures of the baby to her, to my father, and to my mother's mother, my last surviving grandparent. My grandmother was bedridden, but according to my sister, Victoria, who was a reliable observer of our Los Angeles family, she was alert and completely present. I looked forward to the trip.

My mother was first on the family tour. While her new home was being built, she lived with her husband in a leased penthouse on Bunker Hill, overlooking Los Angeles' version of Lincoln Center, the Dorothy Chandler Pavilion. Years earlier my mother had told me that she had been "more than just acquainted" with Mrs. Chandler, a significant social coup in that Mrs. Chandler was the queen of Los Angeles society. I thought that my mother's nuanced parsing of social connection said a great deal about her and what mattered to her.

I had announced our visit weeks in advance, but my mother invited us for drinks only, not dinner. The help would be stressed, she said. This was the excuse that she would use to limit my access to her or her exposure to me for the next twenty-five years. In the present case, however, since this excuse was new to me, I believed her. I could see that an infant, feeding, changing diapers, would tax her household regimes. She was very rigid.

When we arrived at her apartment, I was carrying our daughter. I introduced Alicia, who looked beautiful and exotic. She was noticeably uncomfortable. I did the talking. My mother had a way of being perfectly gracious, both in words and gesture, and at the same time making it clear that she was merely being polite. I offered to let my mother hold the baby. She declined, saying, "I'm afraid that I would drop her." She never touched her grandchild, not on that occasion or any other.

I bluffed along through the evening in a state of denial, pretending that I did not notice her rejection. We engaged in some small talk, admiring the view of the city lights. Finally, I informed my mother that we were going next to visit my grandmother. My mother's reaction was strange. She blanched, almost losing her customary self control. Recovering, she set about trying to dissuade me, arguing that her mother was too frail for the emotional excitement of an infant in the house. I was puzzled; why would my grandmother not want to see a great grandchild? When we left, I knew we were going in defiance of what had amounted to an order, though why I could not imagine.

Andrew, now my grandmother's caregiver in all respects, met us at the door. He wore his usual at-home uniform, a starched white jacket and a black bow tie. He was as slender and wiry as he had been as a young man. He held his arms out and embraced me, gently, for I held the baby. I had known him since I was ten years old, but had not seen him for seven or eight years. Though he had never met Alicia, he embraced her too. I gave him the baby to hold; he cooed and smiled.

We went upstairs, Andrew leading the way. He went into the room first. "Mrs. Kingston," he said, "your grandson is here with a surprise." Because I had sent pictures, I was puzzled by the remark. My grandmother, propped up on huge pillows and wearing a feathered pink dressing gown, stared at the child in my arms with astonishment. She said that she had not known the child existed. Perhaps she was getting senile. I gave the baby to her and she accepted with pleasure, but was clearly confused.

As we left I told Andrew that I had sent my grandmother at least two letters with pictures of the baby, expecting him to say that she was getting forgetful.

"Your mother," Andrew said, "screens her mother's mail and has not allowed your letters to reach her." He gave me a look that was full of compassion and sadness, compassion for me and sadness for his charge, my imprisoned grandmother. Was it that Alicia was Mexican? Or, I've thought in later years, when more of the facts were available to me, perhaps my mother's solicitous concern for her mother was a kind of revenge for being forced into a marriage she did not want, imprisonment in old age as punishment for the prison my mother had been consigned to at age nineteen. I pictured my mother tearing up my letters to my grandmother, discarding the snapshots. How dare she? The anger that I had managed to suppress for so many years came to the surface.

But in spite of this slap, this inexcusable act, I didn't want my feelings about my mother to create a wedge between me and my California heritage. Her family was old California, the pioneer American generation going back to the pre-gold rush days; and I was proud of that heritage. These currents eddied around me as I struggled with my anger over this latest rejection. My mother's family and California were part of my story. They had been pioneers. I was a pioneer as well. It was in my genes, in the instruction manual for living that I had inherited.

I felt strongly enough about the connection to the California story line that for the next twenty-five years, I returned to Los Angeles once a year and kept, politely, knocking at my mother's door. I offered to bring Mariana on several other occasions, but it was always an inconvenient time for my mother. I don't think it was about Mariana; it was about me. My puzzlement about her behavior was a bit like an itch or a wound. Every once in a while, I would scratch at it. It would be years after her death before the scab came off. My mother only saw her granddaughter on one other occasion, and it was a most painful encounter.

We next visited my father who received us warmly and held his granddaughter, unafraid of dropping her. While Alicia took the baby off to my father's bedroom to nurse her, he told me that Dan, my childhood best friend, had killed himself, shot himself with his service handgun in a vacant lot near the golf course behind the houses of our respective families. My father and I reminisced. My father and we two, Danny and I, age about twelve, were at my father's ranch during a great winter rain. A flash flood filled a ravine, and we boys, soaking wet, covered in mud, struggled to build a dam to make, as we imagined it, a little lake that we would stock with trout. We dragged sticks and rocks, and pressed mud into the cracks. My father, also soaking and covered with mud, had been the chief of works. We were not successful, but it had been great fun. That was the Danny that I remembered. He became the man who went off to fight a war in a jungle. Dan had survived the jungle but was a casualty nonetheless. There was no doubt that he had died of war wounds, wounds to the spirit that are now called PTSD. His name does not appear on the wall of the Vietnam memorial on the Mall in Washington D.C. and this strikes me as an injustice.

My father's sadness about Dan's death was genuine. Dan's father was my father's closest friend.

"I'm not good at comforting," he said with tears in his eyes. Alicia returned to the room with the baby. My father took the baby again and cradled her. He smiled at Alicia and said to me, "Tell her in Spanish that the baby is lovely."

Before Alicia and I returned to New Mexico I paid a visit to Dan's mother to offer my condolences. It was on that occasion that I heard the story of my parents' courtship, the sense that it had been a sort of arranged marriage. Dan's mother hinted that despite the fact that my mother smiled at everyone, she was not a happy woman. Alicia had seen the smiles but had experienced my mother's behavior for what it was, a practiced social craft, and as a rejection not just of her, but of our child as well. It was a reasonable interpretation and it did not help Alicia's already fragile emotional state.

When summer came and the Rio Hondo was no longer the icy stream of the spring, Mariana would sit in the stream and splash. It was a delight to watch. But perhaps because things seemed so peaceful, the dark currents that had been always present in Alicia's heart broke their banks. Our lives changed again.

We were sitting outside, under the porch roof, Alicia said, "Harvey, I have something to tell you."

She had never made such an announcement before. I was alarmed. Was she going back to Mexico? I didn't want that. Was she sick? It was, I could tell by her demeanor, a difficult thing to say. She reverted to Spanish.

"Ellos me violaron, tres hombres."

They raped me. Three men.

Alicia began to sob. She said, now speaking entirely in Spanish, that she had been afraid that I would reject her if I had known. This would have been the last thing I would have done or thought. But she came from the macho culture of Mexico where a woman was thought of as male property, and property could be damaged; and she came from the Catholic culture, a tangle of medieval ideas about sin and the body. I understood why she might have feared my reaction. I held her and reassured her.

Now that I knew this terrible truth, her depressions were entirely understandable. I urged her again, now more forcefully, to get help, but cultural and Catholic attitudes interfered. I think depression seemed to Alicia like the sin of despair, a loss of hope, which was tantamount to falling away from God. Or, more prosaically, an admission of failure. Her adventure, taking the risk of coming to America, of running away with an entirely irreligious American, had been a mistake. She had none of my understanding of the unconscious and had nothing of the positive view that I had of the psychological arts.

Alicia had gone from being an enthusiastic college student to being little more than housekeeper and my bedmate, housebound in a closed rural community. Her dream had ended with what I had thought had been a mugging. And now that the real trauma had been revealed, it was more understandable. Violence and evil had found its way into our lives. I tried to think of it as if we had survived a car crash, an accident, but it was worse than that; and I struggled to find the most helpful way to react. I was never sure that I got it right.

Alicia had kept this terrible secret from me for over two years. She kept it from her family. After she died in 2015, with all her siblings dead, our daughter gave me permission to write about it. The event had been a pivotal point in three lives, hers, of course, and, collaterally, ours, thus mine.

∗ ∗ ∗

Time passed. We tried to find a way back to a normal life, to innocence, a time before anything terrible had happened. But we were pretending, playing roles that would be expected of people who had not lived through a terrible accident. I had responsibilities away from the home and chose to honor them. When we were together we talked about the baby, the antics of the animals. But the trauma had already, for almost two years, begun a slow, almost imperceptible erosion, a weakening of our world. Now, with me knowing the cause and Alicia having spoken of it, things might be different, and on the surface, Alicia seemed to be coping. But we were unable to talk about the underlying issues, never about the what she had experienced or how she felt about it. I would suggest that she express what she was feeling, but she could not. It was not that she refused, it was that she was unable. The memory of the experience was simply too painful.

I now felt guilty about many things in respect to Alicia. Our relationship had begun with a spirit of rebellious romance, an innocent love across cultural lines. But I had not anticipated just how difficult the relationship might be for her. I had not protected her. I felt frustrated that neither love nor patience seemed to affect her underlying mood. I thought that I should be able to do more, be kinder, be something better.... and I felt guilty at my frustration with her. And I was angry that Alicia would do nothing to help herself, and feeling angry also made me feel guilty. I felt guilty that I was able to live more normally, more in the present, than she was.

I had preliminary conversations with two therapists, Spanish-speaking women, and had given Alicia their names. There was no question that Alicia understood that what was happening to us was not good. At one point she offered to return to Mexico, where she would at least be in her own culture. But I wanted to continue being a father and so dissuaded her. I felt guilty about that too; she would have been better off in Mexico and I knew it. I kept hoping that her decline would stop, and seeing my commitment to our child, she would realize that that commitment included her, and that she would come out of her depression. But we were no longer the same people who had met in Mexico City four years earlier. Heraclitus' axiom about the river had a corollary: If one has fallen into the river and almost drowned, one never climbs out of it as the person one was before.

Our emotional life became ever flatter and more superficial. I tried to be a responsible person, but I didn't seem to be that person. Without wanting to, without warning or premeditation, I fell in love with someone else. I ended my relationship with Alicia as carefully as I could but without pretending to myself that it would be anything but devastating for her. I did it without delays, without sneaking, without lies, without hoping that she would suggest it, thus sparing me from the guilt. When I told her, she walked out of the house and stood in the night by our vegetable garden and wept. I had only seen her cry once before. There was the sound of a breeze rustling the corn leaves.

The next weeks were a blur. She, with Mariana, now nearly three, moved into a little house in Santa Fe. I put the house in the valley on the market and it sold in a month. Later Alicia carved an apple out of balsa wood and stained it with her own blood, from a wound in her thumb made deliberately with an X-acto knife. It was a very Mexican expression of the broken heart that I had caused.

The woman I fell in love with was named Lee. I had seen her a year earlier at a gallery opening. She had been accompanied, so I did not approach her, but I had noticed her. I saw her next in the summer of 1973, in a bar in Santa Fe. I found out her name, went up to the table where she sat with several woman friends, introduced myself, and offered to drive her home. It wasn't far, close enough to walk, but she accepted. In the car, as if in the grip of some certainty that I had no rational reason to have, I told her that my relationship with Alicia had failed and had come to an end, a finality that I had probably not acknowledged to myself until that moment. I told her that I had a child, that I wanted to change my life, and that I wanted to include her in this new life. How could I possibly think this? This woman who sat in my car, beneath a streetlight on a dirt lane in Santa Fe, New Mexico, was a stranger. It was folly. I didn't know her, but I was sure that I did. For the next three days, Lee and I exchanged notes, some phone calls, and a dinner. It wasn't flirtation, because we both seemed to know that the conclusion was foregone.

Lee was a tall, lithe, athletic woman with short cropped hair and an odd way of looking at one, a cocking of her head, the result of a childhood injury that had left the muscles in one side of her left eye too short, a defect that she compensated for by turning her whole head if you were on her left side. Her arms were long and her legs too, her skin tanned, her fingers graceful. Her lips were full and she had a smile that even today, some forty years later, I think of as being like a break in the clouds. She moved like no woman I'd ever seen, a sort of loping stride, but graceful. By her accent, I knew she had had a patrician, East Coast upbringing, but she had bolted, just as I had, as soon as her majority permitted, had run off with a dashing man, had a child who was ten years old at the time I met her. Lee was thirty-four and I thirty-one.

Within a month of our meeting, I had moved into Lee's house. Her daughter accepted my sudden presence in her world without missing a step. I had always liked children and was happy to have another one in my life.

Our entry into a life together was effortless. We had ignored all the conventional ways of courtship and bypassed all the usual checkpoints. There was no approach and withdrawal, no assessing of each other's strengths and weaknesses, no seduction. None of that was necessary. It was as if we had slipped into a warm current that had always existed but which was unknown until we, for whom it had been intended, came along. We were like a pair of dolphins, swimmers with perfect knowledge of the other's moods and desires. We had found in ourselves, each of us, the capacity to find in another human being an ineffable perfection. The remarkable thing was that we were able to ignore the illogic of such a belief. We had the wisdom, or the audacity, to submit to it as if it was beyond dispute.

* * *

Lee worked as an administrator at a private school and was out of the house each morning at 7:15 a.m. I went each day to my office at the Central Clearing House. Lee's daughter went to school. We cooked together. Lee played the piano and I learned to like Chopin. My daughter Mariana came to visit often and had her own little bed in a room down the hall from ours. Those visits were important because Alicia's depression had deepened to a stage in which she would go for hours without speaking to the child. Alicia herself was concerned about the effect her silence might be having on Mariana. So, off and on, Mariana was a part of my life with Lee. For Alicia, this arrangement was both a relief and a source of pain.

As to the dramas in my political and environmental activities, Lee seemed unconcerned, not minding the dangers and tensions that my work generated. I had been told that a contract would be put out on me if I didn't let up in my efforts against the land developers. Sally had received a similar threat. I dismissed it. Mobsters, lobbyists, fuming senators, corrupt policemen were part of the work environment. If Lee did worry about me, she never complained. It was as if there was a protective shield around us. We felt invulnerable; as if happiness might last forever.

Articles about me appeared in the *Los Angeles Times*, offending my mother who, I heard from a sibling, thought that my views were in bad taste. Bad taste was, for her, a worse opprobrium than a word like "radical." As the result of these articles, however, I was invited by the student body at Harvey Mudd College to give the commencement address of 1972. I was expected to address environmental themes. In accepting the invitation to give the speech, I felt that I was completing the circle of my relationship with my grandfather. I believed that he would have understood me, but this may have been wishful thinking. My father, however, certainly did not understand or approve and did not attend. I was disappointed. This period, when my environmental activities were at their most visible, marks the nadir of my relationship with my mining company executive father.

Not long after the speech, he expressed his opinion indirectly. I received a letter from the bank in Los Angeles that managed the trust established by my grandfather, the trust that was the source of the funds that supported the Clearing House and most of the environmental movement in the state. My father, the letter said, had instructed the bank to cease distributing money to me because he believed that I was on a misguided path. By cutting off the money, my father was silencing the sort of political and public media speech that we did best. He would have succeeded in doing what the developers had tried to do through their lawsuit and the mafia by threats. My clash with land developers, however, wasn't what bothered him; it was my challenge to the mining industry, the copper smelters and coal mine operators. The men who headed these companies were his professional acquaintances and he had heard from them.

I was furious. At thirty-two years, I was a respected advocate for causes supported by growing numbers of the American people. My opponents had not been able to scare me off or out-argue our positions, but they had found a way to suppress both the activity and the expression of opinion. I consulted a lawyer and was told that, by the terms of the trust, my father had neither the right nor the legal power to cut me off. I traveled to Los Angeles to negotiate with him, but got nowhere. I realized that to fight him, I would be challenging not just my biological father, but certain inherited, if unconscious, ideas of authority. The father *is* authority, and even as iconoclastic and unconventional as I was, I had always been inclined to acknowledge a natural authority in my father. But in this matter I couldn't. His reasons were those of the short-term financial interests of a very small segment of the population, certain corporations and their chiefs. I was an advocate for a far wider array of interests and I was pursuing these goals democratically and through persuasion.

I wrote him a careful letter in which I indicated that I would be forced to bring a lawsuit against the bank and him if necessary, a step I would take only as a last resort. It seems that he consulted his attorney and relented. The crisis passed.

Angry as I was, I believed that my relationship with my father had a sound foundation and that this rift would heal. I understood his position. He had a set of values that he could not easily abandon. At the same time, I was sure that my positions were sound from the perspective of the generation that I represented and from the perspective of the new ecological sciences that had emerged since his university days. We knew different things. He knew the mining business in depth. I knew, in as much depth as was possible at the time, what the future held if the world continued with business as usual. Because of this understanding of macro issues, I knew that I stood with the future. I knew also that I was neither a revolutionary nor a nihilist. I sought to reform and modify, but by no means shut down, the engines of the economy through which my grandfather and father had prospered. I thought of myself as reinvesting some of that money in the idea of a more sustainable and conscious economy.

Nevertheless, I knew both of my parents, especially my mother, were more than uncomfortable with both my ideas and my visibility. I inferred from things that she said to my brothers that my mother believed that any questioning of the status quo in America was tinged with disloyalty, both to class and perhaps even to country. She seemed to have an underlying belief that "right" was a quality inherent in wealth and that wealthy de facto meant virtuous. To doubt this belief was somehow worse than mere heresy. It may have seemed to her as a flirtation with something almost as bad as Communism. On one of my annual visits, I tried to discuss these issues. I asked her if the fact that she could no longer see the Hollywood sign from her desk bothered her. Her reply, in effect, was that she hadn't even noticed. Her home was air-conditioned; she had shown me the gleaming mechanical room, with its control panels and glowing green lights.

The financial crisis passed. A personal crisis materialized. Alicia announced that she was no longer able to live in the United States. She wanted to go back to Mexico, to her own people, and to take Mariana with her. This was a blow. I wanted Mariana to grow up as an American. I had no objection to her straddling both cultures and having dual citizenship, but I wanted the American side of her psychological border to be dominant. I was still emotionally engaged with the institutions of American democracy and identified with America. Mexico, at that time, was a sham democracy, a single party state run by oligarchs and generals. Furthermore, I wanted to participate in my daughter's upbringing. But for Alicia, being in the same town with Lee and me was simply too painful. There was no argument that could undo that feeling and my only leverage was financial support. My father's attempt to use financial coercion on me was a lesson I could not ignore. If it had been wrong for my father to do it to me, it would have been equally wrong for me to do it to Alicia. So I helped her pack up her Santa Fe life. They went to Mexico City. I would support her in whatever ways I could.

My heart ached for my daughter. I remembered how my father's absences during the Second World War had affected me. I wanted to be a present and attentive father, to provide more than my father, kept away on war business, had been able to provide for me. I understood that if I lost contact with her now, at age three, she could be emotionally lost to me forever. She would forget who I was and would have to relearn each time I reappeared.

My dilemma became Lee's and then, of course, ours. I had decided that it was important that I go to Mexico City at intervals not much longer than a month and that I stay for four or five days each trip. I would live in a hotel and take Mariana on outings, to the zoo, the parks, the usual things fathers with visitation rights do with their children. I would go regularly and dependably.

Lee understood the issue of the missing father only too well. Her father had been killed in 1944 in a kamikaze attack in the Pacific. She was not sure that she remembered her father, but she knew that she once had one and then she did not. Her mother had taken up with another man in her father's absence, a man she eventually married, a story of infidelity and the replacing of mates that must have been all too common during wartime. So when the news came of her father's death, there was no mourning, only relief on her mother's part. She was free. And since there was no body to return, there was no funeral, no memorial, and no closure.

Lee's loss, the sense of being fatherless, had injured her soul. With my regular departures, she began to relive that loss. She had had a breakdown in her teens. As an adult she had learned to contain her childhood sorrow. Then, by trying to do the right thing for my child, I did the wrong thing for Lee. She recognized that there was a danger to her and to us in the situation, so she began seeing a psychiatrist. But persistent sorrow, memory of sorrow, gradually overwhelmed this beautiful woman whom I loved so much. I watched, helpless, as our relationship suffered. Each time I left, Lee fell into a hole. Each time I returned, it took her longer to recover. It was a reversal of the Orpheus and Eurydice story; each month we wandered deeper into the underworld.

Some injuries to the soul are neither approachable by reason nor curable by any sort of medical practice. Lee was not a weak woman nor was she a sick one. She was one who felt things deeply. Her heart had been injured in childhood, a war wound, a loss, and now the wound reopened.

The loss that I experienced during the war was the sense that the world was a good and safe place. For Lee it was that and much more. The daughter's anguish that is rendered so powerfully in Aeschylus' *Agamemnon*—her father's death and her mother's betrayal of her father even before his death—was Lee's. She was tall and beautiful; she was a good mother; she played Chopin. But she lived a tragedy. She was my Electra.

Lee and I lived in this strained and miserable state for over six months. I kept hoping that this erosion would reverse itself. We never fought. She never suspected me of infidelity. Eventually, exhausted, she had a breakdown and was hospitalized. Her psychiatrist told us that we must separate. We knew it was true and we did. Never in my life, before or since, have I had to choose between two people I loved. I chose the child. Perhaps it was what I owed Alicia.

28

The Study of History

Mexico City became my second home for a period of a year and a half. On one of those regular visits, a historical event changed the way I saw the world.

I had arrived in Mexico City at night and had gone straight to my hotel, the slightly down-at-the-heels Majestic on the main plaza, the Zócalo. I rose late next morning and went up to the rooftop cafe for breakfast. As I stepped out onto the red tiles of the terrace, I saw the volcano, snow covered, serene and symmetrical, the home of gods long since exiled. To see the mountain, Popocatepetl, usually hidden by smog, so clearly was breathtaking, and for a moment I was swept back to the ancient Tenochtitlan, the Aztec capital, with its causeways and floating gardens, the pyramids that echoed the form of the volcano, back to the time before the coming of the Europeans with their guns, their diseases, and their religion, the strange white race that would put it all to the torch.

That morning was September 11th, 1973. Around 11:30 a.m., and seven stories below, I could see people converging on Calle Madero, the street beside the hotel. The usual pattern of foot traffic in the Zócalo is one of pleasant urban disorder, people going every which way, a criss-crossing of pedestrians off to home or work or to market, but clearly, that morning, something had happened. I took the elevator down to the lobby and went out onto the street. There was an agitated knot of young and middle-aged men crowded around the news kiosk. I could hear the news vendor saying, *"Acabado. No hay mas."* Sold out. A short, barrel -chested man with salt and pepper hair and a thick mustache, worked his way out of the cluster by the kiosk and came toward me clutching a copy of *La Prensa* in his hand. He stopped perhaps five feet away, and looked directly at me, not with hostility or recognition, but with bewilderment. Tears streamed down his face. This moment of emotional exposure, his public tears, was a breach in the usual Mexican machismo. He was, for that brief moment, my *compadre,* and I, his.

"Que pasa?" I asked.

"Allende está muerto, asesinado," he said, moving his newspaper up and down as if trying to shake what it contained out onto the pavement. The men around the newsstand stood about in small groups. They looked stunned. The word of the calamity was spreading. Salvador Allende, the elected socialist president of Chile, an inspiration to all Latin Americans who had struggled beneath military or oligarchic oppression for centuries, was dead. General Pinochet's coup was underway. I was witnessing the event from a perspective I would not have had if I had been in the United States.

My reaction to the coup in Chile was anger and dismay; a democracy toppled, an elected president murdered, the subsequent reports of atrocities, summary executions, and disappearances. These feelings were amplified by what many knew, without being able to prove it, that the CIA had had a hand in it. Eventually this was substantiated. In the White House tapes released thirty-five years later, Richard Nixon and Henry Kissinger can be heard congratulating themselves. They had pulled it off.

My feelings, however, were nothing compared to Alicia's. On that visit, we talked about little else. I recognized in her an emotion I've come to think of as political grief. My feelings had a complement to hers, a patriot's sadness that resulted from feeling that, little by little, I was losing the conviction that America acted well and morally in the world. The political philosopher Hannah Arendt described my intellectual situation: "We can no longer afford to take that which was good in the past and simply call it our heritage, to discard the bad and simply think of it as a dead load, which by itself time will bury in oblivion."

These words spoke directly to me. I knew the good part of my heritage, the foundational myth, the heroism of the two world wars, the earnest struggle to overcome the toxic legacy of slavery. But I realized that I had, to the extent I knew it, relegated the bad to the appendix of the book, to the footnotes, as if it were someone else's story, not ours. With Chile, I reached a point at which a reckoning had to be made: I had to open my eyes, to widen my view, to see the whole story of my country. This was a change that had been slow in coming, but perhaps inevitable given my appetite for knowing.

My involvement with the environmental movement had a lot to do with my disillusionment. I had become acquainted with the nation's other self. I encountered willfully ignorant people and consciously deceitful people. It was a world where corruption of the political process by money was considered the norm, where personal interests often came before the country's needs or the common good. Wealth accumulation was seen as unequivocally and unambiguously virtuous. Power was directly correlated with wealth. I had witnessed practices that I considered criminal: corruption called campaign contributions, faking or suppressing evidence, and outright lies.

The environmental struggle against corporate America had destroyed one set of illusions; the Vietnam War had destroyed another. The famous leak known as "The Pentagon Papers," published by The *New York Times* in 1971, had revealed the war for something worse than mere folly. I read "The Pentagon Papers" and related books, like David Halberstam's *The Best and the Brightest* and Michael Herr's *Dispatches*. Neil Sheehan's *Bright Shining Lie*, which appeared in 1988, gave the war the epic scope it deserved: imperial hubris, tunnel vision, willful ignorance, unjustifiable violence, unprecedented waste. Folly and moral cowardice. In these books, one saw evidence of both conscious deceit and unconscious self-deception. I began to understand that war is a form of corporate welfare, destruction as a subsidy. I saw that our political leaders lacked the qualities that I thought should be fundamental to qualify for leadership of a great country, courage, open minds, and the ability to admit mistakes. How a nation behaves depends, I understood more deeply than I had before, on the personality, the values, and the temperament of the leader. When I first encountered Walt Whitman's dirge on the death of Abraham Lincoln, "O Captain, my Captain," I had heard in Whitman's archaic figure of speech what it meant to have a steady, brave, and thoughtful leader. In Lyndon Johnson and Richard Nixon we had not had such a leader. Ego, concerns about virility and reputation, drove both those men into a sort of frenzy that resulted in a violent crime being committed against a people who had intended no harm to America.

I came into my own as a writer in response to the events in Chile. Twelve days after the coup, the great Chilean poet Pablo Neruda died. It was a suspicious death; he had been a strong Allende supporter and was Chile's most prominent world citizen. I wrote a long poem mourning Neruda and the destroyed Andean democracy, and mourning also the loss of my illusions about my country. Chile had pushed me not only out of the bubble of historical ignorance but also out of my artistic shell. It was as if Neruda's ghost had reached out and shoved me into the light.

In the month after the coup, the University of New Mexico, a campus like so many others on the verge of rebellion because of Vietnam, held a rally in support of Chile. Writers and musicians were invited. I had never read any of my poetry before an audience, but I did that night in the UNM gymnasium, before hundreds of people. My voice shook. But the depth of my feeling about the events in Santiago and about the death of the writer whose book, *España en el Corazon,* had helped shape my perception of the world, gave me courage. This was also the first of my poems ever to be published. My career as a writer, such as it has been, thus began with a political statement. A few lines from the poem described how my perspective changed. *My wife, who's Mexican, cried out / as if I had done it.*

"As if I had done it" had a sting to it. She, Alicia, saw things I had never noticed about the United States. I discovered that the United States had acquired an enormous overseas empire. Initially, beginning with the Spanish American War of 1898, an empire began to be assembled. The Founders of the republic had specifically warned against empire building. Initially it was made up of lands conquered and occupied by U.S. troops. The Spanish-American war left the United States in possession of Spain's remote Pacific colony, the Philippines, which we held as an overseas possession for over fifty years. The Philippine people, who thought that the defeat of Spain meant that they were to be independent, were to be disappointed. The new owners had no intention of giving up this strategic base. The Philippine independence movement, which the American press called an insurgency and its fighters savages, was brutally suppressed. Prisoners were regularly tortured; the "water cure," now called "water boarding," first appeared in the American arsenal during this conflict. The invasion of the Philippines was carried out under the banner of liberating its people. In a 1902 Memorial Day speech, Theodore Roosevelt said, "Our armies do more than bring peace, do more than bring order. They bring freedom."

After this initial period of undisguised empire building, objectives of the United States could usually be classified as economic in the sense of preventing alternative economic models, socialism or communism, from getting a foothold. Governments, effectively clients of the United States, allowed American bases on their soil, but by claiming a degree of sovereignty, the United States has managed to have an empire without colonies. Often, however, if the American government was unhappy with what democracy had produced in those faraway places, it engaged in regime change, a practice that goes back a long way in the diplomatic history of the United States.

I am not writing a history—this is a history known by so many that it cannot be considered news—but a personal story of awakening and subsequent disillusionment. It has many chapters, all of them involving people and places far enough away that most Americans never notice.

The facts about all this are, however, undeniable. The United States has installed oppressive, tyrannical, and sometimes murderous regimes across the globe and supports those regimes so long as those governments remain compliant with American demands, its geo-strategic objectives, and demands for natural resources. In Iran, for instance, in 1953, the United States, along with the British, arranged the coup that toppled the elected leader, Mossadegh, and installed the oppressive Pahlavi Shah. The Shah's secret police, trained by the CIA, were so oppressive that conditions under the Shah led inevitably to the Iranian Revolution, and we know where that has led: hostages, Ayatollahs, and Iranian nuclear ambitions. This pattern held in Greece in 1947 and 1967, Guatemala in 1954, Haiti in 1961, Brazil in 1964, and Zaire in 1961. Indonesia, Nicaragua, Honduras, El Salvador, Cambodia, and South Vietnam. In Guatemala, the elected president was ejected by American gunboats at the request of the United Fruit Company. Henry Kissinger is on record as approving and supporting the Argentine generals who "disappeared" thousands of students, teachers, and intellectuals.

I recalled seeing photographs in the newspaper of the president of Zaire, a "strong man" named Mobuto Sese Seki, sitting on a sofa in the White House with President Nixon. Mobuto had been installed after the elected president, Lumumba, was murdered with U.S. approval and CIA assistance. President Eisenhower had called Lumumba a "mad dog" and suggested that he be destroyed, and he was. Mobuto enjoyed public spectacles of the hanging and dismembering of his political rivals, and ruled for thirty-two years by terror and murder on an astounding scale. With the help of American and other western mining firms, he skimmed the mineral wealth of his country and became one of the world's richest men. And there, pictured in the paper, was a mass murderer having a chat with the American president! I was shocked at the time and am even more so today. Mobuto was received in the White House by three American presidents, Nixon, Reagan, and George H.W. Bush. How could any American, much less the president, sit in the same room with such a monster?

What America was, in terms of values and action, mattered to me.

Through my early adult years, I strongly identified with America. I believed that America's participation in the two World Wars had been necessary and that Americans had acquitted themselves bravely and with honor. The Marshall Plan, which put devastated Europe back on its feet, was enlightened policy, a demonstration of generosity and compassion, *and* an application of wealth and power that had practical benefits for all concerned, a very American approach to the world.

Now, little by little, I was becoming aware of how much of American history I had screened out. I had wanted to live within the legend. Chile and the unavoidable suspicion of regime change orchestrated from Washington opened my eyes. Democracy was fine for Americans, but not for others. I had already begun to read more history. In Thucydides I saw that Athens, the birthplace of democracy, had behaved with similar inconsistency toward the other states in its world. The myth of American goodness, liberty, and democracy, no longer worked for me.

Disillusionment may be another word for enlightenment, for knowing the truth of things. The process of reading history carefully that had begun with my discovery of the suppressed history of Arab Spain had taken another step forward. There would be no going back. Once something is known, it cannot be unknown.

Back in the United States, in my environmentalist role, I continued as before: speeches, legislative sessions, grassroots organizing. I occasionally paused to think about the reasons for the intensity of my involvement with these causes. Once, after a hearing before a legislative committee regarding regulation of water usage by a coal mine, a mining executive approached me in the corridor. After confirming who I was, he politely but unmistakably accused me of not sticking together with those in the minerals extraction business, implying that they were a tribe of some sort and that I, by birth, was of this tribe. He seemed to be accusing me of a sort of betrayal. Because there had been no angry words, I was not especially ruffled by the incident, but I had not until that moment given much thought to the possibility that my environmental activism might appear to others as having nothing to do with ideas or convictions, but merely as rebellion.

But it wasn't. My parents, and perhaps their entire generation, lived on a different mental continent; and as I moved forward, theirs was dropping below the horizon. There was no deliberate betrayal on my part. I was finding loyalties that made more sense to me, more sense intellectually and were more emotionally profound. Those objects conventionally offered as worthy of fealty—family, political party, nation— were not exactly false, but I saw them as limited and limiting. Unquestioning obedience to any political party seemed like a mafia virtue; to a nation, it seemed a neurotic bondage. Identity around nation might be legally necessary for travel across national frontiers, but I was continuing to form a political philosophy, cosmopolitan and not ideological, that didn't require national identity at its center.

The planet, I decided, was the ultimate homeland, and I saw that most of the other homelands, especially those defined in nationalistic, ideological, or religious terms, were not only less important, but that those identities were the cause of unnecessary tensions and too often of violence.

My activities as an environmentalist were about more than changing laws. At a deep personal level, they were the expression of the most meaningful sense of identity that I'd yet found; one that I don't expect will be superseded. In nature I found something to which I could be faithful without feeling embarrassed by my commitment, my fidelity to its cause. There was an almost religious aspect to these feelings. I was becoming an "enlightened pagan," as if I were a devotee of ancient deities, Demeter of the fruitful earth, for instance, but with a devotion that was as rational as it was emotional. In effect, I worshiped with my heart what I could understand through science. It was a sort of religion, but one that did not require the suspension of reason.

* * *

When, in 1970, I began to withdraw my energies from my farm in the Hondo valley, I had intended to return to that life, to the simple chores of irrigating my fields and patching the fence. I had been optimistic about the environmental cause, certain that the battles around clean air and water, around energy use, could be won and won quickly, not only because we had reason and science on our side, but also because we had the interests of the widest possible community in mind, one that included future generations. I had thought, therefore, that I could become a commuter between the valley and the wider world. The valley would remain my home, my sanctuary. But my departure turned out to be permanent. I had lost the naïve idealism that had led me there in the first place. I realized that in the final analysis, I could not defend my paradise—if paradise it ever was—against the pressures and appetites of modernity, against the restless activity, commercial and political, that characterizes America. The valley too would change, not perhaps as fast as the rest of the world, but change it would. *Et en arcadia ego.* Even in paradise, there is death.

I recognized, too, that I needed more than what I could find in Arroyo Hondo. I sensed that the sort of isolation that had made the experience difficult for Alicia, would become difficult for me as well. The village was, in the classical sense of the word, a conservative place; it resisted change. I am conservative in one sense, in that I emphatically resist changes that mean the destruction of nature, but as to me, that was another matter. I knew I would tire of life in the valley. So, with regret, with sadness, I said goodbye to my friends, to the stream, to the land.

I moved to Santa Fe. I still owned land in the valley, but since I was quite sure that I would not be returning, I began to sell it off in little parcels for prices well below the prevailing market, to the children of the Hispanic families that had befriended me. Albert Chacon, Clodoveo's son, back safely from Vietnam, bought one of those parcels.

When, by 1975, it was absolutely clear to me that I would not return, I donated two parcels of land, each about an acre in size, to the village.

The land was to be used for recreation and other community purposes. Since all the land in the village was privately owned, the community as a whole had no access to the beauties of our little stream, so one of the two parcels had frontage on the *rio*. I imagined Fourth of July picnics. I got nothing out of it, no benefit, no tax write off, not even the reward of public recognition. There was no ceremony. Before too much time had passed—but years, not months—a volunteer fire station had been established on a corner of one parcel, and there was a basketball court and a softball diamond. My friend, Jim, who had elected to stay in the valley and still lives there wrote me about these developments. I had wanted to give something to the people of Arroyo Hondo in return for what they had given me through their decency and hospitality.

From the men in the village, Clodoveo, Manuel and Marcos Ortiz, I learned how to plaster a wall, tar paper a roof, and plumb a sink. They showed me how to repair a tractor, irrigate a field, and raise alfalfa to feed my livestock. I learned that manual labor, if performed freely and for a useful purpose, is never beneath one's dignity. I understood that feeding one's family and keeping the roof sound were not just useful and necessary activities, but were honorable as well. Above all I learned a great deal about human dignity, my own and that of others. I learned that Jefferson was right; all men *are* created equal. Clodoveo Chacon, Manuel Ortiz and others, along with their wives, were the equals in dignity of anyone I'd encountered in the world of privilege that I had come from. I had experienced a way of living that I see today, among the clamoring agendas of American culture, the pursuit of power, wealth, and fame, as more fulfilling than the never satisfying American Way of Life.

A shovel in the soil, the sun, the sky, the mountain; the clear water from the river. "No eternity," wrote Camus, "outside the curve of the days."

My father with his granddaughter, Mexico City, 1973

HM and Alicia, Mariana's high school graduation, 1988

Part VI
Living and Its Consequences

. . . having neither programme, set theme nor unavoidable denouement, the disheveled improvisation of history is ready to walk with anyone; weave anyone into its line of verse and, if it is sonorous, it will remain his line until the poem is torn up . . .

Alexander Herzen, *My Past and Thoughts*

29

Much Happens

I could calculate the time, a couple of years out, when my grandfather's gift, my inheritance, would be gone. Then what? Inherited money is a mixed blessing. I had not needed to have any sort of training that could have led to a career. I had gone through college thinking of myself as a sort of freelance humanist, which meant that my moneymaking options were limited. There were career paths open to me in the environmental field, perhaps as a staff member of some existing organization. I was well enough connected to find such jobs, but I was burned out, exhausted emotionally. I had not husbanded my energy any better than I had my money.

From a psychological perspective, however, this sudden retirement was not as unsettling as it might have been because I knew what I wanted to do. I would become the writer that I believed I was. So, deliberately and slowly, so as not to send the message to the opposition that we were disheartened or folding our tents, I disengaged from the movement. I left some infrastructure in place, a separate fund within the Sierra Club Foundation (I had served on the board of the Foundation for several years.) to support efforts in the Four Corners states, and a building in Santa Fe. Colleagues with more stamina stayed on. I retired.

My daughter, Alicia, and I became regulars at Mexico City's open air markets with their piles of mangos and clouds of pink helium-filled balloons. My father came once to visit his granddaughter. I was touched that he would make the effort. He was retired from the company and had the time for travel, but Mexico was not on his usual circuit. Mariana was three. I recall that he brought her a stuffed elephant as a present, to remind her; I asked him, teasing, that she came from a family of Republicans? It was a pleasant visit. He did not stay long because he had an active social life that I was just beginning to be aware of. Then sixty years old, he had come with a much younger girlfriend, which was a bit of a shock. It announced a change in his life that would soon become significant in mine.

Alicia's emotional state had improved. She was now back among her extended family, three brothers and four sisters, her own language, and the streets she knew. She told me she felt like herself again. Nevertheless, she acknowledged that the underlying issue of the trauma remained. Even in Mexico City, she declined to see a therapist. After four or five months of a tentative relationship, during which time I still stayed in hotels, Alicia and I reconnected as a couple, once again sharing a bed. We talked and she thought it possible that she could revive her dream of an education. She did not, however, want to return to New Mexico because of bad memories. I agreed that we would retest our relationship and do it in a new place, California. The trial would be for a year. There would be no difficulty in finding a Spanish-speaking therapist or priest with appropriate psychological training, if that option felt more acceptable to her. We chose San Francisco.

Some months after we settled into an apartment on Russian Hill, I began to cough. Then a black gob appeared in my handkerchief. I ran low fevers and was racked by violent coughing episodes that lasted for minutes; the sputum was black, meaning blood. An X-ray revealed a spot on my lung. I was alarmed. Terrified was the better word. I was sure the sarcoma had returned.

A month of tests turned up nothing concrete. The doctor ordered a bronchoscopy of the interior of my right lung, a frightening procedure that involved snaking a fiber optic tube down through the nasal passage and into the damp cavern where the spot had set up camp. The thing was small, but it should not have been there. But this test, too, was inconclusive. The pulmonary specialist in San Francisco referred me to Stanford Medical Center in Palo Alto. I was getting sicker, often spending days in bed.

The specialist at Stanford approached the problem through my medical history, the story of the nine-inch scar on my back, the cancer. He would make a hospital-to-hospital request for my original medical records and, if they still existed, he would call me after he had reviewed them. I went back to the city and waited in a state bordering on panic. Two or three weeks later he called and I drove back to Palo Alto.

I sat on a chair in his examining room; the doctor sat opposite me. On the examining table was a folder, not terribly thick, that looked like an original record because it was faded and dog-eared. He picked it up, opened it, and then looking at me with an odd expression said, "You never had cancer. What they took out was a fatty cyst."

Relief would come later. My initial reaction was horror. I felt as if I'd been hit with a board and had had the wind knocked out of me.

"You're sure?" I asked. "Could fibro sarcoma have been a plausible diagnosis in those days?" A flood of confused emotions washed over me.

The doctor opened the file. "Fatty cysts are as common as impacted hangnails and less significant. They have been identified for hundreds of years. The only reason to remove them is to identify them. Three of the four biopsies had returned unequivocal verdicts of 'benign cyst.' The fourth used the term 'atypical' but in no way suggested malignancy. There is no question of cancer." He turned the file toward me, touching the relevant words with his index finger. "And," he said, with emphasis, "there was no question then."

With the intensity of my emotions beginning to subside, I came to the dark heart of the matter, the reason that my initial reaction had not been celebration and relief. "Then why," I asked, "the major surgery, the story of a fibro sarcoma?" I was remembering my mother in her mourning weeds, greeting the dying child as he came home after five days in the hospital.

"I have no idea," the doctor said. "But if this surgeon is still around, you have grounds to sue him."

I stared ahead, still in shock.

"Not only," the doctor continued, "did he perform an unnecessary surgery, an unethical act that could, and, in my opinion, should cost him his license, but he did it very badly. The incision was messy and excessive." Like a wounding, I thought. I knew what it looked like. But it wasn't the doctor that I was concerned with. It was my mother. The details of those fast moving events in 1953 came back to me, and now what had *not* happened took on new significance. There had been no second opinion, no visit with an oncology surgeon at UCLA, no visits by my father to the doctor who, according to my mother, had made the diagnosis. There had been no family discussion about any aspect of it. The surgery simply happened; my father had been swept along by my mother's depiction of the situation as one that required haste. It was cancer! I remembered the sense of urgency. She had explained to me and to my father that the doctor felt that we should act swiftly. From diagnosis to operating theater took less than a week.

After the revelation that I'd never had cancer, it took me some months to figure out what must have happened. The doctor was part of my parents' social set, but considerably lower on the ladder, and a desire to remain in the good graces of my family probably inhibited him from opposing my mother once she had her mind set on the cancer diagnosis and surgery. She would have known how to exploit the doctor's social ambition. She was an expert at this sort of thing. I'd watched for years as her feminine charms were deployed on my father. I imagined that she played the worried, devoted, and heroic mother, in effect saying to the doctor that if there was even the slightest chance that it might be cancer, they together, doctor and mother, must act decisively to save her beloved son. And he, succumbing to a momentum that my mother had set loose and to his desire to please her, did not argue with her and allowed himself to be unethically used.

Why did she do it? Was she mentally ill? There is a recognized condition called Munchausen's Syndrome by Proxy that afflicts mostly women who, in order to gain attention and sympathy and to be seen as devoted mothers, invent symptoms in their children and persuade a medical professional of their existence. This explanation is unlikely because none of my siblings had ever had any sort of serious illness, real or imaginary. What then? Somewhere deep in her psyche did she want me very sick and possibly dead, and if so, why? Did she need to demonstrate her power over me, the ability to cause pain and fear, and if so, why? Was she threatened by my approaching adolescence and sexual maturity? Was she punishing me for having already shown signs of independence? Or was she actually convinced by the word "atypical" that it might be a cancer and had panicked? But where had the word "fibro sarcoma" come from? Was it the doctor who wanted the drama? Was it some twisted combination of all of these? It would take me many years to even attempt an answer.

Whatever the reason, the cancer story and the surgery had wounded me emotionally. The trauma of the surgery and the awareness of my own mortality, come too early, left me with a fear of death that haunted my youth and early adulthood. The surgery and removal of muscle tissue had adverse effects on my posture that resulted on chronic back problems. Fear of living, which is the worst effect of fear of death, haunted the first half of my life. The Stanford doctor's verbal cure, "you never had cancer," did not immediately eliminate the collateral effects, but as an indication of the recuperative powers of the psyche, I can state that all those negative effects eventually cleared up. Today, I am mostly cheerful, without unnecessary health concerns, and with no back pain.

I never asked my mother for her version of the event. I did not confront her with the Stanford doctor's diagnosis. I did nothing and in that fact, I can see that I was still infected by that most seductive of delusions, hope. Against all evidence, against all common sense, I thought I might have some sort of relationship with her, if not necessarily for myself, but for my daughter; I was sure that a confrontation about the false cancer would have eliminated that possibility.

And there was a second reason that I held back. My mother's life had gone terribly wrong. Her gentlemanly husband had been struck down with an affliction of the nervous system that left him unable to breathe on his own. He could talk, smile, move a glass to his lips, and think, but nothing else. He required around-the-clock nursing care and slept in an iron lung. For my mother, this meant no more travel, no more evenings at restaurants, no more gala openings. On the surface, my mother held up, but I knew she suffered and that she would not ever articulate those feelings of disappointment or even anger that no doubt she had. She had left her first husband, my father who in the main had been a good husband, and after five years of what I presumed was happiness, it had all collapsed. Fate had indeed been cruel. But she remained composed; it was her way, her method. Nevertheless, I suspect that she was psychologically very fragile.

Where she had chosen to live after the divorce had revealed just how fragile. Soon after she remarried, she had sold the family house, which came to her in the divorce settlement, and bought a gloomy Spanish-style mansion *on the same block,* demolished it, and she and her new husband had built an ultramodern fortress of white stucco and electronic security on the site. She had moved only two doors down from our original house and was still just a mile from the house in which she had grown up. Her new husband, who clearly adored her, had done whatever she wanted. Living on the same block where her old life of nearly twenty five years had been spent must have felt somewhat haunted. But she knew where she was.

I don't think that my mother was attached to place. It was, rather, a fear of becoming detached from the known, fear that any displacing, even moving to Beverly Hills, would precipitate a sort of dissolving, a disintegrating. They had only just moved into the new house when her husband fell ill. The disease had imprisoned them both, but she was already a prisoner, of fears that she could not articulate. When I visited, my permitted visits for a glass of sherry, I watched her. Her composure was too perfect. The second reason, then, that I said nothing about the cancer was out of compassion.

And a third reason, the most powerful, was one that I had trouble articulating even to myself. Was I willing to think deeply about the implications of what she had done? Was I ready to entertain the possibility that my mother had wished me dead? What child wants that thought? Further, I was not sure I wanted to risk expressing to my mother, or even to myself, my true feelings about the surgical injury and the psychological damage she had orchestrated. I had undergone the trauma of the knife and had lived for twenty years as someone who was sure he would die soon. I was in fact very angry. Mixed with this feeling was a kind of pity. It wasn't quite a charitable feeling, but it kept me from overt expression of the anger.

Eventually, however, I mustered enough courage to ask her about the limbo to which I had been assigned for the previous ten or so years. I wrote her a letter in which I pointed out that I was never invited to stay in her house although all my siblings were. I speculated about what my offense had been. I wrote that perhaps "the life I have chosen is not what you wanted for me ..." My mother's reply to my letter was, in the main part, as follows:

> Although you may not perceive it, one of my goals always has been thoughtful consideration and kindness to everyone— not just to a small number. This was the guiding rule of my grandmother, and, in turn, of my mother. I am old enough now to be increasingly grateful for this heritage, and I do what I can to abide by it and nurture it.
>
> My deep feelings for you are no different than they are for your brothers and sisters. On their part, they demonstrate a thoughtful and devoted regard for me. In recent years this has been lacking in you, but I would be happy to have it again.

She had hit on at least one truth in the matter; I did not feel devoted regard for her and never had. The cruelties that she had inflicted when I was a child precluded that. The cancer that she had implanted in my psyche now seemed a continuation of a relationship that had been strangely twisted from the beginning. It seemed to me that there was a kind of regal madness in the tone of her letter, the belief that she was someone who merited "devoted regard." My siblings, I knew, only feigned devotion, their manners mirroring hers, but it was courtesy beyond what I could give. Mine was once a year for a glass of sherry.

My lung condition was finally diagnosed as tuberculosis. It hadn't shown positive in the customary skin tests, but I had had exposure in the communes of Taos County and my symptoms mimicked TB so closely that they decided that it must be that. I was cancer free, but with a serious disease, the one that haunts young Edmund Tyrone in O'Neill's *Long Day's Journey Into Night.* The subplot of a young man with a fatal illness had been a major part of the play's impact on me at age sixteen. But I had no romantic notions about tuberculosis. It had killed Keats, whose letters had meant so much to me on my trip to Europe in 1960; I had no intention of emulating him. I took my pills.

After a year's course of medications, I was well again. Since anti-TB medications worked, it proved the diagnosis. I was better than well. I had hovered for twenty anxious years in the limbo of hypochondria. But now I began to see the possibility of still being in possession of the premises in old age.

Cured of cancer, on track to being cured of TB, and in the beautiful city of San Francisco, I could concentrate on my future. Beside my desk, in a plastic box, I had a jumble of notebooks filled with poems written in the previous decade, ideas for poems, pages of scattered images. I set out to mine this material.

I could trace the ambition to be a writer to its origins. When I was eleven, a man who was actually a writer had befriended me. His name was Frank Butler, an Englishman who was a successful screenwriter; he had won an Oscar in 1944 for *Going My Way*, and he had written all

the silly Bing Crosby and Bob Hope road movies that were some of the
favorites of my childhood.

Mr. Butler lived in the beach colony where my maternal grandmother
summered. My grandmother had told him that her grandson was an
avid reader, so he had invited me to visit him in his office whenever I
wanted. I accepted his invitation and visited three or four times. His
office had bookshelves on each wall and a large window that overlooked
the shimmering ocean. There was a wide desk stacked with manuscript
pages. There was a manual typewriter. On the wall behind his desk, there
were signed photographs of Bob Hope, Bing Crosby, Betty Hutton, and
others I didn't recognize. Mr. Butler would chat with me for a few minutes and then return to his typewriter. I would wander quietly in the
room looking at the titles of books. Then I would sit on the oriental
carpet, crossed legged, bony knees, bare feet, and watch this kindly man
as he worked away at his craft. I had never before observed this sort
of behavior, this quality of being intent and focused. I listened to him
write. Click-clack, click-clack, the bell indicating the end of the line,
then the zip of the carriage as it returned to start a new line. After twenty
minutes or so, his wife, a gentle, beautiful woman in her sixties, would
come in with a tray of refreshments for us both, lemonade or cider. I felt
included. And I learned how books came into existence. Someone sat
down at a table and wrote.

Now I settled down to a daily writing routine. I worked on the book that
became *Soulscot* (1976). In that book, there are poems that came out of
my three years as a farmer. My response to the death of Pablo Neruda is
the longest piece in the book, but the main body of the poems dealt with
the anxieties of my wartime childhood and my fear of death. I hoped the
poems would capture, as one catches a firefly in a bottle, those emotions.
With time, some of those fears and dreads died a natural death. Some
live on, flickering in their bottle of words. *Soulscot* is an old English term
that refers to the tithe one was required to pay in order to be buried in
the churchyard. That book was a down payment.

The publisher of *Soulscot* was my own little press, Second Porcupine, which I had formed to publish my book and those of other Southwestern poets who had limited access to more established publishing houses.

The name referred to the newspaper, *The Porcupine*, which my maternal ancestor, Horace Bell, had published in Los Angeles in the 1880s. I kept my press alive for a number of years and published books by five other writers, including a selection of poems by my old friend from Taos, Max Finstein.

Max, disillusioned by the drift of the Taos communes into unsanitary and stoned discord, left New Mexico and joined Alicia and me in San Francisco, living in the spare bedroom. Max's presence was an important influence. His literary sensibility was steeped in Beat culture and jazz, his politics were of the left, and his personality of the picaresque. Max was a man who had always lived by his wits; he was an adventurer. Because I could help him financially, I was a sort of patron. He was somewhat scruffy and had an uneven history. As a consequence of heroin use in a period many years before I knew him, he had only seven teeth left in his mouth, remnant stubs that he called the "magnificent seven." I gave him the present of an extraction and a set of real dentures. He smiled again without feeling embarrassed. But even before the new teeth, he had always been attractive to women. I was friendly with three of his ex-wives; they all still liked him.

Max and I walked down the hill to the cafés and bars of North Beach almost every evening. We usually ended up at the Vesuvio on Columbus Avenue, the saloon that had seen Kerouac, Ferlinghetti, Ginsberg and many others perched on its stools. Max had known a number of these writers and had interesting tales. Max's own writing days were in the past, but he still thought of himself as a poet, and I learned much about poetry from him.

Max's most important contribution to my development as a writer was his belief that poetry was a spoken art. He insisted that I test my work by speaking it aloud. His perspective came from the jazz world, where the poet sometimes shared the playbill with musicians. He trained me to this standard, making me read aloud to him. He would sit on a chair in the kitchen smoking a self-rolled cigarette with a cup of coffee at hand. Mariana would wander through, wondering, I imagine, why her dad kept saying the same things over and over. "No, louder," Max would say, "you have to reach the people in the last rows, the talkers; make them listen." I gradually reached a level of confidence that allowed me to read easily and comfortably in public. And more importantly, he taught me how to compose by units of breath, which comes from speaking, not by formal line lengths of counted beats.

Max and I drank a beer or two on our outings, never more, talked poetry and jazz. Alicia did not go out with us. She said that she preferred to stay with our child. At first I offered to get a babysitter, but she always declined. Her still limited English, her lack of familiarity with the American subjects that Max and I usually talked about and the fact that she had no education beyond high school left her feeling isolated again. She had read some South American literature, Neruda, Juan Rulfo, and Octavio Paz, but couldn't talk about these writers except in the most general terms. She was shy. It was a sad and painful situation that both Max and I were aware of, but making every effort possible to include her helped little. I made appointments for her with therapists but she didn't go. The experiment of living together again was failing.

After a year in San Francisco, Max was restless and unhappy, seeking something. He thought that if he went more deeply into his Jewish identity his feeling of enervation, a nagging sense of alienation and loss of purpose, might be cured. He decided to go to Israel and become, as he put it, a "real Jew." He would live in a kibbutz. I bought him a ticket to Tel Aviv, and for nearly four years, Max disappeared, except for a postcard or two.

With the lease up on our apartment, Alicia and I reassessed our situation. I wanted to return to New Mexico and she was willing. Her bad memories had lost some of their potency. At the same time, we also acknowledged that our relationship was not doing well and was plagued by the same issues as before. She also saw that my relationship with our daughter was important for Mariana, and so she agreed to live in New Mexico so that I could participate in her upbringing. We returned to Santa Fe.

Alicia and I separated definitively. I found a little house for her in Santa Fe and we began the pattern that would last through our daughter's childhood. We worked out a shared child-rearing arrangement, the time pretty much equally divided. Alicia felt it would be good for our daughter if she spent time with me because I talked to her about pretty much everything, even things she was too young to understand. I had brought a half-finished manuscript with me from California and I worked on it during the day while Mariana was in school. I hired baby sitters and went out at night sometimes, sometimes not returning until morning. This arrangement worked for me as a single father, but for Mariana, there were too many uncertainties, instability that, years later, she told me had been harmful.

I was a permissive parent. When my little daughter said "I can do it by myself," or "I can find my way to my friend's house," I tended to believe her. Since I had grown up overprotected, imprisoned by my mother's fears—she was obsessed with the Lindberg baby kidnapping and often cited it as a justification for her rules—I probably went too far in the other direction. If Mariana and her friends wanted to play in the dirt, I thought this was fine. It meant more baths and more laundry. I still believe that in child rearing it is better to err on the side of permissiveness. Mariana is now a successful and independent woman, a songwriter and performer living in Austin, Texas. She is also a doctor of traditional Chinese medicine.

Alicia lived the last twenty years of her life with Mariana and Mariana's husband and son, most of those years battling a slow debilitating illness. The last time I saw her, just months before she died, she was cheerful, but admitted that she was tired. She died in 2015. Mariana took her ashes back to Mexico City.

30

The Writer Emerges

I had come back from San Francisco feeling that I'd made a start at being a writer. I didn't, however, see myself becoming a professional in the way Mr. Butler was. Poetry did not seem to be a profession; it was too haphazard, too dependent on chance encounters with the ephemeral—the smell of raindrops on dry earth, the veins in a beautiful woman's neck—and consequently without much exchange value. How could it qualify as useful work? What an inconvenient question to ask of an aspiring poet. My father's and my grandfather's work ethic always hovered behind me when I worked at my desk. What good is this thing you are doing, what use? A novelist was one thing; there was always the possibility of writing a best seller. A screenwriter like Mr. Butler entertained people, and people need entertaining. I could not imagine more useful work than what Mr. Butler did. But what sort of work was poetry? What was my work? I had that ethic, that value system. I needed to feel that I *did* something. It was a kind of Protestant notion, that a man was not really a man unless he went to the office and brought home a paycheck.

Could poetry change anything? Shelley's statement that poets were the unacknowledged legislators of the world was an appealing idea and Bob Dylan had certainly changed things. Still I had conflicts about it. Farming was the other occupation that I had tried; it required physical labor and I had liked it. I needed to find an occupation that allowed me to do the rather loose work of writing poetry and at the same time produce something measurable in the real world. I needed something grounded, and, once I got over the idea that I had to make a lot of money to prove my worth, I found something.

During the 1971 summer lull in the political season, I stumbled on a project that for many years would make use of my energy in its many forms. I could be a worker on the land, a tractor mechanic, a reader of books, environmentalist, writer, a man in search of the spiritual, or I could simply continue to be a man in search of himself.

Since the age of ten, I had done a great deal of camping, first with my father and then with organized groups like the Boy Scouts, and then at boarding school. When I moved to New Mexico, I made frequent off-the-trail backpacking trips, sometimes alone; five day walks above the timberline, sleeping under the stars. I guided trips into the mountains for friends from the east and California. I could find my way through trackless timber and took pride in the skill. I was happy in the wild, in the pine forests and the aspen groves, on high ridges with vast views. I had many adventures, the most dangerous of which was being chased by a herd bull that I encountered in an open meadow. I dropped my backpack and ran for my life. I made the tree line in time. The bull tossed my backpack around for a spell, then got bored and wandered back to his ladies. Bears and mountain lions are considerably less dangerous.

On one of these off-trail hikes, in the mountain range west of Taos, I came out of a stand of ponderosa pine and found myself in an open meadow. Across the large stream, there was a large log house with huge stone fireplaces. Nearby there were several outbuildings, some very old. The meadow, a little mountain valley, showed signs of having been fenced, so I assumed that it was privately owned. But it was seriously neglected. The buildings had broken window panes and the fences were mostly down. A stream, the Rio Vallecitos, much larger than the Rio Hondo, ran through the valley. Stepping on stones, I crossed the stream and approached the house. It was clearly empty and abandoned. Cattle had wandered through the lodge leaving damage and mess. There were signs of human misuse and vandalism, beer cans tossed about inside and out. But the whole, the valley, the river, and the house, was as beautiful a place as I had ever seen.

I returned to Santa Fe and began inquiries that led to my being able to buy the property with my brother, John, a year or so later. This remote valley in the San Juan Mountains became my spiritual anchor, my writer's retreat. I had read Henry David Thoreau, both *On Civil Disobedience* and *Walden,* in high school. This was my Walden. Wilderness, pine forests, a pond, and a long way from everywhere. I set up a table in an upstairs room where I installed a Royal portable typewriter. And for the next fifteen or so years, restoring and improving the property was my project, my useful work.

The bigger of the houses, the lodge, had been built in 1928. I found the date carved on a cornerstone. The building was relatively sound. The other buildings, a barn, an icehouse, and a cabin, dated to the 1880s, not long after the passage of the Homestead Act of 1862. The name of the pioneer family that had built and lived in the older structures was long forgotten; those original buildings were near ruins, roofs rotten, porch sagging. I had always been drawn to ruins. I knew that with work I could reverse the process of decline and restore all to service. It took a year to assess the scope of the project. Where to start? Fences, plumbing, broken windows, roof. Cleanup was first. I took many loads of trash out in my pickup truck.

I brought Alicia and the baby two or three times, but only once overnight because the lodge was infested with rats. I sat up all that night guarding my sleeping daughter in her crib; I could see the rats scurrying about, their eyes glinting in the faint light from the kerosene lamp I'd set on the table.

This little valley was twenty miles from the nearest paved road and telephone, fifty miles from a supermarket, a doctor, or a hardware store. At eight thousand feet elevation, in the middle of a mountain chain, it was snowbound and inaccessible from November through April, and when it rained heavily in August, the roads in the high country were turned into mud so deep and slippery that even a four-wheel drive vehicle was useless. It suited me. I repaired the buildings, strung new fence, and developed a water system. A friend designed and built a cabin that could be heated and used into the winter. Keeping the place together and improving it satisfied an inner need to be useful in a grounded way. The ranch became a projection of me, a metaphor for what I was about in life.

I was at my happiest in the wilderness. I thrived on the challenges of extreme weather, thunderstorms that shook the rocks, unexpected snowstorms that would have stranded me if I hadn't had snowshoes and the stamina to walk ten miles. It was never total solitude. Friends visited and I had a fine companion in a dog, a golden retriever mix named Pete. I came out of the mountains regularly and joined the world. I was in a sense two people: an introspective solitary, the poet, and an engaged participant in politics and my town.

I lived comfortably with these multiple personalities. I needed the solitude and I liked people, especially women. For a considerable time after my final separation from Alicia, there had been no significant woman in my life. I had been cautious. I recognized that I was not entirely trustworthy in respect to the inclinations and impulses of my heart. Inevitably, I encountered a woman whose needs, or so I believed, met mine well enough. But, entirely befuddled by her looks, I never got around to inquiring deeply into what her needs really were. Shirley became my third wife. She was divorced, with two teenage boys. She had tried for a Hollywood career, had failed and, drifting back toward the places of her origin, she had paused in Santa Fe. At thirty-five, she may have thought that her prospects were beginning to dim, but she was a gorgeous woman and needn't have worried. There would be someone. She had long slim legs and looked marvelous in high heels. And I, perhaps too long single and thus susceptible, fell for her. I would have a goddess, a muse, in residence. Miguel Unamuno, the great Spanish philosopher, described what often happens when a male with inclinations like mine confuses lust for love: I mistook for truth what was only beauty.

Shirley was looking out for herself, considering her future security, and in me she saw a man who was reasonably good looking and adequately provisioned financially, who didn't mind children, and who, being conveniently impulsive, was willing to marry her. I did marry her, having known her for only three months. The marriage wasn't terrible at first. She was an amateur artist, could draw well and paint in watercolor. Our values, however, were very different. She liked to step out at night, "clubbing," I think it is called today. I had no interest in this sort of life so I believe that she was bored with me. She would have made a different sort of man a very good wife. With me she became, over a year or so, irritable and shrewish.

I put together a second book of poems, *Stations,* and published it in 1980. Shirley illustrated it with line drawings. The title referred to the Stations of the Cross, Christ's progress from arrest to crucifixion and death. This bit of borrowing reflected the degree to which I had absorbed the master narrative of Western civilization. I was not the least religious, but I had no compunction about plundering Christianity for metaphors. The meaning was obvious: life had its stations, those moments when we are tested. This wife became one of mine.

I had always intended to write a book about Los Angeles, my natal city: L.A., the city of the angels. I was a fifth generation Angelino and so had deep roots in that strange hallucinatory sprawl, that not-quite-a-city on the edge of the continent. School had nurtured my mind, but Los Angeles had been my true *alma mater.* She was not an especially nurturing mother, but she was my lady of mysteries. They were shallow mysteries, not offering much of a reward if one plumbed them, but they were the mysteries I grew up with. I knew LA. I could name all the boulevards, and knew them before the freeways came: Century Boulevard, Victory Boulevard, Santa Monica Boulevard, Pico and Sepulveda, and my neighborhood's own Third Street, were all we had. I loved LA. And as Randy Newman sings, I was born to ride. Sunset Boulevard, Echo Park to the ocean. And when I was a teen, you could still see the mountains. I did love LA. I found in its moods, its history, and its fictions, a rich inventory of themes—impermanence, existence without clear meaning, the haphazard and inconsequential, the perfect framework for a book that I wanted to write, a cautionary tale about ill formed and unachievable desires, a description of an incoherent but demanding unconscious. LA was the metaphor for my emotional past. Eventually I had left because I felt the place had betrayed itself, that it had gone from grit and glitz to consumer banality, that it had traded the generous gifts of nature, sun and soft air, for mobility and smog. But from New Mexico I could look back and see rich material for a good book.

I made several trips to Los Angeles while writing the book. Because I had to submerge myself in the project, I never contacted either of my parents on these trips and always went alone. For the first part of the book, I imagined how modern Los Angeles would have seemed to an eighteenth century Romantic like William Wordsworth, and so I tried to channel his sensibility and even his vocabulary, his diction, and his repertory of ideas and politics. For the second part of the book, I invoked the bard of LA, Raymond Chandler, and invented the persona of an underemployed and not terribly clever private investigator. To get the atmosphere right, I always stayed in the seediest motels that I could find in iconic sections of the city, Santa Monica and Hollywood. The book that emerged was called *The Plain of Smokes.*

My trips to the coast, my love for the mountains, my bookishness and need for solitude, didn't help my marriage. When I was off on my expeditions, Shirley went out at night. I suspected that she was unfaithful.

As I was finishing the book, I was simultaneously preparing for a long trip to Eastern Europe that had been in preparation, intellectually and emotionally, for many years. My marriage to Shirley was effectively over. In this period, I had an affair with a sweet woman who genuinely cared for me and who helped with the final editing of *The Plain of Smokes.* The relationship remained clandestine because the divorce had turned confrontational over the usual difficulty, money; and I didn't want Shirley to have the weapon of adultery at her disposal. I had seen it used against my father.

By now I had resolved my conflicts about the usefulness of poetry. I think that art of any sort, including poetry, is among the most useful of all human activities. Poetry can frighten the tyrant, free the imprisoned, and nourish the spiritually starving. William Carlos Williams made the case perfectly.

It is difficult
to get the news from poems
yet men die miserably every day
for lack
of what is found there.

HM in LA, 1980

31
Looking Over the Edge

Because I've never been deported, I stay silent. But it is a cry that I am smothering.

Albert Camus, Carnets II

Hamish Robertson had served as an infantry officer in France in 1917. He conveyed to me in conversations that the experience had been "unpleasant;" he didn't provide much detail, maintaining a posture of ironic distance from his experience. "It was a damn long way to Tipperary," he said, "and most of the lads never got there." When he spoke of casualties, it was in a grimly bowdlerized way. I was fifteen when we had these exchanges. I knew about his sojourn in Picardy, the farmer with the calvados, and the farm girl, whom I had met in Paris that same year. The way he had told these stories when I was young had made his Great War experience sounded like a Tom Sawyer type adventure, boys camping out, hideouts dug into the walls of trenches, eating one's mess from a tin plate under the stars. Almost. I intuited, probably from his tone, that it was not, and in my twenties, he began to steer me toward a more real picture of what was an enormous calamity. I read the Great War literature, Robert Graves, Edmund Blunden, Wilfred Owen, Ford Madox Ford, and others in that extraordinary cohort of writers that came out the trenches. Ezra Pound made sense to me:

There died a myriad,
And of the best, among them,
For an old bitch gone in the teeth,
For a botched civilization.
Charm, smiling at the good mouth,
Quick eyes gone under earth's lid,
For two gross of broken statues,
For a few thousand battered books...

T. S. Eliot's *The Wasteland* made sense too. I understood that out of consideration of my youth, Hamish had censored his narrative. It had been far worse than he let on. But because my friend and mentor had been there, had walked along those duckboards in muddy trenches, smelled death and chlorine gas, the First World War became a landmark for me. I lived in a world shaped by those events, shaped by mindboggling folly and a capacity for destruction that would only get worse. Very early in my life, a loss of faith had begun. But it was never total. My years as an environmental activist came certainly out of some sense of hopefulness, something was worth fighting for. Nevertheless, a Janus-like condition existed in my spirit. Disaster was always present and always possible. Indeed, I think the twentieth century can be understood as an almost continuous succession of calamities. Among so many, the most terrible was the Holocaust.

The Holocaust was something that, aged five or six, I had stumbled on without knowing what it was. I had seen a photograph, probably in *Life Magazine*, of a little boy in the Warsaw Ghetto with his hands up. He has knobby knees, wears a hat that is too large, and is clearly terrified. This image had wedged itself into my subconscious and, reinforced by my accidental exposure to the Signal Corp film of the liberation of Buchenwald and exposure to anti-Semitism through the eighth-grade Latin teacher, I had become a student of the Nazis and the Holocaust. It was more than a scholarly interest; it was almost an obsession.

An unspeakable evil, a great filth, something incomprehensible and unimaginable, beyond the merely detestable, sat, smoldering and enormous, in the middle of the road that I believed my life was to take. I believed that if one chose to live in truth, all the facts, all the truths, must be acknowledged. So I read books. I knew the work of the professional historians, Lucy Dawidowicz (*The War against the Jews*) for example. I knew most of the other commentaries, from survivors like Primo Levi, Elie Wiesel, Robert Antelme, and Tadeusz Borowski to scholars like Jean Amery and Terrence Des Pres. What I would make out of these studies, I did not know, but I knew that I had to move beyond abstract knowledge. If I were to understand the nature of my emotional involvement, I would have to move closer. As Robert Capa, the great photographer of the Second World War, said, "if your pictures aren't good enough, you aren't close enough."

From the album titled, "The Warsaw Ghetto is no more," the picture that I saw

I decided that I would go as deep into the Holocaust as I could bear to go. I would go to London to do research for two months and then on to Germany and Poland. I planned to be away from home for six months. My divorce from Shirley would be finalized by the time I returned. My daughter was now eight. Would she understand an absence of so many months? I could not say. But this was something I had to do. It took shape in my mind as a sort of responsibility, something I couldn't let others do for me. I had a need to see for myself.

This need to see, to witness, may have had its origins in the sense that my world contained secrets. As a little boy, I had wandered in dark houses. Now I would wander through one of the darkest places in the human story. My experience with psychotherapy may have contributed to my motivation as well. In therapy, I had explored my personal unconscious; now it was time to know the worst about humankind, nations and societies; what the unconscious is capable of doing when harnessed into an irrational collective.

Vaclav Havel, the Czech writer and later president of his country, wrote, "Nothing that has once happened can un-happen: everything that once was, in whatever form, is forever lodged in the memory of being."

In London, the November days were shorter and it was dark by four in the afternoon. I had obtained a research pass at the British Library and was assigned a cubicle in the main reading room where I could leave my books at night. I sat for eight to nine hours a day reading survivor accounts, speeches by Nazi leaders, the life accounts of ordinary Germans who did terrible things and of those who had resisted. The books came from a mysterious depository far away. Each afternoon, I submitted my requests on slips of paper. The slips of paper disappeared into a pneumatic tube, and the next day memory of those events was recovered; the book would be on my desk. The process brought to mind Orwell's "memory hole," but here the result was reversed. A history had been recorded and one could know it.

During this two-month interlude, I regularly visited Hamish. I hadn't seen him in more than fifteen years. Now in his late eighties, he was physically very feeble, confined to a chair in his study. The man who had once been so full of life, was gaunt and skeletal. He had a racking cough that shook his once robust frame to its joints. The cough was a war injury, a wound that he had carried for sixty years. The story of it, which I'd heard several times, contained for him the horror and folly of the Great War.

"They dumped all us dead men on the body wagon," he told me. There was neither glory nor heroism to die like that, he said, gassed by your own side.

"If it weren't for the poor horses having such a time with the rutted road, knee deep in mud," he said, "they'd have arrived at the pit earlier and I'd have been dumped into it with the rest of them." Raising his glass of single-malt Scotch, he intoned, in his best banquet voice, "so here's to those humble nags so unfairly drafted from milk carts." He had regained consciousness in time, had cried out, and they pulled him out of the tangle of mangled corpses. "Just good luck, young Harvey, that I made it this far. Just good luck."

He took a long pull on his cigarette, a Gauloise, the strongest, blackest tobacco on the planet, and coughed violently. When his body stopped convulsing from the cough, he gave a mischievous chuckle. "The doc tells me that I shouldn't smoke," he said. He took another deep drag. "He said it might kill me." I found such moments irresistible; Hamish had a gift for serious mischievousness and profound mockery. Now he was teasing death. I smoked Gauloises too, a form of hero worship, and took a carton with me on the journey.

He asked about my plans after the research phase at the library was over. My destination was Munich and Dachau, then Berlin, and from there, I would go behind the Iron Curtain to the two most infamous camps in Poland, Auschwitz and Treblinka.

"Poland, in January, young Harvey...?" he had asked. "Only mad dogs . . ."

We talked often about the twentieth century as he had experienced it. He had many observations. Nazism had captured the collective mind of a whole people because the people were "economically insecure, fearful, and resentful, and politically lazy." They had accepted the explanations their rulers fed them, the tale of victimhood, of their special destiny, of external enemies—the rest of the world—and internal enemies, the Communists, those who did not believe in the myths of Germany, and above all, the Jews. The people fell victim to their own emotions, the fears that produced hatreds that the Nazis skillfully manipulated. Propaganda and slogans became facts. Having surrendered the capacity to think for themselves, the German people, the masses, had no reality except what they were told. "The Germans in the 1930s had only radio and the print press," Hamish mused; "I shudder to think of the power of television as a propaganda tool." The German people no longer thought; indeed, the Nazis had made the act of thinking a sort of disloyalty, a betrayal of the Aryan virtues of patriotism, obedience, and strength. At first, thinking was just suspect, demeaned as elitist, and then it became a Jewish vice.

To a man like Hamish to stop thinking was worse than laziness, worse than criminal neglect; it was a sort of mortal sin. "It is a sin against the self and against God," he said. I asked if he believed in God.

"Not anymore," was his answer.

I left for Germany soon after. I crossed the Channel by ferry to Holland, then by train to Germany. I took the slow way, ferry and train, because I wanted to experience the distance as a kind of metaphor. The Holocaust was a very long way from ordinary life, especially the safe and then relatively sane world of America. As the train slid through the dark December day, I asked myself again, what was I doing? I could contribute nothing to the history of the Holocaust. The results of my research, if it could be called that, could only deepen my feelings and give context and awful detail to the things I would see. For the first and only time in my life, I kept a journal.

I went first to Munich, where Hitler's movement had its beginnings, and wandered the well-tended streets. The rubble of war had been cleared away long before and the buildings had been restored. Central Munich seemed almost like Beverly Hills, with trendy shops, restaurants, and chic people. I went to a beer hall where the mood was festive, but the boisterous male aggressiveness was a bit frightening. I took a taxi to Dachau, the first of the Nazi camps. It too had a spruced up look, well maintained as an historical site. It looked as I imagined a minimum security prison in California might look, almost rationally institutional. It had been a camp for political offenders and others unacceptable to the regime, homosexuals and intellectuals, and had been called a labor camp, as if to imply that labor was a form of corrective psychotherapy. Over twenty thousand died there. But Dachau was easy. I was approaching real horrors, the extermination camps, slowly getting used to the idea, perhaps giving myself time to turn back. I had no timetables and no reservations, so, quite easily, I could have. I could have managed to get physically sick.

I went on to Berlin where I spent a week. The days were dark and short. I was strangely inactive by day, staying in my hotel room, lying on the bed reading. I'd taken Andre Gide's *Notebooks* as my only reading material. I was lonely and depressed. Wandering was my favored method for finding direction, so I wandered. By night, my old voyeuristic habit returned, and I went out to find the after-dark life of the city. In after-dark Berlin, there were many bizarre things to see, sexual fetishes, leather, sex slaves, pain, simulated and real, that all converged into a disturbing and repellant strangeness that fit into my search for the darkest side of the human soul. The streets were snow-packed. On a wall, I saw graffiti that said, "We are the people of Mozart. We are the people of Auschwitz." *Wir sind die Leute...*

I went from Berlin to East Berlin on foot, carrying my pack. This geographical transition was more than just political; it was like diving into the ocean, passing through a warm thermal layer at the top into one very much colder, from liberty to oppression. There was a palpable difference. I made a mental note to speak of this to my father when I returned. The things he had said to me about Communism over the years, things that I had sometimes rejected as being the official Republican Party line, had turned out to be right.

Then by train to Krakow, Poland. The train belonged to earlier decades with threadbare carpets, cracked window glass, barely functioning heat. The porter cooked his meal on a gas stove in the vestibule between the cars. I had taken a camera with me, a medium format camera that was hard to use and that would, therefore, require some thought before I tripped the shutter. I was not taking snapshots. I awoke at first light and took a picture of the Oder River as the train crossed into Poland.

I visited the extermination camp at Auschwitz-Birkenau. I walked around the fence that encloses the barracks that housed those selected for death, but who worked until their time came. Many of the Birkenau barracks remain. The walk around the perimeter took several hours. It was the dead of winter now, January, bitter cold. A busload of Polish high school students, boys and girls, arrived for the history lesson that is mandatory in Polish schools. I watched this band of young people, all of them dressed in bright parkas and wearing mittens, as they trudged along the railway track through the main gates. I could not imagine what they thought or felt. I was too far away to get a sense of their mood. Was this an occasion of great import, or was it just another field trip, a welcome break from the classroom?

In the red brick buildings, where the infamous sign *Arbeit Macht Frei,* "Work Makes One Free," still hangs above the gate, there is now a museum. Here the workers with a somewhat longer life expectancy, the crematorium gangs, had been housed. I encountered other visitors, all of whom were solitary, as if the solace of companionship was inappropriate or even prohibited. There was a single red rose on a display case containing the contents of suitcases that had been abandoned on the rail platforms as the trains came in; there were hairbrushes, combs, toothbrushes, books, and children's toys. There was another rose on the threshold of an oven. Fresh roses in the Polish winter. I wondered where they had come from.

I went looking for traces of the synthetic oil plant that I.G. Farben had built and staffed with slave labor supplied by the SS. I had read about the Farben-SS partnership while in London and wanted to see the plant. But no one in the town of Oswiecim seemed to know that it had even existed. All traces of this enterprise had been erased. Farben sold their artificial rubber and motor fuel back to the Nazi war machine at a profit. Labor costs were minimal, a bit of bread and watery soup, perhaps 800 calories per day. A prisoner was worked until he died. He was then replaced. The slave labor was a supply side state subsidy. On the demand side, the German war machine, the consumer of the product, was also state subsidy. It was the perfect money-making machine. As the largest chemical concern in the world at the outbreak of the war, Farben was favored under Nazism as a single-source contractor for essential war materials, including Zyklon B, the gas used in the extermination camps. All the company's senior executives escaped serious punishment after the war, even those who were directly involved in the deaths of thousands. Though the Farben factory at Oswiecim has completely disappeared, razed and plowed under, the corporation itself lives on, reconfigured into three: Agfa, Bayer, and BASF.

I took a train to Warsaw. I explored the city, much of it rebuilt as a perfect replica of what it had been before the Nazis arrived. I discovered well-heated cafés where young people, students and workers, sat around and had intense and hushed political conversations. The Solidarity movement that toppled Communist rule in Poland had begun that winter. At the time of my visit, the outcome was still uncertain and Solidarity was outlawed. Outside the warmth of the cafes, the city was drab and cold, and the skies overcast. Flocks of enormous black ravens strutted about on fields of packed snow near the place where the railhead for the death-trains had been, the *Umschlagplatz*. There is a monument, in several languages, reminding the passerby that there had been such a place. There were no guide books to the Warsaw of the war, but there were plaques on walls, and I went out into bitter cold days to find them.

On one of my days of exploring Warsaw, I crossed a large open space, now snow-covered, surrounded by dismal-looking apartment blocks. There were a few leafless trees. The sun was January low in the sky, a weak source of light, none of warmth. A distance away, as I traversed this almost surreal landscape, I came upon a wooden bench on which sat a very old woman. She was a tiny creature, wrapped in woolen blankets, but since she seemed clean and healthy, I did not think she was homeless or in any danger of freezing to death. As I was about to pass by, she put out her hand and touched my arm. And she held me there, in this vast and cold agora, the only other living creatures being the ubiquitous ravens, with her eyes and with her voice. I was reminded of the scene in Coleridge's "Rime of the Ancient Mariner," the terrible tale of doomed voyage that the mariner wants the wedding guest to hear.

She spoke in Polish and I responded in rudimentary German. She switched to German and I gathered just enough to understand that she wanted me to know something. *Wissen Sie.* From her purse, she removed some tattered and discolored papers and held them out to me to hold and examine. I took off my gloves, fearful that they would make me clumsy handling these ancient documents. They were her war-time identity papers; all had *Juden* stamped on them. *Juden* across the identity photograph. She had been a rather pretty young woman. She smiled and pointed at the picture and then to herself, touching herself on her chest, where she knew her heart must be, the place of her emotions, her courage, her capacity for resistance, all alive still, now hidden inside the wool blankets. She patted herself on her chest, almost as one would a noble and loyal dog. She smiled again. She had her rations card too; it still had a few stamps stuck between pages, stamps that entitled her to some minimal amount of bread: *Brot,* she said and smiled again. My fingers were very cold. I handed them back to her. She said something in Polish, then carefully folded the documents and returned them to her purse. "I had been there," she was saying, "and I survived." Then she stood up and walked away, down the shoveled pathway, toward one of the dismal apartment blocks.

I rented a car and drove to Treblinka, the site in the forest, three hours from the city, where the Jews of the Warsaw Ghetto were exterminated. The cold that day was so sharp that my footsteps through the snow made a snapping sound, like nerve synapses. My heavy black wool coat kept me warm enough. I removed my gloves occasionally, long enough to take a picture and advance the film. Of the extermination operation that went on at Treblinka and which was its only purpose, only the firepit where the bodies were burned remained. They were incinerated to hide evidence of the genocide. The pit, a depression roughly the size of a football field, is surrounded by a scrubby pine forest that forty years earlier had been harvested by slave labor to provide the fuel to feed the fires. Between 700,000 and 900,000 Jews died at Treblinka. Unlike Auschwitz, where perimeter fencing, barracks, rail lines, and ovens are still intact, at Treblinka one finds only symbols.

It is a civilizational cemetery, an arrangement of rough-hewn stones. Granite slabs lying flat on the ground mark where the rail line that brought the Jews from Warsaw ended. These were the unloading docks. The freight cars went back to Warsaw empty and returned the next day crammed full of terrified human beings. There is a giant plinth at the center of what had been the slave workers' camp, the wood cutters. It is built of pieces of granite and is perhaps eighteen feet high, with the words "Never Again" in all the languages of the affected peoples, German, Polish, Hungarian, French, Greek, Russian, carved into the base of the column. A field of jagged rocks, massive splinters of granite, surrounds the central plinth. There are hundreds of these rocks, one for each Jewish community that had been destroyed, each with the name of the community carved in the stone. Some names I recognized, but most were names of towns or villages I'd never heard of and which no longer exist. The boulders, these rough grave markers, range in height from three to six feet, depending on the size of the community destroyed. Wroclaw, as the Poles now call it, Breslau when the SS exterminated its Jews and intellectuals, has a stone higher than most. The stones representing the smallest villages are about the height of an eight-year-old child.

There was not another person at Treblinka that day, but the snowy field was crisscrossed by tracks, not animal, but human. It had not snowed in weeks, so I could see in the tracks the physical signature of two or three others. Just as at Auschwitz, these were solitary people, people who had come, as I had come, for some private reason. I heard the occasional fall of snow from a pine branch. Otherwise it was preternaturally silent, except when I moved and I heard the sounds my feet made walking through the snow. Although Dachau and Auschwitz are terrible places, Treblinka was for me the most terrible. The saddest place on earth.

I thought of Dante's *Commedia*. Nothing in Dante's world matched this, neither the magnitude of the crimes nor the torments of his hell, but as I thought about returning to a brighter world, the regions where life went on, I turned to images from the poem. I pictured the poet and Virgil who, having come to the bottom, had passed through the center of the earth and had begun their slow ascent. They climbed out of darkness, climbed toward God. Without any belief in God, I wanted only to find light, the world uncontaminated by madness and death. I wasn't depressed, but I was emotionally overwhelmed. I decided that I would not return immediately to the United States. For a short time, I would be a deep tourist; I would visit places where civilization had endured, places that had not been touched by the war. I chose Venice. I needed beauty and I needed proof that civilization endured.

I took the train from Berlin. At the Venice rail station, while waiting in the queue for a cab, I struck up a conversation with a French woman of roughly my own age. She was a petite woman with striking violet eyes, handsome rather than pretty, and very feminine in a way that is particularly French. Her English was adequate, so, while waiting for the taxi, we became friendly. Though I had not given it much thought, I realized that I needed companionship. I remembered that I had never encountered couples in the realm of the Holocaust. I wanted, with a quiet sort of longing, to be a couple, and chance had thrown me together with this woman. Her name was Liliane.

We ate lunch together that first day in Venice. It seemed that we were both in a similar mood, lonely, reaching out, needing intimacy, but without any male/female sexual tension involved. Liliane was a teacher in a *lycée* in the cathedral town of Chartres, was married and had three children. She had come alone to Venice, "just to see it," she said, and she added that she had breast cancer and was recovering from a course of chemotherapy. She needed to talk about the cancer and I, having known the sort of fear that cancer induced, could listen. I said nothing about my cancer because it had not been real and hers was. She told me that it was hard to talk about such things with her family, even with her husband. She told me that he was in a state of denial. She was not. I understood.

Somber things were on both of our minds. I told her where I'd been, not in any detail, but enough. I told her that I was researching a book, though at that time, a book was far from my mind. A book provided an easier explanation than to try to explain a strange obsession. What mattered was that we had come to Venice for much the same reason, to find life, to celebrate being alive. To have found each other, someone with whom we could share the experience was a gift, one we made to each other.

Liliane and I spent five days together. We fell into step with each other so quickly one might have thought we'd known each other for years. We were in love in a most unmodern way. We had the highest regard for each other, and since that included a regard for the separateness of our different lives, for the loyalties that lay in our respective homelands, we knew, without ever speaking of it, that we should not confuse or disturb our friendship with desire. We saw ourselves as tourists in a world that contained much that was fragile, and we needed to treat it all, especially each other, with care.

We visited the museums and the churches. We watched the tides rise into the streets and understood that Venice was sinking into the Adriatic and simultaneously being corroded by industrial pollution from the factories across the bay. In the summer, the breath and feet of millions of tourists were eroding the interiors of its famous buildings. The sense of the vulnerability of everything permeated those few days. We wandered through near-empty buildings with famous pedigrees, where plaster had fallen from the walls and fallen on stair landings. I remember standing with her in a cold palazzo, deserted except for an old man in a tattered uniform who dozed on a cane seat chair. We looked out of the tall windows at the fog, at the nearly invisible canal below us. The foghorns of the *vaporettos* made muffled moans.

I came to think of us as emotional convalescents; Venice, in those gray and misty days, was the sanitarium. We strolled arm in arm through its corridors and alleys, through the little piazzas and along the quays that twice daily disappeared beneath the high tides. We were quiet and slow, but we were recovering. We ate dinners together in little, mostly empty restaurants. I would walk her to her hotel, say good night, and return to mine. We talked about the world as if it were an ordinary place where things were comprehensible. On the fifth day, I took her to the train station. When we embraced we fought back tears. She left for France. On the day after, I was on another train, to Barcelona.

I needed to resurface. I needed to hold a living woman in my arms.

I revived my night wandering ways, now through a different city, the bars and clubs that front for brothels in Barcelona. I talked with many girls, but I wasn't attracted to any of them in the way that I needed. I was looking for a quality of playfulness and mischief. When I found her, I knew immediately. "There you are," I thought, and felt as if the world would at last be right again. Her name was Wendy. She was Welsh, about twenty-five, tall and athletic with short-cropped hair and very pretty. She was sweet, not well educated, and not a drug addict; I had asked. Her spontaneity was so obviously genuine that I trusted her, knew she was honest. She was, however, under contract, though how that worked exactly I never quite knew. I had to buy her "freedom." I negotiated with the madam, a formidable lady, buxom, hair dyed black, with lots of bangles on her arms. I wanted Wendy to be my girlfriend for four days, and the madam, thinking this all very romantic and with the money in advance, acted more like a future mother-in-law than a business woman; she gave us her blessing. She opened a bottle of real champagne and we all toasted.

And with this young woman, whom I would never see again, I began to return to the living. I followed the song she sang, a song that consisted of uncomplicated sexuality, frivolity, and cheerfulness. Our time together mimicked an ordinary sort of daily life. Over three meals a day we talked about the Welsh mining town of her childhood, the vagaries of her work, her Jack Russell terrier, and her friends among the girls at the club. I felt that I knew all their stories. We walked her little dog in the park. She brought a small bag to my hotel and we spent four nights together. In the mornings, she went back to her apartment to feed the dog and fetch him. I never saw her apartment because, she told me, her roommates would be jealous of her situation. She had a "boyfriend." I am sure she would have liked to have a real boyfriend, but she was a practical person and took what life offered her. I saw no trace of bitterness in her. She had real self-esteem, a fact that disabused me of stereotypes about the degraded condition of prostitutes. After our days were up, she went back to the club. We embraced and kissed. She gave me a snapshot of herself. We had been pals.

I caught a series of airplanes, Barcelona to London, where I stopped to see Hamish. He was three months older; I could see each of them. I talked about the experience. All of it, from Berlin to my "girlfriend" in Barcelona. He listened, without interruption, to my narrative about visiting the camps. Perhaps because of what he had seen of horrors, the shell-blasted wastelands of the front lines, he seemed to understand perfectly why I had gone. He never questioned it. My description of Venice elicited a quiet exclamation, almost a sign. "Ah, Venice." When I told him that my sweetheart of four days had been a very nice Welsh girl who was also a prostitute, he smiled and put his hand on my knee. "Good lad, young Harvey," he said, "good lad." I told him how gray and flat the world behind the Iron Curtain seemed, with little to buy, little to read, cabbage, potatoes, and fatty sausages to eat. He said "Make sure you tell your father that he was right about Communism" He winked at me and said, "He sometimes thinks that you're a Bolshie." This was the last time I saw Hamish. Then to New York, on to Albuquerque. It seemed that I had been away for a very long time.

32

Aftermath and Beyond

When I returned to New Mexico, it was spring. Banks of dirty snow remained on the north sides of walls, for the nights were still cold, but on the sunny sides of our houses, the snow had melted and the lilacs were in full bloom. The perfume of the flowers, mingled with the smell of mud and rotting leaves, gives the mountain spring in New Mexico an ambiguous quality, "mixing," as T.S. Eliot wrote, "memory and desire." The days grew longer and the air warmed. I wanted to return to the ordinary, to enjoy a life of the senses, to step out of the shadows that I'd been living in for the previous six months. I gave my heavy wool coat away. I felt that it was irretrievably, obscenely soiled. My journal found a place on the corner of my desk. What use I would make of it was uncertain.

America, prosperous, already forgetting Vietnam, seemed unreal. I couldn't connect. I felt like a stranger among old friends and a stranger to myself as well, at least to myself as I had been. I had not returned as a tourist might have, with interesting incidents of travel to recount. There was, in fact, nothing that I could share easily. A local gallery put up a short exhibition of the photographs I'd taken, all with the clumsy Hasselblad, of sights off the normal tourist route: the ruins of the Fuhrer bunker, where Hitler died, a mound covered with snow in the no-man's land between the two Germanys, the grim apartment blocks of Communist Warsaw, the Oder river at first light from a train window. There was no reception for the exhibition, just a notice in the paper. I felt the need

to be separate, to isolate myself, even from women, girlfriends potential
or past. I was having trouble adjusting to America, to a world where it
seemed that nothing terrible ever happened.

There were, however, things that needed tending to. My Los Angeles
book, now titled *The Plain of Smokes,* was still just a manuscript in a
drawer. That project needed to come to a satisfactory conclusion. Because
I was sure that the book deserved wider readership, I had rejected the
idea of publishing it through my own press. I also wanted the book to
include illustrations by a specific artist, Ken Price, who now lived in
Taos. Ken was also from Los Angeles, and, from conversations we'd had
over several years, I knew that our mental image of the city was similar,
ironic, even sardonic, and certainly irreverent: the mythic LA of cars,
spindly palm trees, and babes in bikinis on billboards. Ken was best
known as a ceramic artist, but he had a wonderful drawing style. I com-
missioned him to produce a suite of Los Angeles-themed drawings. We
worked together. I would read him lines that I wanted him to illustrate.
He took to the project. His illustrations were perfect.

The next step was finding a publisher. The publisher I wanted: Black
Sparrow of Santa Barbara, the best literary press outside the East Coast.
But how was an unknown writer to approach Black Sparrow? I knew that
I would need help. Years earlier, I had been befriended by the dean of Los
Angeles's antiquarian booksellers, Jake Zeitlin, of Zeitlin and Ver Brugge.
My grandfather collected rare books and he and Jake had been friends. As
a book-loving young man, I had introduced myself as Harvey's grandson
and over the years Jake Zeitlin and I had formed something of a relationship. I was an acolyte, a disciple. Mr. Zeitlin would take special books
out of locked glass cases and put them on a table covered with green
felt. I remember especially Bernal Diaz del Castillo's *Historia Verdadera
de la Conquista de la Nueva España*, 1632, in its original vellum binding.
Mr. Zeitlin had seated himself opposite me and watched, affectionately
and approvingly, as a teacher might watch a favored pupil. When I was
thirteen I had read an historical novel about the conquest of Mexico,

Captain from Castile. The novel, a romantic epic of conquest without any moral questions about slaughter and slavery to befuddle the reader, had thrilled me and here, before me was the original, the source document. I caressed the pages. My grandfather had purchased his *De Re Metallica* from Jake Zeitlin: I told Mr. Zeitlin about my childhood encounter with that book, the feel, with one's finger tips, of words on a page. Now, fifteen years later, I went to see him, not as one of his students, but as a writer. I asked if I could read him some of my manuscript. I had read no more than five pages when he stopped me with a gesture. My heart sank. Then, on the spot, he picked up the phone, found the unlisted number from his Rolodex, and called John Martin, the publisher of Black Sparrow, a famously inaccessible man. The door opened for me. I know today that there are many very fine writers who do not have the good fortune of having an advocate like the one I had. I was lucky. As is often said, much depends on who you know.

John Martin was an important figure in American literature, an outlier, scouting the writing world outside of the mainstream and academia for renegade talent. He published such writers as Charles Bukowski (*Love is a Dog from Hell*), Ed Dorn (*Gunslinger*), and John Fante (*Ask the Dust*). And he was willing to take a chance on unknowns like me. John's wife, Barbara, designed all the books and gave Black Sparrow a unique, West Coast, aesthetic panache.

John could seem arrogant, but never seemed terribly serious about himself either, a characteristic that gave him an impish quality. He had a kinky sense of humor that sometimes turned a bit cruel. He thought few people were as smart as he was, which was mostly true. With John, I often felt as though I was a mouse being toyed with by a cat, but a cat that would keep me alive for its own purposes, that probably wouldn't eat me. I enjoyed my relationship with both of the Martins, and with John's octogenarian mother, who lived with them, and with the little green parrot who lived by day in John's shirt. I was a frequent guest in Santa Barbara, staying in their guest room. We had long discussions about poetry and about art, specifically about British art between the wars—Wyndham Lewis a favorite of his. Poetry books with illustrations were a dubious proposition for purists like John Martin. Eventually he came around, and when he did it was enthusiastically, deciding to publish a folio-sized edition that highlighted Ken's drawings in addition to the standard book format. A master printer, Gary Lichtenstein, then in San Francisco, produced these in brilliant silkscreens. I spent many hours in Gary's studio, observing and learning.

This process of turning manuscript into book, establishing the connections that made it possible, had taken almost two years. During this period, I began an important relationship with a woman named Anna. She lived in Santa Fe and was a friend of Max's. From the first moment I saw Anna, at a party, I knew that we would come together. She had two sons, the oldest then thirteen; she had a good relationship with the boys' father. She was a graduate of a small Catholic college in upstate New York, but was not the least religious. Anna was the director of an art gallery. I called on her at the gallery the day after the party and we began to get to know each other.

Anna was petite and wiry, not beautiful in the conventional sense, but she was extraordinarily interesting and full of life. She had a shock of thick brown hair that seemed almost like a mane, hence my nickname for her, "Lion." The nickname matched her character. She could be fierce if challenged. Men did not intimidate her. She made it clear that I would have to court her.

It was summer and she was going with her two sons to her family's home on the shore of Lake Skaneateles in upstate New York. She invited me to follow, not come with her, but to follow, to appear a day or two after she had arrived. She would see if I could get along with her parents and her brothers and sisters. I was on trial.

Anna was one of the soundest human beings I've ever known. Her life, its daily existence and its long term direction, was based on values, not on whims or trends. It was not that she was self-righteous or overly serious, it was that nothing was casual for her; not sex, not intoxicants, not each day, and certainly not relationships.

The day after I arrived at her parents' house, she put me to work in the garden harvesting zucchini that her mother made into preserves that she donated to her parish church fund-raisers. We put in long hours in the garden in the humid heat. There were other tests, less useful, whimsical but still tests. In the greenish murk of the water off the family's dock, there was a mysterious object. Some fifty feet from the shore, perhaps twenty feet down, it was a whitish blur as large as a man, a bulky body and a head. As a Californian, I was sure that I swam better than the young men from New York. I had spoken about the abilities of Californians when it came to water, an indirect sort of bragging that fooled no one. A test, then, for the interloper, Anna's suitor, was devised by her brothers. I was to swim down to the object and identify it.

So, holding my breath and descending deeper than I'd ever been before, I swam down through layers of stratified cold and ear-punishing pressure to investigate. The thing turned out to be an old-style refrigerator, with the compressor on top. My report was received with much fanfare. The object was given a name, something fitting the story we then went about inventing. It was an alien spaceman in a white suit, a being that had fallen to earth. It seemed that I had passed the test.

This was the summer of Johann Pachelbel's newly discovered Canon in D Major. It was played almost continuously on Syracuse radio. One night, in an old car belonging to her father, Anna and I took a midnight drive along the west side of the lake. With the Pachelbel in our ears and the windows open, we became part of the night, the mild air, the fields of corn waiting to be harvested, the dark forms of the pine trees across the lake, everything washed with the pewter gray light of a full moon. It was ravishing. The radio in the center of the dashboard, a lighted band with numbers and a red arrow that one moved with a knob to find a signal, seemed like an artifact of some arcane numerology. On the dashboard, behind the Bakelite steering wheel, the analog dials and gauges glowed amber. In one lighted circle, a smoothly ascending and descending needle indicated our local velocity in a universe that was traveling, expanding and moving apart, at the speed of light; but, as if by some odd reversal of relativity, it was as if we were motionless, outside of time, on a journey that involved never departing and never arriving. I felt that there was a great beauty flowing though the veins of the world on that August night, and because the memory is still so fresh, I realize that, despite everything I knew then and know now about human beings, I had experienced a sense of the rightness of life itself. For a handful of summer days and nights, I had surrendered to the immediate, to the simple and particular. It was something that Anna made possible and I am still grateful.

In 1981, Max Finstein returned to Santa Fe. He had found the Jews of the kibbutz extreme and irrational, "nuts" he said. He reconnected with his past as a writer. A mutual friend put out a *Selected Poems* but Max had a falling out with this friend and withdrew the book. Max would not tell what had happened. I know only that he felt betrayed and was very angry. I bought the pages and had them rebound under the Second Porcupine imprimatur. We had 200 copies to distribute to bookstores.

Because I still had occasional business with the Sierra Club Foundation and I still had furniture in storage, remnants of my year in the city with Alicia, I welcomed the idea of a trip to San Francisco. Max had his own reasons: to escape the mud of the mountain spring, to distribute his books, and to see old friends. We agreed that I would cover expenses and he would drive my pickup truck to the city, carrying cartons of his books, and that he would eventually return to Santa Fe with my furniture.

It was March. We set out, traveling together, but in separate vehicles so I could return sooner. Anna was with me. Anna and I were concerned about Max's driving. He looked very small sitting in the cab of a full-size pickup truck. As it began to get dark that first day on the road, we pulled over and, at her insistence, Anna drove the truck the last fifty miles to Ely, Nevada. After we ate, we walked back to the motel in the dry cold of the high desert. Even a few dozen yards away from the buzzing of an old neon sign, "Slots," we were beneath a sky as black as nothingness itself and filled with uncountable stars. I have a memory of Max smoking in the cold, his tobacco smoke mixing with his frosted breath. Anna gave Max a hug and we went to our rooms.

The next morning, Max was coughing. We asked if he was well. Anna offered several times to drive, but Max insisted that he was fine, offended, I think, that we thought him old. He wasn't; he was only fifty-eight. We started off, Max behind in the pickup truck, hoping still to reach San Francisco late that afternoon. The sun was brilliant, the sky clear blue and dazzling, but sixty or seventy miles out of Ely, we hit a snow squall that was so intense that for ten miles, conditions were blizzard-like, and then, as suddenly as it started, we were in the clear again. We encountered only two or three cars on that empty stretch.

As Anna and I approached the next big town, Tonopah, we saw a state police car and an ambulance coming toward us with lights flashing. Our hearts sank, near to panic. There had been so few cars on the road that the possibility that the accident involved Max was very strong. We drove straight to the Tonopah hospital and waited. An hour later the ambulance arrived. We were told that Max had lost control of the truck. It had gone out into the desert, but rather than letting it roll to a stop, he had tried to turn it back toward the highway, and in the wet earth, it had rolled over. He had been alive when they found him, in deep shock, having been thrown from the cab of the truck. He had said to the ambulance attendant, "My friends are ahead of me on the road. Can you radio the police and tell them what has happened?" Those were the only words that the attendant could understand. Max died in the ambulance. How terribly alone he must have felt. I could hardly bear the thought.

The lights in the ER were fluorescent; the stainless steel table on which Max's body lay had a greenish tint, a reflection of the color of the walls. His body was on the table under a sheet that we asked to have removed. I could see no injuries. The doctor said it had been shock as much as anything that had killed him. I took Max's hand. It was stiff and unresponsive. The man, our friend, had gone, and what was left was just the shell. Both Anna and I were struck by how small, how crumpled and old, he seemed in his torn clothes.

I called Max's daughter. I don't think I've ever had a more difficult task. Then came the details of the aftermath, legal formalities, arrangements for cremation, recovery of the cartons of Max's books that had been in the back of the truck, disposing of the totaled vehicle and the drive back to Santa Fe with the urn containing his ashes in the back seat. There was an outdoor ceremony at the New Buffalo commune in Taos and a drunken wake at my house. People came from as far as New York. Robert Creeley wrote a moving elegy, "Oh Max," that appeared in *Mirrors* in 1983.

I composed a prologue and epilogue to *The Plain of Smokes*. The scene, set in Anna's parents' house by the bottomless lake, was a séance, a calling back of the dead. I still think it is some of my best poetry. It included lines for Max.

> *The luminous gray*
> *ghost tatter*
> *of an old Jew,*
> *the wisdom of heroin and exile*
> *burning in him like a votive flame...*

* * *

Anna and I lived together. With us were her two sons, the younger the same age as my daughter Mariana, who was often with us. In June, I resumed the pattern of alternating my time between town and the mountains. Anna came as often as she could. I tended to my regular ranch chores, fences and building repairs, along with a program that I initiated to improve wildlife habitat. Because of a century of cattle grazing and timbering, the section of forest where my property was located could no longer be considered wilderness. So, to help nature, I was returning it to its original condition. I planted native grasses, bushes with berries for birds, and tall grasses to shelter the wintering herds of elk.

I had another, and far more eccentric, project in mind. I wanted to build something that would endure. The native granite of those mountains would last. The monument at Treblinka, a field of granite plinths that I'd seen on that winter day nearly five years earlier, had moved me and that experience was probably the inspiration for this project. My journey into the zone of the Holocaust was still very much in my mind.

But I wanted ambiguity, nothing obviously referential. A shrine, then, but a shrine to what? To nothing that I could easily name. My idea, however, was quite specific and at the same time utterly elusive as to meaning.

I wanted to build a shrine to Icarus, the boy in Greek mythology who, with the help of his father, escaped the labyrinth, but who flew too close to the sun and, the wax on his wings melting, fell into the sea. As metaphor I thought that this contained something of my own story. I remembered that I had proposed to Dr. Frazier, in jest, a diagnosis of "Icarus Complex" to explain my neurotic hesitancies and fears of those days, symptoms including but not limited to an irrational fear of flying. That symptom, among others, expressed a fear that my mother had weakened my wings and I would fall, not to death literally, but to failure, to underachievement, to some sort of shame. The labyrinth from which Icarus and his father, Daedalus, escaped seemed a wonderful metaphor for neurosis and frustrated hopes. Icarus, his father the craftsman, the labyrinth, the wings made by art, the failure and fall into the sea, held multiple layers of meaning for me personally, while the labyrinth as an inescapable maze, had wider metaphorical possibilities. It reflected the plight of the Jews, a whole people who had been trapped in centuries of anti-Semitism. To all that, I added another element, a reference to Michelangelo's *Pieta* in the Vatican, the dead Jesus in the arms of his mother. My Icarus would be like that, wings broken and quite dead, and held in the arms of his grieving mother. Obviously there was a great deal of personal symbolism. At the time, however, during my musing on this, in the hours of quiet solitude in the mountains, it was never literal or specific. I didn't think about it except as "the Icarus shrine," a folly. It is only now, in retrospect, that I have been able to analyze the imagery of the project.

I pitched the idea to my old friend from Amherst and New York, Charles Wells. He was an accomplished stone sculptor. We exchanged several letters. It turned out that he had wanted for some time to build a piece of land art, a solar calendar in the manner of the famous stones of Amesbury in England, and he liked the Icarus idea. I found some foundation money to pay Wells enough of a commission so he could come to New Mexico for two summers with his wife and sons. The Wells family lived in the larger of the two cabins on the property, I in the smaller.

We picked a granite outcrop on a little hill overlooking the valley. Wells built the tower the first summer. He was a meticulous builder; his tower will last as long as the great Anasazi structures of the Southwest. The second summer he carved the statue out of a piece of Wyoming marble that cost $500 to have delivered. It weighed two thousand pounds. Once the statue had been cut, we dragged it on skids with a tractor until we were at the same elevation as the tower and then, with a crew of friends, we built a temporary road through the timber and moved it on rollers, a foot at a time, to the site. It took days. No one saw us. We installed the sculpture. The previous December, I had established the line of sight to the place on the horizon where the sun went down on the solstice. The day had been glorious and cold, ten degrees below zero. We lined up a hole in the sculpture with a hole in the tower with the distant spot on the horizon. We felt like Druids. If anyone ever needed to know the solar date with certainty our calendar tower would have told them the day down to the minute.

In all, the sculpture, the tower, and the process, amounted to a gesture of rare purity. It benefited only those who had participated. Wells's fee was small, but he and his family were able to spend two summers in the wilderness of New Mexico. We had not harmed the earth nor had we exploited anyone. I was pleased with it.

Charles Wells with the Icarus Shrine project.

The Plain of Smokes was a success. The limited, quarto-sized edition attracted considerable notice as fine book making and turned out to make a profit. The book was nominated for the *Los Angeles Times* poetry prize for 1983. I felt that I was on track at last.

* * *

During this period, I had an encounter with my mother which I recount only because it gives her a chance to speak about our relationship in her own words. In Los Angeles, on my way to see John Martin in Santa Barbara, I called her, asking if I could come to visit. She was able to restrict our relationship as she always did in the most reasonable terms, that the staff was so overworked taking care of her invalid husband. She was unable to offer me the guest room, but "do come for drinks."

Bill had now lived for over six years completely immobilized. He required a respirator at all times, but he was determined to participate as much as he could. Strapped into his wheel chair, well dressed in khaki slacks and a blue blazer with brass buttons, he was in the living room when I arrived. An elegant silk scarf was arranged around his neck to conceal the breathing apparatus that entered his trachea. The little air pump, on a platform at the rear of the chair, hissed and huffed. He was welcoming and affable. His live-in nurse, a burly man, patient and self-effacing, in white pants and jacket, had retired to the kitchen for a coffee break, but he was available at the touch of a button or the sounding of an alarm warning of a malfunction of the oxygen pump. Bill always acted as if his condition was endurable. I learned later that he had twice tried to unplug himself but had been discovered and his life saved.

My mother left the room to consult with the nurse. I got up as if to stretch my legs and searched her bookshelves for copies of my books. I had sent them all to her. Books were not an important part of my mother's life so there were few shelves to search. My younger sister had written a book about a bicycle trip she had taken and this I found, but mine, now three, including the well received *The Plain of Smokes*, were nowhere to be seen. I wanted to think she'd given them to some charity or library, but the trash was more likely.

Bill, meanwhile, mentioning that they did not have many visitors, was enjoying the rare social occasion. We sparred about politics, a friendly jousting about the need for government. He, a libertarian purist, believed all government, including the FAA and the FDA, should be abolished. Air traffic control and pharmaceutical marketing would work on a market-driven honor system. My mother returned to the room. She announced that Bill was tired. He protested, saying emphatically that he was enjoying the conversation, but she, smiling graciously as she always did, overrode him and called for the nurse. He was wheeled away. He was a prisoner and not just of incapacity.

I said nothing about her treatment of her husband and suppressed my feelings about the absence of my books. Why, I wondered, did I want contact with my mother at all? And why did she have contact with me when it was clear that she would prefer not to? I think that the second question had to do with appearances. In my mother's world one did not openly expel a child from the family. It might have raised eyebrows and my mother was as sensitive to these social constraints as any grand Victorian lady would have been.

And so the charade continued. On this visit we discussed her art collection and her estate plan. I was interested in what she intended to do with her collection and she actually wanted to talk to me about it. She expressed a desire to keep the collection together and to donate it, in its entirety, to a museum, and I encouraged her to do this. I urged her to consider the Los Angeles County Museum. Los Angeles had cultural aspirations and her collection would give it a significant boost. But when she told me that she had received a visit from the curator of the National Gallery in Washington D.C., I knew that she was being seduced, and I feared that prestige would probably prevail over any thoughts about keeping the collection in Los Angeles. But I did urge her to keep the collection together; it had been her big project. I wanted there to be something in the balance sheet of her life about which I could feel pride. A significant gift to the community, especially to the city of her ancestors, Los Angeles, five generations of them, would cast her, at least post mortem, as a generous person. Since she had lived by appearances, the best of the façade seemed worth maintaining.

The visit lasted no more than an hour. Afterwards, reacting to the discovery that she had not a single copy of my books on her shelves, I wrote my mother a surprisingly plain-spoken letter that violated all my previous self-imposed restraints and abandoned the euphemisms that I had usually used to enable my denial about our relationship. In this letter, I expressed both muffled sadness and polite anger. Continuing our relationship in its present form, I wrote, would be "a fundamental dishonesty," and so I hoped that expressing my feelings might open a dialogue. I began my side of this dialogue with the statement that I was aware of the difference between the way she treated my brothers and me. Then, while acknowledging that I had not followed the path that she had wanted for me, I claimed a few good qualities and embarked on the embarrassing exercise of justifying myself. I cited the visits I had paid to her over the years. Speaking of my activities in the environmental movement, I noted that the values I espoused were no longer considered extreme. I spoke of my various forms of public service, the New Mexico Arts Commission, for instance, an activity that I thought she would approve, even if it was just New Mexico. I spoke of my books and the reviews that they had received. Finally, I wrote that, while acknowledging our differences, I would like to be welcomed back into her life.

Her reply, her half of the dialogue, came a month later. She said that she had "slept on it" and thought that I should have "slept on it too" before writing my letter. The tone was cordial, but the content contained no suggestion that she could let go of what she so strongly felt. Nothing changed.

> Your lack of interest in me and my welfare—and my mother's—gave me great pain for a long time, but I did adjust... But as to your terms of "forgiveness"... if four of your five children consistently gave support and cheer and recognition of your problems and joys, wouldn't you be inclined to give them more of your thoughts and your time than you would to the one whose concerns and whose life seemed to include you very marginally?

* * *

She was accurate in her main point. My concerns and my life had not included her. I'd moved away geographically, politically, and emotionally. I had thought that this, to some degree, was what was expected of a child. I had to acknowledge, however, that my moving away had been more than just out of the neighborhood. I had taken up residence in an entirely different moral and value universe. Without explicitly saying so I had rejected her values and she knew this. Her resentment was, thus, in some ways justified. It was not complete rejection, however, if she'd asked me, I would have affirmed that the proprieties should be maintained, that I knew that manners played a role in keeping society from sliding into a kind of aesthetic disrepair. It was the task of certain people to maintain these standards and she was one of those people. But we never came close to having the sort of open conversations in which such things might have been aired. The summation of her rather long letter was that if there was any forgiving to do, it was she who would have to do it and that she was not so inclined.

My relationship with Anna was under a strain caused by trying to integrate two families with children from previous marriages. Our arrangement turned out to be especially difficult for the older of her two sons. We attempted family therapy, often with the boy's father, who was invariably helpful and supportive. Ultimately, the tension created by the boy's difficulties got to be too much for me and for Anna too. Her first loyalty was to her child, a decision similar to the one I had made not many years before regarding Mariana. We separated but have remained friends.

Meanwhile my European journal lay on my desk. I felt that I had made that trip to fulfill some sort of responsibility, a feeling of obligation that I could hardly explain. The question was still there. Why had I gone? What had I learned?

* * *

I had a lot of conflict around this issue. Not having experienced any-thing even remotely comparable, I felt that I had no moral standing, no right to any part of the story. I certainly had no new information. Nevertheless, the experience had changed me. I knew *something* that I had not known before.

So, five years after the trip, I withdrew into the mountains to attempt a book. For company, I had my dog, Pete. In nature the distress that the world often produces was always eased for me; literally, my heartbeat slowed. I could feel it happen. And so, as I undertook to write about one of the most terrible things that mankind has ever inflicted on itself, I was surprisingly at peace.

My daily practice was almost Zen-like. There was solitude and sim-plicity. Every morning I performed a kind of ablution. I walked barefoot through dew wet grass to the spring that supplied my water. I filled a little metal cup with the clear, cold trickle. Then, while watching the sun rising over the ridge and the dew disappearing from the grass as the sunlight advanced along the ground, I drank the water in a single long swallow. One morning, standing by the spring, I watched as a tiny weasel came to the spring to drink. I stood very still. It approached me and put one front paw on my bare toe. Its entire paw was probably no longer than a quarter of an inch, four tiny delicate toes, each articulated with joints as well made as the fingers with which I typed on my Royal portable. The weasel had no idea that I was a living thing. I was a part of the landscape. I was a tree, a stone. The experience filled me with a quiet joy.

I wrote for five hours every day. The first part of the writing process was to decipher the handwriting in my journal and to transcribe those pages on the typewriter. Then, as the weeks went on, to reflect on what I had written and to transform them into something coherent. That last part of the process, a kind of alchemy that converts raw material into meaning, is something mysterious. I had only the sense that I had a purpose.

I took long walks in the moonlight. In the open meadows, the grass shone gray and the ponderosa pines cast long shadows. One night, a bear came ambling down a rocky slope, a clatter of stones and a dark ball of clumsy motion. I stood stock still, grabbing Pete's collar. He froze, uncertain of the appropriate response. I could feel the rumble of a growl gathering in his throat, but he made no sound and I made no motion. The bear was no more than fifty feet from us when the unwelcome human scent crossed its path. For a moment it stopped. And then it bolted, disappearing into the dark tangles of aspen and fir.

By day, I sat at my desk and pecked away at the typewriter. I was not writing a history; it was, rather, an account of the knowing a history. The journal gradually metamorphosed into a long poem. All I had managed to do was to witness my own witnessing. I accepted that this was all I could ever do.

I continued to be in contact with Alicia. We were friends and were always involved with our child. Alicia finally brought herself to the point at which she thought she could deal with the violence that had so damaged her spirit and so negatively shaped her experience in America. Fifteen years had passed. She was led to this moment because our daughter insisted that she understand the reason for her mother's silence, a condition that she, even at age thirteen, recognized as depression. Alicia found a therapist in Albuquerque that she liked and began the process. She talked about it all with me, what she was learning about herself, things she had never been able to say or to think before. That the rape had affected her so deeply was understandable. What made it worse was that she had internalized it as a kind of punishment for her defiance of the conventions and morals of her Catholic upbringing. "I had not realized that deep inside I was so conventional," she said to me and laughed. She began to get better.

My book about the Holocaust, titled *A European Education*, was finished. The book emerged as a long narrative poem in fourteen parts. It begins as follows:

While Berlin rose
I lay for an hour in the bed
without courage or direction:
an hour which became an aimless week.
I worried unnecessarily
about my health;
I berated myself for laziness and sensuality
and worldliness, a despair
which unfairly riddled
a relatively moral and conscious life.
And I dreamt, full of sweating self pity,
of dying young....

I had answered my question about why I had felt that a personal knowing of the Holocaust was something that I had had to undertake. It had to do with my grandfather's admonition when he put the Assyrian tablet in my hand. "History belongs to the young," he had said. He hadn't meant the little biscuit of fired clay; he had meant the truth of what has happened. Civilization depended on our remembering. Forgetting is a kind of entropy of the spirit. Things fall apart. Truth disappears if it is not maintained. It was like the adobe buildings of my New Mexico. They need to be re-plastered each year or the rains will turn even the most beautiful churches into a pile of mud.

A European Education, illustrated with my own photographs, was published by Black Sparrow in 1986. I had achieved some sort of closure. A chapter of my life came to an end, or almost to an end, for such experiences have no well defined endings. On my desk, I have a four-inch piece of rusted barb wire that I picked up on the ground at Auschwitz. And in that same desk, in a file drawer containing my journal and notebooks. As I rummaged about in these old files, trying to refresh my memory for this present book, I found a letter postmarked Chartres, November 1981, from Liliane. She first apologized for not writing

English well and then she thanked me for sending the book of my poems (*Stations*).

She said that she valued it as a reminder of a friendship. She wrote also that her cancer had returned and that assaults of chemotherapy left her exhausted and depressed. She said that her children seemed unconcerned and that I should not worry either. That she would be concerned for *my* feelings when she was again threatened by cancer touched me deeply. I no longer remember how I replied to her letter, or even if I did, or if she survived. I know only that I found no second letter from her in my files.

Part VII

The Lost Years

No! I am not Prince Hamlet, nor was meant to be;
Am an attendant lord, one that will do
To swell a progress, start a scene or two,
Advise the prince; no doubt, an easy tool,
Deferential, glad to be of use,
Politic, cautious, and meticulous;
Full of high sentence, but a bit obtuse; At times, indeed,
almost ridiculous— Almost, at times, the Fool.

T.S. Eliot, "The Love Song of J. Alfred Prufrock"

33

Error

Inherited money sometimes turns out to be a mixed blessing. Because it allowed me to try out a number of different personae, poet, activist, farmer, among others, no clearly identifiable normative persona emerged. No doctor, lawyer, or merchant chief. Among my multiple selves, there were some rogue elements: a mischief maker, Pan-like, who got me into trouble with women. And there was an inner con artist who persuaded me that I could be a businessman. This last figure represented the confused relationship that I had with my paternal ancestors, businessmen all, and good at it, men I admired.

But in truth I had no interest in business, no training, and no aptitude. Nevertheless, from time to time, I tried being a businessman. It was a role that was utterly inauthentic to my personality.

It had begun when I first arrived in Taos in 1967. Inexplicably I felt that I should do more than farming. I formed a business named after the main character in H.G. Wells' satirical novel about business, *Tono Bungay*, the bumbler Uncle Teddy Ponderevo. The novel is a tale of fraud, folly, and failure. The fact that I called my business enterprise Ponderevo Inc. shows that I didn't take business seriously enough. I was mocking myself. But it was a business enterprise, a gangly mini-conglomerate, engaged in all sorts of things. I built low-income housing, developed a rundown property into retail shops, restored the town's movie house, and opened a bar and restaurant over the theater. I personally ran the bar for several months, dealing with drunks, fights, and acid heads toting revolvers. I lost money. In 1969, when the pollution from the power plant appeared, I found an authentic calling, something I believed in, and I left my businesses in the capable hands of my friend, Jim. He, like me, was also a man of multiple personalities; in his case, however, it was out of economic necessity. He worked as overall manager of my scattered businesses. At the movie theater, he collected tickets and worked the projector.

Involved in politics by this time, I never got even a rudimentary business education out of these ventures. I had no sense of the book keeping, the regulatory issues, the hiring and firing. A business plan was a foreign idea to me. Didn't one just open the doors and turn on the lights? Apparently having learned nothing, nearly a decade later I tried my hand at it again. I opened an art gallery that specialized in antique Native American art. I had enough sense to know that I needed partners. One was a distinguished ceramic artist named Rick Dillingham. If he could be both an artist and a businessman, perhaps I could too. As it turned out, he was much better at managing the contradictions than I was. The gallery, which was in business during my marriage to Shirley, was profitable, but this was due more to the efforts of the partners than anything I contributed. After a couple of years, my partners withdrew for personal reasons and the gallery closed. But the fact that it had been profitable fostered the notion that I might have business skills. Over the decade, I had invested in Santa Fe real estate, buying old houses, fixing them up while living in them, doing much of the work myself, and then selling them. I made money, but in the Santa Fe real estate market of the 1980s, one could not help but make money. Since my business ledger had no column in which to account for good luck, again I thought I'd been clever.

The most serious of my business ventures was an investment in a vineyard and a winery in the Napa Valley of California. I knew relatively little about wine, and to this day cannot bring myself to utter the self-hypnotizing phrases about undertones of this or that. But I was genuinely interested in the farming part of the business, the growing of grapes. Not too long into the venture, however, I became suspicious that some of the other investors, whom I had not known previously, were in the business of importing marijuana on a large scale and were using the winery to launder their profits. The vintner focused on making wine, relied on an informal separate partnership to handle the investments and knew relatively little about his investors. I wrote checks to cover my share, but there was a great deal of cash floating around. Although I had no objection to marijuana as a recreational herb, I had objections to the practices that I suspected were involved when marijuana reached commercial scale, the bribing of public officials for instance. Was I naïve in assuming it was just marijuana? I overheard one of these men boasting about having won a business negotiation by cutting the other fellow's sofa in half with a chainsaw. For a period of months, I allowed myself to be seduced by expensive dinners with bottles of Cristal champagne, all paid for by my co-investors. I began to have concerns. I had invested quite a lot of time. I had put up the money to purchase a dairy farm on a hill that became, after passing through several successive hands, Domaine Carneros. I had seen the potential in the property, but with a sinking feeling, I realized that no matter how much money I stood to make, it was not worth the risk of jail, which might, I concluded, happen if I continued in association with these men. My suspicions were reinforced by a conversation that I had with the former wife of one of the partners; she too had overheard conversations that were unsettling. Denial evaporated and a sense of urgency took over. I sold my interest back to the other investors as quickly as I could and at a sizeable loss. It turned out that I made the right decision. I will never forget the knock on my door several years later; the DEA had come to ask questions. A number of these men did go to jail.

Aida, the former spouse of the partner whose suspicions had confirmed my own, became a friend. She was a tall, slim woman with a striking narrow face and was thirteen years my junior. She was studying to be a psychotherapist. I began dating her. There were good reasons to think we could form a relationship. Our backgrounds were very similar; we were both from families that were among the most prominent in their respective communities, so for a change there was nothing rebellious in my involvement with her. A further reason was that I wanted to have a family, an odd thing, perhaps, for me to want, but apparently I needed to be a father again. Aida had a child, a four-year-old daughter named Jessica whose father showed little interest in active parenting. Aida too wanted another child, even two. On the level of values, Aida was not like my mother, but she had the right manners. The similarities in our backgrounds had another attraction, one even more psychologically tempting: her childhood experience had been as unhappy as mine. There had been many of the same issues, psychological abuse that was hidden behind wealth. Her tormentor was her father, not her mother. There was a perverse sort of symmetry in this.

We married in 1986. The reasons were not the best reasons.

Aida and I had many differences that were not apparent in the beginning of our relationship. She was very accommodating to the needs and wishes of others; I was less so, being very protective of my time and energy. Furthermore, she was an avid all-season sportswoman, tennis, running, and skiing. I did a bit of each, but wasn't sufficiently serious about any to satisfy her needs in a partner. Nevertheless, there was a lot that worked well. My daughter Mariana was fifteen and in high school. Aida was a good stepmother, filling the roles I couldn't take on, mostly involved with female adolescence. I was waiting for *A European Education* to get finally into print. It was a slack period, a perfect situation for additional mischief.

Since I had done well with my houses in Santa Fe, I assumed that real estate was something I knew about. An acquaintance persuaded me to enter into a business partnership with a woman, a licensed real estate broker, whom I will call Angela. She was fat and cheerful, very southern in her manner, calling me "Mister Harvey" and often telling me how smart I was. She told me that she was an expert in how to use leverage.

We formed a partnership to buy and operate student rental units in Albuquerque near the University of New Mexico campus. The buildings were rundown, postwar, cinder block houses, but were easy to rent. At our peak, there were perhaps forty rental units, all purchased with borrowed money, all on appraisals that Angela had arranged.

For a while it seemed to go swimmingly. She assured me that our properties were increasing in value. Things were going so well that she began remodeling a Victorian house that the partnership owned in the old part of the city, intending to use it as an office and her residence. Using money that she said had been a gift from her mother, she installed black and white marble tiles in the entry, thermal pane windows, central air-conditioning and granite counter tops in the kitchen. Reassured by her confidence in the future of Albuquerque, the biggest city in the state, I paid little attention. I lived in Santa Fe, focusing my energy on a new writing project. I had joined a theater collective and wrote a play about Leonardo Da Vinci and the Mona Lisa that was produced to favorable reviews and good ticket sales. And the project of making a family was going well: Aida was pregnant.

One day, Angela called me and said she had to go into the hospital for a minor procedure. She assured me that things would be fine for the few days that she would be out of commission. Deciding to demonstrate my *bona fides* as a businessman, I went to the office. Real men go to the office. I had a key that I had never used. I sat at Angela's desk, in her chair. I opened a drawer. It was stuffed with unopened letters. I opened another drawer, the same. As I took them out and began to open them, a sinking feeling overcame me. These envelopes contained unpaid bills from plumbers, lawyers, and exterminators. When I totaled them up, they came to over $50,000. I went to the hospital and confronted her. She had no answer and retreated into sulky silence and eventually into isolation in the unfinished Victorian. I realized that my partner was either a crook or a con artist or a sociopath, or all of the above.

I knew I would have to sell one of the rental properties to cover these bills. I went to a realtor to get estimates, and was given values that were twenty percent below the mortgages on the properties. Another realtor told me the same thing, and with further research, I learned that with the collusion of a friendly appraiser and a complicit banker the entire portfolio had been over-mortgaged by twenty to twenty-five percent. It was a general partnership and so I was on the hook for the difference, which would eventually amount to hundreds of thousands of dollars. I was facing what the novelists of Charles Dickens's era called "ruin."

Because I had no way of knowing how much I would end up owing, I began living with the prospect of bankruptcy. My mood swung from near panic to depression to self-pity to fury. Aida accepted these dramatic alterations in our financial circumstance with remarkable equanimity and I was very grateful for her composure. In the winter of 1986, I sold my house and BMW to raise money. I drove to Albuquerque every day for a year, a seventy-five-minute commute each way, in a used VW diesel Rabbit that became, in my mind, the symbol of the whole dismal affair. The car was a deteriorating assemblage of bolts, bald tires, and rust that swayed down the interstate barely keeping steering linkages together. I thought of the car as a sort of parade float; it represented the fall to earth of the poet who hadn't been looking where he was going.

A European Education came out that winter. I was in no position to assist in its launch. No readings were scheduled. I was profoundly sad. I'd lost my opportunity. And it was entirely my fault. I could have followed up with another book that Black Sparrow would have published. I would probably have established myself as a poet. But I had to drop all that in order to salvage a financial future. In the midst of all this mess, our son was born, at home. Sam slept his first hours in the world on my chest. I adored him from the minute he was born. I gave up smoking as a gift to him: a father who wanted to stay alive. He is Sam, named for Samuel Clemens (Mark Twain); his middle name, Winston, reflected my admiration for Winston Churchill.

Meanwhile, new troubles kept emerging from the partnership closets. Literally. In one closet, I found all the bank statements, two years' worth, all unopened. I taught myself to examine what passed for the accounts and discovered that my partner had pocketed the difference between the money borrowed from the bank and the price paid for the property and this difference was the source of funds that she was living on. I drove over to the house and confronted her again.

All Angela said was, "Mister Harvey, does this mean that I can't keep my house?"

"That's right," I said, "you can't keep your fucking house." These were the last words I ever spoke to her.

She sank into even greater passivity, refusing to assist in any way. I would call and ask who was who in the address book. When she heard my voice, she hung up. I was too mean.

But when I started liquidating the properties, she came back to life. Because of the structure of the partnership, a formal resolution was required to make a sale, but she refused to sign a resolution. With money from her mother, she hired a lawyer and opposed every attempt I made to liquidate the partnership. I was forced to hire a lawyer. My attorney and I had to appear before a judge to get a court order for the sale of each property. There were eight of these apartment complexes. I would have a buyer. She, putting up none of the carrying costs and having no money of her own exposed to the overall debt, would say the property was worth more than the selling price and that I was destroying her real estate empire. Each time, I was forced to bring in a realtor or appraiser who would tell the judge that the price was market-based and fair. The judge invariably ordered the property sold. Invariably she opposed the next sale on the same grounds. If this process hadn't been so dreadfully wasteful and so grindingly depressing, this woman would have been a comical study of delusional entitlement. She always swept into the courtroom in a new dress and floppy hat, and made the same plea for protection from this corrupt partner who was stealing her treasures, these dilapidated cinderblock buildings with weeds in the yards. She made the same plea over and over to the same judge. He would shake his head and order the property sold.

Eventually it ended. I had sold all the partnership's property and nearly everything I owned personally. Most painful was the loss of the beautiful little valley that I owned in the mountains, where Wells and I had built our tower, the monument to the fallen Icarus. It turned out that the monument was my own. I had fallen back to earth. In the end, however, I salvaged enough money to live on.

I made another discovery about myself. I still had my Army M-14 rifle and had, occasionally, practiced with it out in the desert. During the worst of the Angela crisis, I felt as if I were being shaken like a little chipmunk in the jaws of a rabid terrier. I felt diminished and helpless, but the rifle gave me an illusory feeling of power, of restored manhood. I played out dozens of fantasies of killing Angela. I went so far as setting up a sheet of plywood with her outline spray-painted on it. At 200 meters I found her miserable heart over and over. It was a bit of a shock to find in myself the capacity for even the fantasy of murder. To actually shoot her was never a possibility, but even playacting was against both my character and values. My better self intervened. The rifle contained no meaningful power, unless I wanted to get into real trouble or make an ass of myself. As it says in Corinthians, I put away childish things. I abandoned the fantasies of violence and sold the rifle. I have never owned another firearm.

I considered, when all was said and done, that I had suffered from a delusional condition: I had imagined that I was a businessman. I might just as fruitfully have imagined that I was a tennis champion. The worst delusion was that making more money had been necessary. I should have remembered the adage, "If it ain't broke, don't fix it." My finances weren't broken, but I went out, tried to fix them, and they broke.

Aida had responded calmly to the financial crisis and had helped shield Mariana from the uncertainty and from the anxiety that I felt. I was grateful. But now she had her own difficulties. Her ex-husband had become intrusive and verbally abusive. She felt we should move. I agreed. After twenty years in New Mexico, a certain crust of a life lived had built up around me. Some of the stories about me were true; some were not. The rumors, facts, anecdotes, and, in some cases, outright lies presented a caricature of who I was. The lies troubled me somewhat and for a short time, I considered setting the record straight, but I soon saw futility in this. Those who believed me to be decent and honest always would; those who, for one reason or another, disliked me would continue to believe what they already believed. It was time to start over, with a blank slate.

Thinking about where to move, Aida and I did a considerable amount of research. The criteria we considered included access to higher education, health care, size of the city, crime rate. The most important for me was the politics. Vermont stood out. It was a humane state with good environmental attitudes, no death penalty, and progressive social policies. Vermont's Republican politicians would look like right-of-center Democrats to today's Republicans. Only the winters were a question, but I'd gone through many Taos winters, so was not intimidated. We consulted Mariana who was now a senior in high school. There was an arts-oriented college, Goddard, in Vermont that she wanted to attend. Alicia, who decided to stay in Santa Fe, was in agreement with Mariana's decision. I moved my family to Burlington, Vermont.

Before we moved east, I made another attempt to approach my mother. When our son was born, I sent photographs to her and announced the desire to come to California to introduce my new family to her. To my great surprise, my mother invited us all, new wife, Aida, her daughter, now five, and the six-month-old baby, for an overnight visit at her house at the beach. Overnight! I was stunned, but cautious; I doubted that the invitation represented a complete change of heart. It was likely that my new wife had something to do with it. This suspicion was confirmed when, on arriving at her house, my mother showed me the "lovely note" on monogrammed notepaper from Aida's mother in Minnesota, a note expressing the hope that she would "very soon have the pleasure" of meeting my mother. The two ladies were out of the same social mold, so much so that their handwriting was almost identical.

Before we went on this expedition, I had taken another step toward rapprochement with my mother. I asked her if she would be willing to see a psychotherapist with me, a joint session or two in which we could explore a way back toward a closer relationship. Her reply was prompt. It turned out that she had been seeing a therapist for six years. She offered to treat me to a session with this man, but as to her participation, she had neither the "time nor the energy to be involved," and didn't think it would be "particularly helpful." She had told the doctor to be candid. Figuring that I had nothing to lose and that I might learn something, I made the appointment.

His office was a pretentious facsimile of Freud's Vienna consulting room. Egyptian statuary and little Roman figures were arrayed on his desk. Only in Los Angeles, I thought, the land where a film set was often presented as reality. I described for him the peculiar relationship between my mother and me. Since I had come hoping to restore something, I said nothing about the more disturbing incidents, nothing about the false cancer or about the attempt to seduce me. I stuck to a simpler version, which I had been trying for nearly twenty years to have something like a normal relationship with her. I was candid about the things I thought might be involved from her perspective, my lifestyle choices, my politics, and by not living in California I might be thought of as having rejected her. He, in the manner of psychoanalysts, said nothing. Finally, I asked him directly. "Do you know why my mother continues to reject me? What is the issue?"

His reply was quite astonishing.

"I don't know. All she has ever said is that she is afraid of you. But about what or why, I don't know."

That ended family therapy. We all went to the seashore. My mother met us at the train station in her Bentley and we drove back to the beach compound where she lived in the summer and where I had spent my childhood summers. We had a formal lunch, a salad, a main dish, and dessert, all with cloth napkins and the good china. The Pacific shimmered outside. I have a snapshot of my mother holding the baby. She looks uncomfortable, but almost happy. She is smiling.

* * *

I drove a big yellow truck full of furniture from Santa Fe to Vermont. Our dog, called Extra, rode with me. Aida, with her daughter and our baby, went separately in the car. I crossed Lake Champlain and into Vermont at Crown Point on a June day so gorgeous that I wept with gratitude. The green pastures, the languid herds of black and white dairy cows, the air dry and a perfect seventy-four degrees, and the clouds drifting along the ridges of the mountains that rose up ahead of me all contributed to a sense of relief, even of happiness. Vermont would be my home for the next ten or so years.

I entered a quiet period, a time of psychological and financial regrouping. Financially, things gradually improved. I learned about the stock market and, through long days at a computer, managed to recover some of my previous losses, enough to allow me some maneuvering room.

Believing that I had made such a mess of things because I'd been seduced by the muses, I stopped writing. I experimented with new possibilities. I did volunteer consulting on environmental matters to Vermont State Senator, now Congressman, Peter Welch, hoping this might lead to some sort of career path. It didn't, probably because I found that I didn't fit well in an organization in which I was subordinate and Peter Welch was, appropriately, the boss. I tried teaching in a private high school, where I taught classes in subjects like film theory and art history. I found that I was a good teacher, but no full-time job openings were available for a man of my age without teaching credentials.

As I searched for an occupation, I thought to turn my love for the movies into a possible career writing for film. I wrote screenplays and on the basis of inquiry letters, some people in Hollywood showed interest. I traveled twice to the coast to make the proverbial five minute pitch, but when these producers, who were half my age, saw a man in his fifties, their eyes glazed over. I consoled myself by thinking that all of these youngsters probably had never seen a film by any of the masters, Fellini, Renoir, or Kurosawa. What, I thought, feeling superior, did they know? That snide judgment reflected back on my life. What did I know?

I felt like a workhorse pulling a wagon load of history—a wagon that, subject to the natural law of time, was getting heavier and heavier as more history got piled onto it.

My main focus became my son. I was a full-time father during the first seven years of his life, changing diapers, reading stories, hiking, teaching him to ride a two-wheeled bike and to swim. I tried to be a good parent to Aida's daughter.

In 1990, at my father's request, I brought Sam, now three, to Los Angeles. My father had requested that the visit be between just the two of us, and he wanted to see his grandson. Sam and I paid a visit to my mother and her husband. It was an afternoon event, her usual sort of come-for-tea affair. I don't think we stayed longer than forty-five minutes, just long enough for me to display the rambunctious little boy but to remove him before he made a mark on a table or broke an ashtray. It was the second time that his grandmother had seen him and the last.

My father was now quite ill with what he said was leukemia. His legs were covered with oozing purple sores that smelled, but his spirits were good. He received Sam and me in his hilltop house in Beverly Hills. He was very welcoming. Because his legs were painful, he got around on a little electric cart with rubber wheels. He took Sam for a ride, the cart zipping silently around his living room, my father laughing and Sam squealing with delight as they bumped against the ottoman and the sofa. I put Sam down for a nap on my father's bed and the two of us talked about his health prospects, which, he said, were not good, and then candidly about his death. It was a mature conversation in which he told me that he wanted no heroic interventions if his condition got markedly worse. He was leaving in a few days to receive some special unspecified treatment at a hospital somewhere outside Los Angeles. I didn't understand why he had made this choice, but did not ask.

This was the last time I saw my father. He died some three weeks later. After he died, I thought of the questions I had wanted to ask but had held back because I was not feeling in any way confrontational.

We had, after all, not always been on the same side of issues, or, for that matter, of history. But had I asked, I would have wanted to know if he or the company had had any financial interest in Chilean copper or any involvement with the 1973 coup. I had done research (and have since, using the tools of the Internet) and had found nothing. But since the former head of the CIA, John McCone, was an acquaintance of my father's, I was curious. McCone had been a director of a major corporation, ITT, that was then widely believed to have been involved in the coup; I wanted to hear what my father would say about it. Then, there was an odd rumor that my father had bankrolled the search for the sunken liner, the Titanic, but secretly, out of curiosity and not because he wanted either credit or profit. I wanted to know if he had changed his opinion of Richard Nixon. I wished that I had told him that I was proud of his generosity to the community and above above all of his role in the creation of Harvey Mudd College. He could claim truly that he had done something good and useful with his life. Above all, I wanted to know if he had any regrets.

34

Reputation

Among the laws that concern the dead, this one seems to me to be as solid as any, which obliges the actions of princes to be examined after their death. They are equals with, if not masters of, the laws; what justice could not do with their persons, it should rightly be able to do to their reputations.

Michel de Montaigne

I saw my father cry on only one occasion. Because it was such a rare event, I have remembered it. I was eleven. He was sitting in his chair in the living room listening to a speech on the big Stromberg Carlson radio. I approached him. He hushed me and said, cryptically, "General MacArthur." He filled in the context a little later. The general, whom my father considered a great hero, was making a farewell speech to a joint session of Congress. During the Korean War, MacArthur had wanted to take the war to the Chinese, to put an end to the revolution that created the People's Republic of China. President Truman and the Joint Chiefs thought MacArthur's bellicosity was foolhardy, that a land war in Asia would be a disaster, and ordered him to stop at the thirty-eighth parallel, the present boundary between North and South Korea. MacArthur publicly expressed contempt for this decision and for the President. For this act of insubordination Truman had relieved him of his command.

And now, MacArthur was bowing out of public life.

At the time of the speech, I knew none of the background. But the sight of tears streaming down my father's face, and over something that happened in a faraway place and involving people he did not know personally, made a big impression. History was something unfolding. We lived it.

Not long after the speech, my father came home with an LP recording of the general's speech. It was the issuing of the speech on vinyl that persuaded my father to replace his old 78 RPM record changer with a modern phonograph. The speech was played several times in the coming year. I absorbed parts of it, and, in emotional concordance with my father—we were very close in this period— I too choked up at the general's famous closing lines. "Old soldiers never die," MacArthur had intoned, his voice quiet, "they just fade away." A long pause, then, "Goodbye."

When my brother Tom called to tell me that our father had died, I was surprised. I had seen him only three weeks before and he had not seemed terminally ill. In addition to the sober subjects of our conversation, we had laughed together, teased, bantered, even gossiped. He had not seemed weak, just uncomfortable.

In Vermont, fall was beginning, a bite in the air, and leaves falling. I walked out into the pine forest that backed up to our yard and cried quietly. It was not anguish or a feeling of unbearable loss; I must have intuited that it was coming soon and I suspect my father had too, but had not let on. Besides, I had ambiguous feelings about my father as well as about my mother and I was still trying to sort out this mixture of emotion and judgement.

In my family, I was the outlier, the one who had moved away, but I had not rejected my siblings and had kept in contact. John had had a cardiac event, the result of attempting an iron-man bicycle ride that had induced an episode of ventricular fibrillation that left him brain dead. I had come from Vermont to sit by him, by what remained of him, a perfectly healthy-looking body, but the personality no longer present. There had been hurts and resentments, as there almost always are between siblings. He once told me that he thought poetry was something "that one got over" after one's undergraduate years. And he didn't think that a Mudd should bury himself in the provinces. But despite his judgmental side, I had liked him and respected his intelligence. And I loved him. I believed it was mutual.

I sat at his bedside, held his hand, and reminisced about things we'd done together, about the ranch in the mountains of New Mexico. I touched the tiny white scar on his forehead and remembered how I had smacked him with the sand bucket.

"It is my earliest memory of you," I said. There were medical people nearby talking quietly. The decision had been reached to withdraw life support; crying, I said goodbye to my brother.

As I left my brother's room, I encountered my father. He was standing by a window looking out at the well-tended grounds of the hospital. He looked grim and haggard. We hugged. My father was dry-eyed, but I saw that he was truly stricken.

Complicating the emotion that I felt on the day my father died, the tenth of September, 1990, was a profound sense of disappointment that I felt about him. I felt shame, embarrassment, and even anger about how he had spent the last twenty years of his life. I felt he had wasted something of value. It was reputation. But during this very same period, we had been closer than we had ever been. I felt that I had found him and yet that I had lost him. A paradox. As we grew closer, I often wondered where and why my father had gone. Now, after his death, I had the challenge of making a final assessment. What did I really think of him?

The process of discovering my father had begun when I was in my late teens, a period when the two of us often had long talks about serious matters. With a few bourbons in him, late at night, he sometimes drifted into a self-revelatory mood and told me things that I believed were inappropriate to share with me. I got to know him better than most sons know their fathers. I was ambivalent about these conversations. I appreciated his candor and at the same time I was uncomfortable. I felt that fathers should maintain a certain gravitas. His greater need for a confidant, to be understood, to be seen as a whole being, overrode that consideration. His father, my beloved grandfather, had been a remote figure, unknown and, my father said, unapproachable. He was trying another way.

Apparently he had endured his share of opprobrium, shame, and fear. He described a late-Edwardian world of repressed feelings and a father who was strict and puritanical, an image that I found hard to reconcile with the grandfather I knew. There were warnings about masturbation, "self-abuse" as it was called, and the dangers of "loose women." That one should "save one's self" for marriage was drummed into him. He told me about having nocturnal emissions, an adolescent phenomenon about which no one had told him anything, about his shame over the dreams that had induced these events, and about hiding the semen stained sheets from the maid. His views about sexuality had been so permeated with misconceptions and negativity, that I count myself lucky to have had no father-son chats on the subject. I recalled his discomfort in the ancient Pompeian brothel, the door Hamish had opened to me, a door that had not been opened to him.

My father spoke, again too candidly, of his sexual innocence at the time of his marriage and alluded to early failures of manhood with my mother. He was a man tormented by sexual uncertainty and he had married a woman who, apparently, could offer no help in that quarter. He did not have the peer friendships that allowed for expression of doubts or complaints about intimate matters. He told me that his friends didn't talk about such things out of respect for their wives. He was lonely; and I, without being asked, became his secret sharer. Always, but never spoken, was the fact that he slept in the guest room.

There is no question that my father adored my mother. He showered her with jewelry, gave her as much spending money as she ever wanted, and funded all her remodeling and art collecting projects. He was always opening doors for her, holding her chair as she sat down at the dinner table, standing when she entered a room. Apparently nothing kindled romance in her, neither gallantry nor generosity.

The divorce was the first real disaster my father had ever faced. Up to the day the letter from the attorney told him to pack his bags and get out of the house where he had lived for twenty years, his life had been without drama. He remarried a year or so later. This union failed too, lasting only about two years. He had started seeing escorts on the side from the very beginning of the second marriage. Now in his late fifties, he had apparently come to the conclusion that romantic love, or any kind of intimate relationship, was no longer in the cards for him. He rethought his expectations. Sex, which is the next best thing if you couldn't have love, which for my father would have been the real thing, became the best thing.

My father created a world for himself that was filled with the pleasures that most men only know as fantasy. He established the modern version of the harem. He could afford it. It was a domestic arrangement with a set of rules that he alone wrote without consultation with the other occupants; in return for gifts, good-looking women flattered him, did his bidding, indulged every sexual whim, and didn't talk back. There were eventually seven permanent women, a different woman for each day of the week. They, my father told me, were members of an informal network of present and semi-retired high-class escorts, and were friends. Some had been married; at least one had a child. Jealousy among the ladies was not allowed. Emotional blow-ups or personal problems weren't either. I alternated between being bemused and disapproving, and later, as the arrangement showed no sign of ending, trying to understand and to accept.

His ladies were women in their early to late forties. There were also occasional "treats," one-timers that one of his regulars would bring to him as a present. These were girls in their late teens or early twenties. The core seven made up his new family. He used the terms "harem" *and* "family" to describe his situation. That he even introduced the concept of family was most hurtful, especially since his avid attachment to pleasures and excitement revealed a neediness that I sensed left little time for his real family. He took the ladies individually and in pairs to the best restaurants and on trips to Europe and Hawaii. Flaunting his lifestyle was, I feel quite certain, a form of revenge that he inflicted on my mother for whom appearance was so important. He never said it, but I imagine that he must have been very angry. He had been faithful, generous, and proper for so very long, and still she had withheld herself. It was either that sex was dirty or she simply was not attracted to him. Whichever the reason, there was quite clearly no intimate life except what amounted to the wifely duty. "So look at me now," and he made her look; his life had become an open scandal and everyone who mattered, my mother's friends, all knew. People talked. He had burnt all the bridges that led back to his old life, to his former friends and social position. He no longer cared.

He insisted that the women loved him. Perhaps he was right. I met all the ladies. They were genuine people and I don't doubt that a pleasant and generous older man did inspire something akin to love. I don't have any illusions, however, about the situation or the relationships. He demanded obedience. Miss X was always expected on Monday and she always left on Tuesday morning. These terms were not negotiable. The women, in return, expected to be well rewarded and they were. He gave them allowances, paid for their apartments or condominiums, and bought each a car, always a high-end Lexus or Cadillac and always white.

I tried to think of his ladies as informal wives. They conversed with him, they laughed and made him laugh, and they made him feel good about himself. Aging wasn't so bad after all. In the background there was the uncomfortable truth that money was the basis of the relationships, but since it is also in so many proper marriages, the fact that he seemed genuinely happy made it acceptable, over time, to me. It had to be if I were to have a relationship with him. And I was truly glad to see him happy and relaxed.

There were difficult moments. I had lunch once at the Bel Air

Hotel with my father and a casual date that had been arranged by one of the regulars. It was a grotesque performance, painful to watch. The young woman was an under-educated girl, no older than twenty, who didn't know how to hold a fork. She played her part, calling a seventy-something multi-millionaire "sweetie," and he, looking his full years but dressed in a Hawaiian shirt like a man of fifty, called her by the same endearment. He patted her small hands and their chewed fingernails with his enormous age-spotted hands, the same hands that I, at fourteen, had watched pressing wildflowers into albums. I felt embarrassment for both of them, the exploiter and exploited, and was not sure which was which. Other diners watched them with a sort of morbid curiosity. My father's lack of self-awareness in this public setting was what was most striking; he didn't understand that he was making a spectacle of himself. His lack of social concern was rather like a monarch's arrogance. He could do as he wished.

I visited my father one or two times a year in the last decade of his life. The time we spent was good time, finishing the bonding process that should have happened many years earlier. He was warmer than he had ever been. I liked him *and* I thought that the life he now embraced was wasteful, delusional, and grotesquely self-indulgent. But given the eccentricities in my own history and the many women with whom I'd been involved, I could hardly be judgmental. I liked the women whom I knew best. They were all good natured. None were shrewish, none ill-mannered, none openly calculating. I observed warmth and humor. One had given my father a bronze casting of her bottom, which he had had mounted and hung on the wall of his bedroom.

"At least don't call it art," I said to him.

"I know what I like," was his reply.

When I visited, I stayed in his guest room, but never for longer than two nights, because it interrupted his schedule. I had meals with him and the lady of the day who never stayed the night while I was visiting. He showed an awareness that I might be uncomfortable in the situation. I often felt conflicted. My siblings were less so: they unequivocally disapproved.

I discovered by accident that he approved of me. Once, looking for a phone directory, I opened his desk drawer and discovered a stack of copies of *The Plain of Smokes*; in each was a Xerox copy of the Los Angeles Times glowing review of the book. I asked him about them. He told me that he gave a copy away to almost anyone he encountered and that he was proud of a son who had written such an interesting book. I took this to be an example of his reticence about expressing emotions.

We had easy conversations about the changes in his life, the discovery of a freer way, which included occasional pot smoking. He felt that he had freed himself from all the social constraints that he had lived with for so many years: work, the same brown suit, dinner parties that bored him. He talked about the hypocrisy that existed in many of the marriages that he knew—loveless unions and husbands who were the regular clients of escorts. He fancied himself as a social pioneer, overturning false moralities, bringing the light of liberty into a world of hypocritical conventions and sexual repression.

He often spoke of liberty and freedom. In one conversation, he cited the "life, liberty, and pursuit of happiness" phrase from the Declaration of Independence. "And I am happy," he said. I was not sure if his use of Jefferson's language had been ironic or not. I asked him if he might not be overstating the significance of his personal revolution.

He deflected my question and stuck to happiness. "Jefferson kept a mistress too," he said. "It made him happy."

I couldn't resist adding, "Jefferson's mistress was a slave." Apparently my father had intended no irony, as evidenced by the serious tone with which he replied, "I have seven." There was something in this exchange that he had not understood. It was as if he had not heard the word "slave."

When I discovered that he was seriously ill, I went to see him. It wasn't to cheer him up. He didn't seem to need cheering, from me at least. He was open about his symptoms, a collapsing T-cell count and thrush, a condition in the throat that made swallowing difficult. He made sure that I understood that the condition was incurable. I admired the way he faced his illness and his impending death. While I disapproved of his lifestyle, his last days and months were dignified and stoic. Yet, I felt that he had betrayed himself and his family, abandoning his dignified better self, the man who had raised me, to become a self-absorbed sybarite with the self knowledge of a sixteen-year-old. Yet, I loved him.

In our last conversation, in the late summer when I had come with my son, we talked candidly about his views about inheritance. He had come to think that inherited wealth was not necessarily a good thing.

"Look at me," he said, "look what having so much money did for me. Look what I couldn't figure out."

I thought he was referring to love, that he was aware that he had missed something. As I went back over what he had said that afternoon, I realized that I wasn't sure whether he had said "couldn't figure out" or "didn't figure out." Were they the same? These words, however imperfectly I have remembered them, are, in my mind, his epitaph. He was the man who couldn't—or didn't—figure something out.

Henry Mudd died in September 1990, at the age of seventy-seven, about three weeks after my last visit. There was a memorial service at the college that I did not attend. My trips to the West Coast had put a financial strain on me and, in spite of my tolerance of his lifestyle, I wasn't in the mood to socialize with his harem.

His fortune was concealed in trusts, but rumor is all I would ever know of it and, since I put no faith in rumors, I will stick to saying that I know nothing of his wealth. For all I know he had squandered it. To each of his children, he left an object of little monetary value, but of sentimental importance. I received my grandfather's desk set which consisted of a piece of polished marble with a groove in it to hold a pen to which were attached two little bronze figures: miners, one with a pick, the other with a shovel. He left no money to his children, but we all knew this in advance. He had told it to each of us in person. He believed that the money our grandfather had left us had been enough, and if we'd failed to take advantage of this head start on life, the fault was ours. And he had his own life as a cautionary tale; he clearly had ambivalent feelings about what having more money than he needed had done for him. Of course, I would have liked to have inherited money from him, but in fact I had no argument with his reasoning. He left his principal estate —size unknown—to Harvey Mudd College. He also created income trusts for each of his regular ladies, money to be given to them until they died. This was a deal he had made with each of them as part of their compensation package.

After his death, my siblings and I learned that he had cut one of the regular women out of his will because she had defied him. It had been a matter regarding her child. Because of her status as my father's mistress, her former husband had attempted to take custody of the child. The man called her a "a kept woman," and my father, the man who kept her, had supported the husband's position by writing a letter to the family court. My father apparently thought her morally unfit as well. This, to me, was a dazzling bit of hypocritical double think. I was furious with him, and if he had been alive when all this came out I would have challenged him over it.

The woman had challenged him. She had talked back and he had fired her. "Give back the car, expect nothing in my will." My siblings and I, unified as we never had been about him while he lived, found this behavior inexcusable. I was delegated to help this woman get her promised pension. This drama culminated in a Los Angeles courtroom. I had volunteered to testify as a witness, not to her character, for I knew little about it, but to the fact that my father had often said he had agreements with these women, oral contracts that they relied on. But the most capricious of the Gods, Irony, was still in charge here and introduced a principle straight from *Catch 22*. Having established that sex was one of the services provided, his estate's lawyer argued that since, in California, a contract for sex is illegal, the oral contract was null and void. I had not helped. Several years earlier, before my father and I had made our peace, I had written him a mean-spirited letter in which I had pointed out that that he could get the same services for a fraction of what he was paying. It was a grave insult to a man who believed he had found love. I had forgotten that I had written this letter, which for some reason my father had saved, and now it emerged as evidence that the relationships were essentially sex for money. The other women, who had not talked back to their employer, got their pensions. The plaintiff didn't.

My father called his illness leukemia and that is what the *Los Angeles Times* reported in his obituary. Indeed, his death certificate, confirms that he had chronic lymphocytic leukemia. The more immediate causes of death are listed as advanced cutaneous T-cell lymphoma (the ulcers on his legs and arms) and gram negative bacteremia. Both of these conditions are sometimes associated with AIDS and leukemia is often the euphemism. The sores on his legs matched the clinical description of Kaposi's sarcoma. After his death, I thought about his symptoms and his lifestyle. I remembered a remark he had made two years before he died about "no longer having intercourse with any of them." I think it possible that my father died of AIDS. He had told me that he had occasionally encountered, among his "treats," girls who were intravenous drug users. He had engaged in a rescue fantasy with one of them that lasted months. One of his regular ladies died in her fifties of a disease that my informant, who had been another member of my father's group, was unwilling to disclose. Do I know for sure that my father fell to AIDS? I do not. But it would be no surprise.

In fact, he was, in a perverse sense, the most likely of candidates. Another of the disadvantages of wealth is that it creates not only an attitude of entitlement, but also the illusion of invulnerability. He thought he was above risk and so engaged in very risky behavior. I thought of William Blake: "The path of excess leads to the palace of wisdom." Blake had meant something about how one acquires self knowledge. My father, however, took Blake literally; he had parsed the sentence without the word "wisdom" and had taken the path of the most banal of excesses, consumer and sexual. There was no palace at the end of the path, just the houses and condominiums of his ladies scattered about on the plain of Los Angeles, and each year a new Bentley in his garage.

In the end, as before, I had mixed feelings about him. He may not have been wise, but he had a genuine kind of integrity. His acceptance of his own death had a calm worthy of a Roman philosopher. I suspect, but cannot prove, that my father managed to have an assisted death, and certainly with his kind of money almost anything could be arranged. If he had stayed in Los Angeles, the progress of his disease would have required hospitalization. A slow, humiliating end lay before him. So, like an old dog knowing his end is near, he took himself off to die in private.

My father had started his adult life in as honorable a way as I can imagine. From the 1940s through the 1960s, he was a self-affirming representative of everything that America valued. He had willingly served his country during the war. He was scrupulously honest in his business dealings. He was entrepreneurial and financially successful. He participated in the democratic process, was always well informed and always voted. He believed that capitalism was the best way to bring a decent life not just to himself, but to his fellow citizens as well. He was an enlightened capitalist: he genuinely saw everyone, rich and poor, white and black, as his fellow citizen and believed that they too had rights to dignity and a minimum of security. He never abused his wife or children, neither physically or verbally. He was moderate in his consumption of stimulants, his use of language, and in his political ideas. I never heard him express hatred for anyone. When he disliked or disapproved of something, Soviet style government, for instance, or communism as an economic theory, it was for a reason that he could articulate.

But something happened to him in his middle years, in the 1970s. It was the discovery of something he had always known but had been unable to admit to himself, that his wife, my mother, did not love him and probably never had. He had been living a lie, not his lie, but hers.

To play his circumscribed role in this domestic kabuki, he had been required to sacrifice an important part of himself, his sexuality. When his wife divorced him, he looked around and, no longer having a sure sense of who he was or of what he valued, he adopted what 1980s America was offering up as the good life, a life of consumerism and self-indulgence. It was the Playboy "philosophy" in spades, as if that puerile, self-degrading and woman-degrading nonsense was actually a philosophy.

Our family lost. The larger community of the college and Los Angeles also lost. His behavior tore away the family myth, and it was now clear that we, who were once seen as the best sort of people, often behaved as badly, as foolishly, as tastelessly, as others did. But there was, in my view of things, a gain. We got to truths. My sense, from early childhood on, that my family was a façade behind which there were secrets, unhappy people, and often ugly psychological currents, was vindicated, revealed through my father's behavior, though it was almost certainly my mother who was the cause.

My father, then, the man in whole. There was the politically conservative—centrist by today's standards—capitalist father, many of whose values and economic ideas I had rejected, but who was democratic, ethical, and rational. My exposure as an environmentalist to modern capitalism gave me an appreciation of honorable men like my paternal ancestors. They were, by contrast to most of their present day successors, virtuous men.

Then there was the personal father who had raised me, not perfectly but well enough, who in later years, despite our differences and occasional conflicts, kept faith with me. I loved this man. And in loving him, I tried to see his excesses, not so much as sin or sickness but as an expression of disappointment.

Finally, there was the man who I think of as the transcendent father, the man who carried within himself a portion of the collective wisdom and the lessons of history. He understood that there was such a thing as right and wrong, and that truth was always better than a lie. I remembered that evening long ago, sitting beneath the stars, when he told me the story of Galileo and his telescope, his clash with authority and the official church version of the solar system. My father was then, and on many other occasions, that transcendent father, the guardian and transmitter of a portion of the collective wisdom that civilized men and women have spent 4,000 years accumulating, a man guided by morals and reason, not by appetites, prejudices, or passions.

At the end of his life he had lost sight of this part of himself. But within this strange character, this man who was sometimes arrogant, often embarrassing, and always self indulgent, there was still my personal father, a man I had loved since childhood. He was truly happier than he had ever been and had become a more loving father. He had become my friend.

But it was a sad end. My father wandered off into oblivion. I had watched him go, stumbling at the end on his feet of clay. Oblivion is a very large place, but I have found him there and I have told his story to keep it from disappearing entirely.

My father in his office, circa 1980

35

"Leave her to heaven."

I never saw my mother cry. Not once. Her self-control was absolute. It is tempting to think that she had no emotions, but I don't think this is true. I believe, rather, that she was so totally repressed that what went on in her psyche never had a chance to emerge as an emotion. I think that there was a great deal going on, but it was as unknown and unknowable to herself as to the rest of us. I think of her as being perfectly inauthentic, a screen, but not in the way that Edith Wharton described May Welland in The *Age of Innocence*, as a screen of beauty and manners behind which there was nothing. In my mother's case there was considerable unconscious activity, fears and desires, that produced turmoil and anxiety that she worked hard to contain, deny, and conceal. The aspects of a normal personality that might have created a genuine individuality—loves, regrets, longings, quirks, likes and dislikes, concern about serious matters—were not permitted. She was all appearance. Her interest in art was authentic but even that was restrained, consistent with her style. Ironically the originating passions that created the art that my mother admired were not the sort of emotions that she would have countenanced in anyone she knew personally. Those troubled lives, the intoxicants, perversions, even madness, would have horrified her. She admired Gauguin, Van Gogh, Picasso, and Cezanne, all personalities she would not have allowed into her house. Gauguin, the outlier who slept with dark-skinned women; Van Gogh, mad; Picasso, supremely masculine; Cezanne, an ill-mannered grump. But the beauty that she saw in the art strengthened her, corroborated her resolve to maintain appearances.

My mother was mysteriously psychological. She would have explicitly denied this; she would have said that there was nothing difficult to understand about her. At the same time, she would have denied that she was unemotional. There was the social necessity of dealing with the feelings of other people and for this she had cultivated the most correct words, facial expressions, and social gestures. She knew what to say when someone died or had a baby or got divorced. As to her own feelings, she would have said, if asked about them, that she followed the "rule of my grandmother and, in turn, my mother," giving "thoughtful consideration and kindness to everyone." She believed that she was this person. She was not capable of irony.

She resisted all efforts to penetrate appearance, which meant that she set the limits on truthfulness and intimacy. She believed it was inappropriate to show interest in the inner lives of others. What one thought, felt, believed, or had convictions about—the totality of a self—was of no interest because all that was irrelevant to what mattered most, appearances. This insistent, obdurate superficiality, probably more than any other thing, was what I had rejected about my mother.

I had managed to get over the cruelties and humiliations with which she had tormented my childhood. I never felt that I was either a victim or a survivor of anything. I was just another person who had had a difficult childhood. I had not thought of her as being seriously disturbed until the seduction incident and the discovery that my cancer had been an invention, but even then, I managed to find a place for her in the ongoing story of my life. Stubbornly, some might say neurotically, I kept alive the hope for some level of relationship.

I probably would have been better off if I had just let her go. Or let myself go away completely. If she had abused me in a way that could conventionally be identified as "abuse," or if she had run off with a salesman so that I never saw her again, the conditions of my emotional development would have been different, probably easier, for I would have had something clear to repudiate. As it was, I was always not quite there, apart, in voluntary exile, but still somewhat involved. My mother remained psychologically present through most of my life, a beautiful, gracious, smiling woman whose chair I had often held for her at the dinner table, a woman who spoke of love but didn't know what love really meant. There was something tragic in her. It was as if she lived in a sort of limbo; as far as life was concerned, she was uncommitted.

She was my mother *and* she wasn't. That was the paradox that created the unease in my childhood and that made disentangling my psyche from her so difficult. I had continued to visit, year after year, offering to bring a grandchild, hoping for a shift in the landscape, hoping that I might be invited to stay in her guest room; but I always failed and yet I always accepted the little crumbs with gratitude, hoping that the gracious smile and the flawlessly considerate utterances actually meant something.

In October of 1988, I had a startling, indeed shocking, glimpse into my mother. The event marked a crucial turning point in my relationship with her.

About three weeks after I had seen my brother in the hospital, he died. I returned with my daughter, Mariana, for a memorial service arranged by John's widow, Alexandra. The extended family had gathered at their house in Mill Valley. Mariana, now seventeen years old, joined John's three daughters, her cousins, and cousins from Alexandra's side of the family. All the young people would be camping out in the game room in sleeping bags. I was to sleep in a guest room with Alexandra's brother.

At a gathering the night before the service, I entered the library and stumbled upon my mother and my daughter. I could tell from my daughter's expression that she was very distressed. I approached and heard my mother, smiling graciously, as she always did, say, "Mariana, dear, the house is really quite overcrowded and I think it best if you found a motel for tonight."

My daughter was on the verge of tears. My brother's widow, grieving and bewildered, was sitting nearby. I could tell that this was not something that she had requested. This little drama, so loaded with unspoken animosity, took probably less than two minutes to unfold. It was incomprehensible, but it wasn't. It was not about the crowded house or about Mariana. It was another way my mother had found to reject me. If Mariana had been expelled, forced to find a motel, I naturally would have had to accompany her.

I'd never seen quite so clearly my mother's capacity for cruelty. When directed at me when I was a child, it had always been gloved in that same velvet, the smile and the "dear;" and back then, I had wanted to believe that the touch of velvet meant a secret softness in her heart. But now I saw it clearly for what it was and had always been: cruelty in the guise of propriety. Here was a child who had nothing to do with my supposed flaws and transgressions, who had traveled across the country to show sympathy and support for her cousins; and my mother, not having the ability to throw me out, attacked the child because she was an extension of me. All the negative emotions of my youth came flooding back. All the efforts I'd made, twenty-five years of approach, of thinking something might change, dissolved into that moment. I stopped kidding myself.

I crossed the room and stepped between them. I told my mother that Mariana was staying. I said that her action was "inexcusably vicious." I then backed my mother away from my daughter; I was conscious that I would have used force if my mother had resisted. The older of my two sisters, Victoria, had witnessed this confrontation and joined me in forming a screen between my mother and my child. It was as if we'd encountered a predator in the moment of its kill and had forced it to drop its prey.

I knew where my sister's courage came from. She had had her own struggles with our mother. As children and as teenagers, both of my sisters had been on the receiving end of her cruelty. Now, that night of John's funeral, Victoria and I were united. I comforted Mariana. She stayed, joining her cousins.

But somewhere in that troubled night, in my sleep perhaps, something shifted in me. In the moment when I had directly confronted my mother, when I knew that I would have used my will, even force, to protect my child from her, I was released from my chronic addiction, hope. It had been my worst bad habit. The experience, standing between her and my daughter, propriety dispensed with, with my arm, in spirit if not literally, raised and prepared to strike, had been cathartic. It was as if I had slain her. I felt liberated. My anger surrendered to a kind of realism and, with that, the simple resolve to be as nonreactive as possible.

By the time we came to the outdoor memorial service the next morning, I had allowed myself to understand that my mother's stony composure was, in fact, anguish. The loss of her favorite son had devastated her. I could see it in her drawn face, feel it in her body language. At the service, she would be on her own. Her invalid husband could not attend, and my father, because of the bitterness of the divorce, would have not have been an appropriate companion for her. Tom, looking so like his deceased twin that it was unsettling, stood with John's widow and John's daughters. My sisters were with our father and each other. By default, I became my mother's companion, her support.

I drove her from the house to the service and accompanied her to a folding metal chair set up in the sun. The young people sat on the grass. My mother wore a black and white checked summer-weight suit. She never spoke and she never cried. I stood behind her and put my hand on her shoulder. At one point, we all stood for a vaguely Christian prayer and my mother's knees started to buckle. I caught her by the elbow and steadied her until she could sit without attracting attention. During this whole experience, I could sense that she needed help but didn't want it to come from me. So be it. I drove her to the San Francisco airport that afternoon. We made small talk appropriate to the occasion.

In the aftermath, Tom moved into the place that John had occupied with our mother, becoming her advisor, the favorite. I was glad that he was geographically close enough and that he was willing to do it. I had not wanted it, deserved it, or expected it.

Toward my mother, I began to shift toward a "live and let live" attitude and began, for the first time, to try to understand her outside of the distortions of our relationship. I tried to imagine her as a nineteen-year-old, the year she married my father. I pictured a pretty girl with a normal interest in boys and romance. She may have been in love with someone at the time of her engagement to my father. Those feelings, those normal instincts and impulses, if acknowledged and acted upon, would have wrecked the social advancement project that her mother had set out for her. She was the only child and her mother had an agenda. Upward mobility may have become, with time, my mother's agenda too, but I now suspected that it had come at a great price. Perhaps the mask of perfection that she wore throughout her adult life was to protect herself from feelings of disappointment. She had sacrificed herself in order to achieve the prize of wealth and high social status. It required also the sacrifice of her children—just as she had been sacrificed. We children had to believe that social eminence and the appearances that were the uniform of that social class were of paramount importance. She not only required that the forms be observed— how to set the silverware on the table, how to rise from a chair and for whom, when to hold one's tongue, what sorts of things could be talked about in polite company— but she insisted that these things were supremely meaningful and that we children be true believers. It was a kind of orthodoxy. Any doubt regarding the value of either the sacrifice or the prize would have been heresy. I didn't believe. Doubt may have been the first of my offenses.

After the incident at John's funeral, I lost all fear of her, lost all hope too, and all anger. The result was that a detached sort of connection was possible. I received little and expected little. What I gave, a birthday card, for instance, was now easy. I followed her life through reports from my brother.

Her health declined. She had contracted hepatitis from contaminated blood administered during her back surgery in 1956 and had lived for nearly thirty years with a deteriorating liver. Tom was the only person who had permission to consult her doctors and so interpreted her condition to my sisters and me. As her health got worse, my brother's importance in her life increased. He talked regularly not only with the medical team but also with her attorneys. He became her administrator and was involved with the drawing up of her will.

As she worsened, I made several efforts to see her. As it became clear that she was dying, I thought that it might be a comfort to her if I made such an effort. Did I still secretly hope that some sort of reconciliation might occur? I probably did, but it was compassion that moved me. So I persisted. My efforts, calls from Vermont to my brother did not loosen the boundaries. Her doctors would not permit visitors. Finally, in frustration, I flew to California to visit my brother, essentially to negotiate with him. I stayed in his house in Palo Alto for two nights. Sitting in the hot tub under the benevolent mantle of a California night, we talked about our mother. We both agreed that she had been difficult and he acknowledged that he too had been deeply injured by her.

But I had gone specifically to insist on visiting her, not to complain. He told me that he would advocate for me with her doctors. I went back to Vermont, then, just two weeks later, flew to Los Angeles, heart not exactly in hand, but it was certainly involved. She was fading rapidly. Time for even a partial reconciliation was short. When I got to Los Angeles, I called Tom expecting that I'd received permission, but was told that her doctors still refused to allow me to visit. It wasn't specifically me, he insisted, it was any social interaction that might excite her or tax her remaining strength. I flew back to Vermont.

Eventually, however, I decided to defy them. Doctors could not keep even the outcast son from seeing his mother a last time. Besides, I had begun to have an uneasy feeling that my brother was keeping me from seeing her. Without telling my brother or asking permission as I had previously done, I went to Los Angeles and showed up, unannounced, at my mother's house.

It was eleven in the morning on a Sunday. The nurse let me in after I had showed her my driver's license. She had me wait in the entrance hall while she went to my mother's bedroom. Yes, my mother would see me. I should wait. I waited, sitting on a straight chair in the entry, until, a half hour later, the nurse returned.

My mother was sitting in an easy chair in her bedroom. She was dressed in one of her at-home gowns. White slippers, with a tuft of feathers, were on her feet. Her appearance was a shock. She was a very old, very sick woman. Her face was gaunt and her mouth was drawn back in a contraction of the lips. Her smile seemed to have been painted on. I felt an unexpected anguish, this once beautiful woman, now this specter. I searched for the kindest word, but knowing what she must feel when she saw herself in the mirror, I understood that euphemisms would aggravate what she must feel.

Out of the wide windows, was the golf course, the same view that I had seen as a child. There was "Hollywood" but with the giant white letters now veiled in smog. My mother and I talked awkwardly. I turned, as I usually did, because it worked, to art.

"*The Japanese Bridge* is lovely. It is wonderful to see it again." It used to please her when someone noticed.

As I filled this uncomfortable situation with similar chatter, I surveyed the room. By her bed there was a stand, rather like a lectern or a library bookstand, on wheels. On its sloping face was corkboard to which were tacked photographs of Tom and of John's children. There were no photographs of my children, though I had sent her snapshots regularly over the years. There were none of her daughters either, or of the deceased John, and none of her husband, who, the cook told me, kept to his quarters, to his nurses and his iron lung.

"Tom made that for me," my mother whispered, indicating the piece of furniture. It was beautifully made, of rosewood. My brother was good with his hands.

After fifteen minutes, she indicated that she was tired. I offered to help her to her bed, but she declined. In the four steps to the bed, she fell. I moved to catch her.

"Call Tom," she said, her voice no stronger than a whisper.

"Tom's not here," I said, and helped her into bed. I leaned over her and whispered, "I love you." I had never before spoken those words to my mother. They were difficult to say and I wasn't sure that I meant them. The nurse appeared and I left.

Back in Vermont, ten days later, I received an envelope addressed in an unfamiliar hand. In it was a piece of yellow notepaper that said, "I love you too." She died not long after.

My mother, date unknown, 45 to 50 years old

36

A Conclusion, but Not to Everything

The palms that lined internal roads of Forest Lawn Memorial Gardens were filled with feral parrots, escapees from cages accidentally left open by careless children, or deliberately opened, I liked to think, by the birds themselves, the rebellious ones. The Southern California weather was favorable to parrots and the escapees prospered, reproducing and colonizing the final resting place of Californians who could afford perpetual maintenance at the highest level. No dogs allowed.

My escape, as it turned out, wasn't so successful. My mother had reached out from the grave and had given me what felt like a physical slap in the face. She had disinherited me. Out of a lifetime of injuries, most of them subtle, disinheriting was perhaps the worst. It should not have come as a surprise but yet it did. It declared, now publicly, that her rejection had been absolute. She had, through her will and with the certainty that all would know the contents of it, revealed what in life she had not dared to express. The mask of manners had come off. These were her feelings. Where her little note, the words "I love you too," fit into this, I could not guess.

The word spread quickly. When I had walked into the room where the family had gathered, everyone stared at me. My sister, Victoria, came up and whispered in my ear. Now I knew. Nothing had been repaired. Nothing had been forgiven. It was the logical conclusion to what had gone before, but I admit that I had not expected it. In fact, it had never even occurred to me; I had had some odd version of *noblesse oblige* in my head that allowed me to think that Mudds didn't behave that way. This notion was, of course, silly, because all kinds of people behave that way all the time.

The train of black limos carried my mother's husband, attached to his breathing apparatus, a few of his relatives, some cousins, and my surviving siblings. The officiating minister was an odd feature in the proceedings. He was Church of England, a man my mother had met years before and, as I discovered in conversation with him before the ceremony, only once. He had a rural parish in Kent, England, and my mother, as a tourist with Bill, had liked his church. He had been hospitable, no more than that, and did not claim to be anything more than an acquaintance. In her last instructions, however, my mother had requested that this particular curate perform her last rites. And so, for a substantial fee, he had made his way to Los Angeles, arriving the morning of the service. His bags had been lost, so he had had to borrow robes from a local minister. He was jet-lagged and somewhat bewildered.

Poor invalid Bill, now a widower, sat in his wheelchair with its battery-powered aspirator doing the work his lungs could not. It was hot in the sun and someone had provided him with an umbrella; still, the crown of his bald head glistened with sweat. Close by the graveside stood Tom. He was the director of the event, having positioned the audience at distances from the coffin appropriate not so much as to their degree of connection or emotional closeness, but their position in her will. Standing close enough to touch the sleek, green metal box, he extended his arms in a patriarchal gesture around John's daughters who stood on either side of him. To say that my sisters had not been fond of their mother would understate the case and now they stood somewhat apart from the grouping around the grave. Tom's face showed no grief and I am certain that he felt none, but, borrowing a page from our mother's book, his manner was appropriate to both the occasion and his upgrade in status. He was in possession of a new portfolio of powers.

At forty-nine, he had advanced from being the weaker twin, a cause for worry in earlier days, to being the executor of his mother's will and the manager of her estate. There had been other advancements. When our father died a year earlier, Tom had taken his seat on the board of directors of Harvey Mudd College. He was now the richest member of the family, and so, by default, the alpha male. I stood at the edge of the gathering, for I knew where I stood: outside, as I had always been.

My thoughts strayed. Or better said, they refused to focus on the event unfolding. Looking away from the gathering at graveside, I noticed little puffs of smoke that drifted from behind a berm a couple of hundred feet away. I shifted position and saw the group of four young Mexicans who would finish the job of burying my mother. They were smoking and chatting quietly, white teeth flashing with silent laughter. They would not use shovels: a shiny blue Ford tractor with a front-loader rested, engine quiet, beside them. They would not have understood a word of the service. These men, I reflected, came from a different planet, where the dead were buried in parched and dusty *camposantos* outside their villages, where one put up as large a monument as one could afford, but most managed little more than plastic flowers in a coffee can.

As I sorted through my feelings, I discovered that I wished above all that my mother had left some sort of explanation, a clue that made sense of her unwavering pattern of rejection. I had given reconciliation an effort that had lasted for years, but nothing ever changed. Understanding would have been useful, like recovering the body from the ocean after a plane crash, allowing closure. But there was nothing helpful.

Her will was a carefully crafted piece of legalese that had the effect of dropping a bomb. It sent out shock waves that destroyed any sense of family unity that remained among us. I believe that this was intentional.

She had divided her substantial wealth into eight parts. The size of the estate was invisible to me because I was to receive nothing out of the main body of her assets. One quarter went in trust to John's three daughters. One quarter went to Tom. One quarter went to a distant female cousin of my mother's, a person whom, as far as anyone could figure out, my mother had not seen in thirty or more years. This woman was not at the service, which meant she was in for a very pleasant surprise.

Only one eighth was left to each of her daughters, my sisters. It was a considerable amount of money and they were, I assume, glad to have the windfall, but the fact that their portions were half of their brother's and half that of the female cousin rubbed salt into long festering childhood wounds. Her final gesture toward them had been so deliberately hurtful, such an open act of contempt and cruelty that I was sure the dollars they received would not compensate. "You disappointed me," the gesture said. One of my sisters, Victoria, a filmmaker, had won an Oscar for best feature-length documentary film. Not good enough apparently.

She left me a cash bequest of $50,000 and for my daughter Mariana and my infant son, $30,000 each. These were meaningful sums in real life terms, but a pittance compared to what the others received, in the millions. The bequests to my children and me were not given out of generosity. They were a tactical necessity, representing a move on a legal chessboard. Her will stated that if anyone challenged any aspect of it, that person and, explicitly, his children, would lose everything. She had to pick an amount of money that I would find just enough that I would choose not to risk losing it. If she had left me nothing and nothing for my children, I might have thought it worth the gamble and have hired a lawyer. But the amounts were large enough. I abandoned any idea of challenging the will.

The part of the will that I could see included the disposition of her jewelry. She gave specific instructions about each piece. The inventory was eleven pages long. I saw, in the obsessively detailed descriptions of pieces of jewelry the way her world had been measured. In the jewelry inventory there was a particularly distressing detail. My paternal grandfather, Harvey, had given my mother a piece of jewelry to commemorate the birth of each grandchild, and she returned these pieces to the child with the notation that it had been given by our grandfather on the occasion of the recipient's birth. The piece that he had given her on my birth, the first grandchild and the one who bore his name, was not mentioned.

It had long before been sold or broken up for its valuable parts. My mother had been thorough in erasing me.

What was almost as distressing to me as being disinherited was what she did with her art collection. I had been quite certain that her intent was to gift the collection as a whole to a museum; the only question was which museum. All this had been changed. Only two gifts were made, the Monet *Japanese Bridge* and a little Georges Braque called *Harbor* and of these only half the value was gifted, the other half had to be purchased from her estate. The Walter Annenberg Trust provided the funds so that the National Gallery could have those two works. The remainder of the collection, the Picasso, Homer, Gauguin, Degas, Van Gogh, Cezanne, and the rest were sent like cattle to the slaughterhouse, the auctioneer, Sotheby's of New York. The Victoria Nebeker Coberly collection was accorded a special section of the sale catalogue, along with a picture of her that I knew well. She was standing before an ornate mirror in a fabulous red couture gown. The picture, however, was printed in black and white, an economy ordered by my brother. There, in the auction house, the traditional abattoir of so many dysfunctional families, the collection was dismembered. The Degas pastel of dancers sold for $935,000.

My brother had viewed her art collection as just another asset and had persuaded her that benefiting the family was the best use for it. If she had left it intact and had given it to the Los Angeles County Museum of Art, she might have gotten a commemorative gallery and would have received, postmortem, the gratitude of her natal city. As it is, all she has is a wall label in the National Gallery in Washington D.C. in which they misspelled her maiden name. I was oddly sorry for my mother that her intended legacy of a major gift to a museum had been taken from her. I was furious with my brother.

All in all, there was a very bad taste in my mouth. Males favored over females and a gift to a distant relative that was a deliberate insult to her own daughters. Our brother Tom was the big winner, both in money and position, and my sisters could see this clearly. There was the sense amongst the three of us that much had been done badly and unfairly. Should Tom, as her executer and advisor, have warned us or tried to dissuade her? Years later, when he was quite ill, my sister Victoria asked him if he regretted any aspect of the business. His only reply was that everything that he had done was legal, which of course it was. He was sixty-six years old when he died. If my sister's sense is correct, he felt neither guilt nor shame.

In a letter that I sent to Tom shortly after our mother's death, I had asked him if he knew why she had disinherited me. He replied that the only explanation he had been given was that she was "afraid of you." This was the last communication I ever had with him.

Tom lived a productive fifteen years after our mother's death, using some part of the money to promote scientific education and literacy. He died of pulmonary fibrosis. No cause for his disease has ever been suggested, but I was sure I knew. I had visited him twice in the 1970s, a period in which he was engaged in the restoration of classic automobiles. He had a blue-ribbon-winning 1930s Alvis, a bright red racing car that he had rebuilt from the frame up. On several occasions I watched him at work in his machine shop. He was milling engine parts, bending over a machine enveloped in a cloud of metal dust and sparks. It was a period during which he was drinking heavily and was careless. He wore goggles but no breathing protection. I assume that this unsafe practice had been the rule during all those years. His lung condition was the type caused by environmental assaults, a scarring and hardening of the lung found in metal workers, miners, and sand blasters.

I stayed a few days in Los Angeles after the funeral, spending time with my sisters. We compared notes about our upbringing. Virginia, who had had health issues as a newborn, felt that our mother had instilled in her the idea that she was something of a cripple. And she, Virginia, had responded as an adult by riding her bicycle across the United States, three thousand miles on two wheels. She has become what she calls an "independent Christian" and is an environmental activist living in New

Mexico. Victoria, who became a documentary film maker and film educator, still lives in Los Angeles. Victoria felt that our mother had done everything in her power to destroy in her any pride in the feminine. She, who used her femininity to such manipulative advantage, would deny to her daughters even the smallest piece of that same identity. When, at fourteen, Victoria had begun to develop breasts, she stood up straight and felt proud of her arrival at womanhood. Our mother told her she should stop acting like a slut and that she should stop sticking her breasts out. Our stories were comparable. We three had fashioned our adult selves in creative opposition to her. How Tom felt about his relationship with our mother, I don't know, but the contrast with the rest of us was marked. He had signed on to our mother's agenda, either unconsciously coopted or opportunistically, a sort of career move involving money and dominance. I don't know which it was. We never spoke again.

37

Excavating the Ruins

When I returned to Vermont, my mood remained dark, but there were bright spots. A daughter was born in the spring of 1992, seven months after my mother's death. She spent her first hours in the world asleep on my body, basking like a seal pup on a warm rock. I slept too, a sleep that only the deepest letting go can bring. Born in the aftermath of the collapse of the Soviet Union, she was named for the Russian democracy activist Elena Bonner and for Countess Natasha Rostov in Tolstoy's *War and Peace*, a young woman whose lively nature and open heart I hoped my daughter, Elena Natasha, would share.

But despite the two children, loved by both parents, my marriage with Aida did not go well. At the root of the problem was parenting style, a difference so pronounced that it caused considerable tension. With styles, there is neither right nor wrong, but in our case, we found no middle ground. Many hours of marital therapy did not help. Aida and I divorced, but I stayed in the vicinity, purchasing a condominium and sharing in the raising of the children. Sam and I threw footballs and baseballs depending on the season. I taught them both to swim in the cold, clear waters of Lake Champlain. In the dark winter days, we built cities out of blocks on the living room floor. I exposed them to the classic movies like *Philadelphia Story* and *Shane*. I called the program Mandatory Movies and, once resistance to black and white movies was overcome, it went well.

This phase of my life lasted nearly ten years. My work became the children. I was happy in their company, watching them grow, but because I had stopped writing, I experienced those years as at least partially lost.

Still, I was happy. It was a dynamic time, daily challenges with the children, great pleasures, and surprisingly few crises, but despite this, I was incomplete, as if a part of me had been left behind, stuck in that ever present past, stuck like Brer Rabbit in his argument with the Tar Baby. The question that I had been poking at for thirty years was still the question. I still wanted to know why my mother had rejected me. I had come full circle, as I had before. I thought that these issues no longer mattered to me, but not so apparently. I decided to go back into therapy.

Since my mother was the issue, I decided that a female therapist would work best. In the therapy discipline, an hour every two weeks, I would do some detective work. I suspected that there were clues buried in my unconscious, memories, dots that I had not before been able to connect.

The clues I started with were the several versions of my mother's state of mind that I could look at. There was a letter that her lawyer had written me. I dug up the letter. "While she never went into detail about this with me, each time your mother spoke of you I had the impression that she felt deeply hurt by you in some way. She did not seem vindictive, rather more accepting of the fact that you had chosen a path that made your inclusion in her estate inappropriate in her mind."

Here, indeed, in one letter, were valuable clues. The first was that my mother had been "deeply hurt," and the second, that I had "chosen a path" that she had not approved. Perhaps both explanations were true. The wrong path explanation, whether of politics or lifestyle, had always seemed possible, but I was not convinced. It was true that I had wanted to change American society in respect to environmental issues, but to send the *ancien régime* to the guillotine, never. More important, however, in thinking about the wrong path explanation, was that I was quite sure that her rejection had begun long before I had shown any signs of being either artistic or politically progressive. The false cancer had occurred when I was thirteen.

There was a third clue. Tom had said that our mother was "afraid" of me. This was the strangest of all the clues, but significantly, one that had been corroborated by her therapist. Afraid, but of what? I had never been violent except on the occasion that I had smashed the martini pitcher to dramatize my emotional state and never physical with her except when I had broken her grip on my arm on the night of the seduction episode. The incident at John's funeral had occurred years after her therapist had used the word "afraid." Perhaps it was not physical violence that she feared. Something else, but what? Afraid of her own feelings for me? Afraid of what I knew about her? I kept at it. It was like fiddling with a Rubik's Cube; I was trying to get things to line up.

I knew, of course, that I could never really know because the only witness was also the chief suspect and she, my mother, had gotten clean away. But I did want to be able to say "case closed" so the Tar Baby would let me go and I would be done with it.

One day in therapy, I found myself talking about the sequence of poems that dealt with my childhood memories of the war. One especially, titled simply "Childhood I," places a little boy, myself, anxious and uneasy, in the context of his wartime awareness, and who, as the little night wanderer carrying his teddy bear, was frightened because he had heard noises.

Shhh, I say to Bear;
we hear the noise again.
And we descend.

What caught my attention was the image of descending, of going down the stairs; another poem in the same book, titled "Childhood II," contained the same image:

Sounds in the big house, darkness;
I, small, hand on banister, descend.

Sitting in the therapist's office, with Lake Champlain frozen solid outside the window, I was engaging in a different sort of literary exercise, not parsing lines of a poem, but tracking the sources of those lines, their inspiration. In "Childhood I," near its end, I had written:

> *I swear into the night's ear*
> *that I will never tell*
> *the things I've seen…*

"The things I've seen" line suddenly jumped out at me as being the key to the events that lay behind the poem. Previously, when I thought about that poem, I'd considered that those lines referred to a child, myself, exposed through pictures in the magazines and newspapers to the horrors of the war and that somehow the child must keep these things secret, as if, magically, remaining silent about them would reverse history, or un-know things that were untimely known.

But now it seemed to me that this was an intellectual overlay, a rationalization. Perhaps "the things I've seen" was something more personal. Now my attention turned toward the content of the child's voice. The final stanza reads:

> *See,*
> *I told you so,*
> *I did not die.*
> *I have this tiny cross.*
> *It protects me;*
> *See, it opens:*
> *inside*
> *is my father's voice*
> *and a dry relic*
> *of my mother's heart.*

These lines contained, I now could see quite clearly, a child's view in a very intimate and personal way. It had nothing to do with the war, with history. It had to do with my own small world. My father, the often-absent Navy officer, is present only in the child's memory of his voice. And there is my mother, her heart somehow "dead" to me. I was now certain that the poem contained more, or at least different, information than I had previously suspected.

Whenever I talked about my mother with the therapist, the line of muscles that lay beneath the scar on my back contracted and my right shoulder rose noticeably, as if clinching, cringing, fleeing the scalpel. I was amazed at how easily the memory, a body memory, of that surgery was activated. Had my mother wanted to punish me? She had cut something out of me, the tumor that wasn't a tumor. Why had she done that? Back and forth I went, from the past where things had happened, to the present where the psychic work, the detective story, was in progress.

Outside, always that winter, was the frozen lake, sometimes on sunny days, sometimes under grey skies. There is a local legend about a Loch-Ness-type creature that lived in Lake Champlain. The analogy appealed to me. It was out there, trying to break through the ice, emerge from the depths. . .

And then it did. On a brilliant winter day, the sunlight on the ice so bright one could not look for long, as I sat in the chair facing the therapist, looking out at the lake, something long forgotten came back. It emerged, came in a rush. As the memory returned, the poem finished itself. It was the rest of the story that had been concealed in the poem.

There I was, in 1944, standing at the top of the stairs. I was holding the teddy bear in my right hand. I had heard a noise, a squirrel scampering along the roof or a shutter banging in the wind, I don't know what, and was frightened. I went in search of my mother. I descended the stairs, my left hand on the banister. On the table in the entrance hall was a Navy officer's hat, one with braid on the brim, a hat I recognized as belonging to a friend of my father's, a man of higher rank. Once, the man had let me wear it. The living room door, to the left as I came down the stairs, was closed, but a light came from under it. I pushed open the door and went in. In the faint light from a single lamp, I could make out my mother sitting on the sofa close to the man. I could not tell what they were doing, for my eyes, coming from the dark stairway, had not quite adjusted. I entered and announced my presence, "Mommy," probably no more than that, and abruptly all became a blur of motion. My mother leapt to her feet. The folds of her loose skirt, which had been somehow pulled up, came down and flared as she crossed the room. Her face was contorted with an emotion that I understood as fury. I was terrified. She crossed the room in two or three strides and struck me hard, with her open hand, on the left cheek. I had never been struck before and have never been since.

As I remembered this, the memory was released. It seemed that in the deepest layers of my brain the experience still lived, the memory of something happening, an event, was burned into the cells themselves, recorded as if on a disk. And now it replayed. My hand leapt involuntarily to my cheek and my cheek felt hot.

I had howled with pain, fright, and bewilderment. My mother grabbed me by the arm and dragged me, screaming, out of the room and up to my bed.

There came a flood of similar memories, none so dramatic, but of the same script. I could see myself again, wandering about the house, first in Washington D.C. and later in Los Angeles, listening to voices downstairs, and later in the nights, when the house was dark, listening at my mother's bedroom door. It seems clear to me now that I had stumbled upon activities that I now think had been infidelities. In respect to the specific incident that I witnessed, I had no comprehension of what I had seen. I was only four. But what I did understand, and understood immediately, was that it was something that I should not have seen, and for that I had been struck.

I had found the dark kernel from which had grown a noxious weed that had crowded maternal feeling out of my mother's heart and allowed fear and paranoia to take their place. There *was* a secret. The secret was what had contaminated my childhood. The burden on my mother was no doubt very heavy. She lived with the fear that I would somehow let the secret out, that I would tell my father. The repressions, rigidity, and punishments that characterized my childhood stemmed initially, if I am correct, from her fear of exposure. What began as a sacrifice, marrying my father, became her essential identity, but if her husband, my naïve and unsuspecting father, ever got wind of the man (or men) who shared her body, there was no telling how he might react. Divorce probably, on grounds of adultery. My mother's settlement would have been modest. My father had not yet arrived at the financial heights that he was destined to reach, so staying the course was essential. I was the threat to this. My mother feared that her infidelities would not simply decay into oblivion. There had been a witness.

But there had not been a witness. I was clueless. But my poor mother was never able to allow herself the thought that I knew nothing. Even if I had seen something, I would not have known how to describe it, much less interpret it. I was, in fact, so clueless that I would have had no idea what to say to my father even if I had been moved to. "Mommy hit me" was the worst I could have come up with. But since she knew what she had been doing, she assumed that I must know. She became hypervigilant in respect to me and I think came to see me as the enemy. The reports, from both my brother and her psychiatrist, that she was afraid of me give some support to this hypothesis. This may explain the worst aspects of my childhood, especially her use of force against my body, the enemas, which emphasized her power over me, and the cancer and the surgery, which expressed her unconscious wish that I die, taking with me secrets that I didn't even know I had. By that time, however, ten years later, I am not sure she even remembered what her fear of me was about. She was that repressed.

The expression of fury that I'd seen on my mother's face that night in 1944 when I blundered into her secret life was the same that I saw in 1969, the night she attempted to seduce me. By seeing these two events as being linked by sex, the most heavily guarded area of my mother's unconscious, I began to understand why her relationship with me had become so fraught.

The leitmotif of this story is fairly simple. I knew something about my mother that she had wanted hidden. It was not just what she had done that she wanted concealed, but who she was. Seducing me would have brought the witness, the secret sharer, into the unconscious psychological conspiracy that she had maintained with herself for so many years. In that moment in 1969, removing her stockings while sitting beside me, the all-but-spoken invitation to join her in the bed, she had given herself away. She had been caught again. And I could not be forgiven. My transgression had been the knowing.

Our last meeting at her bedside in August of 1991, when I had forced myself to speak words I had always wanted to say, "I love you," not because I really felt them but because I had always wanted to feel them, was the final act in this sad tale. I had whispered, "I love you," and she had responded, weeks later with a little yellow note, with the same words. Had we, without intending it, forgiven each other?

The sad tale was not quite over. Years later, after I'd moved to France, I woke one morning thinking, for no reason that I could identify, about a book in my library that, strangely, I knew nothing about. I could see the book in my mind, dark blue cloth, somewhat scuffed, no dust jacket, with the title on the spine so faded that it was illegible. Like many bookish people, I know virtually every book in my library and usually could remember where and when I purchased it. This book, however, was an enigma. I knew only that it had come from my mother. When it had appeared, in 1990, in my mail box and when I realized, from the return address, that it had come from her, I had treated it lightly, casually. I was trying to damp down my reactions to her, to feel neither anger nor disappointment, so I had put it in the bookshelf without even bothering to open it.

Because I had always been aware of my odd avoidance of it, I found the book easily. Now, with a strange sense of foreboding, I opened it.

It was a true first edition of James Joyce's *A Portrait of the Artist as a Young Man*. New York, B.W. Heubsch, 1916.

A slip of paper fell out of it, a note on onionskin paper. The writing was in my mother's hand. Tentatively, gingerly even, I unfolded the paper. It was dated February, 1990, six months before her death and sixteen months after the dramatic confrontation at my brother's funeral, the event, almost violent, that had begun to free me from her.

The note read "to Harvey, who introduced me to the joy of motherhood—with my love on his fiftieth birthday. February 28th, 1990."

She had made an extraordinary gesture and I had not even noticed.

I had not acknowledged it. No wonder, I thought, she felt as she did.

Part VIII

Where Things Stand So Far

. . . I have already scratched out, amended, suppressed, or gagged so many things in myself that I am tired of doing it. Everything has its limits, and I am a big enough boy now to consider my training completed. I have other things to think about. I was born with all the vices. I completely suppressed many of them, and have indulged the rest, but slightly. God alone knows the martyrdom I suffered during this psychological breaking in; but I have finished with it.

Gustave Flaubert to Louise Colet, 1854

38

Reinventing Myself

Are my parents' stories, the mysteries of their characters that I claim to have solved, believable? I cannot be sure. Perhaps all I have done was make them into characters that function, as in a novel, to confirm a plot line. But since there were things that I am sure of, things for which I have evidence or had observed in person, and since the pieces seem to fit, I have decided I will stand by the story. What of course is missing is their own versions of who they were and what they did—and, perhaps more important, how they saw me. I have a nagging sense that I have misjudged my mother's character in some significant way, missing components of her story that would reveal it as, if not tragic, profoundly sad. It is easy, however, to miss things that were carefully kept hidden. That was her way and it puts her at a great disadvantage.

My father, on the other hand, at the end of his life was utterly transparent, ridiculously so. But he had died happy, in the company of attractive women who were unconcerned about social niceties, while my mother had spent her final twenty years with an invalid, imprisoned by her fears, by the tyranny of appearances.

After these discoveries, these revelations, I felt quite liberated. Not a single received belief, things most men call essential, remained. I retained little, not belief in God, not nationalistic patriotism, not adherence to a political party or to an ideology, or to any fine sentiments about family. The long process of what Montaigne called "a general overthrow of all (his) ancient opinions" was complete.

In this process of this general overthrow, I had acquired some life skills: the capacity, for instance, to distinguish between the merely pleasurable and the truly good, between the reprehensible and the seriously bad. And with a greater sense of ambiguities and nuances, I became less absolute in my views, more comfortable with the gray areas in my personal life and in the history of my country. I accepted, albeit reluctantly, that it was sometimes necessary to do bad things to prevent worse. I understood that situations and individuals had to be judged in their contexts. And I accepted that, within my reverence for the truth, there could be permissible untruths, a concession that did not compromise my belief that outright lies about serious issues, matters concerning life and death or the fate of the nation, were inexcusable.

I accepted also that if my perceptions turned out to be wrong and if I made mistakes, I could, like the jazz musician, start over. Embarrassment, I decided, was a temporary condition and not a defeat. I was developing the ability to discern what was important and what was not, when it was necessary to act and when it was not, to be able to sit still in the midst of silliness or hubbub. And finally, out of the maze at last, I might be able, perhaps for the first time, to accept my self as the creative person that I believed I was.

Thus, on a fresh spring day in 1994, I awoke with an inclination to revisit the Cézannes in the Museum of Modern Art (MOMA), pictures that I'd first seen in my mother's company more than thirty years earlier. It was a sign of how I'd changed. I could seek out the things that she had liked, but now for myself. I chose Cézanne because he had changed the way we see and think about the visual world and since I was interested in challenging my perceptions about myself in life, Cézanne offered a sort of metaphor for my own project.

By the next day I was in New York City at the MOMA. After studying

Cézanne for a spell, I wandered through gallery rooms until, by chance, I found myself in front of the collection's largest Jackson Pollock drip painting, *One: Number 31, 1950.*

I had long before concluded that the art world was full of frauds and fads, and now, a bit prejudiced by the usual slurs about Pollock, "my child could have done that" or "linoleum patterns," I was skeptical but didn't want to dismiss Pollock as a fraud or fad without a bit more reflection. There was a bench in front of *One: Number 31.1950*, so I sat for a while, thirty minutes perhaps, and looked. This painting, with which I was superficially familiar through art history books, suddenly snapped into mental focus. It was a classic epiphany. I understood what I had not before, that the field of drips and loops was not chaotic or accidental at all. The moment was thrilling. I suddenly understood that the painting was rigorously coherent and intensely organized, but was so according to logic that defied ordinary analysis. *It was faithful to its own laws* and thus the more remarkable. This moment renewed my capacity for complex emotion in response to art. And so, beginning with a famous Jackson Pollock, I decided that I would not go back to poetry, but would try my hand at painting. Thirty years earlier I had decided to become a farmer in a similar moment of insight and inspiration.

I followed a self-directed education in aesthetic theory and art technique. I integrated my appreciation for the Italian *Quattro Cento*, Giotto for example, who was one of Hamish's great loves, into a wider understanding of art that would soon include Robert Motherwell, Arshile Gorky, and Mark Rothko. I studied Cézanne's composition, learned the formulas for glazes and washes, and studied the masters' uses of color. I came by the most important part of this education by eavesdropping on conversations between practicing artists and the clerks at New York Central Art Supply on Third Avenue. With time I acquired enough of the artist's vocabulary that I could ask intelligent questions of these always-knowledgeable young people. Later I discovered a virtual apothecary of colors called Kremer Pigments, a tiny store where the entire range of the Renaissance palette was displayed as powders on the shelves: ochres, dozens of them, azures from ground lapis. yellows from toxic orpiment, the mineral my grandfather had had displayed as brilliant yellow crystals on his coffee table, lead white, also toxic, that Velazquez had used to weave the lace on Juan de Pareja's collar in the Metropolitan. I mixed my own paints. I responded to color more than to line or to content. From years spent in Mexico, and from the emotion that I experienced in the presence of Titian's blues and blacks and Bellini's green, I became a color painter. I experimented endlessly. Mixtures of color with different mediums, rabbit skin glue for instance. The chemistry and properties of the materials interested me just as the geological properties of the earth had when I was younger. I experimented with making my own colors; curry was a beautiful yellow, but it was not lightfast, fading to dusty gray in less than a month. I bought a roll of cheap canvas and a couple of wide brushes. I took no lessons and could hardly draw, but I could assemble colors.

Painting required a space. My apartment, a studio on West 93rd St., was barely large enough for a bed. I rented a room in a former factory building in Long Island City. Every day I went to my studio, passing through the subterranean world of the Times Square subway station, riding escalators that rose out of Piranesian caverns or descending on stairs overhung by layers of mold and dirt, and joined the throngs of men and women, mostly from the Third World, who did the heavy lifting for the rest of us, people who used Times Square as the turnstile between sleep and labor. I took the 7 Train, the "Immigrant Express" as it is called, to Vernon Boulevard, Long Island City, and walked through a working-class Italian neighborhood to my studio. The building next door was still industrial, a manufacturer of gaskets for engines and pumps. The work force consisted of very young Mexicans, all probably undocumented.

Each afternoon they, boys and girls, would pour out of the building, their hair combed and shirts clean, flirting and laughing. Their exuberance buoyed my spirits. When a young woman who worked in the factory was hit by a car and killed, a painted sign was stapled to a telephone pole; it told her name and brief life story—she was only seventeen— and requested, in rudimentary English, donations to send her body back to her family in Mexico. There was a two-quart pickle jar, with a slot cut in the metal lid, duct taped to the pole; I watched for a week as coins and small bills accumulated in it. It was never disturbed. After a time, it disappeared and a handwritten sign replaced it, thanking the neighborhood for its generosity. I often returned to Manhattan late at night and experienced the streets as always safe because, someone told me, a lot of "made" guys lived in the neighborhood and "they don't tolerate no trouble where they live." It was a real-life New York neighborhood, a hidden province behind the Pepsi sign.

I painted large, bright abstractions. I liked oil because it was slow to dry and because I could scratch out or scrape off my mistakes before they set. Life's mistakes are harder to amend, but I liked the metaphorical suggestion of the slow-drying paint, that the past was a sort of *pentimento*, a sketch that underlay the present.

When my marriage to Aida ended, I refreshed an old friendship with a woman I'd known for several years. She, Jami, was my son Sam's godmother and had been married to Aida's brother. In respect to degrees of separation, some thought this not enough. But despite that, we began to date. She lived in Washington D.C., where she was a public school administrator. She was a blonde with chocolate brown eyes and a full figure, in her late forties, and very beautiful. I took the train to Washington on weekends and stayed in her guest room. In the course of events, we fell in love. Her background, a peripatetic military family, had made her cautious. I was more impetuous, but we had no fundamental differences, not in our politics or, and very important for me, in the matter of raising children. After a year of occasional cohabitation, we married. Jami retired from her job and we set ourselves up in a tiny one bedroom apartment on the Upper West Side of Manhattan.

Jami had no children of her own, but like me, she had wanted a family. I brought mine to her. She was loving and accepting, but tolerated no nonsense and in that respect was a perfect co-parent. Her touch was gentle but always firm. Both of my younger children, Sam and Elena, have turned out well, with sound values and are pursuing interests that suit their personalities; Jami contributed much to making this possible. She joined me in traveling back and forth between New York City and Vermont. The Vermont winters are long, the spring short, but when the snow melts and the back roads finally dry out, summer comes. The brief Vermont summers are glorious. We swam in the lake and rode our bikes.

Our apartment was near the Museum of Natural History. For me, it is a shrine to the natural world—the plants, geology, fauna both ancient and modern, the heavens, all framed in the language and concepts of sciences, a perfect fit for my way of seeing things, an emotional connection with nature but always in a rational context. I went through a period of study inspired by our proximity to the museum. Over the next few years, just by walking across the street, I was able to explore the physical universe from top to bottom, from the stars and galaxies that the telescopes brought down to earth to the lowly invertebrates, the most diverse and numerous species on the planet, the mollusks. In a corridor by the stairs, an out-of-the-way corner for creatures not as sexy as the T-Rex or Grizzly bear, there is a glass case with hundreds of mollusk shells, each named, each coming from a different part of the world's oceans, some edible, some accidentally useful, Tyrian Purple, for instance, the dye for the robes of the Roman emperors, pieces of the vast shambling epic of life. For Charles Darwin they had provided important clues to his great insight, that of evolution, that all life had emerged from what had come before. The natural history museum contained traces of my past. My grandfather had donated the musk ox diorama in the Hall of North American Mammals. I stopped by often to see those homely shaggy beasts, life size but lifeless, behind glass in their perpetual snow.

They stand there still. A bronze letter in my grandfather's name, in the plaque below the case, has fallen off.

* * *

During this period, I brought my daughter Elena to New York. I wanted to show her Jackson Pollock, *One, Number 31, 1950*. I was, unconsciously, repeating an event from my own childhood, the visit with my mother to see *The View of Toledo*. The memory of that visit and the awareness of its importance in my life added a curious *frisson* to the moment. The MOMA, with its smooth walls and even light seemed an unlikely place to encounter my mother's ghost but there we were, meeting across an emotional divide bridged by a painting. In the *Odyssey* the divide is described as a fosse, a ditch, and there in the underworld, Odysseus meets his mother. Odysseus too had neglected his mother.

My little daughter and I stood before the Pollock. Her mind uncontaminated by textbooks, looked at the painting for as long as ten minutes. I asked her what she thought it was about; she looked at me as if I were being silly.

"It's not *about* anything, Dad," she said. "It's a whole thing." Indeed, a whole thing. That was the answer I was looking for. Or, if not the answer, the way to frame the question.

My daugher, Elena, with Jackson Pollock's One, number 31, 1950

39

The Center Does Not Hold

By reframing the question as *a whole thing*, I began to see history as a four-dimensional puzzle, as a single event, a perpetual *ongoingness*, in which time provided the fourth dimension. History is better understood not as sequence but as a sort of hologram that contains both past and present, or more inclusively, that contains all the ideologies, all the follies and delusions, all the accomplishments and catastrophes. More of the same in the future was not just probable; it was certain. This insight would, or so I hoped, prevent one from falling into complacency during easy times, keep us from believing that an eventless present meant that we had come to the end of history.

But one could be tempted by those thoughts: who would not prefer peace and common sense to disorder and danger? I was relatively content and the year 1998 had started out quietly, directionless, neither too weird nor too bland, nothing too urgent, temperate political weather. The Soviet Union was finished. The Cold War was over and the Berlin wall had come down. America's financial situation was the best it had been in decades, the debt going down, and employment going up.

Then, like a tornado out of a clear sky, the Clinton impeachment fell upon the country. The storm clouds had been gathering, but I had been too busy, too involved in my life to notice.

The impeachment, for acts that I saw as having no relationship to the "high crimes and misdemeanors" that the Constitution specifies as necessary for the removal of a president, revealed something about America that I had not understood before: that the Republican Party was fueled by an ideology that rejects the tendencies toward tolerance and social justice that the other party represented. These were not disagreements about policies which reasonable people could resolve through compromise. This was uncompromising ideological opposition and they had declared war. The impeachment of President Clinton was the opening skirmish.

Where did the fever, the passion, come from? Was it just a continuation of the painful divisions that the Vietnam War had produced, an act of political revenge for what many on the right had felt was a "stab in the back," the refusal to allow the military to win that war? But there was certainly more to it than one event. I think the Clinton impeachment can be explained as a part of America's hidden meta-narrative, an ongoing but never acknowledged class warfare. Clinton favored the wrong classes. He was genuinely friendly with African Americans and actually sympathetic toward the poor. He wasn't radical by any definition, but he leaned, ever so slightly, toward a redistributionist tax policy; it was a drift toward the socialist model of the relationship of the state with its citizens, and even that little bit was unacceptable. Franklin Delano Roosevelt was hated for similar reasons. This class warfare is a symptom of something perhaps even deeper. Something in American culture, or in all human beings.

It was clear to me, as I observed those events, that America had lost its sense of common purpose. When I thought about the passions of the Civil War, of the persistence of Jim Crow, the isolationist Americans—a majority for a time—who sympathized with the Nazis and would have let Europe go, I wondered if there had ever been a purpose or an ideal that all Americans held in common. Across the breadth of the land, I saw Hobbesian struggles, money against restraints, man against man, and the only goal was to be richer. And it was a zero sum game; the powerful got more powerful by making the weak weaker. I came to the conclusion that the central issue was a struggle to ensure the continued economic dominance of male white people. Money, at the very bottom, was the issue. Hobbes was right.

Glued to the television, I saw a dangerous part of the national character, something ugly and vicious, but proud of itself, preening, self-righteous, and relentless. I saw hatred and I was frightened by it.

I reread Alexis de Tocqueville's *Democracy in America*, and noted that, with remarkable prescience, he observed that the Constitution's vague provision for impeachment will someday create "an almost irresistible impulse to the vindictive passions of parties."

It was a drawn-out political "night of the long knives." I realized that behind the veneer of material abundance and what is called "The American Way of Life," there are many who, in order to keep dominance and wealth in a certain class and to solidify their own power, would undo the bonds, constitutional and communal, spiritual even, of the republic itself. I recalled reading about the debates in the Congress about slavery in the 1840s when little else but the justification for slavery was on the minds of Southern senators. Slavery, these Americans argued, was a necessary good, necessary in order to preserve a social order, one oligarchic and authoritarian in which force and money ruled.

I concluded that America has long been at war within itself and with itself. I saw the republic as afflicted with a sort of societal auto-immune disease. But in this case, the presidency and the constitution survived. It was by just two votes, both by Republicans who refused to sacrifice the country for party. One was Senator Jim Jeffords of Vermont. He was my senator. I wrote a letter thanking him. The Republicans drummed him out of the party.

A sigh of relief. The long Vermont winter enveloped us, days of gray, days of blowing snow, days of brilliant sun on snow that sparkled. My daughter and I took long tramps through deep drifts, going to a rock outcrop in the tall trees, a rock we designated as the North Pole.

Part IX

Leaving

God alone can be omnipotent, because his wisdom and his justice are always equal to his power. There is no power on earth so worthy of honor in itself or clothed with rights so sacred that I would admit its uncontrolled and all-predominant authority. When I see that the right and the means of absolute command are conferred on any power whatever, be it called a people or a king, an aristocracy or a democracy, a monarchy or a republic, I say there is the germ of tyranny, and I seek to live elsewhere...

Alexis de Tocqueville, *Democracy in America*

40

The National Crisis that Became My Crisis

I had been alarmed by the impeachment incident. Many were eager to call it a farce and, indeed, it had elements of farce, but I saw it as a direct assault on constitutional government. My political immune system went into a sort of high adrenaline alert. I think that I was predisposed to have this strong reaction because, despite all my disillusionments about the United States, there was still some trace of idealism in me about the Idea of America.

So I followed the news carefully and engaged in serious reading about politics, political theory, and modern history. I discovered thinkers like John Locke (liberal), Edmund Burke (conservative), and Thomas Paine (revolutionary).

Other crises followed. The Florida ballot recount was the most serious. The Supreme Court's order to stop the vote counting was a politically motivated decision that I saw as a judicial coup d'état. For the Democratic challenger, Vice President Gore, there was no higher tribunal, nowhere to go except to the streets, a remedy that ran contrary to the American tradition of the peaceful transfer of power. Graciously, Gore withdrew.

I thought the court's reasoning spurious, and the action almost treasonous, but I agreed with what Gore did. To fight the court decision would have made things worse. Then things got worse. Within a month of the inauguration of George W. Bush, it was clear that the

Republicans envisaged a radical remaking of America, oppressive and inequitable within, aggressive and unaccountable in the rest of the world. Words like "exceptionalism" floated about. The return of rule by "isms."

Bush withdrew the United States from the treaty creating the International Criminal Court, abrogated the Kyoto Climate Protocol and the Anti-Ballistic-Missile treaty with the former Soviet Union. In 2003, the United States invaded the nation of Iraq, a country ruled by a brutal dictator, to be sure, but one that posed no threat to the United States. To the arrogance and ignorance that produced the tragedy of Vietnam was added a policy of naked aggression. Chuck Hagel, later Secretary of Defense, then Senator, said in 2007, "I am saddened that it is politically inconvenient to acknowledge what everyone knows: the Iraq War is largely about oil." But that fact had to be kept from the American people, so the administration had subjected the country to a year-long barrage of propaganda, the Weapons of Mass Destruction campaign. I had kept notes from my readings in the British Library and I found a quote from *Mein Kampf* that struck me as relevant. "The intelligence of the masses is small," Hitler wrote, "but their power of forgetting is enormous. In consequence of these facts, all effective propaganda must be limited to a very few points and must harp on these in slogans until the last member of the public understands what you want him to understand..." Cheney, Condoleezza Rice, and the president kept saying that we did not want "the smoking gun to be a mushroom cloud." They said it over and over, and Americans, already traumatized by 9/11, cowered. Hermann Goering had said in an interview, "The people can always be brought to the bidding of the leaders. All you have to do is tell them they are being attacked." Slogans were pitted against the evidence that there were no WMDs. The slogans won.

I became an obsessive observer. I consumed newspapers. As a current popular expression has it, I was a man with his hair on fire. I was very angry, an unhealthy emotion, but one I was sure was necessary, virtuous and justified. There was so much that was distressing, that was wrong. The systematic disenfranchising and suppressing of minority voters appalled me. The intrusion on private communications, the torture, secret prisons, and kidnappings, all those acts were the tactics deployed by regimes that ruled by fear, Nazis, Stalinists, and the Argentine generals; there are no euphemisms that modify the truths of what they did. "Enhanced interrogations" was torture. Bush refused to tax Americans to pay for the invasion of Iraq. Instead he borrowed from China, the only power with the ability to dislodge the United States from its place at the top of the world order. And there was the war itself, not just botched but truly terrible in human terms, with an estimated half a million Iraqi civilian deaths, thousands of American casualties and enormous waste of treasure. I felt shame as an American, just as I had during Vietnam, and I felt outrage. The Bush regime's machine of folly and ineptitude rolled on. When it came to the unraveling of environmental protections, the issue to which I had given many years of effort, I felt personal loss. I watched with dismay as anti-science became almost policy, especially as it concerned climate change, a posture dictated by the petroleum industry.

My ability to enjoy life atrophied. I was joyless and humorless. I took to emailing commentaries, a reprise of my broadsides of 1968, to everyone I knew. I was, I don't doubt, something of a bore. I was quite impossible to live with. My marriage suffered.

With the 2004 election campaign, Bush running for a second term, I became an activist again, but now down in the trenches. It was just a gesture, honorable but meaningless in a political environment where money, the loudest megaphone, drowns out all else. Jami and I joined a non-partisan organization and became volunteer poll watchers. We were sent to Colorado Springs to observe. We paid our own way. The Republican masses, with their heads full of slogans, went to the polls, then returned to their TVs. They were like the groundlings in the pit at an Elizabethan theater; they had come to watch a spectacle, an entertainment called "democracy."

* * *

During the Mexican-America War and with the futile efforts in Congress
to end slavery in the background, Henry David Thoreau had written,
"As for adopting the ways that the state has provided for remedying the
evil, I know not of such ways. They take too much time."

By "the ways the state has provided" he meant the vote. I too saw
that the vote is seldom able to provide a remedy for a current ongoing evil. In fact, the vote often legitimizes wrong, even gives wrong
permission. In 2004 the voters had endorsed the anti-democratic and
militaristic policies of Bush and Cheney. In a democracy the belief is
that the people, the majority, in the collective meeting of their minds in
the voting place, are supremely wise and that they know best. Clearly,
they didn't. I knew what had been done to those minds; I'd watched the
propaganda campaign that had begun with 9/11. "We, the people," were
no longer people endowed with the capacity for critical thinking; "we"
had become a mass that had been brainwashed by Fox News, a Madison
Avenue style brainwashing, and had been deprived of their wits. I could
neither respect their decision, nor go along with it.

Shakespeare tells us in *Macbeth* that life is "a tale told by an idiot, full
of sound and fury, signifying nothing." Macbeth's kingdom, founded on
violence, collapsed into a nightmare of disorder. Over time, I saw that
my own country was similarly afflicted. It had ceased to be guided by
moral principles or by common sense. It too had become a disturbing
story, a tale told, if not by an idiot, then by men whom I could neither
honor nor respect. I believed that I understood enough of the situation, the political, social, and moral dimensions, the historical roots too,
and, more important, the implications for the future, to make moral
judgments, to form reasoned opinions. I saw a trend and felt sure it
would get worse. With dismay, with sadness, I realized how much the
republic's affliction, its disunity, affected me. A portion of the American
people had become my enemy. I could not defeat them and I feared

being defeated. America, the democracy, the republic, had become a country occupied by a foreign power.

It had become a place "full of sound and fury," and signifying I no longer knew what.

41

"When in the Course of Human Events ..."

Thoreau suffered a similar disconnection with the America of his times. He reflects on all these issues in *On Civil Disobedience*. He finishes the line, quoted above, "the ways the state has provided..." with these words, *"take too much time, and a man's life will be gone."* I had reached an age where the words "a man's life will be gone" was beginning to mean something. Thoreau continues:

> I have other affairs to attend to. I came into this world, not chiefly to make this a good place to live in, but to live in it, be it good or bad. A man has not everything to do, but something; and because he cannot do everything...

I had read *On Civil Disobedience* for the first time when I was fifteen or sixteen. Thoreau's words suggested that there could be situations when refusal or resistance would be an appropriate, even morally justified, response. His ruminations have stuck with me these many years, as if unconsciously I was checking in with him, checking myself against his thoughts. In one important respect, however, I had a different perspective than he had: I have children and he had none. Since my children would inherit my place in the world and they in their turn would have children, I had thought that as an environmentalist I could leave for them at least a piece of the natural world as it should be, unspoiled, clean, and alive. I could not do everything, but I could at least do that. Nature, I believed, would survive even if the ideas of America's Founders do not. I am no longer sure that even that is possible.

But I had done what I could and it has taken a toll. Michel de Montaigne, reflecting on his father's life of public service, described him appearing old and bent, "his soul cruelly agitated by this public turmoil." My soul too has been cruelly agitated. "And a man's life will be gone," warned Thoreau. Gone, swallowed up in public turmoil, exhausted by encounters with the unyielding,

"I have other affairs to attend to," Thoreau had said. I decided that I did too. I decided that I could attend to those affairs better in a peaceful state of mind, with my heart more at ease than it would be in the United States. In *Walden*, Thoreau wrote, "I went to the woods because I wanted to live deliberately…to see if I could not learn what it had to teach, and not, when I came to die, discover that I had not lived."

Thoreau went to the woods. I moved to France.

42

The Whole Thing in Some Parts

By the *other things* Thoreau meant activities like gardening, sawing wood, listening to the breeze in the pine trees, following the tracks of the fox or the mink in the snow. He also meant reading books or writing them. Inherent in all these activities was an improvised sort of spiritual practice, something that one does to protect the soul from the indecencies of the world, the assaults on truth, the offenses to conscience. It was slavery and the Mexican War that aroused Thoreau's disgust and anger. Thoreau's inner problem was similar to mine. His solution is one that I, in my own fashion, have tried to emulate.

Nearing the end of my life, I have decided to take better care of my soul, my psyche. This was not a religious quest. It was detachment that I sought. I would not ignore the realities of the world, but I would not be overpowered by them. I would pay more attention to what I might know and less to what I can't and probably never will know. I find my self to be a subject of interest, and ask questions of myself, questions asked before, but never answered satisfactorily. So they get asked again.

Have I done better as I moved away from the youth that I once was? And if I have done better, what should get the credit? Psychotherapy? Art? Love? Determination? Perhaps the mere fact that the paths I took, some chosen carefully, some less so, some pleasant, some fraught with spiritual dangers, kept branching and pushing on into the future. It was a process rather like evolution, the haphazard journey, full of accidents, that led the simplest creatures to pull themselves out of the ancient seas and onto the dry land. Was it randomness only—time and movement combined with good luck—that has brought me to a condition of relative peace with myself? A history of choices and accidents. It is a question of great interest to me. How did I end up where and who I am? What am I to do with the time and the life that remains?

Paris remembers its history. Streets are named for doctors, statesmen, military officers, and actors, for battles and significant days, liberation, the fall of the bastille. The reminders are everywhere. Plaques on walls with names of people who died resisting the Nazis or killed during the liberation of Paris. Everywhere there are plaques recalling the most terrible event of the past, the Holocaust.

In the ninth arrondissement, where I lived when I first came to France, one of these memorial plaques was installed shortly after I arrived in the neighborhood. On a polished black granite slab, three feet by two feet, gold letters catch at our hearts as we walk past. Remember, the words say, the children of the neighborhood who had been murdered by the Nazis in 1942.

I stumbled on the dedication ceremony for this plaque.

The event, public but not advertised, was held in the courtyard of the same school building, at the corner of rue Milton and rue Hippolyte Lebas, where the children had been pupils. There had been sixteen of them, identified as Jewish by their surnames, ages six to fourteen. They had been called out of their classrooms, marshaled in the corridor, and marched by the school principal and a uniformed German officer down the stairs. I imagined the scene: the leather heels of the children's shoes making a discordant clatter on the wooden floors, contrasting with the heavy confident tread of the German officer in his shiny black boots. The younger boys wore short pants and their legs were spindly after two years of rationing,. They went out into the air and onto the street where a canvas-topped truck was waiting. Three or four soldiers stood by with rifles. The presence of a French policeman gave the event an aura of grotesque legitimacy. Seized, without their parents, herded together with hundreds of other children, they must have been terrified. The younger ones must have wailed.

The day of the ceremony was clear and very cold. I sat shivering on a folding chair. The sun, sliding below the tallest of the surrounding buildings, raked the rooftops and the chimney pots with golden light. The courtyard was in shadow. I looked around at the members of the audience. Most were old and most, probably, were Jews who had somehow survived. Those in the audience who were my age or a little older, who had been children during those nightmare years, perhaps remembered hiding under their beds or had faint images of people's faces, those who went away and did not return. The name of each dead child was written on a piece of paper attached by a length of string to a white helium-filled balloon. As an older child, a sixth grader, read the name of one who perished, a third grader released the balloon into the January sky. The late, low sun caught the balloons as they floated away. I cried.

The ceremony came to an end. The dignitaries removed their tri-color sashes and mothers claimed their children. I sat and gathered my emotions. I thought about the principal of the school in 1942. What did he think when the children, whose only crime was to be born Jews, were taken away? I wanted to understand him, and through him, to understand how to deal with a political crisis that becomes a human catastrophe, an encounter with evil.

Some people offer resistance, consciously and deliberately refusing to participate. This is passive resistance only, but it is often the only feasible option, especially if there is a job to go to and children to raise. These covert resisters keep the civilizational values alive, waiting, hoping for the liberators to arrive. But many just look away, denying the truth of what is happening around them. These are the sleepwalkers and are probably the majority. Then there are the opportunists, willing to cooperate with the new order in order to advance themselves in an amoral universe, where every man is out for himself. Then there are the sympathizers, the bigots, anti-Semites and racists, and xenophobes who silently approve.

And there are the ideologues, the true believers, who identify with the narrative the leader has fashioned and are enthusiastic participants.

There are heroes too, those whose resistance entails great personal risk, but they are few. Most people are afraid when faced with an arbitrary and ideological state, one which threatens violence or imprisonment for dissent. Fear is a powerful motivator, a stimulus to do nothing. The principal of the school was not a hero. What, or even who, he was, I doubt that anyone knows today. He was everyman.

What would I have done if things had reached such a point, when children are rounded up and taken away? I confess that I cannot be sure.

But sitting in the fading light, very cold now, I recognized that if I were to continue to think of myself as a conscious being, one still involved with the troubled affairs of humankind, someone who believed that certain core civilizational values, tolerance, mercy, and truth among them, are worth defending, I must continue to engage in this kind of reflection. And in introspection too, uncomfortable as some of it may make me.

It was, thus, on that winter afternoon in Paris, that I decided to write this book.

To achieve equanimity of thought and emotion has long been a goal of mine. It was not possible in my younger years when emotions ruled, but the possibility of it has emerged in the last twenty or so years. And from that to maintain an inner balance that would permit me to remain upright in a world that does everything in its power to deny us peace of mind. Michel de Montaigne called this the "privilege of insensibility;" it is a balance between engagement and distance. Albert Camus described something like it; he called it "lucid indifference." I've used this time to assemble these reflections, this patchwork of memories that make up my life and opinions. And having done that, I will take up other things, perhaps the simplest ones that Thoreau recommends. I have lived and of that I am certain. And that I am, as Montaigne put it, *entier et non tranché*, "whole and unsolved." I am glad to leave some of the riddle intact.

Epilogue

When Donald Trump won the presidency in November 2016 I decided to spend the days around the inauguration in Paris. I wanted to feel the continuity of western civilization, the tradition of values that Trump despises and will shred if he is able. Paris is one of those places, part stage, part repository, a keeper of the memories, a place where the worst had been witnessed. A city matured by hard experience. I've been in France now for over a decade. In 2012, I left Paris for the south, the Midi. I went in search of a quieter life and more sunlight. Paris can be very damp and gloomy in winter; and as I got older, I was generating less and less of my own warmth. In early January 2017, as Barack Obama moved toward the end of his time at the center of the American drama, the realization that Americans, and the world, would no longer see this decent and intelligent man at the head of the republic, made me profoundly sad. I thought I should wear a black band on my jacket sleeve. I think it is reasonable to fear that the constitutional America that the Founders envisioned will not survive.

I would take up the political pen again, but that decision lay a month or so in the future. For the moment, I was thinking of myself again as the poet, the self I liked best.

* * *

My Paris is its streets. The sidewalk café was my office and I had favorites in several arrondissements, in the 8th and 9th and 18th. In all weather except rain, I would sit outside and watch the human world, dark skin and light, hurried and slow, young and old, go past. Now, wrapped in coat and scarf, I sat in the cold and resumed my watching. The little black notebook that I always carry lay on the round metal bistro table, the ball point pen close by. I have always done this, a way of waiting for a poem to pass my way.

Down the street, on Martyrs, was my hotel. The room was small, with a single bed pushed up against a wall. An amateurish oil painting of the church of Montmartre hung over the bed, its tones muted by the aging varnish, while on the opposite wall was a similarly amateurish painting of French peasants hoeing in a field, potatoes probably. The sun, in this scene, was setting, a somber image. I thought of Millet's image of the peasants, with their heads bent, who are believed to be burying their child in the field. There was a basin in the corner and a tiny WC. The room was plain and clean, a bit cramped but perfectly livable. There was a good reading light by the bed and an ample window overlooked the busy street.

Each morning, I listened to the little stream of life that runs through the neighborhood. I heard the motorbikes, the first #67 bus of the day climbing the hill to Pigalle, and the click of women's heels on the pavement. My movement toward morning and wakefulness was slow, reluctant, but quietly acknowledged as necessary. I let myself be carried along toward consciousness as if by a drowsy stream, a warm current that teems with swarms of the psychic plankton that inhabit the depths of the unconscious and that nourish the complex creature that apparently I still am.

Aware of my sleep, my body seemed like a well-worn suit of clothes, nearly old now, a bit rumpled, showing signs of wear. My arms and legs felt empty, without tension. I was filled with something almost like happiness. It has taken me a lifetime, nearly complete now, to reach this point. I have not always been so calm, so unconcerned that I could allow myself to drift like this, momentarily without concerns or obligation, to enjoy what flows around me and through me.

At eight in the morning, the air fills with the delighted squeals of first and second graders in a school around the corner. The children are like puppies, chasing, tugging, and teasing. The school yard is graveled and I can hear the crunching of children's feet in the pebbles. The bell rings. It is a hand bell, not mechanical. The school day begins. This school is parochial, Catholic, and so was spared the round-ups of the Jewish children in 1942. Having that thought brings me back to the present and the awareness that I have never been completely free of sadness. I have a slight emotional limp, what Bob Dylan called a toothache in the heel. This is not a complaint. Most of us who have lived would report similar feelings.

At twilight, I took the metro down to Place de la Concorde. A giant Ferris wheel, a holiday tradition in Paris, was spinning its circle of white lights in the sky. I saw it as the mechanical metaphor for the Tantric wheel, an image that seemed a bit incongruous in the country that prides itself on its respect for reason, the country of the Enlightenment. I walked along rue de Rivoli to the Galignani bookstore to browse. I spent an hour in the history section. Wars, kings, and tyrants. Floods and famines. Victims and refugees. Beautiful women who wore long gowns and attended the opera. Nations. Grand achievements, the building of dams and canals, the conquest of space, the vanquishing of diseases. Conspiracies. Follies, fantasies, and run-of-the-mill wickedness. And a great deal of serious evil. Books in French about the rise of Trump and *Trumpisme* have already appeared. A new age of "isms" appears to be upon us, a political dysfunction centered on the cult of a person. These always have been terrible times.

I strolled back toward Concorde. Where that graceful Napoleonic arcade of rue Rivoli meets rue Castiglione, near where the emperor's bronze effigy once stood atop a column, there is an entrance to the Jardin des Tuileries. Just inside the gate is a monument, not to kings or heroes, but to the laws of the jungle. Life size, in black-green bronze, a rhinoceros plunges its horn into the chest cavity of a lion as another lion tears at the rhino's armored flank. It seems strange to find such a terrible image in Paris, and here especially, at the gate to a garden used by so many children. The statue is all surging muscle, massive bodies locked together in a convulsion of violent death. The rhino's horn up thrusts into the lungs and heart of the lion.

It had rained earlier, but the clouds went, leaving only a few stragglers. The short winter day was easing its way out, and the sky slipped from pastel cerulean blue, to pink, and then became a darkness that shimmered, that almost had texture. There is a moment, between the pink and the black, when the winter sky of Paris takes on a color I've never seen in any other place, a trace of very deep violet blue. I watched for it again, as I have many times before. It is like the voice of a young girl singing a long way off, a voice so beautiful that all living things stop to listen.

I walked back to the Metro through the almost empty gardens. The little merry-go-round was still turning slowly. A stubborn little boy rode happily on a wooden pony. His father stood in the shadows watching. The merry-go-round was an island of warm light amongst puddles and bare trees. How beautiful it all was!

Automobiles, the Peugeots with their rampant lions, the Citroens with their chevrons, slid along the boulevards. The headlights seemed to disassociate from the host machines and become just particles of light, like cells, flowing in the dark bloodstream of the city. The warm, amber light of the cafés spilled out onto the sidewalks bringing scraps of conversations and music from jukeboxes that float like pollen carried on a gentle breeze. I hear snatches of Gainsbourg, Sinatra, and Piaf, of the Rolling Stones too, "You can't always get what you want..." That last is an old anthem of mine. The words are true most of the time, but, as the song says, I have managed to get what I need. More than enough.

As the night deepened, sinking toward the silence of the early morning, the streets emptied. I went back to the hotel. The night clerk was asleep, but the bell finally roused him. From my room, out the window, I saw starlight, then, presently, I saw the running lights of an airliner crossing a field of stars that is as chaotic and disorderly as the pebbles in the playground around the corner. The airliner was bound perhaps for the old French colonies, Dakar or Timbuktu. I imagine those places as hot and sunny. Or to America, where the republic I so admired, a nation founded on the noblest ideas, is floundering and may, I fear, fall back to earth and fail.

HM in France, 2015

Notes

Part I
The quote from St. John of the Cross is from the John Frederick Nims translation.

Chapter 3
The preparatory school was the Thacher School in Ojai, California. My English teacher, David Lavender, a professional historian, introduced me to literature and was a major influence in my life.

Chapter 18
In 2006, Disney Studios made a film, *Glory Road*, about the Texas Western Team.

Chapters 25, 26
Giving credit where it is due:
The other names that deserve notice include Dr. Peter Montague, a Ph.D. researcher into all manner of environmental issues, Em Hall, a professor at the UNM School of Law and author of several Southwestern histories, and Don Devereaux, an investigative reporter who helped us understand the Mafia connections. Dr. Philip Schultz and Beryll Asplund were among the first "citizens" to join us. Our staff, especially Marilyn Price and Linda Velarde, made it possible. Bob Miller provided

critical support during the fight with the land developers and the mob. There were many others.

I should name a few of the politicians and government officials who deserve recognition and thanks. All are either retired or deceased. The state's chief water officer, Steve Reynolds (RIP), was often in opposition to our positions, but his integrity and professionalism stand out. In the water department was Attorney Paul Bloom (RIP). In the state legislature there were a number of men—no women in those days—who went to bat for environmental issues. Representative Jami Koch (D.), Senator Mike Alarid (D. RIP), Senator Fred Gross (R. RIP), Senator Jack Eastham (R. RIP), Senator Herb Taylor (D. RIP), Senator Arturo Jaramillo (D.), Representative David Salman (D. RIP), Representative Tom Foy (D. RIP), Representative Bill Warren (D), Representative Alfonso Vigil (D.), Representative Al Castillo (D.) and Representative Max Coll (D. RIP), former Land Commissioner Jim Baca, Governor Toney Anaya (D.), and U.S. Senator Jeff Bingaman (D).

Four Corners Generating Station:
The web site of the Wild Earth Guardians has links to multiple reports about the plant and its legal history. Search for "four corners."

The "brave friend" has not wanted to be identified.

"Californication" was a term we coined. Its reappearance as TV sitcom in the 1990s may or may not be coincidental.

Brant Calkin stayed in the movement as an activist for the rest of his working life. He is now retired. He managed a fund called Frontera del Norte that I had established to provide grants for environmental projects in the four contiguous Southwestern states and Mexico. The Frontera Fund is a part of the Sierra Club Foundation. He continued as a "free-lance" environmental activist and as a consultant with the Southern Utah Wilderness Alliance (SUWA.) He is the quintessential professional environmentalist.

Sally Rodgers continued in the movement for forty-plus years. Experience had convinced her that grass roots citizen involvement was the key to achieving environmental goals and to that purpose she has focused her efforts. In response to a question I put to her about the effect and effectiveness of Central Clearing House (CCH), she wrote the following note. I had asked if we had accomplished anything significant.

CCH was the grandparent of the kick-ass organizations that define the activist/political landscape of today. CCH set many standards to follow. Its direct descendant was the Conservation Voters Alliance. The "child" of CVA is now Conservation Voters New Mexico. Further CCH inspiration, I would argue, is The Environmental Law Center.

CVA and CVNM have achieved two of our goals. 1. To stop any and all bad, regressive legislation (bills, memorials) from passing. That is an unbroken record (between the two organizations) of over thirty-five years. 2. The organization's work has been THE reason why many good guys have been elected and THE reason why many bad guys were booted from office. Good guy candidates actively seek CVNM endorsements and support and that support is provided in ways you and I couldn't imagine in the 70s. I often feel like a very proud Grandma even when the current generation has no clue who I am. You should have a comparable Granddad pride.

Chapter 34

Harvey Mudd College: The inspiration for the college came from my father, Henry T. Mudd, and his mother, Mildred Esterbrook Mudd. It was founded in 1955, two years after my grandfather's death. He, Harvey Mudd, had left a significant sum of money to the Claremont Colleges, but with no direction as to its use. He probably would not have approved of a college named for him. It is now one of America's preeminent science colleges. My father, modest as was his father, always gave much of the credit for the successful launching of the college to its first president, Joe Platt, and his wife, Jean.

Chapter 28

Hannah Arendt: The quotation is from *The Origins of Totalitarianism*.
Assertions about Nixon and Chile:
Nixon and Kissinger, Robert Dallek, 2009

Kissinger on Argentina: John Dinges, *The Condor Years*, 2005; The National Security Archive Electronic Briefing Book, No. 133 George Washington University, National Security Archives, March 23, 2006

The donation of land that I made to the village of Arroyo Hondo in 1975 became a problem. Nearly forty-five years later, a wealthy Anglo, relatively new to the valley, challenged my gift, claiming that the uses of it disturb "the peaceful enjoyment of his property." He has sued the organization that holds title to the land. They have, he says, created a nuisance. He has sued me as well because I started it all with my gift. He has apparently bottomless financial resources and hopes to wear us down, bully us into selling it to him. Our lawyer is Clodoveo Chacon's grandson, who grew up in the valley and recalls swimming in the stretch of the rio Hondo that flows through the disputed parcel. I represent myself. Over the years I have learned a bit about the law. In 2018, a judge ruled that his lawsuit had no basis and the case was dismissed. There is now a small community park.

Chapter 30

Vallecitos Ranch: My brother, living in California, could not use the property enough, so I bought him out after a year or two. Twenty years later, when I could no longer afford to keep it, but could not bring myself to develop it, I sold it to a non-profit organization headed by my old friend and colleague from the CCH days, Grove Burnett. My younger sister Virginia was instrumental in making this happen. It is now the Vallecitos Mountain Ranch, a wilderness retreat center with an emphasis on Buddhist practice.

The picture of the boy with his hands up:
Remarkably this little boy survived the camps. He was identified and was later discovered living in the United States as a physician.

Chapter 36

A GOOGLE search for the Victoria Nebeker Coberly collection will bring up pictures of the paintings my mother donated to the National Gallery.

My sister Victoria, with her co-director Maria Florio, won the 1985 Oscar for best feature length documentary. The film, *Broken Rainbow*, documents the forced removal of Navajos from ancestral lands on Black Mesa, Arizona, as a part of the effort by utilities and mining companies to gain access to the coal resources of the region.

My political newsletter is called "Vue from here." Back issues are posted on my website. www.harvey-mudd.com

Acknowledgements

A memoirist takes as much of the life as he or she can dredge out of memory and maneuvers it into a plausible narrative that goes somewhere more satisfying than the realization that what he did with his life has not mattered all that much.

But since a memoir is not fiction, it can easily become incoherent if all the subplots and all the real-life characters who passed across the stage are included in the narrative. The result would be an encyclopedic excess, a recipe for certain tedium. In such a memoir there would certainly be no satisfying finale that solved all the story lines; the reader would be left, as with the real life, with a tangle of loose ends. A memoir has unity only through the memoirist who has filtered the facts and has given them an order that may show cause and effect, growth or lack of growth, release from constraints and tensions, or not, as the case may be. Since I have had a relatively long life—may it continue for many years to come—there were many stories, incidents, relationships and friendships that were left out in order to suggest that there was a sort of coherence to the life, or at least to the narrative. Is it a "life" or is it only art?

It is not, however, a fiction. As I surveyed my life, thinking about what I had left out, I realized there have been many people to whom I owe something, people who contributed to the making of the person that I became, who shared an adventure with me, who stood by me in tough times, or, the corollary, whom I stood by. It seems appropriate to at least give them names, to acknowledge them in a positive way: to say thanks for participating.

First there were those who helped with this book. Jami Miller was there when the book was conceived and who read earlier versions of a book, one very different from this present book. This acknowledgement of her very important role is offered in lieu of the book's formal dedication. Jim Levy, in addition to having been an essential actor for most of my life was also a most helpful editor and proof reader. He read earlier versions, killed some outright, and had valuable suggestions that kept the project on track. Similarly my friend Susan Lynner. Katherine Moore a professional editor gave valuable advice. My daughter Elena, and my son-in-law, Michael Kurko, were the copy editors. A final edit was by Elizabeth Aldred. My daughters, Mariana and Elena, and my son, Sam, were steadfast in their support and in their belief that sensitive subjects should be discussed openly. The most critical and constructive edits, additions and deletions came from Ellen Kamarck Davies. The book would not be what it is today without her unstinting help and willingness to stand up to authorial defensiveness.

Of special importance in respect to my intellectual foundations, there were David Lavender, who introduced me to literature, Robert Miller, my Spanish teacher at Thacher, who gave me the key to a second language, and Eugenio Villicana, who led me into the great books of the Renaissance. In terms of my own writing, Lyn Redding helped bring *The Plain of Smokes* to a successful conclusion. Eleanor Caponigro showed me what book design was all about.

But not having had a direct role in my writing life has not meant that the others, the friends and colleagues who populated the last six decades, were not important. It would be impossible to rank all these people as to their importance, so I have not tried. I see them in my memory as if in a single event of long duration, a scene that reminds me of the finale of Federico Fellini's film, *8 ½,* a parade, with clowns and musicians, and some ghosts. Those who were the more frequently present and for a longer period of time are at the head, but some who had brief parts were equally important. There are girlfriends, people I

worked with, lawyers, drinking buddies, artists, writers. No one, however, who did me harm is included. To the extent that I am tempted to
settle scores, I do so by omission. Anyone mentioned in the text is not
included in this list.

Ellen Kamarck Davies, Dr. Norman Levy, Kay Levy, Katherine
Hall, Marianna Lands, Leonard Newcomb, Lynn Newcomb, Tom and
Elise Noble, Patrick Noble, Kate Noble, Phaedra Greenwood, Linda
Wylie, Jennifer Francoeur, Avra Leodas, Maryann Cassidy Kapoun and
her children, Bob Kapoun, Lexi Rome, Bill and Norma Lumpkins,
Reggie Cantu, George and Joyce Robinson, Talley Mingst, Maria
Florio, Jorge and Sandra Midon and their two boys, Renee Queen, Lisa
Queen, Karen Arch, Jack and Becky Parsons, Edith Alexander, Polly
Reichenbach, Owen Lopez, Kathleen and Jonathan Altman, Charlie
Ramsburg and Michelle Zackheim, Linda Velarde, Glenda Young,
Belinda Bolte, Marilyn Price, Bill Mingenbach, Jean Pieniadz, Michael
Diaz, Tom Brady, Joshua Brady, Whalen Brady, Jocelyn Fisher, Roger
Thomas, Margaret Vangelisti, Steve and Holly Baer, Gary Dryzmala,
Jami Wehe, Bernie Lopez. Katie Lopez, Robin and Connie Doughman,
Marlou Quintana, Gerry Peters, Alyce and Larry Frank, Sally Howell,
Rena Rosequist, Ernesto Mayans, Bill Gersch, Brooke Tuthill, Fred Fair,
Michael Duncan, Christina Griscom, Jack McCarthy, Paul and Kay
Zenaty, Chris Von Trapp, Duke and Barbara Cozart, Steve Natelson,
Frank Concha, John Randall, Jan Sultan, Betsy Sultan, Judy Chicago,
Donald Woodman, Ed Abbey, Malcolm Brown, Rachel Brown, Tom
Popejoy, Susan Carr, James Reid, Randy Greene. Elise Whittemore,
Ann Jamison, Olaya Perez, Hueri Fair, Ellen Powell, Charles Bell, Gary
Walker, Sandy Bell, March Kessler, Bobby Gleason, Cynthia Nowak,
Lauren Greenwald, Alice Sealy, Dave Dodge, Andy Smith, Carl Roberts,
Carylla Potts, Luke and Coco Dowley, Anne Harris, Donna and Bob
Korn, Pabla Miller, Craig Murray, Ed Morgan, Judy Roberts, Nancy
Sutor, Sarah Lovett, Judy and Ray Dewey, Stewart Bluestone, Lonnie
Miller, Jeff Miller, Susan Miller, Alison Miller, Howard Rome, Sasha and
Tomas Undarraga, Joe Becker, John Kimmey, Sandy Snow, Sue Mack,
Marcia Goldstein, Jeanne Yeatts, Preston Mohr, Nick Potter, Adrian

and Mindy Davies, Owen and Laura Davies, Tino Kamarck, Elaine Kamarck, Morgan and Erin Davies, and Brett Walker.

The animals were important too. Cat: Tibet. Pig: Mariposa. And the dogs: Jet, Cockie, Bravo, Otter, Charlie, Apollo, Cora, Pete, Simba, Moe, and Extra. It would have been quite a different experience without them. Jim Levy is the author of two books published by The Porcupine Press: *The Poems of Caius Herennius Felix* and *Joy to Come.*

The photo titled "HM in France, 2015" by Ellen Kamarck Davies, with permission.

Suggested Reading

Some classics.
> Virgil, *The Georgics*, trans. Janet Lemke
> Michel de Montaigne, *The Essays*, trans. Donald Frame
> Ralph Waldo Emerson, *Essays*
> Henry David Thoreau, *On Civil Disobedience, Walden*

The 20th century
> Czeslaw Milosz, *The Captive Mind*
> Raymond Aron, *Thinking Politically: a liberal in the age of ideology*
> Isaiah Berlin, *The Twisted Timber of Humanity*
> Albert Camus, *The Plague*
> George Orwell, *1984*
> Geoff Mulgan, *Good and Bad Power*
> Vaclav Havel, *The Power of the Powerless*
> Hannah Arendt, *The Origins of Totalitarianism*
> Tony Judt,
> > *Thinking the Twentieth Century,*
> > *The Burden of Responsibility*
> > *Ill Fares the Land*
> Robert O. Paxton, *The Anatomy of Fascism*

Richard J. Evans
  The Coming of the Third Reich
  The Third Reich in Power
  The Third Reich at War

The past as a lens

Alexis de Tocqueville, *Democracy in America*
Harry V. Jaffa, *Crisis of the House Divided*
William Lee Miller, *Arguing Slavery*

Specific issues

Judith Nies, *Unreal City: Las Vegas, Black Mesa, and the Fate of the West*

Colophon

…historians must and ought to be exact, truthful, and absolutely free of passions, for neither interest, fear, rancor, nor affection should make them deviate from the path of the truth, whose mother is history, the rival of time, repository of great deeds, witness to the past, example and advisor to the present, and forewarning to the future. In this account I know there will be found everything that could be rightly desired in this most pleasant history, and if something of value is missing from it, in my opinion the fault lies with the dog who was its author rather than with any defect in its subject.

Miguel de Cervantes, *Don Quixote,* trans. Samuel Putnam